THE GREEKS

Texts by

ROBERT BROWNING · A. M. SNODGRASS · CLAUDE MOSSÉ
A. A. LONG · J. M. COOK · PETER LEVI · MICHEL AUSTIN
AVERIL CAMERON · JUDITH HERRIN · SPEROS VRYONIS, JR.
NIKOS SVORONOS · GEORGE YANNOULOPOULOS
RICHARD CLOGG

EDITED BY ROBERT BROWNING

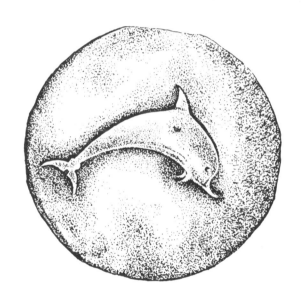

THE GREEKS

CLASSICAL, BYZANTINE AND MODERN

PORTLAND HOUSE
NEW YORK

ISBN 0-517-67418-1

Printed and bound in Yugoslavia

hgfedcba

CONTENTS

PROLOGUE:LAND AND PEOPLE

ROBERT BROWNING

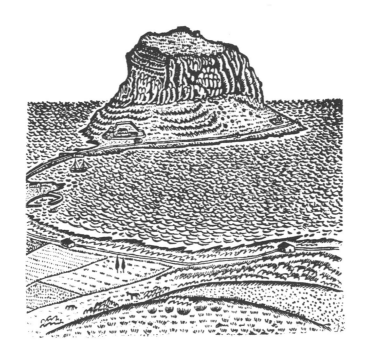

'HELLAS AND POVERTY are foster sisters' is a saying recorded in the 5th century BC by Herodotus. It invokes a continuous theme of Greek history: the natural poverty of the land has acted as a spur to the enterprise of its inhabitants.

The remarkable beauty of the country has usually distracted the attention of outsiders from the difficulties faced by Greeks in making a living out of the land. The sea which surrounds and penetrates so much of Greece is essential as a source of food and a means of communication, yet the Mediterranean is not abundant in fish and her treacherous winds and currents made navigation a difficult skill to acquire. The hot, dry summers, the extensive mountain ranges, the thin soil that barely cloaks most of the rocky land and the scarcity of rivers all impede agriculture.

None the less, by their labour and skills Greek communities usually managed to prosper. Yet if disaster struck – war, plague, bad harvests or earthquakes – they had few resources to sustain them. This constant awareness of the precariousness of their livelihoods has given the Greeks an acute appreciation of the natural forces with which they are surrounded. In their art they celebrated the fertility of the vines and olive groves; the courage of their mariners; the hardiness of mountain-dwellers; the treasured gift of water from natural springs. In ritual and tragic drama they confronted the omnipresence of death. The pictures in the following pages depict the setting of Greek civilization – the land, the sea and the communities that have shaped the Greek character and way of life.

Greek holy places
still have a strange, almost mystical, appeal, deriving as
much from the landscape itself as from the man-made
setting. In the natural forces that gather round them it is not
difficult to feel the presence of the gods and to understand
their meaning in the ancient world. Greek architecture, too,
seems to grow out of the ground beneath it – partly because
it is formed of the same rock, partly because three thousand
years of weathering have almost transformed it into a
product of nature rather than art. Yet no architecture is
more intellectual than the Greek, no lines more calculated,
no intervals more subtly balanced. Perhaps it is this
combination of opposites that gives these buildings their
unique power, a power that survives even in ruin. *Right:*
The temple of Poseidon at Sounion, built about 445 BC,
with Poseidon's kingdom, the sea, majestically spread
before it. (1)

Fortunate winds

Communication between different parts of Greece, and between Greek cities and their colonies, was by water; it depended on calm seas and prosperous winds. But they were wayward elements, explicable only in terms of the enmity or favour of the gods.

The winds were frequently personified in Greek art. Boreas, the north wind, appears (*above*) on the north side of the Tower of the Winds in Athens – built in the 1st century BC as a sundial, water-clock and weather vane. Aeolus, the god of the winds, shepherds the winds into his cave – the opening of the knuckle-bone-shaped vase on which they are painted (*above, right*). (2, 3)

The land also draws its benefit from the wind. Greek windmills are lighter than those of the north but equally efficient. They serve many purposes, including that of water-pump, as here on one of the Aegean islands. (4)

The sea has been a prominent theme in Greek literature and art since the *Odyssey*. The two ships under sail (*left*) are depicted on a vase of *c*.520 BC. Each has a bear figurehead; lookouts stand in forecastles at the prow. At the back each boat has a landing ladder, and we can see the helmsmen steering with long oars which act as rudders. The sterns are carved into swans' heads. Sitting on a tendril on the right is a harpy, half-woman, half-bird. (5)

11

The unchanging land

The physical structure of Greece, with its mountains dividing one region from another, its large tracts of barren land, its deep inlets encouraging communication by water, has largely determined the course of Greek history. That structure remains.

Every hill has associations with myth or legend, so that it is impossible to look at the landscape untroubled by the past. This is the citadel of Argos, once a mighty city. For Homer 'Argive' was synonymous with Greek. (6)

The islands are in many ways miniature versions of Greece itself. *Right:* Assos, on Cephalonia, one of the Ionian Islands. *Below:* Mykonos, in the Cyclades, its whitewashed houses hugging the quayside. (7, 8)

The farmer at his plough: *above* in a detail from the Nikosthenes cup, 6th century BC; *below* in a scene from a Byzantine illuminated manuscript of the 11th century. In 1700 years the plough has become more complicated – it has an adjustable metal ploughshare, whereas the ancient example is entirely wood – but little else has altered. (10, 11)

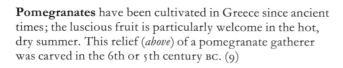

Pomegranates have been cultivated in Greece since ancient times; the luscious fruit is particularly welcome in the hot, dry summer. This relief (*above*) of a pomegranate gatherer was carved in the 6th or 5th century BC. (9)

The first farmers in Greece grew barley and wheat. Since then the range of crops grown has increased greatly, but the problems of a difficult climate and unyielding soil remain. The gods of harvest were among the most respected of the Greek pantheon.

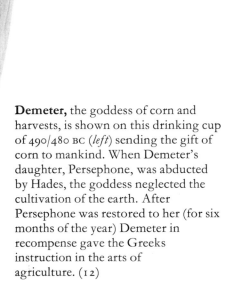

Demeter, the goddess of corn and harvests, is shown on this drinking cup of 490/480 BC (*left*) sending the gift of corn to mankind. When Demeter's daughter, Persephone, was abducted by Hades, the goddess neglected the cultivation of the earth. After Persephone was restored to her (for six months of the year) Demeter in recompense gave the Greeks instruction in the arts of agriculture. (12)

Dionysus, the god of wine, is represented on this archaic votive tablet (*above*) with vine and drinking cup. His cult involved the death and resurrection of the god, an image – like Persephone's descent to the Underworld and eventual reappearance – of the cycle of the earth's fertility. Christianity took over some of this symbolism. Grapes, the source of the eucharistic wine, stand for Christ's redeeming sacrifice. Two Orthodox priests (*left*) prepare to bless grapes before the pressing starts – a photograph from the village of Liopessi, near Athens. (13, 14)

Water in a dry land

In the hot summers of Greece, rainfall is scarce and water is precious. The land has few rivers, but many springs, which rarely fail. In ancient times their importance caused them to be regarded as sacred.

Women draw water from a fountain (*right*) chatting with their slaves before carrying it away: a 5th-century BC vase painting. (15)

The sacred spring at Delphi (*above*) was a place of cult worship from very early times. It was dedicated at first to Ge, the goddess of earth, and later to Apollo. The Pythia, the high priestess of Apollo, purified herself here before delivering the oracle's replies to questions put to it by suppliants from all over the Greek world and beyond. Here too anyone who came to Delphi to worship was ritually cleansed. (16)

The water of life: an 11th-century mosaic (*right*) at Daphni, near Athens, shows the Annunciation to St Anne, an incident from the apocryphal Gospel of James. Here water symbolizes the fertility of nature, from which Anne thought herself excluded. (18)

On Delos, one of the most important religious centres in Greece, water that fell on the theatre was collected in a huge vaulted cistern (*left*) and used for the needs of the town. Many of the smaller islands still depend on rainwater collected in the winter. (17)

17

Mountain dwellers

Greece is a mountainous land. Infertile, often precipitous, cut through with deep gorges, the mountains have posed a harsh challenge to those who lived among them. But they have also nourished a race of hardy fighters who proved their worth in times of unrest or national struggle.

Mount Olympus (*left*), on the borders of Thessaly and Macedonia, stands between Greece and invaders from the north. Greece's highest mountain, its grandeur led the ancients to see it as the home of the gods. Snow lingers on its northern flanks throughout the year. The village *below*, its sturdily built houses clinging to the steep slopes, is in the foothills of Olympus. (19, 20)

Shepherds tending their flocks are
the mountain's chief inhabitants, for
the soil is too poor to support crops.
Over the centuries they have provided
an important point of contact between
different communities, which often
have to share the scanty summer
pastures. The shepherds *above* were
photographed in the Gorge of Kanalio
in the Pindos mountains; those on the
far left are vividly depicted observers
of the Nativity, from a 14th-century
mosaic in Thessalonica. Shepherds
have often doubled as traders,
smugglers or soldiers: the armed
mountaineers on the *left* were
photographed *c.*1917, during the First
World War. (21,22)

The gift of toil

The olive harvest was by tradition the gift of Athena, but it was a gift not easily bestowed. In large parts of Greece every square yard of soil has to be won by hard labour and kept by constant maintenance. Nothing is more expressive of this vast effort than the terraced hillsides, built up to conserve moisture.

The olive harvest uses methods that have hardly altered in thousands of years. On this storage jar of *c.* 520 BC, gatherers (one sitting in the branches) use long sticks to knock down the olives, which are picked up by the crouching figure. Nothing has changed apart from the costumes in this painting of 1933 by Theophilos (*below*), which depicts peasants on Lesbos. (23)

The olive groves of Lesbos (*left*) have been famous since antiquity; they still provide the main source of income for the island's inhabitants. (24)

Grief and joy

Ritualistic patterns recur in Greek society as constantly as the passage of the seasons, shaping the expression of people's emotions throughout history.

Gestures of mourning strikingly link these women of different epochs. Mourners at funerals appear (*above*) on a clay plaque of *c.*540 BC, and (*right*) in a photograph taken during the Turkish invasion of Cyprus in 1974. The painter of the mid-16th-century icon (*top right*) employs similar gestures in stylized form to intense effect in this depiction of the lamentation over the dead Christ. (25, 26, 27)

Dancers join hands to celebrate a happy occasion. The three girls (*above*), led by a flute-player and followed by a boy, are shown on a relief from the Acropolis in Athens of *c.*500 BC depicting a religious festival. In a Boeotian terracotta of a hundred years earlier (*below*) a musician stands in the centre of the dancing figures. The dance photographed *right* is at Andritsaina, a town in Arcadia. (28, 29, 30)

THE LAND – and in the case of Greece the sea also – sets a limit to what men can do. And men in their turn transform the land by imposing upon it a pattern of cities and fields, pastures and plantations, irrigation and drainage works, roads and fortifications. Sometimes by their actions they frustrate their own long-term purposes, as when they burn the forests for charcoal and leave a desolate waste of prickly maquis that not even goats can live on. The sea is harder to transform. But there too there are harbours and breakwaters and lighthouses, and a network of criss-crossing seaways. And human waste may pollute the sea. Since man first appeared on the earth there has been a two-way relation between him and his environment, which has made both into something vastly different from what they first were.

Mountain and sea

The Greek environment is a complex balance of land and sea: land surrounded and penetrated by sea – nowhere in central Greece is more than 60 kilometres (38 miles) from the sea, nowhere in the Peloponnese more than 52 (33 miles); but also sea surrounded and penetrated by land – there is no point in the Aegean from which land cannot be seen in conditions of good visibility. The Greeks (says Socrates in Plato's *Phaedo*) live round the sea like frogs round a pond.

The land is mountainous. Only 18 per cent of the Republic of Greece is classified as arable land, and it consists mainly of small plains and valleys separated from one another by ranges of mountains. The mountains belong to two different geological systems. In southern Macedonia, Thessaly, Euboea, part of Attica, and the Cyclades a massif of primary rock has been thrust up and is now embedded in later formations; to this massif belong Mounts Olympus, Pelion, Ossa and Othrys on the mainland and Dirphys on the island of Euboea, as well as the islands of the northern and central Cyclades. Surrounding this massif on the north, west and south is a complex system of secondary and tertiary folding arising from the same tectonic movements as those which created the Alps with their outliers in southern and eastern Europe. This system includes the Pindos range in the north, the Ionian islands, the mountains of the Peloponnese, the southern Cyclades, and the islands of Crete, Karpathos, and

Rhodes. Much of the Greek landscape is geologically recent, as is shown by the volcanic activity in Thera, the volcanic rocks in Melos, at Troezen and elsewhere, and the frequency of earthquakes in many regions.

The mountains are not high in comparison with the Alps, the Himalayas, or the Rockies. Only Olympus exceeds 10,000 feet (about 3050 metres). The Parnassos group reaches 8245 feet (2513 metres), the highest point in the Peloponnese is about 8000 feet (a little over 2400 metres), Mount Ida in Crete just under 8300 (2530 metres). But Greek mountains are often precipitous, and traversed by deep gorges with steep sides. And they often rise straight out of the sea or from a low-lying plain. Thus they appear higher than comparable peaks in the interior of continents, and they have always been a serious barrier to movement. They are largely formed of limestone, usually resting on a less porous base. The top-soil is thin, and near the summit there is often none. So the rains of winter are partly carried off as flash-floods down short water-courses to the sea, and partly penetrate the porous rock. Therefore there are few perennial rivers. The Axios and the Hebros rise far beyond the confines of Greece in a very different climatic zone: the Acheloos, the Arachthos, and the Peneios can change in hours from easily fordable streams to torrents which sweep away everything in their path; most other rivers are reduced for much of the year to a thin trickle among the pebbles, or dry up altogether. So there is no scope for the river-based irrigation practised in the Near East, nor for the use of the water-wheel as a source of power. Modern hydro-electric technology can make use of Greek rivers, but it calls for colossal capital expenditure and is of limited efficiency. Yet the scarcity of perennial rivers is compensated by the countless springs which issue from the bases of the mountains, and most of them never fail. They have always been of importance to those who lived on the land.

The land-locked Mediterranean Sea is virtually tideless and is unaffected by the great oceanic currents of the Atlantic. The surface water warms up rapidly in summer, reaching a mean temperature of 28 degrees centigrade. The loss of water by evaporation is made up only in a very small measure by rivers. A larger contribution is made by the steady current flowing through the Bosphorus and the Dardanelles from the Black Sea, which has a much lower rate of evaporation and is fed by many great rivers. But by far the largest contribution is that made by water flowing in continuously from the Atlantic through the Straits of Gibraltar in a five-knot current five miles wide and two hundred and fifty feet deep. So the passage from the Mediterranean to the Black Sea or to the Atlantic can only be made against a stiff current and through a difficult channel. It took ancient mariners a long time to

Three ages of Greece – classical, medieval and modern – are juxtaposed in this photograph of the Agora, the assembly-place of ancient Athens. In the foreground is the beautiful late 10th-century Church of the Holy Apostles; behind it is the Hephaisteion, an excellently preserved Doric temple of *c*.450 BC. In the background rise the buildings of the modern city. (31)

learn how to do it. The surface water becomes salty because of the high evaporation, and therefore denser than the water beneath it. As it cools in winter, so it sinks, and is replaced by water from the depths. This vertical circulation leads to a complex system of underwater currents, the main direction of which is from east to west.

The warm surface water is poor in nutritive material – from two to twenty times less rich than Atlantic water in comparable latitudes. And the limited extent of the continental shelf, together with the lack of tides, prevents the rich development of fixed and bottom-living marine organisms found in offshore waters of the Atlantic. So the Mediterranean is not a rich source of food for man. The main edible fish are the tunny, the sardine and the anchovy, with the swordfish coming far behind. Students of ancient Greek literature, who read in Athenaeus or the fragments of Middle Comedy descriptions of banquets in which fish were the principal delicacies, or casual visitors struck by the variety of sea-food served in tourist restaurants, can easily form a wrong idea of the role of fish in Greek diet. The truth is very different. The total catch of fish in the whole of the Mediterranean in the 1950s was only a third of that caught by Norwegian fishermen, and less than a quarter of the South Korean catch; and very little of that was taken from Greek waters. The rarity of sea birds in the Aegean compared with the coasts of western Europe is an indication of the poor nourishment offered by the

sea. So fishing in Greece has always been a small-scale activity. Boats are small, manned by two or three men: they do not venture far from their home port; their equipment was and still is backward and for most fishermen fishing has been a part-time occupation. Yet fish has provided a source of protein for the inhabitants of Greece for many thousands of years.

The absence of tides means that no estuaries are scoured out at the mouths of rivers, providing both safe harbours and routes of penetration into the interior. The silt that the rivers of Greece bring down with them is not carried away, but accumulates to form a delta or sometimes a shallow lagoon behind a sand bar. This alluvial land may be fertile, as is the delta of the Nile. But if it provides pools of water in which the Anopheles mosquito breeds, it becomes unhealthy or even uninhabitable. The same is true of the few low-lying and flat stretches of coast. Modern drainage and pest-control may enable the potential value of such land to be exploited. But through most of history it lay desolate and pestilential.

A tideless sea permits building to be continued right to the water's edge. Modern Greek coastal and island towns are often so constructed. But throughout much of history considerations of security have led men to settle some way inland on a site which could easily be defended. The coast was often left bare and uninhabited. Or there was a relatively small port settlement serving a city some miles away. Examples are Athens

Several characteristic features of the Greek landscape appear in this view of Hydra: the mountainous terrain; the sea penetrating the land; the community on the water's edge.

Karitaina is a medieval town spectacularly positioned on a high hill overlooking the plain of Megalopolis and the river Karitaina (as the Alpheios is called at this point). The peak is crowned by a Frankish castle.

and Peiraeus, or Corinth and its twin ports of Lechaion and Kenchreai (the modern city of Corinth, on the coast of the Corinthian Gulf, is not on the site of the ancient city, which lay about two miles inland). In tidal waters a sailing ship can clear the coast on an ebb tide. In the tideless Mediterranean this manoeuvre is impossible. Sometimes a land breeze will carry a ship out of the lee of the shore. But in many cases it has to be rowed out until it catches the wind. This set a practical limit to the size of ships which could be sailed, over and above that imposed by methods of construction and steering, of which more will be said later.

Sun, rain and soil

The Mediterranean climate is one of winter rain and summer drought, and the further east one goes the more marked becomes this feature. It is the direct opposite of a monsoon climate, with its hot, rainy summer, and its cool, dry winter. The details vary from place to place. Eastern Crete averages over seven months per year without rain, Sparta four to five, Thessalonica three to four, the Pindos region in northern Greece one to two. In general there is more rainfall in the west than in the east. Epirus, Acarnania, and the west coast of the Peloponnese are notably greener than Thessaly, Boeotia, Attica, and the eastern Peloponnese, which lie in the rain-shadow of the mountains. Temperature and precipitation also vary strikingly with altitude. The modern traveller who takes the motor road from Igoumenitsa in Epirus to Trikkala in Thessaly across the Pindos mountains, or that from Sparta to Kalamata across the Taygetos range, passes through a series of climatic zones, from parched lowlands, where the only green visible in summer is the dark foliage of the olive tree, to alpine meadows, above which tower peaks covered with snow for most of the year. The importance of this vertical climate zoning for the human geography of Greece will be discussed later.

Summer temperatures in Greece are often higher than those in the tropics, thanks to the cloudless skies. However the Aegean area is cooled during the summer by the steady north-east wind – the Etesian winds of the ancients, the *meltemi* of today – which usually begins to blow in the early morning and dies away at nightfall. Winters are generally mild at sea level throughout Greece, but the temperature falls rapidly as altitude increases: Jannina has long and severe frosts with frequent snowfalls; the uplands of Arcadia are cold and

27

wet and often frosty; and throughout the country the higher mountains are snow-covered; there are even patches of permanent snow on the north-facing slopes and gullies of Olympus. Regions exposed to north winds channelled through gaps in the mountains may experience periods of severe cold in winter: an example is the area round Thessalonica. But there is nothing to compare with the devastating Bora of the Dalmatian coast, or even with the mistral of southern France.

The autumn rains begin when a collapse of the high pressure over the Mediterranean allows a mass of colder air from the north to come in contact with the warm and humid Mediterranean air mass. These autumn rains are striking in their suddenness. The first sign of their coming is a rapid improvement in visibility as the cool, dry air replaces that laden with water from evaporation. As one looks south-westwards from the Acropolis of Athens, first of all Aegina emerges from the haze, and within an hour or two the mountains of the Argolid stand out in sharp detail. Then the downpour begins, and a few inches of rain may fall in as many hours. As one moves south the onset of the rain comes later and later. In Epirus in September, in Attica in early October, in Kalamata at the end of October, in Crete not till December or even January. During the rest of the winter the rain – or snow – falls in short and severe bursts, separated by long sunny periods; the drizzle of the north is rare. There is often a period of more frequent showers in spring, as the summer anticyclone establishes itself. Then the rains cease, the temperature rises sharply, and summer begins again. The Greek spring is short and spectacular, as plants flower and complete their vegetative cycle before the summer heat dries out the top soil. However, though the soil is parched in summer, the absence of rain means that salts and nutrients are not leached out, as they are in regions where precipitation is less concentrated.

Warmth and moisture are needed for plant growth. The dissociation of these two conditions, typical of the Mediterranean climate and especially marked in the eastern Mediterranean, severely limits the range of plant life, whether natural or cultivated. Leafy perennials can flourish only in specially sheltered situations. The climate favours woody plants which put down deep roots, plants whose thick and leathery leaves limit transpiration, rapidly growing annuals which can complete their life cycle before the summer heat dries the soil, and quick-flowering perennials, like the asphodel, which survive the summer as tubers or bulbs. It is thanks to the last two groups that the Greek countryside is suddenly carpeted with flowers in spring. The first two groups provide the trees and shrubs which form the natural climax. Typical of most of the country are various species of oak, deciduous in the north, evergreen in the south. In the mountains of Attica and the Peloponnese a variety of conifers form the natural climax. The beech forests of the Pindos mountains represent an intrusion into the Mediterranean world of the typical central-European vegeta-

tion pattern. These ecological areas are not clearly distinguished, there are many regions of mixed forest, especially in western Greece, and poplars of various kinds are often intermixed with oaks, pines and beeches. What is important to bear in mind is the instability of Greek forests. If the forest cover is destroyed by natural catastrophe or by human activity, it is at first replaced by low-growing xerophytic plants of the typical Mediterranean maquis or *garrigue*. The forest reestablishes itself very slowly, if at all. The maquis is much less able to retain the soil on sloping ground than is the true forest. Hence loss of forest cover is followed by severe erosion, which can sometimes permanently prevent the regeneration of the forest. This process of deforestation and erosion had already gone far by the 4th century BC, set in motion by natural causes, including probably a drastic climatic change around 5000 BC, but aided by man and his voracious companion the goat. Men were aware of what was happening. Plato speaks of the earth having slipped down from the mountain tops, leaving no covering of soil to speak of, and the mountains protruding like the bones from an ailing body (*Critias* 111A–B). The smaller islands were probably the first to be denuded, then the mountain slopes of the Peloponnese and Attica, later those of central Greece. The forest covering of Pindos, of the Olympus massif, and of the mountains of Macedonia and Thrace were preserved well into classical times and beyond.

Much of the soil of the valleys and plains is very fertile. Macedonia has a rich and heavy soil, but until recently much of it was marshy and ill-drained. Land-locked Thessaly was and still is renowned for its deep, rich soil. That of Attica is thin, but fertile enough. In the Peloponnese the plain of Argos is fertile, that of Laconia – very large by Greek standards – has good soil and a copious water supply: springs rise from the base of mounts Taygetos and Parnon, and the Eurotas has a perennial, though in summer often niggardly, flow. The plateau of Arcadia has rather poor soil, which is slow in warming up in spring. Messenia has extremely fertile soil and plentiful rain and sun, and was and is one of the most productive regions of Greece. The small plains and valleys of Crete can produce rich crops if they get enough water. It must not be forgotten, too, that the summer heat enables agriculture to be successfully carried on at much higher altitudes than would be possible in central or northern Europe. Wheat is now grown up to about 4900 feet (1500 metres) and vines up to about 4100 feet (1250 metres). Nevertheless the area suitable for agriculture is less than a quarter of that occupied by inhospitable mountains.

The soil of Greece contains mineral deposits. Many of these, such as magnesium and manganese, have only recently become of interest to mankind. But silver has long been mined in the islands of Siphnos and Thasos, and southern Attica contained rich and easily worked deposits, now exhausted. Copper was mined at Chalkis and in Mount Taygetos, lead in Attica in association

One of the earliest Greek works of art is this Palaeolithic engraving of a wild horse, found in a cave near Mount Pelion. The comparative scarcity of Palaeolithic remains in Greece is an indication of the limited quantity of game for hunting.

with silver. But the whole area is almost devoid of exploitable deposits of iron ore. The limestone mountains provide almost everywhere a ready supply of good building stone, and marble of various kinds and qualities is found in many parts of the mainland and the islands. Obsidian was mined from very early times on the island of Melos.

The human landscape

The scene has been set in the shape of land and sea, mountains and plains, summer and winter. The principal actor, man, has already occasionally peeped from the wings. It is now time to let him take the centre of the stage.

Remains of Neanderthal man datable to about 70,000 BC have been found at Petralona in Macedonia. Homo sapiens is traceable somewhat later. Palaeolithic man can never have been numerous in Greece, where the terrain did not provide much game for him to hunt.

Recent discoveries in a cave at Franchthi, on the west coast of the Argolid peninsula, have dramatically illuminated the history of early man in Greece. The deposits furnish a continuous sequence of Palaeolithic, Mesolithic and Neolithic habitation. Mesolithic man lived by hunting and fishing and by gathering, but not cultivating, a variety of food plants. At a level in the Mesolithic deposits datable to between 7500 and 7000 BC there were found tools made from obsidian from the island of Melos, some 120 kilometres (75 miles) away, and the bones of large fish not found in inshore waters. So the men of Franchthi must have been able to build seaworthy boats that could sail in open waters. The islands of the Aegean, inaccessible to Palaeolithic man, could now be explored and settled. A thousand years later the Franchthi deposits contain the bones of domesticated sheep and goats, the seeds of wheat and barley, which do not grow wild in Greece, and sherds of rough hand-made pottery. Civilization had arrived, no doubt through contact with the Near East. Freed from the need to follow his source of food, Neolithic man could live from generation to generation in a permanent home, and bring the land about him under his control. The village community which came into being was the precursor of the *polis* or city. In a sense we can see at Franchthi the birth of political society. What men made in Greece of their new opportunities will be dealt with by other hands in later chapters of this book. The present chapter will examine some of the constraints, positive and negative, which the land of Greece imposed on those who dwelt in it.

First, the mountains and the plains. With the exception of Thessaly and eastern Macedonia, continental Greece consists of small valleys or coastal plains separated by mountains. The flat land is often fertile if it gets enough water. But it must be emphasized again how little there is of it – 18 per cent of Greece, compared with 34 per cent of Portugal, 39 per cent of Spain or about 35 per cent of Italy. Greece is a land dominated by mountains.

The relation of mountain to plain is a complex one. In the first place, mountains are a barrier to movement. An army which can march irresistibly 1000 miles over level ground can be stopped by a few hundred feet of vertical difference. The steep and scrub-covered mountains of Greece isolated the valleys and plains from one another. Economic and political units have tended to be small. The typical classical Greek *polis* comprised a city, often with a defensible citadel or *acropolis*, and the surrounding territory as far as the crests of the mountains or the sea. Some were tiny, only a few square miles in extent. A small island might contain several such cities, each of which in antiquity was a sovereign state. Even the largest, like Sparta or Athens, were no bigger than Rhode Island. In principle, the citizens lived off the produce of their territory. If the yield was low because of drought or disease, or because hostile neighbours made a sally across the mountain pass and cut down or burned the crop, men starved. With the best will in the world, transport of bulk supplies of food across the mountains was impossible, and transport by sea, as will be seen, was often impracticable. Political isolation often went with economic isolation. There was no pan-Hellenic community until 1830, and even then it left more Greeks outside its frontiers than within them. Fierce local patriotism marked the city-state of antiquity, and it was a notable feature of Greek life in modern times; sometimes it was institutionalized in the form of patron-client relations, which until recently dominated much of Greek public life. The relations between city and city, village and village, island and island, has more often been one of rivalry than of cooperation.

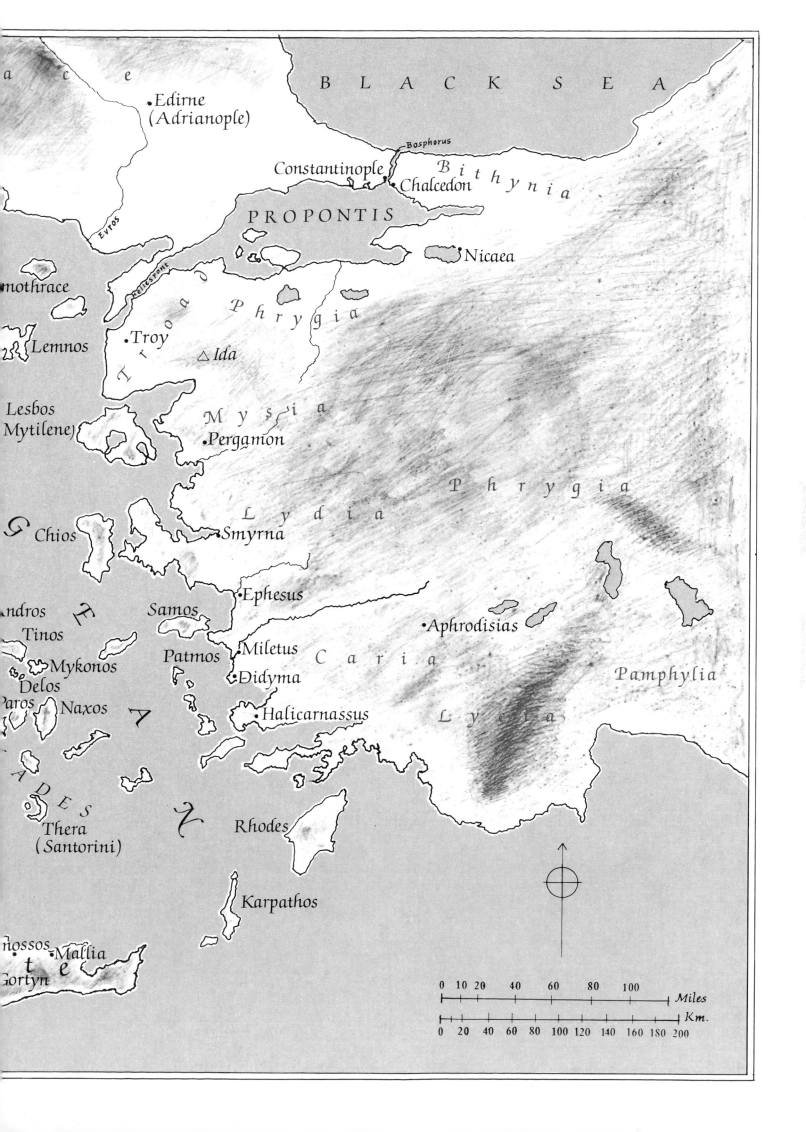

Yet at the same time the mountains could become a zone of communication between the lowland communities. Their flocks of sheep and goats shared the high summer pastures, for the climate imposed short-distance summer transhumance. No doubt there were disputes about grazing rights between neighbouring cities in antiquity, as there have been between neighbouring villages in modern times. But the shepherds from different communities could meet on equal terms in these mountain borderlands. It was in the high pastures between Thebes and Corinth that the infant Oedipus was handed over by a Theban shepherd to his Corinthian colleague. The young Orestes too was spirited out of the territory of Argos by a shepherd. In later years smuggling and clandestine trade in high-value goods have often gone on in the mountains. The Vlachs, who since the early Middle Ages have pastured their flocks in summer in the heights of Pindos have always combined stock-rearing with trade. Before 1912 they moved freely between Greek, Ottoman, and Bulgarian territory, circumventing the customs control of all three states. In the Second World War they often had valuable consumer goods which the settled inhabitants of the lowlands were ready to pay well for. Communities which included mountain areas in their territory, and thus had access to two different climatic zones, enjoyed great advantages. Not only had they summer pastures for their flocks, with the possibilities of external contacts which this entailed. They could also grow crops which did not thrive in the lowlands – apples, walnuts, chestnuts, and the like – and they might well also have access to valuable timber supplies. Many of the smaller communities, and particularly those in the islands, had no such access. Their life was correspondingly impoverished and threatened. The Spartans possessed a large and fertile plain, and a great area of high mountain, which contributed to their leading position among Greek states in antiquity, just as it did to the prosperity of the Despotate of the Morea in the later Middle Ages.

Another role of the mountains was the result of their very inaccessibility. They could become refuges, islands of freedom in an unfree world. 'The steepest places have at all times been the asylum of liberty', wrote Baron de Tott in the 18th century, thinking of such regions as Switzerland, Montenegro, or Lebanon. In Greece it was often impossible, or just not worthwhile, for those who ruled the lowlands to enforce their authority in the highlands. The Arcadian cantons – there were no cities until the foundation of Megalopolis about 366 BC – retained their freedom when most of the Peloponnese was firmly controlled by Sparta. Slavonic peasants held out for centuries against Byzantine and Latin rulers in the heights of Taygetos. The Turks left many mountainous regions to the control of their own notables or of a local militia – the *armatoloi* – who lived in a kind of uneasy symbiosis with the *klephts* – men who had taken to the mountains to escape the Turks and often to fight against them.

The tough mountain shepherd, with his herds of goat and sheep, has been a familiar figure throughout Greek history: above, the herdsman Euphorbas with the infant Oedipus; below, goats in a vineyard.

'Brigands' operated in some of the Greek mountains until late in the 19th century. And invasion, occupation, or civil war have always seen men take to the mountains to defend freedom as a principle, or simply to escape the intolerable constraints of the lowlands. Once there, they ran their affairs in their own way.

Then the mountains often provided a reserve of manpower – tough younger sons with the skills of the mountaineer. Most of the 10,000 mercenary soldiers who marched with Xenophon to the heart of Persia and back again to the sea, seem to have been Arcadians. The armies of the successors of Alexander came largely from the mountainous regions of Greece and Macedonia. The Byzantines had élite units of Tsakonians, men from the inaccessible highlands south of the Argolid and east of Laconia. The *stradioti* who fought for the Republic of Venice were mainly Greeks and Albanians from the mountains. In more recent times men from the mountains have come as workers to Athens or Thessalonica, or gone as *Gastarbeiter* to Germany or as emigrants to America or Australia. Mountain manpower, often welcome, occasionally threatening, has been a constant feature of Greek society.

Lastly, the mountains could be a source of timber, the most important raw material in antiquity and the Middle Ages, and in particular the material of ships. 'Could be', because it was not enough that oaks or pines still covered some of the mountainsides. It had to be transportable to where it was needed. Greek rivers were unsuitable for floating logs down. Forest-covered mountains near sheltered seacoasts were what was needed. Ancient states sometimes made great efforts to gain and retain control of such sources of timber. Solomon and the cedars of Lebanon, or the Vandal rulers of Africa with their outposts in Sardinia and Corsica are cases in point. Throughout antiquity and the Middle Ages this was a factor in the politics and strategy of Greece. Athenian interest in Thrace was partly prompted by the need for accessible supplies of timber for the fleet, a fleet which in its turn was needed to maintain control of the routes to the timber sources. The Byzantine fleet maintained ship-repair yards in ports near pine- or cypress-covered slopes. The main shipbuilding centre was in Constantinople itself, but there were subsidiary naval shipyards in Euboea, Lemnos, Samos, and Smyrna.

Sea and ships

The sea was both a source of food and a means of communication. But fishing was relatively unproductive. Its small-scale and local character hardly made it a training-ground for sailors, nor did it call forth the ingenuity and inventiveness that lead to technical advance. No major improvement in navigation or seamanship is of Greek or indeed Mediterranean origin. It was in western European waters and in the China Seas that men learned to master the ocean. Ancient Greek ships were all carvel built – with the planks laid flush with one another – and readily sprang a leak. The clinker-built ship – with the planks overlapping – is not found in the Mediterranean until the later Middle Ages. Ancient Greek ships were steered by large oars, and could not sail close to the wind. The hazards of sailing in the ancient Mediterranean are graphically illustrated by the adventures of St Paul. There was, of course, plenty of skilled seamanship in the Greek world. But it was concerned largely with warships propelled by oars, be they Athenian triremes, Byzantine *dromons*, or Venetian or Genoese galleys.

Though most voyages in the Greek world could be made without losing sight of land if the weather was good, travel by sea was none the less dangerous. Even in summer sudden squalls can sweep down. In winter there was virtually no sailing anywhere in the Mediterranean until the 15th century, and little until the advent of steam. In antiquity the sailing season began at the end of March and ended in October; Pisan regulations of 1160 prescribe the same limits, as do also the maritime statute of Venice of 1284 and that of Ancona of 1387. The islands were therefore cut off from one another and from the mainland for half of the year, and forced to survive on their own resources. The island in the sun could be a prison in winter. Coastal communities on the mainland could maintain touch with one another only by difficult journeys on foot or on mule-back across mountain paths. Being a sailor was not a full-time occupation, to which a man might devote his whole life. There was consequently no reserve of men for whom the sea was their natural element. The rise of the Greek shipping industry in the early 19th century, which made Greece by the middle of the 20th century one of the world's great maritime powers, was due to Greek mercantile enterprise and to a conjuncture in the relations of the European powers with one another and with the Ottoman empire. It did not happen because Greece was a land of 'natural sailors'.

Centres of shipping have always been determined less by considerations of local trade than by those of naval policy and long distance trade. Athenian sea-power was the creation of the Persian wars and of the simultaneous fulfilment of a number of economic, social, and political conditions which will be examined later. Rhodes became a great centre of maritime trade in Hellenistic times on the basis of long distance commerce between the eastern and western Mediterranean. Crete and Chios owed their importance as entrepôts to Venetian trade with the Levant and Genoese trade with the Black Sea. Small, almost barren islands like Hydra, Psara, and Oinoussai became centres of a Greek merchant marine engaged in conveying goods between the Ottoman empire and western Europe, while their larger neighbours slumbered on in their age-old isolation. Syros prospered in the 19th century while nearby islands faced starvation or emigration. Today Andros and Chios are centres of world-wide shipping networks, while most of the Cyclades are depopulated or depend on the uncertainties of tourism. So it was and is with the coasts of the mainland too. There was much

shipping in the Saronic Gulf and the Gulf of Corinth in antiquity, but the Peloponnese, in spite of several excellent harbours, remained inward-turned and self-sufficient, as Thucydides observed. Epirus made nothing of the splendid natural harbour of the Gulf of Ambracia, so conveniently situated for trade with Italy. One form of maritime activity was at certain epochs regrettably prevalent in Greek waters – piracy. Nestor asks the crew of a strange ship whether they are merchants or pirates (*Odyssey*, Book 3, lines 71–4). The absence of a strong naval power always led to the growth of piracy, whether in the 1st century BC, when the end of the conflict between Rome and Mithridates of Pontus left a power vacuum in the eastern Mediterranean, or in the 9th and 10th centuries of our era, when the Byzantine fleet was unable to prevent Arab corsairs from Crete from raiding and devastating the coasts of the Aegean. In a way pirates were the only professional sailors of the Greek world, and the clandestine encouragement of them by the great powers at the end of the 18th and the beginning of the 19th century probably made some contribution to the rise of the Greek merchant marine.

Fruits of the earth

When men began to grow their own food in Greece, they had to take account of the constraints which limited the natural vegetation of the country. They had to cultivate either deep-rooted, woody perennials or quick-growing annuals which produced their seeds before the full summer heats. The olive, the vine, and perhaps somewhat later the fig – all of which have non-Greek names – belonged to the first category. The second was represented by autumn-sown wheat and barley, and by various beans and other legumes. All had already been domesticated in the Near East. Of these the staples throughout history have been olives, vines, and wheat. The latter two can be cultivated in virtually every region of Greece. The olive is more demanding, above a certain height, which varies with latitude, or at more than a certain distance from the sea, it will not fruit. Consequently much of central and northern Greece and almost all of the Arcadian highlands are unsuitable for olive-growing. As the fruit of the olive and its oil were used throughout Greece as food, as fuel for lamps, and for anointing the body, there must have

been from very early times internal trade between the regions where the olive grew and those in which it did not. Simple subsistence cultivation has never been frequent in Greece.

The wheat grown in Greece since antiquity is bread wheat (*Triticum aestivum*), the result of prehistoric hybridization in the Near East. But emmer wheat (*Triticum dicoccum*) was also cultivated. Its prominent role in sacrificial ritual both in Greece and in Italy suggests that it may at one time have been the wheat principally cultivated. Pliny in his *Natural History* says that it was 'the first food of ancient times' (*primus antiquitatis cibus*). It does not make good bread. In modern times much more wheat is grown than barley. In antiquity it may not have been so. An inscription recording the first fruits of the Attic harvest offered to the temple of Demeter at Eleusis in 329/8 BC suggests a harvest of 363,000 *medimni* of barley and only 39,000 of wheat. We do not know how these figures were calculated nor how typical they are, and in any case Athens imported much of the wheat it needed. But there is no doubt that a great deal of barley must have been eaten in Attica, even if some of the crop was consumed by animals. Bread of a kind can be made from barley and was made in antiquity. Much of it, however, must have been eaten in the form of some kind of porridge or polenta.

Pulses formed until recently the most important source of protein in the Greek diet. The main dish served in the messes of the Spartans was a black broth of beans, perhaps not unlike the excellent bean soup which figures daily in the menu of the United States Senate cafeteria. Aristophanes makes Herakles a glutton for *etnos*, a kind of thick bean soup. Green vegetables of various kinds were eaten as salads or cooked. But they were scarce in summer. The only root vegetables largely cultivated were radishes of different kinds. Gourds and melons have always been cultivated, but they depend on irrigation, and cannot have been so frequent in the past as they are today.

As time went on many Greek communities – or their ruling class – found it more advantageous to practise specialized agriculture rather than to aim at self-sufficiency. In particular the cultivation of cereal crops was reduced in favour of olives and vines. Such specialization presupposes the availability of alternative

Sea and ships: two lines of rowers prepare to propel this ship (left) – a scene from an archaic vase painting thought to depict the abduction of Helen. The fruits of the earth: right, a farmer ploughs with his ox while his wife scatters the seed behind him.

sources of cereals, and the demand for oil and wine and the ability to pay in silver or gold; it also calls for reliable sea transport, merchants with adequate capital, a market structure extending over a wide area, and so on. Athens was probably the first Greek state to specialize in this way, importing grain from Egypt or from the Bosporan kingdom on the north coast of the Black Sea, and exporting oil and wine both there and elsewhere. Throughout history a great deal of Greek agriculture has been devoted to the cultivation of cash crops for sale on an external market. In early modern times, for instance, the vine was cultivated in Crete and Corfu to the almost total exclusion of cereal crops. In this way the Greek farmer turned to his advantage the features of terrain and climate which limited much of the country to olive-growing. There was a danger here. Greek interstate warfare usually took the form of sending a small force of armed men into a neighbour's territory just before the harvest to seize or more often to destroy his crop. If a portion of the year's corn was lost men could tighten their belts and survive. But olive plantations take twenty-five years to regenerate. To cut down, grub up, or burn a neighbour's olive trees is to inflict a mortal blow. The law of Moses forbade the Jews to cut down their enemies' olive trees (*Deuteronomy* 20.19–20). The Greeks usually observed similar self-restraint. But the rules could be, and occasionally were, broken, with devastating effect.

Because the Greek farmer has been since antiquity involved in production for a market – in modern times for a world market – he has always been aware of conditions outside his own area, and able and willing to make economic decisions. Greek readiness to emigrate, Greek commercial enterprise, and perhaps Greek intellectual curiosity, owe much to this long tradition of production for an external market which must be studied and understood. One manifestation of this openness to new ideas and new practices is the readiness to accept and adopt new crops to supplement the basic wheat, olives, and vines. Many of these new crops have from the first been produced mainly for a distant market. The almond and the mulberry may have been introduced in the archaic period. The cherry (its name is Akkadian) was brought from Persia in classical times. The peach (*persica* in Latin) and the apricot (its Greek name *verikokko* is derived from Latin *praecox* via

Arabic) were introduced in the heyday of the Roman empire; their ultimate origin was in China. The walnut (*karyon pontikon* or *basilikon*), the chestnut, and the pistachio were all importations from the east. Rice, sugar, and citrus fruits were taken over from the Arabs in the Middle Ages; sugar cane was once cultivated in Crete and Cyprus. All these crops were originally domesticated in China or south-east Asia. The discovery of the New World brought many new crops to Greece as to the rest of Europe. Maize, tomatoes, peppers, and tobacco flourish in the Greek climate, and the potato grows well in cooler and damper regions such as Arcadia and Epirus. Recent times have seen the introduction of the avocado and the banana, among other exotic crops. These innovations have transformed Greek agriculture and enriched Greek life, and at the same time strengthened the links binding the Greek farmer to a world market. Some of the new crops require irrigation. Conservation of soil moisture by terracing hillsides, and the channelling of spring water into fields go back to the remote past of Greek agriculture. In some regions the digging of wells provided an additional source of water. But until very recent times not much more could be done. Nowadays water is pumped from artesian wells in many regions, such as the extensive citrus plantations of Messenia. The practice has its hazards; the reserves of underground water are not unlimited; and continuous irrigation of the thin, friable soil may leach away some of its valuable plant nutrients. In Greece, as elsewhere, there may be a contradiction between short-term profitability and the conservation of the resources of the land.

Of domestic animals the sheep, the goat, and the pig were introduced in Neolithic times. The sheep and the goat are admirably suited to the practice of summer transhumance. However, the goat, by eating the young shoots of trees, helps to prevent forest regeneration. The removal of the flocks to the high pasture in summer means that droppings are not available to manure the crops, and so reduces the fertility of the arable land. The pig eats the by-products of the olive-press and the wine press. Cattle, other than working cattle, have always been rare in Greece. The high pastures are inaccessible to them; and in any case their grass is much less nutritious than that of Alpine meadows, consisting as it

35

does mainly of steppe grasses. In the lowlands there is no green grass in summer. So beef, veal, cow's milk and its by-products have never until modern times been prominent in the Greek diet. Working oxen until very recently provided the only source of energy in Greek agriculture other than human muscle. But in antiquity the shortage of summer pasture meant that they had to be fed on barley, so competing with human consumers. The introduction of lucerne (in Greek *medike*), probably in the 5th century BC, enabled more oxen to be kept. Both the horse and the ass and their bastard offspring the mule have been known in Greece since the Bronze Age. The horse eats the same food as man – and much more of it. It was never a working animal in Greece as it was in northern Europe. It was either an instrument of war or a status symbol. Most Greek cities could not field an effective cavalry force. The Athenians won the Battle of Marathon because they were able to attack when the formidable Persian cavalry had ridden off to water their horses. The collapse of the Crusader regime in the Peloponnese in the later Middle Ages was partly due to the difficulty of maintaining a force of mounted knights in Greece. The ass and the mule have always been used both for riding and as pack or draught animals. Their less tender digestion enables them to live off the Greek countryside. Not least among the domestic animals of Greece are the bees. They gather nectar from the countless flowers that cover the mountainsides in spring, and their honey provided the only concentrated source of sugar until the importation of cheap cane sugar from the West Indies began. Greece still exports large quantities of honey.

The scope of Greek agriculture has been constantly increased since the inhabitants of the Franchthi cave first began to cultivate barley and wheat. Every advantage has been taken of the long summer sunshine and the often copious winter rain. But Greece is not a bounteous land. Herodotus makes King Demaratos of Sparta tell Xerxes that Hellas and poverty have always been foster-sisters. Not the crushing poverty that breaks men's spirits, but a poverty that encourages them to examine their situation and find ways of bettering it. It was a commonplace of ancient Greek thought that poverty was the mother of invention, the source of arts and crafts and wisdom. As Anaximenes of Lampsakos remarked in the 4th century BC, 'Poverty makes men cleverer and more skilled in the craft of life.'

While life may have been tolerable enough for most Greek communities most of the time, it took very little to tip the balance between sufficiency and hunger. A bad harvest, an enemy raid, the loss of its young men in battle, an earthquake, could all speedily reduce a small community to starvation. A large and powerful – by Greek standards – state, like Sparta or Athens, could usually weather the storm and protect the living standard of its citizens. But great and small communities alike were from time to time faced by a rise in population beyond what their resources could feed. Internal migration has throughout history both helped

to ease local disparities in productivity and to create new ones. First of all, there has always been a drift to the cities, the historical demographers tell us, because no ancient or medieval city could maintain its population without constant reinforcement from outside. Urban mortality was much higher than in the countryside. Peasants from Attica and craftsmen and others from different regions of Greece flocked to Athens in the 5th and 4th centuries BC. In the Ottoman period there was constant movement from the countryside to the towns. The headlong growth of Athens and Thessalonica in our own time is a phenomenon of the industrial world, but its effects are similar to those of earlier migrations. Men often moved in search of work, as mercenary soldiers or as labourers. Thessaly in the 17th century relied on immigrant labour from central Greece and even from Attica to cultivate its fields of grain. Such migration can become emigration. In the Ottoman period men moved from Greece to Constantinople or Smyrna, and often stayed there. In the 19th century there was similar movement to Odessa and Egypt. Much of the work on the Suez Canal was done by labourers from the island of Kasos. Many of them stayed on in Port Said. But sometimes there was a reverse movement from the towns and the lowlands to the mountains to escape an oppressive authority. This was not uncommon in the period of Turkish rule. The migrants sometimes returned, changed by their life in the mountains; they lost their peasant passivity and their city softness. Sometimes, however, the flight to the mountains was the beginning of permanent emigration.

Poverty: the options

When for one reason or another the population of a Greek community, whose territory was determined by the geography of the country, rose sufficiently to threaten its standard of living, there were several courses open to its citizens, quite apart from individual emigration. The first was to seize the land of its neighbours, expelling or subjugating the original inhabitants. It was some such situation that underlay the Lelantine war between Chalkis and Eretria in the 8th century BC. An extreme example was the conquest of Messenia by the Spartans in two long wars in the late 8th and early 7th centuries BC. There was little scope for such direct conquest in later times, when Greece was dominated more and more by one or other of its own leading cities or by external powers.

The second option was to send away part of its own people, as a bee-hive sends out a swarm. The great expansion of Greek 'colonies' – independent city-states founded by the initiative of one or more existing cities – during the 8th to 6th centuries BC is the most obvious example. Formally the procedure harks back to an ancient tribal ritual in which a portion of the young men is sent away to form a new community; there are parallels in early Italian society. By the 6th century a new 'imperialist' type of colony makes its appearance,

Dancers in a row: a delightful 19th-century embroidery from Crete.

sent out to be a strategic outpost of its mother-city. Finally, after Alexander's conquests, Greek and Macedonian colonists settled in the new cities in the east Mediterranean. We have few figures, and not all of them are reliable. But it is clear that a mass movement of population was involved. The territory of Antioch was apparently divided into 10,000 lots, probably distributed to 10,000 original settlers and their families. In the 1st century BC the Roman census recorded 117,000 citizens of Antioch (i.e. excluding women, children, slaves, and dependent peasants); but many of these may by this time have been descendants of Hellenized Syrians. Diodorus recounts that after the departure of Alexander 23,000 Greeks were massacred at Bactra, between the Hindu Kush mountains and the river Oxus, in present-day Afghanistan; the figure has been questioned by modern historians. Such officially sponsored emigration was rare in the Roman, Byzantine, and Turkish periods, though the Byzantine authorities did on occasion transfer whole populations from one region of the empire to another. In modern times there are occasional examples of something similar. The wholesale recruitment of the men of Kasos for work on the Suez Canal has been mentioned. There are islands in the Aegean whose inhabitants regularly settle in a particular city in America or Australia. The extreme example is the tiny island of Kastellorizo, off the south coast of Asia Minor; the large majority of the natives of the island now live in Sydney. The emigration of Greek *Gastarbeiter* to Germany was not always left to individual initiative, but was in large measure organized by German employers. Some of these points will be more fully discussed in the chapter on the Greek Diaspora.

The third course of action open to the rulers of a community under population pressure is to change the internal social and economic structure of the community, and consequently the distribution of the social surplus among its members. Something of this kind seems to have happened in early Sparta, when a part of the population lost control of the land which it cultivated and was forced to pay over part of its produce to those who owned the land but did not cultivate it. The precise origin of the Spartan helots is disputed, but it must have involved the political and economic subjection of a part of the original population. In Thessaly too the bulk of the population had by classical times been reduced to a serf-like status of subjection to a small hereditary aristocracy. In early Athens the peasants were in part becoming sharecroppers, in part debt-bondsmen, and even being sold into slavery abroad as a small ruling class tightened its grip. The political victory of Solon and his supporters arrested this process by cancelling debts and abolishing debt-bondsmanship, and set Athens on a new course.

A fourth option in the face of population pressure is to improve the productivity of the land. One aspect of this is the constant introduction of new crops which has already been mentioned. Minor improvement was always going on by way of terracing, channelling of springs, and building up of river banks. But extensive irrigation or bringing of new land under cultivation calls for a concentration of capital resources impossible for a small community. Hellenistic kings and Roman or Byzantine emperors did occasionally provide funds – and technical skill – for major works of improvement, but very little of this came the way of Greece. It was only with the foundation of the Greek state, the expansion of new commercial activities such as shipping, and the creation of a world-wide credit system that major betterment schemes could be carried out. The draining of Lake Copais in Boeotia in 1886 made available a large area of new and fertile land. In many parts of Greece afforestation projects have sought to reestablish the forest cover on the mountains, both to provide a crop of timber and to reduce flash-floods and soil erosion. There is still much less being done in the way of land improvement than could be done.

Finally, the challenge of rising population can be met by importing food and exporting something else in return, be it precious metal, cash crops, manufactured goods, or services. Such a policy, in ancient times as in modern, depended on the fulfilment of a number of necessary conditions. When at the beginning of the Peloponnesian War in 431 BC Pericles told the Athenians that they need not fear the devastation of their land by the Spartan army, and the city and its port of Peiraeus formed a kind of island that would be supplied by sea, he was alluding to the success of an unprecedented policy of non-dependence on local food resources. Athens got its corn from Egypt or the Black Sea. It had to have something to export in return – wine and oil and manufactured goods in time of peace, silver from its own mines if its land was raided or occupied. This policy presupposed a powerful war fleet to ensure uninterrupted supplies. This in turn required access to timber in Thrace and elsewhere, reserves both of skilled craftsmen and of men freed from the demands of agriculture to row the ships, and willingness of the citizens to forego immediate enjoyment for future security. It was in fact during the Persian wars that Themistocles persuaded his fellow-citizens not to share out the profits from the silver mines at Laurion but to use them to build a navy; and later the threat from a hostile Sparta replaced that from Persia. This is an oversimplified view of a complex transformation of the relation of man to the land and of man to man. Within our own lifetime even more radical changes have taken place in Greece in both these domains. Yet the basic constraints imposed by terrain and climate remain.

Greece may be the foster-sister of poverty, yet its ever-changing natural beauty, its agreeable climate, its richness in vines and olive trees, its ready access to the sea, have all drawn men to settle there. The first speakers of the Indo-European language that later became Greek probably arrived in the peninsula from the north – or possibly from the east – about 2400 BC. The invaders brought with them not only their language – and perhaps patterns and themes of poetry – but new tastes in pottery and building. Their religious beliefs and rituals were fused with those of the older inhabitants; Zeus, ruler of gods and men, is an Indo-European god.

Newcomers to Greece

In a similar fashion later immigrants and invaders learned from the earlier inhabitants ways of life imposed by the environment, but they brought new contributions of their own too. In the late 6th and early 7th centuries of our era there was heavy immigration and settlement by Slav tribes, particularly in north-western Greece and the Peloponnese. Traces of their earliest settlements have recently been found at Argos and Olympia. The Slavs, who from the beginning were involved in economic, political, and cultural relations with the Greek world, were gradually absorbed into it. Only in the fastnesses of Taygetos did they continue to speak their own language until the 15th century.

The third major wave of immigrants were the Albanians who flocked into central Greece, mainly in the 15th century. Their movement was part of a great expansion of the Albanian people southward and eastward from their mountain homeland. In Greece they were welcomed as mercenary soldiers by the Latin rulers and later by the Ottoman Turks, and settled on the land. They clung tenaciously to their language and lifestyle. At the end of the 18th century the island of Aegina was almost wholly Albanian in speech, and Athens was a Greek town in the middle of an Albanian countryside. There are still villages on the slopes of Mount Helicon and elsewhere where Albanian is the everyday language. In others only the older generation still speaks Albanian. However, the Greeks of Albanian origin neither feel themselves nor are felt by others to be outsiders. They are part of the Hellenic community. Many of the leaders in the War of Independence were of Albanian stock, as are many who are prominent in Greek public and intellectual life today. Another community which has been absorbed into the Greek amalgam is that of the Vlachs, descendants of the Latin-speaking population of the northern Balkans who took up a pastoral way of life and moved southwards into Greece in the Middle Ages. The frequence of Italian family names in Greece reminds us that there was much intermingling in areas long under Italian rule, such as the Ionian Islands, Crete, and Chios. Vintzentsos Kornaros, the greatest of the flourishing school of Greek poets in 17th-century Crete, has a purely Venetian name, and was probably of Venetian descent; but he was a Greek by the criterion of the 4th-century BC writer Isocrates, who claimed that language and culture rather than descent made a person Greek. There were flourishing Jewish communities in Greece in the 12th century, when Benjamin of Tudela visited the country. In the 15th and 16th centuries they were joined by many of their co-religionists who fled from persecution in Spain and Portugal. For centuries Thessalonica was a largely Jewish city. Many Greek Jews perished during the German occupation in World War II. But the community survives as an integral part of the Greek nation.

All these groups, and many others, have in the course of millennia been absorbed by the Greek world, and made their own enriching contribution to it. They have met and surmounted the challenge of the land, and in so doing have transformed the land, building cities where there had been only villages, planting useful crops from every corner of the world, learning to exploit its hidden riches, first silver and copper, today lignite and magnesia. They have learned to sail first their own island-studded waters, and later the oceans of the world. They have formed since the Bronze Age a link between Europe and the Near East, and many Greeks today are keenly aware of this role which has been given them by their geography and their history. In doing all these things they have made contributions to world culture quite out of proportion to their own small numbers.

I · PRELUDE

I
The Age of the Heroes
*Crete and Mycenae in
the Bronze Age*

THE GREEKS always believed that their culture had its beginnings in what we call the Bronze Age – the age of Crete and Mycenae, of the warriors and heroes immortalized in the Homeric epics and the great cycles of tragedy: Oedipus, Achilles, Odysseus, Agamemnon. The sensational discoveries of Heinrich Schliemann at Troy and Mycenae in the 19th century seemed to confirm at least the background of these legends, while Arthur Evans's excavations at Knossos, which first revealed the ancient civilization of Crete to the modern world, made the story of Theseus seem almost credible. In recent years, with the establishment that the language of the Mycenaean world was indeed an early form of Greek, myth and history have drawn even closer together. The most sober archaeologist finds it hard to suppress the image of the past which the Greeks themselves have passed down to us.

The first high civilization to emerge in the Greek-speaking area of the Aegean was that of Crete. Around the beginning of the second millennium BC a highly centralized state was established, with palatial buildings at Knossos, Phaistos, Mallia and elsewhere, a sophisticated religion with elaborate rituals, a hieroglyphic script and a wealth of mature art forms that included fresco-painting, pottery and jewellery.

The relationship between Minoan Crete and the urban centres on the mainland, such as Mycenae, and the Cyclades, is still problematical. To what extent were they interdependent? Which was dominant at which times? What caused their rise and – even more intriguing – their fall? All that now seems likely is that about 1200 BC all these great centres suffered some sort of catastrophe. A dark age of several centuries descends upon Greece, a reversion to primitive levels of life, before a new dawn: the beginning of classical culture.

Goddess, priestess or queen?
Minoan religion and Minoan government, if indeed they are separable, are equally enigmatic. The deciphered Linear B tablets shed little light on the earlier Minoan world, and all that we have are images in painting and sculpture – frescos of bull-leaping, scenes of sacrifice on sarcophagi and gems, clay figures with upraised hands or these so-called 'snake goddesses' (*opposite*) of faience, found in the palace of Knossos. The bare breasts suggest the mother-goddess. The snakes have analogies with Egyptian religion; one encircles her waist; one is draped round her arms and shoulders, the head in her left hand, the tail in her right; a third rises above her headdress. (1)

The art of the Cyclades forms a prelude to Minoan civilization. Flourishing in the 3rd millennium BC, it left mysterious remains in the shape of near-abstract sculptures of men and women (*above*), their features reduced to simple geometric patterns. (2)

Harvesters return from the fields, from a black steatite vase found at Hagia Triada, in Crete. They carry tools which seem to combine sickle and flail. (4)

Women bring libations which they pour into a large mixing bowl standing between two double axes: a scene from a painted sarcophagus also from Hagia Triada. The second woman has two vessels on a pole over her shoulder. The third is a musician playing a lyre. (5)

The empire of Minos

Minoan civilization takes its name from the legendary King Minos, lord of the labyrinth and of the minotaur. We now know that a cult involving bulls did indeed flourish at Knossos, and there is some evidence that human sacrifice was practised in Crete.

In the heart of the Palace of Knossos, Sir Arthur Evans discovered what he believed to be the royal throne (*left*). The wall-paintings are much restored but are based on surviving traces. (3)

Minoan buildings are known partly from excavations and partly from representations in painting and pottery. *Right:* stone rhyton from the palace at Kato Zakro, a new site excavated in 1962. The relief depicts a mountain sanctuary. The entrance doorway at the bottom is decorated with spiral designs, a common Minoan motif. Wild goats above it attend the local mother-goddess. On the right are ritual 'horns of consecration', also plentiful at Knossos, while a bird of prey hovers over the gateway. (6)

About 1500 BC a volcanic explosion tore apart half of the island of Santorini, or Thera, and covered the rest with a thick layer of ash and pumice. Only since 1967 has this layer been penetrated and a whole town been revealed, with tall houses, lavish wall-paintings and pottery.

'The flotilla' one of the best preserved of the paintings, shows a harbour town and a fleet of ships. Some of the houses are several storeys high. Men and women crowd the roofs and quaysides to watch; in the background a lion – unknown in the Aegean islands – pursues a herd of deer; a stream rises in the hills and encircles the town. The fisherman from the same room (*above*), proudly holding a bunch of fish, is perhaps the first male nude in secular European art. (7, 8)

Mycenae

Mycenae was the Homeric capital of Agamemnon and Clytemnestra, the setting of Aeschylus' 'Oresteia'. Crowning a low hill and surrounded by ramparts, it is still one of the most atmospheric of Greek sites.

Miniature heads in ivory from Mycenaean graves give some indication of costume and armour. The helmet is covered with boars' tusks; a crest would have been fixed to the knob at the top. (10)

The citadel of Mycenae (*upper right*) occupies an irregular triangle. In the photograph we are looking north-west, with the Lion Gate (*right*) in the re-entrant angle in the foreground and Grave Circle A a little to its right. This circle, marked by a double line of upright stones, contained the shaft-graves excavated by Schliemann in 1876. (11, 12)

The gold masks that covered the faces of the dead evoke a world of barbaric splendour and grim warrior princes. It is difficult to resist identifying them with the doomed house of Atreus and saying with Schliemann: 'I have looked upon the face of Agamemnon.' In fact, according to archaeology, they must date from the 16th century BC, some three hundred years before the presumed date of the Trojan war. (9)

47

I
The Age of the Heroes

*Crete and Mycenae in
the Bronze Age*

A. M. SNODGRASS

The bull cult is the subject of two exceptionally well
preserved gold cups found at Vaphio in southern Greece.
In this detail (*opposite*), a hunter, having lured the bull with a
decoy cow on the right, is tying a rope to its hind leg.
These reliefs, dated to about 1500 BC, are among the most
sophisticated works in the whole of Mycenaean art, looking
forward in their easy naturalism to the art of classical Greece
a thousand years later. (13)

This chapter has inevitably to be more tentative – and more controversial – than the chapters that follow it. During the last hundred years great advances and momentous discoveries have been made concerning the Greek Bronze Age. But they have tended, disconcertingly, to contradict as often as to confirm the prevailing opinions of the time. Progress has therefore been a series of steps backward as well as forward, each step being marked by scholarly quarrels of varying degrees of rancour. The notorious debate over the language of the Linear B tablets – that is, the language spoken in Mycenaean Greece and, for a time, in one or more of the centres of power in Crete – has now reached a point of widespread agreement: they are written, if not necessarily exclusively, in Greek. But some equally crucial questions, especially of dating – when Greek speakers arrived in the Aegean, when Knossos fell and Santorini was destroyed, when the successive layers of Troy were formed – are still hotly debated. Assumptions in virtually all areas of our subject are likely to be overturned without warning. Our picture of the Minoans, for instance, as easy-going, life-loving people has been shaken, to say the least, by recent discoveries suggesting that they practised human sacrifice and cannibalism. Any account claiming to be comprehensive, therefore, is bound to be largely provisional. We are assembling clues rather than summarizing facts.

We are, for example, very uncertain when the first Greek-speakers entered the Aegean region: the likeliest date is towards the end of the 3rd millennium BC. But in any case their advent brought with it no swift or dramatic change, and they undoubtedly shared the environment with peoples of different stock. Geography and climate made for continuity; the ubiquitous presence of the sea, however, encouraged a life-style fundamentally different from that appropriate to the Balkans further north. The numerous islands invited maritime exploration in a way that did not arise elsewhere in the Mediterranean. The mountainous terrain of the mainland discouraged centralization. Fertile land was limited; there could be no agricultural expansion to parallel that of Asia Minor. And since there was no scope for elaborate irrigation, society did not become stratified in the way that irrigation systems facilitated in Mesopotamia.

The early villages were located with an eye to the best arable land: during the Neolithic period the plains of Macedonia and Thessaly were more thickly settled than

The high civilization of mainland Greece produced fresco paintings equal in scale if not in quality to those of Minoan Crete, but what remains is too fragmentary to be restored. This water-colour reconstruction is part of a fresco from Tiryns and shows two young women setting out in a chariot for a boar-hunt.

southern mainland Greece, and many of the smaller islands were apparently not yet permanently inhabited at all. Even though on one of these latter, Melos, an important natural source of obsidian had already been located, its extraction seems to have been conducted in a fairly haphazard way by parties of visitors landing periodically on the island. There are no signs of the existence of a clear social hierarchy; evidence for warfare and fortification is rarely found. Cereals form the main basis of subsistence, with wheat, in various forms, the dominant crop in northern Greece, though barley came to supplant it in parts of the southern mainland and, presently, in the islands. Animal husbandry is dominated by the sheep and the goat.

In the Early Bronze Age, covering very roughly the third millennium BC, the picture appears to change so radically that at first we are inclined to overlook the constancy of the most deep-seated features. One of these features is the persistently small scale of most operations in the prehistoric Aegean. It shows itself most clearly in the size of settlements: even at the height of the Minoan and Mycenaean cultures, it was a rare settlement in the Aegean which attained even five per cent of the area of Uruk in Mesopotamia, while the typical settlement of the Aegean Early Bronze Age was very much smaller still.

That said, we must recognize that the changes that took place in the Early Bronze Age Aegean were not only striking in themselves, but also a foretaste of many later achievements and proclivities of the people of Greece. To begin with, it is in this period that we have the first evidence for the building of oared longships or galleys. These craft, with a beam:length ratio of about 1:12 and a probable overall length of at least 50–60 feet (15–18 metres), made regular Aegean navigation feasible for the first time, opening up new possibilities for migration, exchange and innovation. The distribution and density of settlements over the Aegean area increases. The basis of subsistence is transformed by the much greater importance of cattle and pigs, by the wider cultivation of barley and pulses, but above all by the domestication of the wild olive and vine. Thus were laid the foundations of what we now recognize as the staple regime not only of Greece but of many Mediterranean lands. Greater craft-specialization now developed: it was one (but only one) of the factors behind the appearance of works of art – particularly the marble figurines of human subjects – of a quality unrivalled in their day, and admired without condescension even in our own. That carved stone should be the medium in which some of the greatest successes were attained is another prophetic trend, even if its full exploitation had to wait another two millennia. On a monumental scale, too, the lasting association of stone-working with the Aegean begins in funerary architecture and fortific-

Consonant	A		E		I		O		U	
J-	JA	目	JE	※			JO	↑		
K- G-CH-	KA	⊕	KE KWE?	Ψ ℙ	KI	⫯	KO	♀	KU	⟲
N	NA NWA?	☰ ⋇	NE NEKO?	Ψ ⊕	NI	Ψ	NO .	⫯	NU	⏸
S-	SA	⅄	SE	⊩	SI	坐	SO	⅄	SU	⊟

In 1952 Michael Ventris was able to show that Linear B script was syllabic and that the language was an early form of Greek. Above: Ventris's grid for four consonant-plus-vowel clusters. Applying it to the tablet on the left, the first four signs in the bottom row read: [Ko-]no-si-jo ('Knossians'). Below: a line combining syllables with straightforward pictograms for chariot, corselet and horse.

ation. With the latter sphere one naturally associates another new feature, the appearance of a wide range of weapon-types. Underlying all these innovations, however (most obviously the last named), is the greatest single advance of all, the mastery of metallurgy and especially of the copper–tin alloy, bronze.

The adoption of bronze carried with it the acceptance of a whole new economic system based on bronze. Bronze tools made possible new and very much higher standards in agriculture, carpentry and stone-working; they therefore conferred enormous advantages on those who had access to the metal. At the same time, bronze weapons transformed warfare, and so gave the same people the chance to consolidate their advantage by force or coercion. Its value meant that bronze could also act as a medium of wealth in itself, rather than merely the means of creating wealth (just as on occasion it could form the material of works of art, besides that of the tools used to create them). Finally, since the nearest sources for one of the two ingredients of the alloy, tin, seem to have lain not much less than a thousand miles from the nearest Aegean shore, this placed a high premium on the maintenance of the long-range contacts which would ensure supplies. It is no wonder, therefore, that the adoption of bronze metallurgy brought about great changes in Aegean society.

For a period in the middle phase of the Early Bronze Age, covering several centuries around 2500 BC, the new culture of the Aegean has the appearance of prosperity and relative stability. Settlement is spread fairly evenly, though not densely, across the landscape of Greece and its islands; important cultural divisions have emerged, though intercommunication across these divisions is frequent and widespread. Especially significant is the fact that the most advanced regions, on almost any criterion, are now those of central and southern Greece, the Cyclades, Crete and the north-eastern Aegean (including the Troad and the off-shore islands of Lesbos, Chios and Lemnos); Thessaly and Macedonia seem hardly to participate in the new age, and it was not until two or more millennia later that either area fully made up the lost ground. The shift of emphasis was thus a lasting one. But the new culture itself was less permanent. Not many centuries elapsed, for example, between the first erection of stone fortifications and their first violent destruction. The last phase of the Early Bronze Age and the greater part of the Middle Bronze Age comprise, for much of the Aegean, the first of a series of episodes, widely-spaced in time, in which some kind of material stagnation, if not actual recession, seems to have occurred. Against a variety of symptoms in one way or another suggestive of decline, we cannot in many cases set any material advance more striking than the adoption of the fast potter's wheel.

The enigma of Crete

The most important exception to this trend is Crete. Nothing in the previous history of the island prepares us for the appearance, at the beginning of the Middle Bronze Age, of the 'First Palaces' of Minoan Crete, the most impressive social artefacts of their age in the Aegean area. What we know of earlier Cretan society is largely derived from the communal tombs. These tombs are evidence of the cohesive family-groupings which formed the foundation of a wider social hierarchy, soon to be represented in at least three separate centres on the island – Knossos, Phaistos and Mallia – and culminating in a ruler whose political dominance seems matched by his (or just possibly her) surveillance of religious practices, production and storage. To the regalia of a more traditional kind there was presently added a new bonus in the form of literacy: the palaces developed a native hieroglyphic script, in which the jumble of signs and symbols, already engraved on pottery and seal-stones in the Early Bronze Age, was reduced to a coherent system and used for the economic

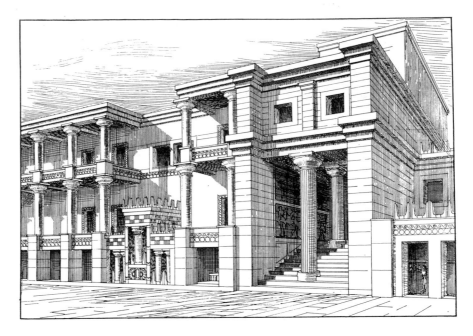

Reconstruction of part of the palace at Knossos. Most of the details are conjectural and reflect the ideas of the original excavator, Sir Arthur Evans. But the overall impression must be close to reality.

and religious purposes already alluded to. The whole of this new superstructure, finally, was given an architectural setting more impressive than anything yet seen in Europe.

The modern visitor to a Minoan palace-site will not find many visible traces, in architectural form, of its earliest phases. But excavation has shown that, as early as about 2000 BC, these buildings were already extensive and elaborate; while the artefacts which they and their associated cemeteries have produced show unprecedented aesthetic quality – notably the gold jewellery and the fine polychrome pottery known as 'Kamares ware'. These early attainments, however, tend to be overshadowed by those of the mature Minoan civilization of the 17th, 16th and 15th centuries BC, just as the early palace-plans are overlaid by those of their more sophisticated successors. Minoan Crete, at its zenith, has the appearance of a self-sufficient and self-confident society. The palace centres, by now numbering at least five, exude an atmosphere which extends, in diluted form, to many of the other sites as well, and particularly to the numerous isolated 'villas' in the countryside. The impression is conveyed that other ends – aesthetic polish, leisure, even downright luxuriousness – are considered at least as important as merely practical ones. Thus the consummate masterpieces of gem-carving go far beyond the functions of mere seal-stones, and the dark-on-light decoration of the 'Marine Style' pottery of about 1500 BC has a sophistication that is unprecedented and unmatched, even in Greece, until a thousand years later. The world of the Minoan fresco, too, appears as one of nearly timeless leisure, almost untroubled by incident or narrative. As for architecture, the palaces may have had extensive storage-space (as the content of the later Linear B tablets from Knossos suggests), but in their plans it is very much subordinated to the needs of gracious living and religious ceremonial and, as a result, somewhat un-

economically deployed. Religion – though this is a problematic issue – seems to obtrude, in the palaces especially, in almost every part of the building. The profusion of religious cult-places elsewhere on the island, particularly in caves and on mountain-tops, further reinforces this emphasis on the spiritual life. The Minoan palace system was to remain for more than five hundred years as an imposing back-drop to the endeavours of the mainland population, by now definitely Greek-speaking, on which we shall concentrate our attention.

It was not for some centuries that the rest of the Aegean world produced anything to match the complexity and pretension of the Minoan system; and when it did arise, it was to have a very different appearance. If we compare the Middle Bronze Age palace of Mallia in Crete with the contemporary citadel of Troy VI in the north-eastern Aegean, we are looking at two paths which have irrevocably diverged. Mallia is an integrated whole, while Troy has preserved the principle of separate, free-standing structures at some cost to the economic use of space; Mallia has staircases, showing that we have the remains of only the lower (and almost certainly less prestigious) floor of a structure of at least two storeys, whereas the Trojan buildings seem to be single-storey; Mallia is unfortified, Troy has fortifications of an elaboration which seems almost out of proportion with the small area that they protect; Mallia is a structure which palpably combines several functions in one arrangement, while Troy's plan betrays little beyond the domestic and defensive purposes: stripped of the latter, it would look like the glorified village which it really is.

The case of Troy is relevant because it has some points of resemblance with the settlements of the same period on the Greek mainland. Although they wear a more modest appearance, it is likely enough that Troy represented the same kind of social and economic unit

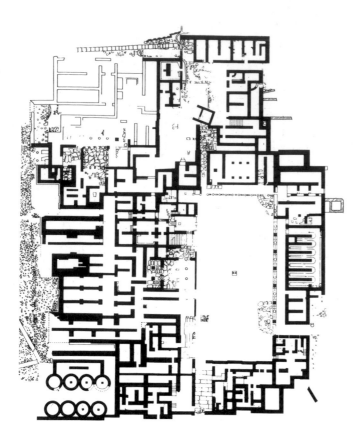

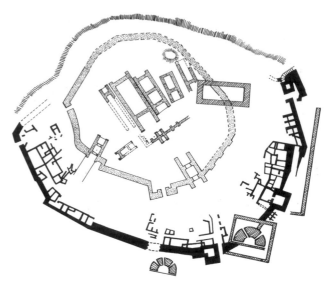

The palace at Mallia in Crete (left) and the citadel of Troy VI (above) are roughly contemporary in date but offer interesting contrasts in layout. Where Mallia is compact, ordered and open, Troy is irregular in plan and heavily fortified. The black lines indicate the remains of Homeric Troy.

that was beginning to prevail in mainland Greece: the general order of size is the same; both areas produce a characteristic pottery-ware, the 'Grey Minyan', which shows closely similar tastes and techniques. There seems, however, to have been a time-lag between the two, with the mainland features finding their counterparts not in contemporary but in earlier phases at Troy.

The apparent stagnation or recession, which as we have seen is often inferred for mainland Greece and the Cyclades during the Middle Bronze Age, needs closer scrutiny. The counts of sites, local or general, show a marked drop from the level of the Early Bronze Age to that of the Middle Bronze Age, but we should pause before attributing this to depopulation or general depression: two other explanations might well apply. First, the sites, though fewer in number, might be larger in size, a process known as nucleation; and second, the fact that the Early Bronze Age was more than twice, perhaps even three times, as long as the Middle Bronze Age, means that the possibility that sites were not in contemporary but in successive occupation is very much greater for the earlier period than for the later. Nevertheless, it remains a fact that there are certain areas where at the very least a slowing-down in the rate of population-growth must be accepted: the clearest cases are Laconia and the large off-shore island of Euboea.

Arguments about apparent decline are important because this period presents symptoms of a kind which will recur several times in later Greek history. On the mainland, the grave-goods become poorer and the burials on the whole less pretentious; architecturally, no building has been found to match the most ambitious Early Bronze Age structures; metallurgy becomes less innovatory; and burials are found within settlements, often under house-floors, a practice which has been seen as a resurgence of more primitive standards.

Few of these features, however, are found in the contemporary Cyclades. Three islands, Melos, Keos and Thera, are the best known, from the excavation of one of the principal settlements on each and from subsequent field-work. The settlements exhibit many Cretan features, but it is doubtful whether they should be classified simply as Minoan colonies. Phylakopi on Melos, however, may represent Minoan influence in another respect: earlier, the population of the island had been widely scattered (some thirty-odd sites of the Early Bronze Age are known), but in the Middle Bronze Age the number drops abruptly; by the first part of the Late Bronze Age, Phylakopi has become the one proven site of habitation on the whole island, and meanwhile its size has grown to that of an appreciable town – an extreme instance of nucleation. For Thera (or Santorini), great interest has been aroused by the discovery and excavation, since 1967, of the site at Akrotiri. Even now, it is probable that only a small proportion of the original town has been uncovered, but the quality of the finds and, above all, the preservation of the architecture have been spectacular. This is because Akrotiri was buried under a deep layer of volcanic ash, after the explosion of the volcanic core of the island. The date and the effects of this explosion have been hotly debated, but the recent evidence tends overwhelmingly to support the view that it was *not* contemporary with, and therefore not directly instrumental in, the final destructions of the palaces and other major sites on Crete. At Akrotiri, however, it has preserved for us the streets and houses, standing to two storeys in some cases, of a Cycladic town. There are many features in the architecture, in the wall-paintings and in the finds which remind us of Minoan Crete, as is also true of the sites on Melos (Phylakopi) and Keos (Ayia Irini), but there are differences too, and all three sites had been occupied long before the period of the strongest Minoan influence.

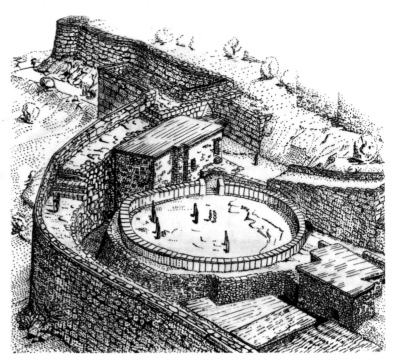

Mycenae's Grave Circle A, immediately inside the Lion Gate, was the royal burial ground, raised on a stone substructure and surrounded by upright stones. The graves were amazingly rich. Besides the famous gold masks, they contained gold and silver vessels and ninety bronze swords.

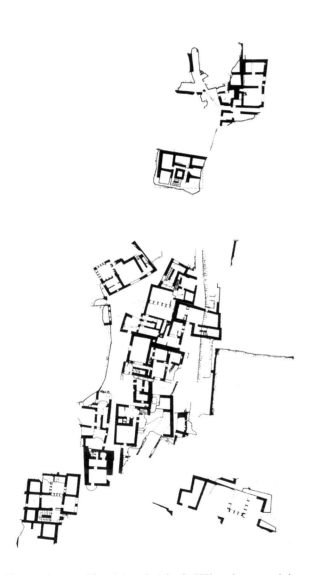

Excavations at Akrotiri on the island of Thera have revealed a whole buried town complete with streets, houses and frescos. They were covered under volcanic ash after an eruption in the mid-2nd millennium BC.

The Mycenaean Age

At length we come to the famous Shaft-graves of Mycenae, which represent an obvious contrast with standard Middle Bronze Age practice in that they are burials of unprecedented wealth, in graves of some structural pretension, set in apparently consecrated ground outside the then walls of the citadel. Everyone recognizes them as the beginning of a new era, not least because of the exceptional reverence with which they were treated later on in that era. Their inception, with the first interments in Grave Circle B, may prove to date earlier than the 17th century BC to which the conventional chronology assigns it, while even Circle B itself may have incorporated parts of a yet earlier circle. The whole notion of the Shaft-graves as an abrupt efflorescence, requiring some such dramatic explanation as the arrival of new immigrants or the achievement of a devastatingly successful plundering expedition abroad, must today be rejected. The extraordinary wealth of the latest burials in Grave Circle A can now be seen to have accrued gradually, over a period of much more than a century.

Nevertheless, this wealth attained a spectacular level. Shaft-grave IV of Circle A, for example, contained eleven gold and five silver vessels, besides a much larger number of lesser finds in gold. In the male burials, the provision of bronze weapons was profligate: some ninety swords are recorded as having been originally found in one of the graves. The famous gold face-masks serve to exemplify the artistic quality of the Shaft-grave finds, for they range from the masterly to the mediocre, providing an obvious contrast to the polish of contemporary Minoan work. Other differences are equally clear: the subject-matter of the human figure-scenes concentrates heavily on warfare and hunting, and exhibits an anecdotal, if hardly yet a true narrative, content. The sheer ostentation of the burials, and the acquisitiveness which they attest, are not matched at any period in Crete. The artistic media chosen for some of the most ambitious work are not those favoured in Crete: gold- and silver-relief, inlay on bronze, and shallow carving on the upright stone slabs which served as grave-markers. Grave Circle A was in use at the time of the destruction of Akrotiri on Thera and, as in the Cyclades, its finds do also reflect considerable Minoan influence in some fields. But, once again, the influence of Cretan craftsmanship and the importation of some of its products, and the parallel links with the Cyclades in the field of pottery, can be shown to have had some humbler predecessors on the Greek mainland. Finally, the whole phenomenon at Mycenae no longer stands alone, even in its own time: comparably precious objects, in smaller quantities, have been found at Peristeria in Messenia, housed in tombs of a type that has a more lasting significance for Greece, the *tholos* or vaulted tomb; Shaft-graves of similar date, though robbed of their contents, occur at Lerna.

The Shaft-graves of Mycenae, in short, are an emphatic local demonstration of tendencies which were soon to become widespread in Greece: the opening-up of contacts with places far beyond the Aegean basin; the increasing admiration for a representational art in which the human figure played an important role; the ostentatious display of wealth; a proclivity for warfare, reflected both in the nature of the objects buried with the dead and in the subject-matter of the scenes with which some of them were decorated; and a political system which allowed, and perhaps encouraged, the glorification of its rulers. These are among the permanent qualities which distinguish what has been generally called, since Schliemann's unveiling of its origins in 1876, the Mycenaean civilization.

How well-merited is the last term in that title, the word 'civilization'? There are definitions of this term whose requirements the Mycenaeans would certainly satisfy; others, equally certainly, they would fail to fulfil. Their culture was evidently capable of a high degree of organization, even if it can be shown to have achieved this only in those few localities where major archives of Linear B tablets have been discovered. These texts, with their lists of commodities, livestock and people, document the administration and supervision of extensive territories (as can be shown from the study of the place-names mentioned), and particularly of the means of production in these areas. The palaces seem to have an interest at every stage, from manpower and raw materials to finished products, which can only be explained by the assumption of a central ownership and control. The Mycenaeans were able also to undertake major corporate enterprises: if it is hard to believe

that the sheer physical laboriousness of some of their constructions, like the citadel of Gla in Boeotia, was matched by their practical value, then we may recall that similar reservations are often expressed about the parallel undertakings of the Romans, a millennium and a half later. In both cases, the values reflected are those of a society which had access to abundant conscripted labour. The Mycenaeans achieved, at the same time, a notable degree of craft-specialization; they also produced a wide range of works of art in a decidedly coherent, even homogeneous style.

The repetitive profusion of Mycenaean pottery is the most obvious illustration of this, but other media such as ivory-carving, gem-cutting and terracottas give equally clear evidence. The products of the central Mycenaean periods are easy to distinguish from those of other cultures, and indeed from the short-lived exuberance of the earlier Shaft-grave epoch; but it is extremely hard to distinguish any regional difference *within* the Mycenaean world.

Yet there are qualities of civilization which, in the Mycenaean world, we look for in vain. Their towns, as already noticed, are disappointingly small and can seldom have housed more than a few hundred inhabitants. Nor did the Mycenaeans apparently find it appropriate to create major ceremonial centres, whether for secular or for religious purposes. Each of these last two observations can plausibly be connected with a conspicuous feature of their culture, the compulsive concentration of their rulers on self-aggrandizement of a largely personal kind. The most impressive Mycenaean settlements tend to be the fortified citadels, each centred on its palace; the nearest approach to a monumental ceremonial centre is the palace itself. Such hierarchical structures existed in other prehistoric civilizations, but they were usually built on a broader and older foundation; the Mycenaean princes have the inescapably *arriviste* air of those who have taken a short cut to supremacy, and one does not get the impression that they have taken their subjects with them very far along the road to civilization. There is, for example, a detectable separation between 'palace' art and 'popular' art as represented by the decoration of pottery or the painted figures on the sarcophagi found in the last twenty years at Tanagra.

Mycenaean culture, which lasted for at least 500 (possibly more than 600) years, was not static, but showed an appreciable progress through time. The period has been conventionally divided by archaeologists into nine phases, characterized by pottery types, but of very unequal duration. From the first of these nine phases (which includes the span of the Shaft-graves of Mycenae) to the seventh (whose latter stages are marked by a wave of destruction of Mycenaean sites), i.e. between 1650 and 1200 BC, Mycenaean culture advances and expands continuously, at least in quantitative terms. The Mycenaean princes prospered mightily, and began to display their prosperity in more practical ways than the obsessive accumulation of precious grave-goods which had characterized the Shaft-graves. The main new feature that they introduce is monumentality: unlike the Shaft-graves, the *tholos* tombs proclaimed their magnificence even to the casual passer-by while their built façades were visible, and even when covered over they usually left a suggestive hump on the ground's surface. At the opulence of their contents we can in most cases only guess, since their conspicuousness made them inevitable targets for tomb-robbers in times of unrest. But even as empty shells, the *tholoi* display the pretension of this ruling class, the constructional skills they had at their disposal, and above all the steady move towards homogeneity, at least in the material remains, over the whole of Mycenaean central and southern Greece.

The distribution of the chamber-tomb is roughly co-extensive with that of the *tholos*, though predictably much denser. The grave-offerings in them have often survived unplundered, and they give us another clear illustration of the homogeneity of Mycenaean culture: a number of clay vessels, a bronze or two and, in the late phases, terracotta figurines are the typical accompaniments of each burial. The numbers of these tombs, and especially the frequency of burials in them, teach us something else: there is a steady increase in the number of people using this form of burial, and therefore presumably in the total population (since no other tomb-type even approaches this in popularity), until the fifth, sixth and seventh of the nine phases. By the 13th century BC, Greece is more thickly settled than it had ever been before (or, one might add, than it was to be again for at least five centuries).

The same century saw a 'peak' in many of the other material categories by which we judge Mycenaean

Three hundred years after the 'Shaft-grave dynasty', the ruling family of Mycenae were burying their dead in tholos tombs, large underground chambers with domed roofs. The most elaborate is the so-called Treasury of Atreus, entered through an ornate doorway with patterned columns and tympanum.

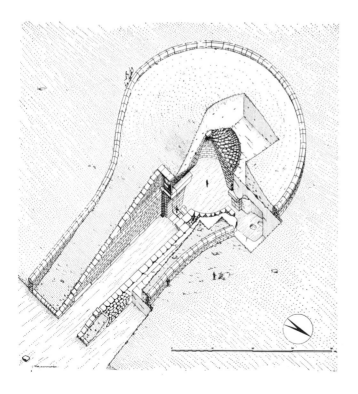

progress, but not, however, in the qualitative attainments of their art. Mycenaean art reached its zenith disconcertingly early, under a spell of powerful Cretan influence, and then embarked on an extended decline covering at least three centuries. Nowhere is this more clear than in the most plentiful class of material, the pottery – although a high technical standard was maintained even when production was so markedly increased in the later stages, it is the second and third of the nine phases which produced most of the known masterpieces of shaping and decoration. A similar story could be told of the less representative surviving selections of gold jewellery, carved gems, bronze vessels and weapons, or modelled figurines, though this

57

Schliemann discovered this early 12th-century vase, with its line of marching warriors, in a house in Mycenae. It is of unique value in showing military dress and equipment.

is hardly true of *every* art-form – not, for example, of ivory-carving or fresco-painting.

In the later phases, however, it is as if the energies of the community were being drawn more and more into architecture, and especially into defensive construction. Here at least is a category in which the sixth and seventh phases offer an undoubted climax: most of the great surviving citadels, fortifications and palace buildings so characteristic of the Mycenaeans belong to this time and, though their construction has necessarily removed much of the evidence for their predecessors, we can usually be sure that these were less ambitious.

Mycenae and Tiryns give the completest picture, but the same concerns are reflected in the more fragmentary traces visible at Iolkos in Thessaly, Thebes in Boeotia and the Acropolis of Athens. These sites have the appearance of fortress-towns, but closer examination shows in almost every case that the overriding aim was the protection of the palace itself, which with its appurtenances covers much of the area within the walls. Many lesser Mycenaean sites have fortification-walls, but the thickness and height of those at the main palace sites are of a different order of magnitude. Within, the plans of the palaces themselves are very much less complex than those of the Minoans. The nucleus, in every case where a true palace function existed, was formed by an enlarged version of the 'megaron' type of house, already seen in Troy a thousand years earlier. This consists of a large oblong room, often wide enough to require internal supports, entered through a door in the centre of one of its short sides from a columned porch of equal width, often with an ante-room intervening between the two, and a fourth unit at the back of the main hall. The whole complex has a strong symmetry about its central axis. In its simpler house-form it had been conceived as free-standing, but the palaces show an accretion of smaller rooms around

the sides and back which do not obscure the plain dignity of the central unit. At Mycenae and Tiryns, the palace occupies the highest ground within the citadel, which itself dominates the lower ground on which the extramural houses stood, thus underlining the predominance of the rulers in the starkest physical terms. The latest additions to these two citadels were the work of people who put their trust not only in sheer mass of masonry, but in acute tactical design as well. And with reason: this same period produces more evidence of violent destruction than the sum of its predecessors.

The end of Mycenae

The end of the Mycenaean period presents particular difficulties to the historian. It is reasonably certain that all the great sites experienced some sort of disaster from which they never recovered. But were they natural disasters (this part of the world is especially prone to earthquakes) or were they man-made – invasion, revolution, war? Were they nearly simultaneous or were they separated in time?

Current opinion seems to be veering strongly towards the view that they were indeed the components of a single horizon of disaster around 1200 BC; some would include in this horizon not only the long-attested cases of Mycenae, Tiryns, Pylos and a few lesser sites, but also two much more problematic instances of palace centres, Thebes in Boeotia and Knossos in Crete (which at the period immediately before its destruction – whenever that was – had been subjected to such a degree of control or influence from the mainland as to lead to the adoption of the Mycenaean Linear B script in the local rulers' bureaucracy). Experience does not, however, encourage the belief that 'current opinion' will remain constant for long.

Both Thebes and Knossos seem to me to present severe obstacles to the 'single destruction horizon' hypothesis. In Thebes the orientation of the buildings suggests successive destructions followed by rebuilding, all within the span of the Mycenaean culture and the use of Linear B. Knossos, structurally the more unified, is stratigraphically more complex still: the range of dates which have been advanced for its main destruction by fire bracket a full two centuries: detailed documentation, and often impassioned advocacy, is offered by the supporters of each date.

I believe that time will show the argument in each of these two cases to have been unduly influenced by the deep psychological hunger for political narrative and interpretation which has pervaded Mycenaean studies, and by the insistent search for 'events' on which to base such an interpretation. The question of the date of the Thera eruption, mentioned above, gives another example of the effects of this urge. Yet, for the 13th century BC, even the most committed advocates of the 'single horizon' have to concede that there were other destructions of Mycenaean sites in this general era, both earlier and later than the major wave: this is proved, if by nothing else, by the discovery of two or three successive conflagrations in the selfsame part of the same site, a phenomenon documented both at Mycenae and at Tiryns. Military violence had become part of the way of life of Mycenaean culture in its last stages. This makes it unlikely that the Mycenaean world formed a political whole, a kind of unified empire under the overall rule of Mycenae itself. This has been, and still is, argued on the grounds of the general homogeneity of the culture, the picture presented by certain passages in the *Iliad*, and the references in Hittite documents to a kingdom called Ahhiyawa, identified by some with the Achaioi of Homer. Yet the material evidence, supported by other passages in Homer and by the Linear B tablets, points rather to a number of powerful, independent and often mutually hostile kingdoms within the Mycenaean culture.

The solution to this problem of dating is of great importance for the last and thorniest of Mycenaean problems: that of explaining the causes of the downfall of the culture. Where previous generations inclined towards simple conquest theories, bringing in invaders from further north in the Balkan peninsula, discussion today has turned to hypotheses of internal revolt, of famine and drought, and of economic disaster brought on by an excess of intensification and specialization in agriculture. Some combination of these factors is more than likely to have been in operation. We must also, I believe, inject into any interpretation the evidence noted just now for the internal unrest and strife, documented by the history and perhaps by the very existence of the heavily-fortified citadels of the later phases. In any case, if Mycenaean culture was anything like as divisive socially as was suggested in our earlier discussion, it is hardly surprising that its structure proved fragile when put under economic or military pressure.

Further insight into the Mycenaean decline is given by the consideration of the aftermath, the eighth and ninth phases of the pottery-sequence. The picture presented by this era is not one to encourage sensational interpretations of what had happened before. For what we find are not innovations of a non-Mycenaean kind, but a continuity of Mycenaean features at a generally lower level. The Mycenaean tradition in the shaping and painting of pottery continues for well over a century after 1200 BC; the settlements are often reoccupied even where destruction has occurred and, when they are, they show the same dominant building-plan which, on a grander scale, had been that of the palaces themselves: the rectangular 'megaron', with a single entrance in the middle of one of its short sides. At other sites again (including one or two palace centres), there had in any case been no sign of damage in the time of the 'destruction horizon' and the settlement survived, sometimes falling victim to a *later* destruction instead. Chamber-tomb burial continued for several generations, to be slowly replaced by single burial in cists, with grave-goods remaining doggedly Mycenaean in character. Of the two major and unquestioned innov-

Mycenaean religion is still a mystery. This gold signet ring found at Tiryns seems to show four dog-like beings (demons?) bringing offerings to a seated goddess.

ations in the material culture of the post-Mycenaean age, the adoption of cremation and the transition from bronze to iron as the main practical metal, the one spread fitfully and the other gradually across the Greek world, and both did so too late to be plausibly connected with the events around 1200 BC. Faced with this body of evidence the general reader, remembering perhaps the important fact (see p. 51) that the Mycenaeans had already been Greek-speakers, might well ask why anyone should regard the fall of the Mycenaean culture as an event of more than internal significance, or even as an 'event' at all.

But there is another side of the story. Later Greek tradition was insistent that the Heroic Age had been brought to an end by a period of unrest which involved substantial migrations of peoples (though nearly always purely of Greek-speaking peoples), and within these strict limits the evidence of archaeology and of the Greek dialects does support tradition. The archaeological record may show continuity of Mycenaean features in mainland Greece, but it shows other things as well. First, these same features appear, in strikingly concentrated form, in new locations both at home and abroad. The classic cemetery site of this aftermath phase, Perati on the eastern coast of Attica, is in a new location without evidence for a Mycenaean presence before the very end of the preceding phase; Mycenaean artefacts of the aftermath phase are found in unprecedented quantity on some Aegean islands, especially the Dodecanese, but also much further east, in Cyprus and at Tarsus in Cilicia; westwards, too, there is a concentration of late Mycenaean finds on some of the Ionian islands and, across the Adriatic, at sites near Taranto. All of this has been rightly taken to suggest a period of great restlessness, in which whole communities of Mycenaean refugees migrated overseas, while movements on a smaller scale brought new inhabitants to settlements within Greece, if only from a few miles away.

The second important point is that, although Mycenaean artefacts are still absolutely characteristic of these closing phases of Mycenaean culture, they are not quite alone. Some years ago it was noticed that there is a scatter of new bronze types appearing in the Aegean at this time. Although some of these types, including new forms of sword and spearhead, resemble central European models, many of the actual specimens found in Greece were evidently made there, and some of the types in question actually made their first appearance in Greece before rather than after the great horizon of destructions. They cannot therefore be used as evidence of invasion or conquest from central Europe. But then, in the 1970s, excavators began for the first time to notice a more significant phenomenon: alongside the characteristic wheel-made Mycenaean pottery of the eighth phase, settlements started to produce burnished, hand-made pottery of a kind prevalent further north in the Balkans as well as in Italy, but unlike anything produced in Greece hitherto. Has the trail of the post-Mycenaean newcomers at last been picked up? It is still too early to give a definite answer to this question; this pottery has been observed only at ten or twelve sites, mostly in the Peloponnese, and nowhere is it the predominant ware. Nor has a precise area of origin outside Greece been located for it yet, and it may in fact turn out to be no more than another local response to the changes of economic circumstances and the loss of specialist skills, to set alongside the other, more certain cases which characterize this period – the decline in the use of monumental masonry, whether for fortifications or for full-sized *tholos* tombs; the disappearance of fresco-painting, gem-carving and indeed most other media for representational art; and, in a different way, the eventual abandonment of multiple burial in family vaults over much of Greece. All these features could have resulted from the general loss of continuity and security.

The silent centuries

A long interval of silence now descends on the Greek world: silence in written documents, since there is a gap of about 450 years between the latest Linear B texts and the first inscriptions in the utterly different alphabetic script; silence in Greek tradition, which did not (and did not pretend to) record any major events or personalities between the last generation of the heroes (which might correspond to the early 12th century BC in our terms, since it was the generation of the sons of those who fought at Troy) and the beginnings of continuous Greek history some 400 years later; silence in the records of literate foreign powers, who likewise find no occasion to mention Greece or the Greeks for five centuries; silence even in the representational arts, which had provided illustrative, and on occasion almost narrative, comment on the doings of the Mycenaeans. It will be our final task in this chapter to see how far this gap was bridged by the later Greeks of historical times, as well as to sketch in the developments which modern scholars, mostly from the evidence of archaeology, believe to have taken place in the interval.

By tackling the second part of this task, we may set the stage for the understanding of the first. The negative side of the picture is usually, and reasonably, given the greater prominence. To begin with, the Greek mainland and many of the islands must have suffered from a catastrophic depopulation in the post-Mycenaean era: the decline indeed begins in the eighth Mycenaean phase (in the 12th century BC), continues in the ninth or Submycenaean phase in the years around 1100 BC, and reached its absolute nadir perhaps in the years shortly before 1000 BC. The emigration of refugees must be responsible for a small part of this fall in population: to the movements already mentioned, we may add another, historically much more significant, which seems to have begun in the 11th century: the permanent settlement of Greeks along the western seaboard of Asia Minor and in the larger off-shore islands of that coast, both of them areas hitherto mainly occupied by non-Greek-speakers. This movement created Greek Ionia, whose contribution to later Greek civilization, beginning with Homer himself, was of major significance: and it also ringed the Aegean Sea, for the first time, with Greeks on all but its northern coast (Crete, too, having by now acquired an almost completely Greek-speaking population).

But neither this nor any migration could do more than mitigate partially the demographic disaster which struck Greece itself. The abandonment of sites, which in the earlier case of the Middle Bronze Age could be offset by the evidence for nucleation of settlements, presents this time an unanswerable case: all the evidence suggests that those few settlements which continued in occupation were smaller in size than previously; while the stark truth is that, on present evidence, something like four-fifths of the former Mycenaean sites had been altogether deserted by about 1000 BC. Virtually all the luxurious appurtenances of Mycenaean culture had disappeared, and with them vanished other features hardly to be classed as luxuries. In architecture, not only monumental masonry but even, for a time, rectangular building-plans seem to have been abandoned, at least on the mainland: mud-brick, timber and thatch became the standard materials. For all the diaspora of Greeks overseas, there is a period of well over a century during which neither Greek artefacts on foreign sites nor foreign imports to Greece are known. The agricultural regime on which Mycenaean culture had been founded can only have suffered drastically with the loss of man-power: in places people may have returned to a purely pastoral way of life. Politically, although the institution of monarchy undoubtedly survived in name, the extensive Mycenaean kingdoms were swept away by the tides of unrest and fragmentation. At the most humdrum level, we may even note the apparent temporary disappearance of razors and lamps from the Greek world.

On the positive side, there were new features which, in the course of time, formed the basis for a fresh start. The adoption of iron and the mastery of its working, even if originally motivated by the shortage of bronze,

By the 8th century BC, the historic Bronze Age had become the legendary Heroic Age, enshrined in the two epics of Homer. This detail of a shipwreck from an early Geometric vase has been interpreted as an episode from the Odyssey, with Odysseus sitting astride a capsized boat while others lie drowning in the sea.

eventually gave Greece and other cultures a practical and economical alternative base for industry, agriculture and war. The wholesale movements of communities encouraged a fresh start socially, and must to a great extent explain the startling difference between the Mycenaean and the later Greek models of society. The fact that Greek pottery production, for the first time in six hundred years, underwent a radical change of direction with the emergence of the style called 'Proto-geometric' in the 11th century, was in the end to have far-reaching consequences. The Geometric, of which this is the beginning, is the first and universal style of historical Greek civilization.

At the most fundamental levels, meanwhile, there was much continuity. The Greek language, in its various dialects, survived this 'dark age' and developed steadily through it; it is the geographical distribution of the dialect-groups which provides some of the most convincing evidence for the movements of Greek-speakers around the Aegean area. Although historical Greek religious practices, and their settings, show radical differences from Mycenaean ones, there is a strong case for thinking that religious *beliefs* were maintained through the intervening centuries. Above all, Greek epic poetry not only blossomed in this period – Homer is only the last and greatest of a long line of bards who composed without the aid of writing – but it took as its favourite subject-matter the doings of the heroes, and to a lesser extent of their gods, thus inaugurating an interest that was to persist as long as Greek civilization itself. The historical basis of this 'Heroic Age', in so far as it exists at all, seems to be located exclusively in what we call the Mycenaean era.

The making of the Heroic Age

A comparison between the Mycenaean and classical ages is indeed not only of great interest in itself, but it also sheds light on the way the Greeks regarded their own past. Somehow, between these two eras, the people of Greece underwent a change of spirit too profound to be explained simply in terms of social progress. In the classical Greek world, the deepest division within humanity was seen as being that between Greek and barbarian, between the speakers of one language and the upholders of one system of values, and the rest. In Mycenaean times, there seems to have been no such division: the material remains present a cosmopolitan picture, at first especially towards the upper end of the social scale; by the end, with the breakdown of the Mycenaean culture and the probable mass-migrations of people from Greece eastwards to Cyprus and the Levant, it appears that cultural divisions are altogether obliterated at every social level. The surviving documents, too, seem to contain personal names from a wide mixture of stocks, an impression which later Greek legend would reinforce; further, it is most likely that the stubborn resistance of some of the Linear B texts to decipherment as Greek is to be explained, at least in part, by the fact that the very word-forms are non-Greek.

Rather than the antithesis between Greek-speaker and barbarian, it is other oppositions which stand out clearest in the record: between palace-dweller and countryman, between rich and poor, above all between rulers and ruled. By classical times – and not only in the democratic states – these contrasts had paled considerably in importance. The change can be given precision by taking a number of examples. Of the two political systems it is hazardous to speak in any detail, since we know so little of one of them, but at least it is clear that the Mycenaean system of government was monarchical, and that the political unit was sometimes a large one by Aegean standards, with a kingdom embracing many towns and a substantial stretch of territory. The classical ideal of the *polis*, a state embracing a city and its territory, independent of other states but with no internal differentiation between town and country, seems the antithesis of the Mycenaean pattern. Turning to the material remains, we find that there are still citadels in classical Greece, but that they serve either as refuges for the whole community or as the setting for the main state sanctuaries, and often as both. In many cases the 'Acropolis' of a classical city had been a Mycenaean citadel in its time; but a Mycenaean would have been astonished at the uses to which it was now put. Or we may take burial practices: there are few Mycenaean monuments more familiar than the great *tholos* tombs in which their rulers were buried; moreover, the chamber-tombs which many of their subjects hewed from the rock (and which, predictably, at times simulate the shape of a *tholos*) reflect the same principle of the family vault, in which successive generations will be laid to rest, sometimes with a degree of pomp and a provision of grave-goods which necessitate sweeping the ancestral bones to one side in a cavalier way to make room for the new interment. The classical Greek burial, in a single grave (sometimes a cremation) and with little ostentation in the matter of grave-goods, once again provides an antithesis.

Some classical Greeks at least will have shared the

insight of Thucydides, who observed that the customs of earlier Greeks had resembled those of contemporary barbarians. But at the popular level, the Mycenaeans were remembered entirely through one medium, the legends of the Heroic Age. Clearly this memory of the Heroic Age represents some kind of bridge between the Mycenaean and the historical Greek cultures. But how strong was the bridge? It was Arnold Toynbee's thesis, in his last, posthumously-published work *The Greeks and their Heritages*, that the Mycenaean legacy to later Greece was slight, the bridge a flimsy one, and furthermore that this fact was an important element in the making of classical Greece and its extraordinary achievements. His argument seems, at least in a theoretical way, a convincing one. For as a reading of Homer's epics shows, little detailed knowledge of Mycenaean culture survived, at least by the time that his poems were shaped in the 8th century BC. Certain essentials were remembered: among the most impressive of these was the knowledge of which Greek cities had been important places in heroic times. So, too, the untiring bellicosity of the heroes, their network of personal contacts overseas, their fondness for amassing treasure, their use of bronze, even the very fact that they spoke Greek, all appear true to Mycenaean reality. But on the other side, the complex organization of the Mycenaean kingdoms was lost to Homer's simpler age, their scale of operation was underrated and the majority of the detailed observations on society and on material culture have been updated to a greater or lesser degree – sometimes the inspiration seems to come from the experience of Homer's own generation.

Outside the sphere of epic poetry, that generation and its immediate predecessors had also been establishing independent links of other kinds with the Mycenaean age. Many Mycenaean sites were now being reoccupied for the first time in four centuries, and this process can only have led to a greater appreciation of the 'heroes'. Some have indeed argued that early monumental architecture in historical times took inspiration from Mycenaean remains; more certainly, some of the minor arts reflect their Mycenaean antecedents in a way which is easy to understand if small, portable Mycenaean objects were coming to light in quantity; and we may note that Homer, too, when he gives his rare convincing descriptions of Mycenaean objects, mainly does so either with portable artefacts or with features, such as the 'shield like a tower', which we know to have been commonly represented on minor Mycenaean works of art. One of the very clearest cases of all is provided by the rediscovery of Mycenaean tombs in this era: there are more than forty cases in Greece and the islands where modern excavators of *tholoi* and chamber-tombs have found that they have been anticipated by Greeks of the 8th and 7th centuries

BC, who placed pottery and other small offerings of their own in the 'ancestral' graves, treating them in effect as hero-shrines.

We must, I think, concur with Toynbee's conclusion that this degree of imperfect survival and partial rediscovery gave the historical Greeks exactly the amount of inspiration that they needed for their own endeavours. As often, the very distance of the Mycenaean age lent it an enchantment; any detailed programme of revival (which would have been disastrous for the emergent Greek civilization) was excluded by the completeness of the intervening break; but fanciful emulation was another matter, and the classical Greeks practised it to the utmost degree. There was almost no social or political act for which one could not invoke, with advantage, a precedent from the Heroic Age. If there was a war to be fought, then no pretext was more respectable than revenge for some injury committed twenty generations earlier and recorded in legend; if there was territory to be annexed, then no claim could be stronger than to show that one's heroic ancestors had once possessed it; if there was a cult to be promoted, then a legend of its foundation by a hero was a flying start (or, better still, the hero himself could be worshipped): if a personal supremacy was sought, then a demonstration of heroic ancestry was half the battle. It would be wrong to take too cynical a view of the Greeks' enthusiasm for this game, for there are many signs that they were quite sincere in their beliefs about the Heroic Age. Nor were all their beliefs by any means erroneous: there is, for example, a suspiciously close correlation between the routes used for the colonial expansion of the early Greeks, one of their greatest achievements in the 8th and 7th centuries BC, and those pioneered by Mycenaean navigators five hundred years earlier, and it is not impossible that the memory of these Mycenaean exploits had survived by means of oral transmission. It is beyond question that many heroic legends were kept alive by ordinary story-telling within families and other groups, in addition to those commemorated in the epics.

In these ways, their Mycenaean heritage was indeed an invaluable asset to the classical Greeks. The very vagueness of heroic legend permitted of wild anachronisms, such as the crediting of Theseus with having in some way founded Athenian democracy. The historian who is too censorious of such absurdity may be forgetting the part that it played in promoting real political progress. The Greeks of the historical period were in fact founding an entirely new world: if they themselves chose to give a large part of the credit to undeserving or individually fictitious ancestors, then who are we today, on the mere basis of our probably superior knowledge of those ancestors, to say that they did wrong?

II · ACHIEVEMENT

2
Between the Persian Wars and Alexander

*the flowering of the
classical world*

3
Thinking about the Cosmos

*Greek Philosophy
from Thales to Aristotle*

FOR ARISTOTLE, what chiefly distinguished men from animals was the fact that they lived in cities. The word he used was *polis*, which can also be rendered 'city-state', and is the origin of our words 'politics' and 'political'. It implied a community large enough to defend itself and exist independently, and sophisticated enough to have a clear view of its aims and nature. As we have seen, the geography of Greece encouraged such a system. It stood in sharp contrast to those states that had existed before, that surrounded it in Aristotle's time, and that were eventually to succeed it.

This is not to say that the Greek cities had very much in common politically. Aristotle classified them as tyrannies (or, as we might say, dictatorships), which were governed by a single autocrat; oligarchies, where a restricted class exercised power; and democracies, in which power resided with the people as a whole. Each had its merits and its drawbacks. Pericles eulogized Athenian democracy in his famous oration at the funeral of the soldiers killed in the first year of the Peloponnesian War; Plato was more critical, contrasting it with the efficient totalitarianism of Sparta. Later historians, especially since the Renaissance, have tended to idealize the Athenian system, seeing in it the seed-bed of all the western political virtues – the rule of law, respect for the individual, the development of personal talents, the encouragement of free intellectual inquiry and artistic expression. Other features, such as its foundation upon slavery and its subjection of women, have until recently received less attention.

Judged in terms of overall political stability, the *polis* was a failure. Local autonomy made nationhood impossible. The separate cities could never unite under common laws and leadership. Rivalry was inevitable, war almost continuous. After miraculously surviving one threat from a powerful empire organized on totally alien lines – that of Persia – the Greeks succumbed, a mere century and a half later, to another: Alexander's Macedon. Within the comparatively short span of a century and a half between those two struggles lies the highest achievement of Greek culture.

It was fitting
that the divine patroness of Athens – the nurse of tragedy, comedy, philosophy and history – should be Pallas Athena, goddess of wisdom and of the liberal arts. In Aeschylus' symbolic retelling of the origin of human justice in the *Oresteia* she institutes the court of the Areopagus in order to try Orestes. Another myth tells how she successfully contended with Posidon over the most useful gift to mankind. Posidon produced the horse, symbol of war, Athena the olive, emblem of peace. She was also the reputed inventor of ships and protectress of the Argonauts.
In all these aspects, Athena reflected the Athenians' view of their own destiny. To her they raised their greatest monument, the Parthenon. It was in her honour that their most lavish festival, the Panathenaia, was held, the subject of the Parthenon frieze. And she is constantly represented in Athenian art, together with her attribute, the owl. This detail (*opposite*) is from a cup by Douris dating from about 480 BC. Athena is shown watching Jason being disgorged by a dragon. A gorgon decorates her armour (instead of, more usually, her shield) and a black sphinx her helmet. Above Jason's body can be seen the Golden Fleece. (1)

Craftsmen and traders

At the top of Athenian society was a small group of rich landowners; beneath them, the largest class, the small farmers; beneath them again, the landless craftsmen and shopkeepers. These classes were not distinct. Some of the rich also engaged in trade.

Potters and sculptors were highly valued, pots in particular being exported in vast numbers. *Top left:* a potter burnishing an unglazed vase. *Below left:* sculptor at work on a herm, a figure of Hermes marking a boundary. *Right:* a bronze-smith's workshop. On the left is the furnace, with plaques hanging on the wall; on the right the limbs of a statue being assembled. (2, 3, 4)

Weighing merchandise, perhaps grain, on a balance, one of several scenes from the world of marketing and the exchange of goods. (5)

The first stage of pottery-making (*right*) was to dig out the clay, shown here on a terracotta plaque from Corinth. One man digs, another collects the clay in a basket, a third hands it up over the edge of the pit. (8)

An oil-press (*far right*): the olives are on the right, the oil running out at the bottom into a large vessel. To increase the pressure, not only have two large weights been tied to the beam, but one of the men has climbed on to it himself. (9)

Fishmonger and cobbler – two of many vivid scenes from Greek pottery illustrating everyday life. The fisherman carries his wares to market in a basket; the cobbler sits at a bench surrounded by tools and half-finished shoes. (6, 7)

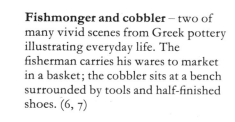

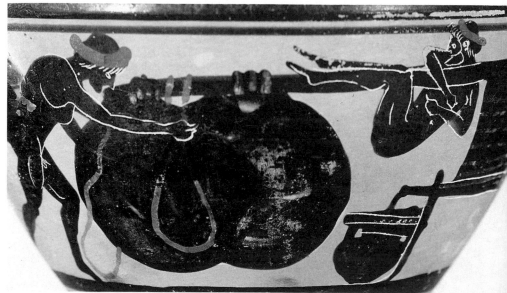

State of war

War seemed a natural condition to most Greeks. Even Plato's ideal republic is geared to the requirements of military strength. But the Greek warrior depended heavily upon sophisticated armour – sword, helmet and shield – which in turn depended upon a supply of iron. The needs of war were thus one of the spurs of trade.

The hoplites were the fighting men of the Greek army and have given their name to a social revolution brought about by military tactics. Up to the 7th century, war had been an aristocratic privilege. That code could not survive the use of the massed infantry phalanx: the soldiers of the phalanx demanded political equality. *Above:* a hoplite's bronze helmet, early 5th century, found at Corinth. *Below:* detail of the Chigi vase, late 7th century, showing warriors clashing in battle. The piper on the left is leading another (unseen) line of soldiers. (10, 11)

'The point of the spear passed right through the lower part of the skull, under the brain, and smashed the white bones. His teeth were shattered; both his eyes were filled with blood; and he spurted blood through his nostrils and gaping mouth. Then the black cloud of Death descended upon him.' (*Iliad*, Book 16). Rarely does art express the brutality of war with the same vividness as Homer's verse. This detail of a falling warrior is from the Nereid Monument at Xanthos, in Asia Minor, erected by Greek artists *c*.400 BC. (12)

Anatomy of a city state

Discussion of Greek politics inevitably centres on Athens, since it is through Athenian writings that virtually all our knowledge comes.

The life of Pericles spans Athens' greatest period. Born in the year of Marathon (490 BC), he lived to see the outbreak of the Peloponnesian War in 431, in which Athens was defeated by Sparta. He presided over the formation of the Delian League, Athens' decisive bid for power in the Aegean. Thucydides made him the supreme spokesman of the Athenians' democratic system, who stressed their freedom under the law and their responsibility for their own government. (13)

Demosthenes, as clearly stands at the end of Athenian greatness. Dedicated to the ideal of Greek freedom (an ideal by now tarnished and fading), he foresaw long before it actually happened that a powerful ruler such as Philip of Macedon could mean the end of the whole democratic tradition. By the time of his death in 322 BC his fears had been realized. (14)

Slavery remained part of the Greek way of life, though its nature varied from city to city. Athenian slaves (*left*) were mostly individuals captured or purchased from abroad. Spartan slaves (helots) were a hereditary subject class. (15)

Tyranny was repudiated by Athenians up to the very eve of Alexander's take-over. This stela (*right*) is inscribed with a law safeguarding the rights of the people passed in 336 BC. The figures represent Democracy crowning the Demos (people) of Athens. (16)

Women

Women were given respect but not equality. They seldom left their homes, though lower-class women might go out to work, and their status was wholly defined by reference to men.

Wife and mother: child-bearing was woman's chief function, in Sparta virtually her only one. This detail (*left*) from an Attic Red-Figure vase dates from the 5th century BC. (17)

Mistress of the household: women in Athens seem to have had full responsibility for running their husbands' homes. In this detail (*right*) from a white-ground lekythos (oil flask) the mistress is dressed in a chiton and carries a scarf. The little servant girl, in black, carries a chest, possibly a jewel casket. Above the girl hangs a mirror and a lekythos. We get a glimpse into the lives of women in plays like Aristophanes' *Lysistrata*. (20)

Courtesan: slave-girls provided social and sexual entertainment – as flute-players at banquets, as dancers and as prostitutes. Here a girl is being undressed by an older man. (18)

Friends: the charming terracotta group from Tanagra (*left*) dates from slightly later than the classical period (*c.*300 BC) but its manners and mores are those of a century earlier. (19)

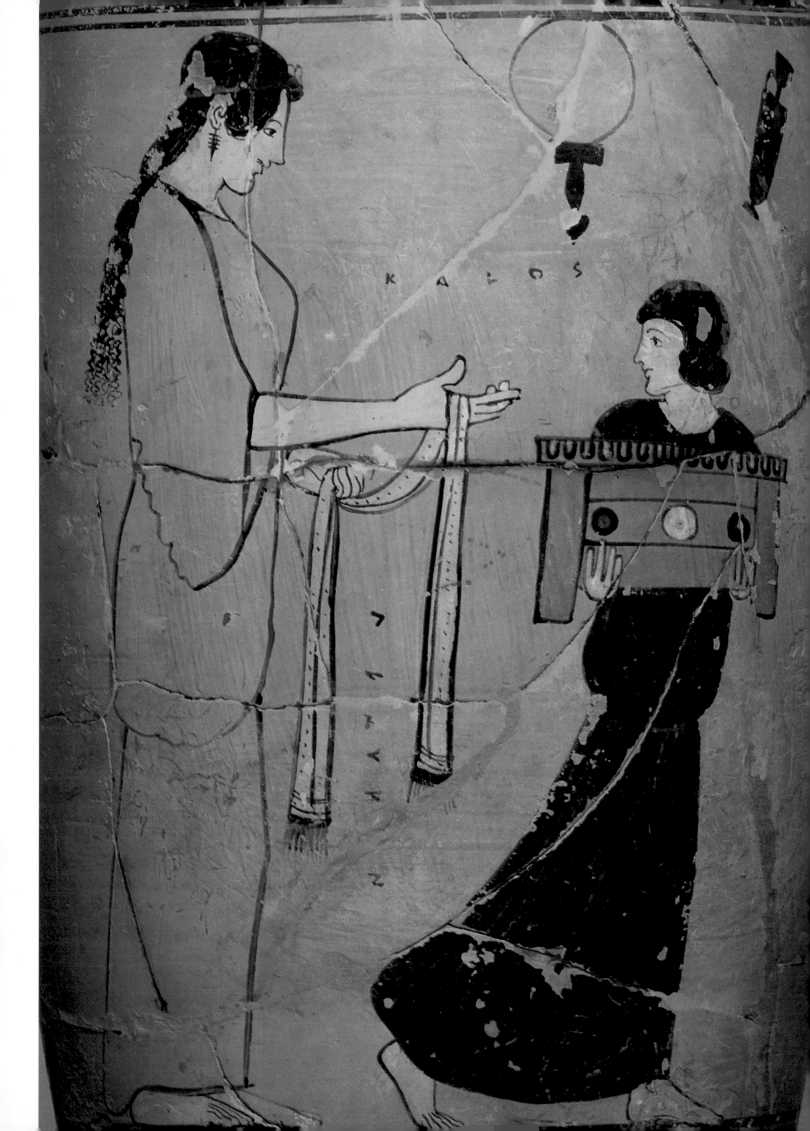

Public observance, private experience

There are two aspects to Greek religion. One is associated with the Olympian gods and shows itself in established rituals, processions, sacrifices and observances at shrines. The other, associated with Dionysus and with fertility cults, is concerned with mystical experience and personal salvation.

Delphi was one of the oldest sacred sites in Greece. Here, within a cave, the Pythian priestess gave forth her prophecies, inspired by the god Apollo, and around her grew up a complex of temples, shrines and treasuries, together with a theatre and a stadium. The Pythian Games, at which all the Greek city-states came together, were held every four years. In this view we are looking from the top of the theatre to the Temple of Apollo. (21)

Dionysiac orgies released pent-up emotions and satisfied deep-seated psychological needs. Here (*right*) Dionysus, god of wine, watches while a maenad abandons herself to music and dance. (22)

The Olympian gods demanded public animal sacrifices (*below*), whose prescribed rituals were the framework of civic religion. (23)

2

Between the Persian Wars and Alexander

*the flowering of the
classical world*

CLAUDE MOSSÉ

Startling new discoveries can still happen in the world of
Greek archaeology, adding fresh masterpieces to those
already known from the classical age. In August 1972 an
amateur fisherman off the coast of Calabria came across two
life-size bronze statues. When rescued and cleaned, they
proved to be works of the highest quality, dating from the
5th century BC. An exceptional amount of detail survived.
One of the heads (*left*) had eyelashes and teeth of silver, with
eyes composed of vitreous paste to give colour. Their
identity remains a mystery – gods, heroes or mortals? (24)

TRADITION applies the term 'classical' to the zenith of Greek civilization in the 5th and 4th centuries BC, but to understand how this classical civilization could come into being and flower, we have to go back in time to the first appearance of that institution peculiar to the ancient Greek world, the *polis*, the city.

The dawn of the 8th century BC appears to have seen the formation of those *poleis*, small self-contained states consisting of an urban centre with an indispensable area of surrounding territory to support it. Archaeology is often our only guide in tracing their growth, first in Greece and Asia Minor and then, from the middle of the 8th century BC, on the west coast of the Mediterranean, in southern Italy and Sicily. True, later Greeks did possess a body of tradition, on the basis of which modern writers have tried to reconstruct the genesis of these cities (at least some of them – those destined to enjoy enough fame to make their memory worth preserving), but such accounts are essentially mythical or legendary. In these stories, the origin of cities is usually a charismatic founder, a hero or king, whose descendants reigned over the city for several generations, and whose sanctuary marks the limit of their territory. This seems to reflect a historical process by which the stabilization of populations and the development of agriculture that we associate with the end of the 'Dark Ages' coincides with the foundation of small communities whose unity is expressed through the cult of the founding hero.

These communities were essentially rural. They were dominated by an aristocracy who were either horse-breeders, as in the cities of Euboea, where they were called *hippobotai*, or simply 'well born', like the Eupatrides at Athens. It was also a warrior aristocracy, which implies the existence of craftsmen specializing in metal work; which in turn implies, for a land with few iron mines, some means of obtaining supplies of this precious metal. Recent studies have emphasized the role this aristocracy may have played in the development of Greek craftsmanship and commerce. Only major landowners were in a position to equip ships, send them to sea and – aided by the tenant farmers and craftsmen who formed their clientage – exchange the products of their estates for precious or commonly used metals. They were at the root of the vast expansion, incorrectly called Greek 'colonization'.

The creation of legal codes by the city-states of Greece marked the beginning of constitutional government, one of the fundamental features of classical Greek civilization. The 'municipal laws' of Gortyn (left), of 500 BC, are part of a process of codification that had begun 200 years earlier. Each alternate line is in mirror script, a method called by the Greeks 'writing as the plough-ox turns'.

Greek 'colonization'

This huge expansion of the Greeks across the Mediterranean began towards the middle of the 8th century BC and ended in the middle of the 6th century. After this date there were only a few new foundations, most of them established by Athens or by Syracuse in the time of Dionysius the Elder.

It is true that Greeks had earlier, in the decades following the fall of the Mycenaean palaces, settled on the coast of Asia Minor but, although later tradition credited this earlier colonization to Athenian initiative, it seems more likely that it was simply one of those movements of population common in the Mediterranean world at the end of the second millennium and the beginning of the first. From the middle of the 8th century onwards, on the other hand, there was a much more substantial expansion, which seems in particular – although many obscurities remain – to have been much more carefully organized, in so far as the initiative came from cities that were already well established.

There has been much discussion about the origins of Greek colonization. Late traditions concerning this or that foundation rarely reveal the motives of those who set out to found a new city. Some are supposed to have been personal. The Corinthian Archias, the founder of Syracuse, for instance, was said to have been forced to flee after committing a crime, while the Partheniae ('bastards') were supposed to have been banished by the Spartans because of their illegitimate birth. Other alleged reasons are circumstantial. Famine was said to have compelled part of the population of the little island of Thera to settle in Africa on the site of the future Cyrene.

Sometimes, however, a more general phenomenon is mentioned – *stenochoria*, lack of land, which obliged the inhabitants of a city to find land to cultivate elsewhere. Obviously the historian cannot content himself with repeating ancient traditions. He has both to understand the reasons for this *stenochoria*, and to ask whether other factors may not also have played their part in setting in motion this vast process of emigration.

On the first point, various hypotheses can be advanced. *Stenochoria* could be the result of an increase in the population making the cities' territory (*chora*) too small. But it can also be connected with the phenomenon of the concentration of the land in the hands of the most powerful, a concentration which may have been accelerated by the practice of splitting up patrimonies. This practice put the poorest people at the mercy of their richer neighbours. However that may be, it remains certain that the need for land was one of the essential factors in Greek expansion, and that the siting of the colonies on the rich soil of eastern Sicily, southern Italy, Libya and the shores of the Black Sea, as well as certain traces of land partition brought to light

The ear of barley on this early 5th-century silver coin from Metapontum proclaims the source of the city's prosperity.

by archaeologists, confirm that Greek colonization was primarily an agrarian colonization, and not (as was once thought) a search for outlets for Greek industry.

But was it only that? Continental Greece is relatively poor in iron ore and in metals in general. Now the 8th century was the time when the panoply of the hoplite, the heavy-armed infantryman, was being developed and when, as we shall see, the task of fighting, hitherto confined to a small aristocracy, was spreading to larger and larger sections of the population. It is true that the phalanx was not generally adopted in battles until the dawn of the 6th century, but there can be no doubt that the need for metal had been continually growing during the preceding decades. The regions of the Mediterranean where the indispensable metals – iron, copper, tin – could be obtained were not particularly numerous. There was the region of the Anatolian plateau, but this was controlled by powerful states the interior of which there could be no question of reaching. The island of Elba and the Tuscan hinterland on the one hand and distant Spain on the other were important sources for metals. It is thus not surprising to find that the first Greek establishment in the west was that of Pithecusa (Ischia), where archaeologists have discovered numerous traces of workshops for smelting ore, which was certainly imported from the island of Elba. Herodotus tells the story of one Kolaios, a ship's captain from Samos, who, while making for Egypt, was driven by a storm towards the coast of Spain and could thus have come into contact with the king of Tartessos, a country which is supposed to have been the modern Andalusia.

These commercial relations should obviously not be conceived as regular, organized exchanges, but they

may have determined the choice of certain sites – all the more since they were probably in the hands of men dominant in the cities, rich landowners who alone could offer products in exchange for the coveted ores. By no means all the Greek cities took part in this trade, but those which had sizeable fleets – Corinth, Samos, Phocaea, the cities of the island of Euboea – certainly played an important part.

We can distinguish two main periods of Greek colonization. The first extended from the middle of the 8th century to about the middle of the 7th. The colonists came at first from the island of Euboea – from the cities of Chalkis and Eretria – then from the Peloponnese and the isthmus of Corinth. They sailed on the whole to southern Italy and Sicily. Chalkidians settled on Pithecusa around 770, then at Naxos in Sicily and Cumae in southern Italy in about 750, and finally on the two sides of the straits of Messina, at Rhegion and Zancle, around 730. Megarians founded Megara Hyblaea in 750, Corinthians Syracuse on the east coast of Sicily in 734. At the end of the 8th century other Greeks from the Peloponnese founded Sybaris and Croton in southern Italy, not far from Tarentum, the colony founded by the Partheniae exiled from Sparta after the first Messenian War (*c.* 736–716). Finally, at the beginning of the 7th century, Greeks from Locris founded Locri in the south of Italy, and Rhodians in association with Cretans founded Gala in the south-east of Sicily.

The second period, which began towards the middle of the 7th century, was characterized by greater diversity in the origin of the colonists and a considerable extension of the areas colonized. In addition, new foundations were established by some of the oldest colonies. The western Mediterranean remained one of the favourite regions for Greek expansion. New colonists came to reinforce the first settlers and helped in the creation of new cities such as Poseidonia (Paestum), founded in Campania by people from Sybaris about the middle of the 7th century; Himera in Sicily, created about the same time by the Zancleans; and Acragas (Agrigentum), founded about 580 by Greeks from Gela. But the main feature of this second period of expansion in the western Mediterranean was the activity of the Phocaeans: towards the year 600 they founded Massalia (Marseilles) near the mouth of the Rhône, a few decades later Velia, some twenty miles south of Poseidonia, and finally Alalia on the east coast of Corsica. During the late 7th century cities founded by Greeks from the Aegean islands and Asia Minor were springing up in virtually every part of the known world, from Libya and the Nile delta to the shores of the Black Sea and the Crimea.

What were the consequences of this vast expansion of the Greek world? One important point must be made first. Those Greeks who, for various reasons, left their native city to settle elsewhere were not colonists in the modern sense, people who remained bound to their mother-city. Their new city became their homeland. A

Syracusan was no longer a Corinthian; a Tarentine was no longer a Spartan. It is true that links – essentially religious ones – could continue to exist between mother-city and daughter-city. This is particularly true of cities in the eastern Mediterranean; Miletus kept close links with its colonies; so did Paros with its colony Thasos. The mother-city could also on occasion send new colonists to the daughter-city to reinforce the first contingent, or even to help the daughter-city found a colony of its own. But in so far as the colonists had been forced to leave their native city they also broke all links with it. This seems to have been reflected in particular in the adoption of institutions which often differed from those of the mother-city.

There seem to have been no privileged commercial relations between mother-cities and colonies, except possibly for the Phocaean colonies, which served as staging-posts for Phocaean commerce until their mother-city fell under the blows of the Persians in about 540. On the other hand, there can be no doubt that the geographical enlargement of the Greek world must have favoured the development of trade between the old world and the new world created by colonization. The diffusion of pottery bears witness to this. However, the colonial cities soon developed their own manufactures, and the study of the distribution of coins reveals that most trade was between colonies, rather than between colony and mother-city, although certain mainland cities like Corinth or Phocaea certainly maintained strong trade links with their colonies. Such was the situation up to the 6th century; after this, the lead begins to be taken by Athens, a city which, it should be remembered, had previously founded no colonies at all.

But Greek colonization also had other consequences, this time affecting the regions where the colonies were established. It is clear that these regions were not devoid of inhabitants and that the Greeks therefore had to face the problem of living with the indigenous populations in the midst of whom they settled and whose land they took. The ancient sources do not tell us a great deal on this point. At the most they mention difficulties or conflicts: for example, settlers at Cyrene are described as falling a prey to the Libyan natives who had at first welcomed them warmly. On the other hand, touching stories of friendly relations are also recorded, as in the history of the foundation of Massalia (Marseilles). In addition, we know that in the classical period there existed on the territory of some colonial cities a class of dependent farmers who were probably the descendants of native populations subjugated at the time of the colony's foundation.

In recent years, archaeology has provided valuable information on this point. If we take the example of Sicily, three main types of penetration of native areas by the Greeks can be traced. The Chalkidian cities were the oldest Greek foundations in Sicily. Contact with the natives seems to have been close. Excavations have revealed the presence of objects of Greek manufacture

This late 5th-century silver coin from Acragas in Sicily shows the city's emblem, the crab, above Scylla, a monster which terrorized sailors in the Straits of Messina.

in the cemeteries of the interior, the early hellenization of native sites and the spread of a Greek type of habitat. The impression is of peaceful cohabitation of Greeks and natives, with the former not exercising any domination over the latter. Greek penetration in the hinterland of Gela and Syracuse looks quite different. There we note the existence of Greek forts, which seems to indicate a constant threat from the indigenous population. The discovery of weapons in typically Greek tombs confirms that there was military occupation of the hinterland. Finally, in the west of Sicily, contacts between Greeks and natives seem to have been much looser; the presence of Greek objects in native cemeteries reflects commercial relations rather than any effective hellenization of the interior.

Similar conclusions could certainly be drawn from the excavations carried out in other parts of the Mediterranean world. Where the native population was not politically organized, hellenization was rapid, as a result either of permanent contacts and trade or of the direct domination of enslaved populations. Where, on the contrary, the native population showed greater cohesion, it posed a permanent threat, and military occupation of its territory became a necessity. One last remark must be added: where the Greeks settled in order to find land, they had to dispossess the natives, either by pushing them back or by enslaving them. When on the other hand they were mainly seeking bases to procure metals and other raw materials from the hinterland, they had every reason to maintain peaceful relations with the natives. Greek 'colonization' could thus assume very different aspects. That said, and in spite of its many different faces, the extension of the

81

The extension of the army beyond the ranks of the upper classes eventually led to a profound change in Greek society. Because the common people, the demos, provided the foot-soldiers, or 'hoplites', they soon demanded greater participation in government. On the left is part of the 'panoply' – the hoplite's equipment – breastplate, helmet, short sword and massive round shield. Tactics in warfare changed between archaic and classical times: the massed ranks of identical hoplites on the right, each with a shield bearing an image of a sacred tripod, have abandoned the cult of the individualist hero, familiar from Homer.

Greek world obviously contributed to the spread of Hellenism throughout the Mediterranean basin. The gods of the Greek pantheon were introduced wherever the Greeks had settled, both by the Greeks themselves and by the natives, who adopted them, even if the deities venerated under the name of Hera or Demeter were really old local divinities.

The 'hoplite revolution' and its consequences

However, not all the Greek cities took part in 'colonization'. Some had first sought to extend their territory at the expense of the neighbouring communities, by absorbing them or making them dependent. This was the case with Athens, which incorporated the small neighbouring communities into its territory, and Sparta, which conquered Messenia and reduced its population to the state of helots. But to do this one had to have a military force superior to that of one's adversary and consequently to renounce the aristocratic privilege which restricted fighting in wars to the well-born. This is what was done at a fairly early stage by cities such as Argos, Sparta and Athens, and in the end by most of the cities that adopted the phalanx of hoplites (heavy-armed infantry) as their fighting formation. This 'revolution' in military practice was to have considerable social and political consequences. It took place, so it would seem, in the second half of the 7th century. From that time onwards, war was no longer a matter for aristocrats alone, but for all those who had the means to acquire the panoply – the hoplite's equipment: the breastplate, greaves, lance, sword, helmet and the famous round shield, held on the left arm, which gave the phalanx its massive character. Now the extension of the warrior's role at once led those who fought in the same line to claim an equal share of the booty.

It is instructive to compare the examples of Sparta and Athens. At Sparta, if we are to believe tradition, the share-out was effected by the legendary law-giver Lycurgus; and in fact it does seem to be historically true that the land of Messenia was so divided after two long wars. At Athens, on the other hand, in the first decade of the 6th century, the archon (chief magistrate) Solon, faced with a similar demand by the *demos*, the common people, who felt themselves threatened with poverty and servitude to the Eupatrides, refused to allow such a share-out, but did promulgate a series of decrees establishing the same laws for both Eupatrides and *demos*, and making the enslavement of poor Athenians by the aristocracy legally impossible.

In Sparta, therefore, a certain 'economic equality' was established which did not entail political equality, and in Athens an equality before the law was created which allowed economic inequalities to go on existing.

Elsewhere the crisis of the 'hoplite revolution', usually accompanied by an agrarian crisis provoked by unequal land division, was not always resolved by the intervention of a legislator inspired by the gods, as Lycurgus and Solon were traditionally supposed to have been. The fact that it provided hoplites for the army gave the *demos* political weight. Men arose to champion its rights, and these men aimed principally at seizing power. They did not necessarily belong to the *demos* themselves. They might equally well be aristocrats. But they knew how to take advantage of social divisions, how to exploit any prestige acquired in a military campaign and, by acting as the defenders of the *demos*, how to gain control of the city. Greek tradition applied to them a term borrowed from Lydian, the term 'tyrant', which from the 4th century onwards, and particularly in the work of the philosophers Plato and Aristotle, was to acquire the pejorative meaning that it

has for us today. But the tyrants of the 7th and 6th centuries were not all despots, even though tradition built up round them a whole folklore whose effects we can detect in the works of the Greek historian Herodotus. Among the most famous were Periander, the tyrant of Corinth, Cleisthenes, the tyrant of Sicyon, Pittacus of Mytilene, Polycrates of Samos and above all Peisistratus of Athens, who first seized power in 561 thanks to all the discontent which Solon's measures provoked, both among the poor, thwarted by his refusal to share out the land, and among the rich, dispossessed of their exclusive powers. Peisistratus is the tyrant about whom we are best informed, and it is significant that his reign was regarded, even by the bitterest opponents of tyranny, as an epoch of equilibrium and prosperity for the city. This prosperity is confirmed by the archaeological evidence: it was then that the city of Athens began to develop, that Athenian pottery became sought after throughout the Mediterranean world and that the policy of maritime expansion which was to characterize classical Athens was inaugurated. At Corinth, at Sicyon, in Samos, and later in Sicily with Gelo and Hiero, the age of the tyrants often coincided with the moment of the city's full flowering, with the erection of public buildings and the flourishing of artistic life. The tyrants' courts were often the centres of a brilliant and sophisticated intellectual life.

But tyranny is by definition an ephemeral regime. If the founder of the dynasty succeeded in retaining his power and in passing it on to his son or heirs, the latter soon came up against the discontent of all those whom the tyrant had excluded from power. The dynasty of the Orthagorids at Sicyon is said to have dominated the city for over a century, but most of the rest disappeared in the second or third generation. Thus at Athens Peisistratus handed over power in 527 to his sons Hippias

and Hipparchus, but Hipparchus was assassinated in 514 and Hippias was forced to flee in 510 as a result of the intervention of Cleomenes, the king of Sparta, who had been called in by the Athenian aristocrats. However, the fall of the tyranny at Athens was to have consequences which went far beyond the internal history of the city. For when the Athenian aristocrats, brought back by the king of Sparta, attempted to re-establish in Athens the regime existing before the laws of Solon, they met opposition from the *demos*, which had found a leader in the person of Cleisthenes, himself a member of the aristocracy but also, through his mother, the grandson of the tyrant of Sicyon, whose name he bore. Cleisthenes did not confine himself to re-establishing the laws of Solon; he went much further and proceeded to carry out a complete re-organization of the city, laying the foundations of what would later be called democracy, that is, a political system in which the *demos*, the people, held the *kratos*, sovereignty. To do this he began by dividing Attica in a way which served as a foundation for the whole political organization: he created ten tribes, themselves divided into three trittyes, each of which contained a certain number of demes. Each Athenian thus found himself a member of a deme, of a trittys and of a tribe, and was designated by his 'demotic' (his deme of origin). The division was made in such a way that the different sections of the population were mixed up together; the same tribe had necessarily to include urban, rural and coastal demes. The aristocratic clientages were thus broken up and all Athenians placed on the same level, though this did not mean that social inequalities disappeared. Moreover, to strengthen the weight of the *demos*, Cleisthenes incorporated into the civic body foreign elements who had come to settle in Athens as a result of the development of the city during the period of the tyrants. Aristotle even claims that the main function of the demotic was to favour the integration of these new citizens by making the patronymic disappear. The other measures ascribed by tradition to Cleisthenes were less important, apart from the creation of the Boule of Five Hundred, a council whose members were elected by lot every year, fifty from each tribe; this was to become the city's principal organ of government, and we shall have occasion to return to it. But the 'Cleisthenic revolution', the first step to the future Athenian democracy, also marks the end of what is known as the archaic age, not only in the history of Athens but in that of the whole Greek world. Less than two decades later came the start of the Persian wars, which mark the opening of the classical age proper.

Between two wars: the classical flowering

If we try to situate the classical Greek world chronologically, we find that its flowering took place between two great periods of conflict. In both, the Greeks, or at any rate certain Greek cities, were faced by an adversary alien to the world of cities – the king of Persia at the beginning of the 5th century and the king of Macedon after the middle of the 4th. And in both it was Athens that bore the main shock and ensured the common defence. The city emerged victorious from the conflict with the Persians, but was conquered by the Macedonians. Why the victory, and why the defeat? It is this double question that gives the history of classical Greece its meaning.

According to Herodotus, the Persian wars were among the greatest conflicts ever known to history. At the root of these wars lay the increase in Persian power in the reign of Cyrus, who, starting out from the Iranian plateau, succeeded in conquering Mesopotamia, Asia Minor, Syria and Palestine, leaving to his son and successor Cambyses the task of conquering Egypt. Among the peoples who thus passed under Persian domination were those Greeks who lived in the cities of the west coast of Asia Minor. Some submitted without any problems, others – such as the Phocaeans – preferred flight, and others again were forced to accept the protection of the conqueror, a protection usually exerted through a tyrant loyal to the king. Why one of these tyrants, the one who ruled in Miletus, should have tired of his position and called upon the cities of Ionia to revolt is a question to which the ancient tradition itself provides no certain answer. But in all events the revolt of Ionia was to have serious consequences. The Athenians, called upon for assistance by their brothers in Ionia, sent twenty ships. This force took part in the burning of Sardis, the capital of the Persian province of Lydia. The revolt was none the less suppressed, but Darius, who after a period of disturbances had succeeded Cambyses, wished to exact vengeance for this insult and in 490 he launched against Athens an attack by sea which ended in a defeat on the plain of Marathon, where the Persian expeditionary force had landed. Ten years later, in 480, Darius' successor, Xerxes, mounted

a new offensive on a much vaster scale, with a double expedition by land and by sea. This time the Athenians did not have to sustain the assault alone. The Spartans sent a contingent of élite troops who, however, in spite of their heroism, were unable to halt the enemy at the famous pass of Thermopylae. But the Athenians, under the leadership of Themistocles, won a decisive naval victory over the Persian fleet in the straits of Salamis, and although the Persians succeeded in gaining possession of the Acropolis in Athens they were forced to withdraw hastily. In the following year a Persian army that had remained in Greece was beaten at Plataea. The Persian wars were over.

Their consequences, however, were to be extremely important for the Greek world as a whole. Athens, victorious by sea, extended her victory by undertaking to liberate the Greek cities of Asia from the Persian yoke. To do this she concluded with a number of Aegean cities an alliance usually called the Delian League, because its centre, on which the common treasure was kept, was situated in the island of Delos, where there was a sanctuary of Apollo venerated by the Ionians. In a few decades the League was to assemble around Athens the majority of the Aegean islands and of the Greek cities of Asia Minor. However, at the same time the role and influence of Athens in the League became preponderant. From the foundation of the alliance in 478 it had been agreed that most of the allies would contribute to the common defence in currency; only a few big islands like Chios sent a naval contingent. The sums obtained by this tribute were to be deposited in Delos, but the Athenians very soon started using them for their own purposes and in the end moved the common treasury to Athens. At the same time they intervened in the internal affairs of the allied cities, not hesitating to impose on them regimes favourable to themselves and harshly repressing any attempts at independence. To keep a better watch on them, they even established permanent garrisons of Athenian citizens, who received for their subsistence lands (*cleroi*) confiscated from the recalcitrant allies; hence the name 'cleruchies' given to these garrisons. According to Plutarch, ten thousand Athenians were thus endowed with lands at the expense of the allies. We shall return to the consequences which the development of this imperialism had on the internal evolution of the city. As for the consequences on the equilibrium of the Greek world, they were beneficial in that they favoured the development of a unity of culture and civilization which was to be felt particularly in the following century, but harmful to the relations between individual cities. Sparta never accepted the hegemony exercised by Athens over part of the Greek world, and when Athens – with the foundation in 444/443 of the panhellenic colony of Thurii in southern Italy – turned her ambitions towards the western Mediterranean, Corinth joined Sparta to put a brake on Athenian expansion. The eventual result was the Peloponnesian War, a war that lasted more than a quarter of a century and pitted two Greek leagues against each other: the Delian League and the Peloponnesian League. The theatre of operations extended from the Hellespont to Sicily, and the war ended with the dramatic defeat of Athens, who was forced to give up her empire, her fleet and her democratic regime and join the Spartan alliance. This defeat was apparently not a lasting one, for not only was democracy reintroduced after a few months of an extremist regime, but in 378, a quarter of a century after her defeat, Athens succeeded in re-establishing her empire. Nevertheless, it was a real defeat, and the Athens of the 4th century would never again be what she had been before. A prey to growing financial difficulties, she did not succeed in maintaining her position in the Aegean. Sparta for her part had certainly won only an ephemeral victory. In particular, even more than Athens, she found her institutions, which until then had put her in the front rank of Greek cities, breaking up. Defeated at Leuctra in 371 by the Theban Epaminondas, Sparta never really recovered. But the Theban hegemony which followed the Battle of Leuctra was equally short-lived. It was thus a divided Greece, torn by internal quarrels, without any city capable of taking in hand the common defence, that was to face the ambitious Philip, who had become king of Macedon in 359 and who in some twenty years, by dint of intrigues, diplomatic skill and military successes, made himself master of the Greek world. Immediately after the victory that he won at Chaeronea in 338 he summoned to Corinth the delegates of the Greek cities to call on them to recognize his hegemony, a hegemony which he claimed to put at the service of the Greeks, to help them avenge the insult inflicted on them by the Persians, by mounting an expedition which he himself would lead. Philip was assassinated before he could put his plan into effect, and it was his son, Alexander, who took it up, on a scale that neither Philip nor the Greeks could have imagined.

Alexander's conquests mark the end of the classical period and the beginning of a new era, the Hellenistic age, in which the Greeks were to find themselves in contact with different civilizations. Thus the classical period proper lasted a little over a century and a half, but this century and a half was one of the richest periods in the history of civilization. It is therefore a matter of some consequence to understand how these little Greek communities were able to develop a civilization to which, twenty-five centuries later, we are still the heirs.

City and city-state

At the heart of this civilization there was first the city, the *polis*, the nature and characteristics of which we must now try to define.

The problem is not a simple one, for the term *polis* is ambiguous. Does it denote a state, as the term city-state would imply, or an urban agglomeration? Scholars have sometimes wanted to contrast the two terms *polis* and *astu*, the former indicating the state, the latter the town. This is sometimes valid, but not always. And the

The sacred owl, attribute of Athena, with a spray of olive, the goddess's gift to the Greeks. An Athenian coin of c.480–460 BC. The inscription reads ATHE(NAI).

A hoplite fights an Asiatic soldier, probably from the Persian army (the hoplite's nudity is an artistic convention, designed to distinguish Greek from barbarian). The spectacular Athenian victories over the Persians at Marathon in 490 and at Salamis ten years later were the origins of the city's imperialist ambitions.

term *acropolis*, formed on *polis* (with *acro*, 'high'), takes us back to the urban concept. Some scholars have also wanted to rid the term *polis* of any territorial connotation; according to this view, the *polis* would be first of all the community of citizens. This would make it possible in the last analysis to conceive – in the words of a German scholar – of a 'city without territory'. In fact, the Greek cities were fairly large states comprising an area of land and an urban agglomeration. Sometimes there was a separate port as well, as was the case with the Athens–Peiraeus complex, but usually the port was an extension of the city itself, as at Miletus, Syracuse, Rhegium, Cyrene and other places. Sometimes the city was virtually landlocked, like Sparta. The excavations carried out at certain colonial sites, in southern Italy in particular, show that there was total continuity between the city and its territory. In these cities created out of nothing by Greeks whom necessity had forced to abandon their native city, the layout of the territory was simply an extension – as has been demonstrated at Metapontum, for example – of that of the city. This shows that there was no opposition or dependent relationship between town and country. In any case, originally the urban centre was only a meeting place, a religious and administrative centre where those who controlled the life of the city would live. However, in the classical age things had changed. The city had also

Ostracism was an Athenian device for sending into temporary exile citizens whose absence would benefit the polis. It required 6000 votes, in a secret ballot, to exile a man. The system was named after the potsherds ('ostraka') on which candidates' names were written by the voters. Some are shown above, inscribed with the names of Aristides, Themistocles and Pericles.

become a place of exchange, a market and sometimes even a centre of craft production. But its basic function remained political and that was the really original feature of the Greek *polis*.

For what characterized the Greek city was the fairly large degree of participation in common decisions of the citizens as a whole, that is, the adult men who formed the body of citizens, the *politai*. Theoretically at least, all the citizens met to form the assembly, but the form of the regime varied according to whether the meetings of these assemblies were periodical or not and according to whether their deliberations resulted in sovereign decisions or not. During the 4th century, philosophers preoccupied with the problem of finding out what was the best constitution (*politeia*) were accustomed to distinguish between democratic and oligarchic regimes. The former were characterized by the sovereignty of the *demos*, the whole body of citizens, the latter by restrictions to this sovereignty such that only a small number of people, the *oligoi*, could hold power, *arche*. In fact, there were numerous intermediate possibilities, but the definition fitted the two principal Greek cities, Athens and Sparta, pretty well. At Athens the assembly of citizens, the *ecclesia*, was the source of all decisions and the origin of all power. It met forty times a year. Since the time of Cleisthenes the civic year had been divided into ten periods of thirty-five or thirty-six days called prytanies, and each prytany embraced four ordinary meetings of the assembly. Its agenda was fixed by the Boule of Five Hundred, which submitted to it draft decrees dealing both with questions of internal policy and with alliances, war and peace. Any citizen had the right to speak and to propose an amendment to the motion tabled by the Boule and the decision was then taken by a show of hands, except in certain special cases where a secret vote was required, for example when it was decided to use the procedure of ostracism against a citizen suspected of threatening the regime and to exile him from the city for ten years. In this case too a quorum of six thousand was required, which reveals the relatively small proportion of Athenians who actually took part in these assemblies. It has in fact proved possible to estimate the number of citizens towards the middle of the 5th century at about forty thousand. This means that barely a tenth of them usually went to the assemblies on the Pnyx Hill. And the ancient writers themselves admit that it was mainly the country people who hesitated to make a long journey and spend a whole day in the city, for the meetings of the assembly began early in the morning and often did not finish until late in the evening. Moreover, although any Athenian present could speak, usually the majority remained silent, leaving the confrontations to the orators, the men who can well be called the politicians, whether or not they held any official office, and who were called demagogues by the opponents of democracy.

Yet the sovereignty of the assembly remained real, as is shown by the very criticisms formulated against the

These 4th-century BC ballot-discs, discovered in the Athenian Agora, were used by jurors in the law-courts. They dropped the discs into a box to record their verdict; those with solid hubs stood for acquittal, those with hollow for condemnation.

regime by those who did not admit that the crowd could take decisions. And the system functioned, continuity between the sessions of the assembly being ensured by the Boule, which, since the measures taken at the end of the 460s by one Ephialtes, was endowed with very extensive powers both in matters of general policy and in the realm of financial and judicial affairs. One last institution put the finishing touch to the sovereignty of the people: this was the Heliaea, which the same Ephialtes had endowed with extensive judicial powers to the detriment of the old aristocratic council of judges of the Areopagus. The heliasts, six thousand of them, were chosen every year by lot and formed the courts which had to try all public and private cases. Moreover, since the days when Pericles (*c.*490–429) had guided the destiny of the city, councillors and heliasts received a daily payment – five obols for the former, three obols for the latter – which enabled every Athenian, whatever his means, to devote himself for a year to the service of the city. However, the sovereign people delegated part of its sovereignty to the magistrates responsible for executing the common decisions. These magistrates were either elected annually – such was the case with the generals (*strategoi*) and the treasurers – or chosen by lot, like the archons, the magistrates responsible for supervising judicial affairs. They formed colleges of five or, more often, ten members, and were subject to close supervision by the Boule, which put them through an examination before they took up their duties and required them to give an account of their stewardship at the end of their term of office. Those to whom large public funds were entrusted were personally responsible for them, which explains why treasurers and generals in particular were recruited exclusively from the ranks of the richest men. Thanks to the Persian wars, the generals had acquired very great authority in the city at the expense of the archons, once the supreme magistrates. Most of the important politicians of the 5th century were generals at one time or another in their lives – Miltiades, the victor of Marathon, Themistocles, the victor of Salamis, Aristides, the founder of the Delian League, Cimon, who enlarged it, and finally Pericles, who was re-elected

fifteen times consecutively to this office. He shared it, certainly, with nine colleagues, but it enabled him to direct the policy of Athens when she was at her zenith. In the 4th century, on the other hand, after the Peloponnesian War, when financial affairs assumed growing importance, it was the men responsible for financial affairs – Eubulus and Lycurgus, for example – together with orators like Demosthenes or Aeschines, who occupied the forefront of the political scene. But whether they were generals or financial magistrates, they remained subject to the strict supervision of the assembled people, who could bring them before the courts and prosecute them if their activities seemed contrary to the interests of the city. Many generals were thus convicted for exceeding their orders or for pursuing a policy different from the one which they had been commissioned to carry out. One of the most famous of these affairs is recounted by the historian Xenophon. In the last years of the Peloponnesian War the Athenian fleet met the Peloponnesian fleet off the Arginusae islands. The Athenians won the day, but after the battle several ships were destroyed by a storm and their crews drowned. The generals who had not had time to pick up the shipwrecked crews were impeached before the *ecclesia*, converted for the occasion into a high court of justice, and a fierce debate took place before the people, a debate which ended in the death sentence for the generals. The procedure was irregular, for the generals were judged *en bloc*, not individually, and the affair caused a good deal of controversy. It helped in no small measure to reawaken the partisan passions already aroused a few years before by the failure of the Sicilian expedition, which had been followed by the partially successful attempt by the opponents of the regime to overturn the democracy in 411. It would, in fact, be a mistake to imagine that the Athenian people were not divided by contradictory opinions. There was certainly a consensus about the empire and certain aspects of the constitution, but on this or that particular problem opinions could differ, without making it necessary to speak of political 'parties'. However, in the last few years of the 5th century there developed in Athenian opinion, thanks precisely to the military defeats, an oligarchical movement which succeeded twice – in 411 and 404 – in securing the triumph of its policy. Those who defended it were generally admirers of Sparta; they belonged for the most part to the wealthier section of the Athenian population and saw in the Spartan victories a confirmation of the excellence of Sparta's form of government. On both occasions they failed and democracy was re-established, but the 'Spartan mirage' which they had helped to create was to go on developing in the following centuries.

It is precisely this 'Spartan mirage' which makes it so difficult to analyse the very original institutions of that city. To the Greeks of the 5th century, it was the very symbol of oligarchy. And in fact the citizens as a whole, who called themselves the Peers (*homoioi*), played only a very limited role in political decisions. It is true that there was an assembly, the *apella*, but its meetings seem to have been very irregular and the people had no power either to pass or to amend the proposals submitted to it. The real authority lay in the hands of a council of elders, the *gerousia*, together with two kings and a college of five ephors. The twenty-eight members of the *gerousia* were appointed for life. The double monarchy was hereditary in the two royal families of the Agiads and Eurypontids. Only the five ephors were elected; chosen annually, they were endowed with extensive judicial and supervisory powers, which extended even to the two kings, whose functions were mainly military and religious. Politically, therefore, Sparta, where authority lay in the hands of thirty-five persons, the majority of whom were irremovable, was an oligarchy, even if later, thanks to the idealization of Sparta already mentioned, people were to attempt to find democratic elements in it.

Varieties of political experience

Sparta and Athens represented the two extremes of a very wide spectrum of political regimes. Democracy had been established in a number of cities during the course of the 5th century, as a result of the hegemony that Athens exercised over the Aegean world, but it did not everywhere take the same radical form as at Athens. One difference was that public offices were not remunerated, which kept the poorest people out of them; another was that economic conditions or social criteria excluded certain people, sometimes the poorest, sometimes the craftsmen or the tradesmen, from political life. The *demos* was certainly sovereign, but it was a *demos* consisting only of landowners or those who could afford to serve as hoplites. Similarly, there were different forms of oligarchy, with varying numbers of citizens eligible to hold office. Aristotle, who gives a long analysis in the *Politics* of the different kinds of government, counted among the moderate oligarchies Massalia (Marseilles), where people otherwise excluded from all political activity were allowed to hold certain magistracies. We are not well enough acquainted with these institutions to be able to go into details, but it is certain that in this realm Greek experience was particularly rich and it is not surprising that it very soon led to reflection on political affairs.

However, it is important to make it clear that the *polis* was not the only form of state known to the classical Greek world. Whole regimes remained apart from the

process of evolution whose origin and development we have tried to trace. Even in the 5th century, Aetolia, Locris, and parts of Arcadia and Thessaly were still at the stage of what Aristotle called the *ethnos*, that is, a form of undifferentiated community whose members were dispersed in villages and met round a common sanctuary. We know little about the institutions of these *ethne*, which can only be glimpsed at a relatively late period. By then the framework of the city tended to be accepted everywhere, but the still close links between the various components of the *ethnos* led to the federal states which developed in the 4th century and the Hellenistic age; the most striking examples of these were the Achaean, Aetolian and Arcadian confederations. What characterized them was the existence, over and above the civic institutions, of federal organs responsible for managing the common treasure, which was usually deposited in the federal sanctuary, and for taking decisions in foreign policy. However, in the view of Greek thinkers of the 4th century, these states, some of which were to play a by no means negligible role in Greek affairs in the following period, were still only primitive forms of human community and it was the city and the city alone which should be the natural milieu of men. That is why, when they thought about the best constitution in relation to society, it was always the city and urban living that was in the forefront of their minds.

At the start, as we have seen, the civic community was essentially a rural community consisting of those who owned land. In the classical age this was still the case in many cities, where membership of the civic body implied the possession of landed property. Such was Sparta, where the loss of the *cleros* automatically involved exclusion from the ranks of the Peers. Tradition, as we have seen, ascribed to Lycurgus an equal division which guaranteed every Spartan the same quantity of oil, wine and corn. In fact, this share-out probably affected only the land conquered in Messenia, but the possession of a plot of land remained none the less the indispensable condition for belonging to the civic body. That is why the number of citizens was to decrease catastrophically from the moment when – probably at the beginning of the 4th century – people were allowed to dispose freely of their shares of land, which until then had been inalienable. This led not only to a decrease in the number of citizens, but also to concentration of the land in a small number of hands. This identification of land ownership and civic rights very often also meant, both at Sparta and in other cities, that one had to abstain from all activities except those connected with the land, and that merchants and craftsmen were excluded from the civic body. At Thebes, according to a law mentioned by Aristotle, one had to have given up any mercantile activity for ten years in order to qualify for citizenship.

At Athens things were different, although it is true that the majority of Athenian citizens, too, were landowners. An ancient writer tells us that if a proposal

put forward at the beginning of the 4th century, which aimed to restrict citizenship to those who owned land, had been adopted, five thousand Athenians would have been deprived of their civic rights. At that time, as a result of the losses incurred in the Peloponnesian War, the number of citizens was not much more than about thirty thousand. If these indications are accepted as accurate, it would mean that five-sixths of the Athenians owned a piece of land. The fact remains that the other five thousand presumably drew their income from other activities of a mercantile or manufacturing nature. It is Athens about which we are best informed concerning the social structure of the civic body. After Solon's time, if we are to believe tradition, Athenian citizens were divided into four property classes. The qualification for each class, at first based on income from land, was in the classical period estimated in cash, which made it possible to count among the members of the first class rich men whose income came from craft workshops or maritime loans. In the 4th century, the only period for which we have precise data, the rich numbered twelve hundred. These rich men were the ones obliged to perform 'liturgies', that is, to make 'voluntary' contributions to equip a trireme, to train a choir or to organize a public banquet; they also had to bear the weight of the *eisphora*, the special war tax. Big landed proprietors were certainly to be found among them, although – as numerous studies have proved – the land was very much split up in Attica. But there were also, and more significantly, men whose fortune comprised simultaneously land, slaves (who were sometimes employed as craftsmen), credits in the form of maritime loans granted to merchants and also concessions in the silver mines of Laurion. Some fortunes included no land at all. Such was the case with the father of the orator Demosthenes, whose fortune amounted to fourteen talents (84,000 drachmas) and consisted mainly of credits and of two workshops of slaves, who worked as cutlers and cabinet makers.

The politai, or citizens, of Athens were the entire body of adult males. Political sovereignty was theirs and they had considerable opportunities for participation in the decision-making process. Above, a group of citizens eagerly arguing among themselves. Slaves – excluded from that process – gave the wealthy time for political activity: below, a slave prepares the wine for a feast.

Alongside this minority of rich men, who formed the first two classes (*pentacosiomedimni* and *hippeis*), there were the small owner-farmers, who tilled their land themselves, rarely went into the city and formed the bulk of the combatants in the phalanx of hoplites. It is they whom Aristophanes depicts in most of his comedies and whose side he takes against the war-mongers and demagogues. The plays of Aristophanes are contemporary with the Peloponnesian War and bear witness to the very heavy price paid by Athenian farmers during this period: fields devastated, vineyards and olive groves destroyed. As usual the poorest suffered most. However, today scholars hesitate to deduce from this real misery in the war years that it led to an exodus from the countryside and a concentration of land in a few hands. In fact, Athens remained a largely peasant democracy until the end of the 4th century, and a large number of these country people lived on strips of land just big enough to support them. Proof of this is supplied by a piece of evidence from 322 BC. When, after suppression of the revolt against Macedonia which broke out after Alexander's death, Athens had to adopt a constitution which excluded all those who did not possess property worth at least 2000 drachmas, 12,000 out of a total of 21,000 Athenians lost their civic rights.

However, among the *thetes* (the lowest class) there were also a number of small craftsmen and tradesmen. The crafts had developed in Athens during the course of the 6th century, thanks partly to the great popularity of Attic vases (first black figure, then red) and partly to the development of the Athenian fleet and the exploitation of the silver mines at Laurion. The profession of craftsman was certainly despised, but at Athens it did not prevent participation in civic life. What is more, the craftsmen who lived in the city or at the Peiraeus found it easier than the farmers to attend the meetings of the assembly and as a result exerted more influence on the common decisions. This was one of the major grievances of the opponents of democracy. In time of war the craftsmen usually served as oarsmen in the fleet, since their incomes were not big enough to entitle them to be listed as hoplites. Wildly enthusiastic supporters of democracy, in 411 they caused the failure of the revolution fomented by the oligarchs among the Athenian sailors stationed at Samos. However, there were also rich craftsmen, men who owned a workshop of slaves and lived on their income, like landowners. It was men like this who achieved political office at the end of the 5th century – men such as the tanners Cleon and Anytos or the potter Hyperbolos. Demosthenes' father, who owned two workshops of this sort, belonged to the same circles, but his fortune also included maritime loans. For there was no bar to Athenian citizens taking part in commerce any more than in manufacturing. However, it is important to distinguish between those whose business consisted in lending money to merchants and shipowners and those who were businessmen themselves. The former were often rich men who made their money grow by lending 'in bulk' a fortune usually drawn from the land or from working the mines. The latter, on the other hand, were men of much smaller means for whom commerce was their main occupation. It should not be imagined that mercantile activity at Athens was a very large-scale affair. The main object of maritime trade was to guarantee the provisioning of the city, particularly in grain – vital because Attica did not produce enough grain to feed its population – but also in wood for

shipbuilding, and in slaves. In addition, the Peiraeus was a reliable port, where merchants from all over the Aegean basin could be sure of finding customers and a sound currency. But the merchants themselves, who usually went to sea with their cargo, after coming to an agreement with a shipowner, were people of relatively modest means, often resident foreigners, but also, as we have seen, citizens, at the mercy of a storm or dishonest partners. As a matter of fact, it is because disputes often arose between the merchants and those who lent them money, and because these disputes involved court cases, of which the pleas have come down to us, that we are reasonably familiar with Greek commercial conditions. The cases in question concern only matters relating to maritime trade and banking. Here, too, one must be careful with words and the meaning which we are tempted to give to them in the 20th century. Those Athenians who are called bankers were money-lenders and money-changers, in close relations with the activities of the port, but playing mainly the part of intermediaries. It is striking, moreover, that the few bankers whose names have come down to us were for the most part freed slaves. There were no influential financial circles any more than there was any business middle class. The Athenian economy – and it is practically the only one on which we can base any deductions – was certainly not a primitive subsistence economy, but it was not a 'capitalist' economy either, and trade occupied only a relatively modest place in the life of the city. As for internal trade, the trade that took place in the *agora* (market place), it was still more modest, and the small merchants, the *kapeloi*, belonged to the poorest strata of the population.

The Athenian political and legal system is well known through her writers and orators. Evidence for the other Greek cities is much more meagre. A certain number of cities of Greece proper, of Asia and of the west were organized along similar lines to Athens. At Miletus, Corinth, Syracuse and later at Rhodes, there was also intense seaport activity, regular exchanges with the Aegean world, a large number of craftsmen and consequently a diversified civic community. But elsewhere, where commercial activities and craft production were less important, the civic community was more homogeneous, consisting mostly of landowners, and the unequal division of such property was the primary reason for the antagonisms which developed in the community. This was particularly the case with the Peloponnesian cities, and it was not by chance that demands for the division of the land often appear there in connection with political disturbances, especially in the 4th century, provoking a recurrence of the phenomenon which had characterized the archaic age, tyranny. This does not apply, of course, to Sparta, where not only was the civic community composed of landowners and citizenship tied to the possession of a *cleros*, but in addition all activity other than political and military activity was forbidden to the citizens. This naturally implied the existence in the Spartan state of disfranchised social groups who performed commercial and craft work and also cultivated the soil, since even agricultural activity was prohibited. However, it would be too simple to suppose that the class known as the *perioeci* satisfied the first requirement and the helots the second. In fact, the *perioeci* were Laconians who had kept their own towns but had renounced all independence and put themselves completely in the hands of Sparta. Most of them were farmers, as is proved by the fact that the tradition relating to the division of land in Laconia and Messenia included them among those who received shares of land. But there were also craftsmen in the cities of the *perioeci*, and it is reasonable to assume that trade, unimportant as it may have been because Sparta controlled the rich cornlands of Messenia and possessed sufficient quantities of metals, was the concern of the *perioeci*. On the other hand, there is no doubt that the helots did all the agricultural work on lands belonging to the Spartan citizens.

The Greek colonial world experienced a history and development somewhat different from those of continental Greece and of the islands. In particular, the rhythm of its evolution was different. Tyranny, for example, exhibited features different from those which distinguished it in Greece proper; it was at the same time more military and less populist. Aristocratic values did not predominate for so long, yet democracy did not appear until relatively late and even then in somewhat peculiar circumstances. For example, in Syracuse at the beginning of the 5th century, the *demos*, in order to seize power, had to ally itself with the indigenous population against the landed proprietors, and in any case was very soon robbed of its power by the tyrants. Finally, in so far as this colonial world was an 'experimental laboratory', it played a far from negligible role in the history of Greek thought and art. Before Athens came to be 'the school of Greece', it was at first mainly Sicily and southern Italy that were to develop large-scale architecture (Acragas, Selinus) and the philosophical ideas associated with the names of Pythagoras and Empedocles.

Slavery is to us the least acceptable institution of Greek society, but it was barely questioned by the Greeks. Slaves were usually of 'barbarian' (non-Greek) origin. The one shown on this 5th-century BC perfume bottle is Ethiopian.

The problem of slavery

One of the major problems in the history of the classical Greek world is that of slavery. It is a problem that has caused many controversies and aroused many passions, as Sir Moses Finley recalled in *Ancient Slavery and Modern Ideology*. However, there can be absolutely no doubt that Greek society of the classical epoch was a slave society. We can assert that not so much because of the number of slaves – the subject of so much acrimonious debate – or even because of their fairly large role in the production of material goods, but because slavery was a fact accepted by everyone and never questioned, not even occasionally by those who were the victims of it. It has even been said that slavery was the very condition of the Greek man's freedom, a freedom that must be understood in the sense which the Greeks themselves gave it, that is, the freedom to do as one liked with one's person and to participate in the life of the community to which one belonged. The slave was in fact a piece of property, a possession that one could buy, sell, pawn and bequeath to one's heirs. Deprived of any personality, he obviously could not have a family, and his children, if he came to have any, did not belong to him, but were the property of the master of the woman who had borne them. In this general framework the real condition of the slave could vary within narrow limits. Here again we have to base our reasoning on the Athenian example, the only one about which we are slightly less ill informed. At Athens in the classical period there was a considerable number of slaves, about a hundred to a hundred and twenty thousand; no precise estimate is possible. Large gangs of slaves were employed in the silver mines of Laurion. Thucydides reports that in the last four years of the Peloponnesian War twenty thousand slaves escaped thanks to the occupation of part of Attica by the Spartans, and there is every reason to think that these were slaves working at Laurion. They were the worst-off ones, working in wretched conditions with little hope of improving their lot. The fate of the rural slaves was certainly less hard, whether they worked under the supervision of a bailiff, himself a slave, on a large estate or toiled at their master's side on a little strip of land, sharing his troubles but also sometimes his joys, as is shown by the plays of the comic poets. The same is true of the slaves working in small workshops, sometimes even established on their own account and paying their master a sort of rent or due, the *apophora*. Accounts of public works reveal that on the same site, performing the same tasks, were to be found citizens, foreigners and slaves, and that the wages were the same for all, the slave doubtless handing over part to his master. A pamphleteer of the end of the 5th century even claimed that at Athens nothing distinguished the slave from the poor free man, adding that there were also rich slaves. In fact, some slaves who enjoyed the confidence of their master could manage a workshop or bank for him, or represent him in a foreign market. And there is no doubt that such slaves, rare as they may have been, had the chance of growing rich. The famous banker Pasion was a former slave, freed by his master. At his death he left his heirs a huge fortune amounting to over fifty talents. But even if the slave was rich he could not dispose of his property as he wished unless he had been freed. He was at the mercy of the good will of his master, who could do as he liked with such property. Athenian law may have punished a master guilty of murdering a slave, but this did not imply any particular 'mildness' on the part of Athenian democracy in the treatment of slaves; it was simply a question of not letting a crime go unpunished. At Athens, as elsewhere, the slave was subject to corporal punishment and his testimony was only valid if given under torture. Yet we do not know of any slave revolts in the history of Athens. However, there is nothing surprising about this. We know from numerous pieces of evidence that the slaves came from every shore of the Mediterranean, mainly the eastern. There were certainly Greeks among the slaves – prisoners of war or people captured by pirates – but, especially in the 4th century, the majority of those employed at Athens were of barbarian origin – Lydians, Carians, Scythians, Egyptians, Thracians and so on. They were thus people of diverse origins, who often did not understand each other and whose sole aim, if they ever escaped, was to flee in the hope of getting back to their native country. It was not by chance that Plato recommended having slaves who did not speak the same language. However, there is no doubt that in doing this he had in mind above all the Spartan helots, who frequently revolted.

To Athenians of the classical period the helots were in fact slaves, but slaves of a particular kind also found in the Cretan cities, at Syracuse, in certain cities on the eastern coast of the Aegean and in Propontis. What distinguished them from the chattel slaves used at Athens and in the cities which, like Athens, supplied themselves with manpower from the Aegean markets, was that they were natives – Greeks or barbarians – and that they formed a homogeneous population, reproducing itself naturally. They were also farmers, cultivating the land of the cities to which they were attached and paying their masters rents usually in kind. We are reasonably familiar only with the status of the Spartan helots and that of the Cretan *clarotae*, the former because Greek authors wrote at length about their lot, the latter because we possess a long inscription from Gortyn containing useful details of their legal status. Even in antiquity the helots were regarded as the primitive inhabitants of the soil of Laconia, reduced to servitude by the Dorian conquerors. Modern scholars have generally accepted this view, though it has nevertheless been contested, at any rate so far as the helots of Laconia are concerned. As for those of Messenia, there can be no doubt that the conquest of their lands by the Spartans marked the beginning of their dependence. The ancients particularly emphasized the harsh treatment inflicted on them by their Spartan masters, especially the notorious *crypteia*, which involved the nocturnal hunting-down of helots by young Spartans, a sport which certainly reflected ancient initiation rites. And they saw in this harsh treatment the cause of the helot revolts which several times endangered the city. However, comparison with the condition of the Cretan *clarotae*, as it emerges from the Gortyn inscription, shows that these dependants enjoyed relative freedom, and a late grammarian describes them as existing 'between slavery and freedom'. They could in fact own their own tools and house and do what they liked with their harvest, once they had paid the rent due to their master. This rent was certainly very high and doubtless the helots remained poverty-stricken peasants. However, since they could not be sold and were sure of remaining on the land to which they were attached, they were not pieces of property to be dealt with as their owners pleased. It is this semi-freedom, even more than the harsh treatment, which explains their frequent revolts, the aim of which was precisely their integration in the Lacedaemonian community. It is also striking that all the slave revolts mentioned by our sources concern dependants of the same type – the *penestae* of Thessaly, the *cyllyrii* of Syracuse, the *mariandyni* of Heraclea Pontica and so on. These forms of dependence were to be found in a number of colonial cities, where the Greeks had reduced to servitude the natives in the midst of whom they had settled. But after several centuries of living together these hellenized natives were ready to demand incorporation into the civic community, and if the latter was torn by social antagonisms, as was often the case in the 4th century, it was tempting for one or other of the opposing factions to seek the support of this mass of manpower in return for the promise of land and civic rights. This is what happened at Syracuse on the accession of Dionysius the Elder, at Heraclea Pontica when the tyrant Clearchus seized power towards the middle of the century, and later at Sparta when the reforming King Cleomenes and then the tyrant Nabis freed the helots to gain their support for the revolution which they had set in motion. The existence of these dependent populations did not of course exclude the use of chattel slaves. This is certainly true of Syracuse, and possibly of Sparta from the 4th century onwards. But these slaves represented only a marginal element in comparison with dependants.

This leads us to emphasize a point which has been the subject of many controversies. Greek slaves did not form a class in the sense in which this word is understood today, and it is a mistake to regard them as the equivalent of the modern proletariat. As we saw above, slaves and free men often shared the same activities, and the relation between the slave and his owner was not that between wage-earner and employer but that between a piece of property and its owner. The very diversity of economic and working conditions of slaves, together with the persistence within the most highly evolved cities of family structures, made things even more complex. Paradoxically it was at Sparta that the relation of dependence between Spartan and helot was the most direct, with the reservation, however, that the helots belonged to the Spartan community, not to this or that individual. It was also at Sparta that intermediate categories between the fully fledged citizen and the helot were to be found. These did not exist elsewhere, where the contrast between free man and slave was radical.

Finally, to complete this picture of Greek societies in the classical period, we must describe the status of the foreigners who for various reasons – political exile, mercantile activities, intellectual interests – settled in cities as residents. At Athens they were called *metics*. Free to pursue any activity which suited them, and obliged to pay taxes and to do military service, they were nevertheless barred from political life and forbidden to own land, the exclusive privilege of the citizen. Some of them were very rich, like the father of the orator Lysias, who owned an arms workshop employing a hundred and twenty slaves. Others were of more modest means; they were to be found mainly in the neighbourhood of the port, where they pursued all kinds of minor activities connected with commerce.

Greek religion in the classical period

One of the most important factors affecting both social cohesion within the states and relations between them has not been mentioned so far: Greek religion. By the classical period the Greek pantheon was complete and the great myths had acquired their definitive form. Those divinities, Dionysus in particular, who might

The cult of the Olympian deities was largely a matter of public ritual: above, Apollo in his shrine at Delphi; he is sitting on the omphalos, the stone that marked the centre of the world. The worshipper's emotional needs were satisfied by the mystery religions, of which the earliest was that of Eleusis. In this 5th-century relief from the site (below), Demeter, on the left, gives an ear of corn to Triptolemus (founder of the Eleusinian mysteries), while Persephone places a wreath on his head.

have seemed a shade marginal had been incorporated into the religion of the *polis* and shorn of some of their original features. Tragedy, by giving shape to the conflict between the old world of the heroes and the budding city, helped in the establishment of a religion that was more concerned with ritual than with dogma.

It is in fact ritual that best enables us to form some idea of the different manifestations of religious life in the city of the classical age. At its centre lay the sacrifice, which established between men and gods not only a division of rights and privileges but also a close relationship. It preceded all the acts of public and private life and was conducted in accordance with a precisely fixed sequence: choice of the animal when a blood sacrifice was involved, cooking of the meat, sharing out of the flesh, bones and entrails, and so on. Offerings and processions were the other features of this religious life, which followed a very precise calendar. Thus at Athens the pattern of life was fixed by the great festivals in honour of the divinities who protected the city. First of all there was the Panathenaea, involving an annual procession – conducted every fourth year with particular solemnity – which ascended the Acropolis to offer to Athena the *peplos* (a

ceremonial robe) embroidered by the city's maidens. Then there was the Thesmophoria, a festival in honour of Demeter and Kore in which only women could take part. The Dionysia and Lenaea were festivals in honour of Dionysus; they were the occasion of the dramatic contests in which the tragic and comic poets competed against each other and were crowned by the people at the end of the day. These four were only the most important of the festivals.

The relationship between religious life and civic life was so close that most of the priesthoods were in fact magistracies open to all citizens and usually salaried. Only a few priesthoods attached to ancient cults remained the privilege of certain aristocratic families such as the Eumolpides and Kerykes at Eleusis. The priest who presided in Athens over sacrifices and the various other manifestations of religious life, the king-archon, was a magistrate elected by lot every year. The city also appointed the sacred ambassadors sent to consult the Delphic oracle or to represent the city at the Olympian or Isthmian games.

It was at the great pan-Hellenic sanctuaries that the unity of the Greek world was affirmed. The famous athletic games, which attracted spectators from all parts

The order of ritual: a procession to the shrine of Apollo in Athens. The girl leading the procession is known as the 'Kanephoros'; she carries on her head the basket containing the sanctified corn that will *be sprinkled on the sacrificial animals to consecrate them before they are killed. The Kanephoros was chosen annually from among the city's noble families. On the right is Apollo's sacred tripod.*

The frenzy of worship: priestesses mix wine in front of an image of Dionysus. On either side of them are maenads, followers of Dionysus, each clutching a burning torch and a thyrsus, the ivy-twined stick that is an attribute of the god.

of the Greek world and were the occasion for oratorical and political jousting, took place every four years at Olympia in honour of Zeus. The sanctuary of Posidon at the isthmus of Corinth and that of Apollo at Delphi were also important centres of Greek religious life in the classical age. Even if the reputation of the Pythia was somewhat tarnished by the attitude of the priests of Delphi at the time of the Persian invasions, when they gave contradictory – and initially defeatist – advice, the oracle none the less remained a far from negligible element in the life of the Greek cities. In the 4th century the sanctuary was to become the stake in inter-city conflicts, and first Thebes, then Philip of Macedon tried to use the Delphic Amphictyony (an ancient league of local communities connected with the cult) to impose their authority on the Greek world.

It is easy to understand that such an essentially civic religion could not satisfy the need for consolation and hope that leads men to seek divine help in troubled times. However, there was also another side to Greek religion, partially concealed by the civic rituals, but still full of vitality. This found expression in such violent outbursts as the Dionysiac orgies, in the mysticism of the Eleusinian religion (which, as far as one can understand, was a cult of personal salvation) and the inclination, especially from the 4th century onwards, to adopt foreign cults like those of the Thracian goddess

Bendis, the Egyptian Isis, and Adonis, whose nocturnal rites attracted women particularly. Finally, there were in addition the numerous manifestations of popular religion which found expression in the countryside – on the occasion of the rural Dionysia, for example – in games, mirth, ribaldry and rites often inherited from very ancient practices like the seasonal feasts observed by anthropologists in present-day peasant societies.

Civic religion, popular religion and forms of mysticism are, taken together, a reminder that Greek religion in the classical age was more complex than the apparent 'secularism' of intellectual life might lead us to suppose.

Woman's role

Women, of course, had no political role in the city, but the wives of citizens ensured the reproduction of the civic community by providing legitimate heirs for heads of families. Marriage was thus an institution essential to the life of the city. At Athens and, one may suppose, in most cities, it was the father or guardian of the girl who chose her a husband. Marriage was a private act, often effected before witnesses who also guaranteed the handing-over of the dowry, which the father could recover if the marriage was annulled. For this purpose he registered a claim on the property of the future husband. The girl then left her father's house to go to live in her husband's house, of which she became the guardian, watching over the stores and directing the work of the domestic slaves. She practically never left her home again, except to take part in religious festivals, some of which – such as the Thesmophoria at Athens – were festivals specially intended for women.

One of Greek women's chief occupations was the manufacture of clothes. The two weavers shown here are working on a warp-weighted loom. They walk to and fro, passing the bobbin through the threads.

Evidence for the daily life of women in classical Greece is not abundant. Some of the most memorable images are on grave-stones: this exquisite monument to Hegeso shows the dead woman examining jewellery proferred by her maidservant.

Apart from this function as mistress of the *oikos*, the household, her principal duty was to give her husband legitimate sons to inherit the patrimony and to be inscribed, when they were old enough, on the civic lists. But she had no legal existence apart from her husband. In theory at any rate, she could not own property. If she was widowed, she went back to her father or legal guardian, who made himself responsible for finding her a new husband, unless she stayed with her son if the latter had come of age or unless she was too old to marry again. Of course, procedures were not always followed strictly, and numerous lawyers' speeches which have come down to us prove that in reality things did not always happen quite like this. In any case, this procedure applied to women belonging to 'polite society'. In lower-class circles the women often assisted their husbands in their work or were obliged to work outside, particularly as nurses, and were less closely confined to the women's quarters. In addition, although since ancient times monogamy was the rule, the master of the house quite often had, besides his *gamete gune*, his legitimate wife, one or more concubines, usually daughters of poor or foreign families, whose children could sometimes be legitimized if the legal wife was barren or if – which came to the same thing – she had only given her husband daughters. An only daughter could not inherit the family fortune. When such a situation occurred, the heiress, known as an *epicleros*, had to marry her nearest relative on the

paternal side, which was liable to create extremely complicated situations. Although the husband was free to bring concubines into the house, and could have sexual relations with slaves, the woman was expected to remain faithful to her husband. Adultery was severely punished; an ancient law authorized the husband who caught his wife *in flagrante delicto* to kill the lover without incurring the slightest penalty. Usually things did not go so far and the matter was settled more peacefully. But an adulterous wife was regarded as a criminal; she was forbidden to take part in religious festivals and she was to some extent banned from society. Here again, the main object was to preserve legitimacy of descent, to guarantee the master of the house legitimate heirs to keep the patrimony in the father's family.

At Sparta the situation was somewhat different, although based on similar principles. There, too, marriage was intended to ensure the reproduction of the civic body, but the Spartan woman did not have the same domestic functions as the Athenian woman, since the Spartan contented himself with receiving the produce from his property, which was cultivated by the helots. She was first and foremost a child-bearer, and it is not by chance that all the anecdotes and traditions emphasize the Spartan mother, the person who brought into the world well-formed children destined to be vigorous soldiers. According to the admirers of Sparta, it was to ensure that this reproductive function was

citizenship, erected a monumental tomb for his mistress, the courtesan Pythonike. This simple example illustrates the changes which had taken place in attitudes at the end of the 4th century, changes which were only one of the aspects of what has been called 'the crisis of the city' in the 4th century. We shall conclude this short picture of the Greek world in the classical age with a few words about this crisis.

The crisis of classical Greece

The term 'crisis' must be used with great caution because of its modern connotations. One must take care in particular not to talk about an 'economic crisis', as people have sometimes been tempted to do on the basis of certain data – for example, the obvious decline of Attic pottery or the strict grain laws adopted at Athens from the beginning of the 4th century. Similarly, one cannot really speak of an 'agrarian crisis', although it is true that the Peloponnesian War, by causing the destruction of many vineyards, olive groves and harvests indubitably increased rural poverty in the decades following Athens' defeat. But the existing division of landed property seems not to have been much affected and the crisis can only have been temporary, while, as we have seen, Athenian commerce remained extremely active during the whole of the 4th century. Indeed, the second half of the century saw the introduction of new forms of maritime loan, the speeding up of business transactions and the expansion of the whole 'world of the *emporion*'. Elsewhere our information is too thin to enable us to draw general conclusions. At Sparta there was unquestionably a concentration of land in a few hands, but this was the result of political rather than economic factors. The freedom to do as one liked with the *cleros*, abetted by the influx of wealth after the military operations in the Aegean, certainly led to a serious imbalance which was to grow steadily worse during the course of the century.

Although one must take care not to speak of an economic crisis and avoid imposing on ancient societies the patterns of the modern world, the fact remains that the 4th century was an unstable one and that the Peloponnesian War was the decisive factor in this breakdown. As Thucydides had already emphasized, the war had everywhere exacerbated the antagonisms in the cities between the small minority of rich or powerful men and the mass of the poor. The defeat of Athens, by depriving the Aegean world of a hegemony which had its positive side, accentuated the imbalance still further. In most of the cities oligarchs and democrats clashed, and the victory of either one or the other was accompanied by massacres, proscriptions and confiscations, while almost everywhere tyrants reappeared – adventurers who at the head of a band of mercenaries would seize cities, free slaves and share out the land. The Peloponnese in particular, where Sparta's writ had ceased to run, was the scene of violent civil strife. But in Magna Graecia (the Greek colonies in Sicily and southern Italy) too, the cities tore themselves

carried out in the best conditions that Spartan girls received a physical education comparable with that of the boys, and trained half-naked at the gymnasium. It was also to guarantee the city vigorous young people that – again according to the ancient writers – the law authorized an elderly man to 'lend' his young wife to a more vigorous man so that she could bear him fine children. These practices filled Sparta's admirers with enthusiasm, and it was on the basis of this real or imaginary model that in the ideal city of the *Republic* Plato envisaged the community of women for the guardians of the city, that class of warriors based on the Spartan citizens.

But in this point, as in many others, Sparta was a city apart in the Greek world. Elsewhere, women were first and foremost, as at Athens, the guardians of the domestic hearth, underprivileged citizens deprived of any legal rights, yet integrated in the city of which, as Plato, and after him Aristotle, says, they formed half. But here again, citizenship was the essential criterion. Legitimate marriage meant union with the daughter of a citizen; a foreign woman could only be a concubine or a courtesan. Pericles himself did not escape the rule, for which he had been largely responsible; he could not marry the woman he loved, the famous Aspasia of Miletus.

A century later Alexander the Great's treasurer, one Harpalus, who had fled with part of the royal treasure and after taking refuge in Athens had been granted apart, making themselves vulnerable to any ambitious men who arrived upon the scene. After the tyranny of Dionysius at Syracuse, anarchy prevailed in the island for several decades, until the Corinthian Timoleon arrived to re-establish a provisional peace.

Athens escaped these disorders. After the two vain attempts of 411 and 404, the oligarchs gave no further sign of life and no one dreamed of overturning the regime. However, increasing financial difficulties and the growing independence of the military leaders led to a breakdown of democracy. The mass of the people, a prey to poverty aggravated by the loss of the empire and of the material advantages that went with it, seemed to take less and less interest in the life of the city, in spite of the introduction of payment for attending the meetings of the assembly, while the politicians fought and savaged each other, substituting personal quarrels for the great intellectual debates of days gone by. Lawsuits multiplied, especially in moments of crisis, and the situation was to grow worse after 359, when the ambitions of Philip of Macedon drove an even deeper wedge between the factions. The oratorical duel between Demosthenes and Aeschines, the former an advocate of obstinate resistance to Philip, the latter possibly a convert to his claims, is significant in this respect.

This deflection of politics to personal ends reflects the decline of Athenian democracy. It was also at the origin of what might be called the birth of political philosophy. It was no accident that the Peloponnesian War precisely coincided with the appearance of the first writings, sometimes in the form of pamphlets, that sought to define the best *politeia*, the best constitution.

However, it was especially in the 4th century and at Athens that political theory really took shape, first round Plato and the Academy, then round Aristotle and the Lyceum. The institutional crisis, the aggravation of social conflicts and the growing imbalance of classes led to the propagation of remedies. For some people, such as Isocrates, the remedy consisted in going back to the past, to the 'constitution of our ancestors', which had managed to combine the authority of the 'best men' with the sovereignty of the *demos*. He thought that those who endangered the internal balance of cities by their demands should simply be sent away – Asia would be a convenient place of exile whose conquest would be easy if the cities would only agree to unite and forget their quarrels. For Plato, things were not so simple. His master Socrates had been sentenced to death because the city would not tolerate his criticisms. What mankind needed was another kind of city, described in the *Republic*, an ideal city based on justice, where the conflict between rich and poor would be ended by a strict separation of function.

The producers of material goods would be excluded both from military activity, reserved for the guardians, and from political activity, reserved for the philosophers. And among the guardians, who were to be ultimately responsible for the peace and equilibrium of the city, all private property would be abolished, including the particular form of property that came under the heading of wives and children. Plato had no illusions about the chances of ever seeing such a programme put into effect. That is why in the second of his great political dialogues, the *Laws*, he gave up this ideal scheme in favour of the creation of a colony whose citizens, though forbidden to take part in any productive activity, would none the less be landowners, but average landowners, since the share of the richest could not be greater than four times the share of the poorest. This 'average' solution was also advocated, less systematically, by Aristotle in the *Politics*. Without rejecting any of the existing political forms, he nevertheless advocated the adoption of moderate forms of oligarchy or democracy, within which sovereignty would lie in the hands of the middle class, identified sometimes with the land-owning peasants, sometimes with the hoplites, but excluding craftsmen and tradesmen, whose presence in the civic community was judged undesirable. Even monarchy, the rule of a single individual, which in the Greek world conjured up either the barbarians or tyranny, was seen as a possible solution, provided however that the king was subject to the all-powerful law.

It is difficult to know whether these speculations, produced in a narrow circle of philosophers surrounded by disciples who had come from all over the Greek world to follow the teaching of Isocrates, Plato or Aristotle, had any effect on the destiny of the city. Modern scholars differ on this point, for although it may be true that the conquest of Asia – to be carried out by Alexander – was advocated by Isocrates, and although it is no less true that the theories about the 'good king' concerned for the interests of his subjects and respectful of the laws were to feed the monarchical ideology of the Hellenistic epoch, the fact remains that the political thinkers of the 4th century had been unable to conceive what the Macedonian conquest was to bring into being. Thinking purely in terms of the *polis*, they could not foresee those vast states in which the Greek heritage and the oriental heritage would merge to give birth to a new world.

3
Thinking About the Cosmos

Greek philosophy
from Thales to Aristotle

A. A. LONG

LOOKING BACK at more than two hundred years of Greek speculative thought, Aristotle suggested that philosophy arose out of 'wonder' or 'puzzlement'. That impulse fits the cast of his own mind, but his suggestion was not simply a transposition of personal interests. It helps to characterize distinctive features of Greek philosophy, features which, to the best of our knowledge, were not to be found in the culture of the Greeks' Mediterranean neighbours nor in that of any other ancient society. The older civilizations of Egypt and the Middle East had elaborate myths and religions which probably contributed to archaic Greek beliefs about the world. From a remarkably early date the Babylonians kept astronomical records with a level of accuracy that enabled them eventually to predict solar eclipses. Yet these indications of imaginative and precise discoveries, impressive though they are, do not appear to have constituted any impulse to ask speculative questions in Aristotle's sense. Babylonian astronomy was an instrument for religious cult. The creation myths of Sumeria and elsewhere are narratives that close rather than invite empirical inquiry into our origins and the way the world actually works.

Greek speculative thought, as it began in the 6th century BC, had a tenor of its own. This showed itself partly in the discarding of myth and poetic and religious symbols, thought there was no immediate rejection of all the previous cultural tradition. But the most significant aspect of early Greek philosophy is its open-endedness and completely uninstitutionalized character. So far as we can tell, the Ionian thinkers (whose thought will be described shortly) had no impulse to speculate about the world other than that suggested by Aristotle. Their philosophical work was not a means of earning a living, or fulfilling a specific function in social, political or religious life. Biographical details about these men are scanty and unreliable. They may have invented various measuring devices and provided practical advice to statesmen. In their own communities they acquired reputations as 'wise men' quite generally. Anaximander and Anaximenes, if not Thales, wrote books, using the new medium of prose instead of the hexameter poetry which the later thinkers, Parmenides and Empedocles, would continue to employ. But 'schools' of philosophy, as institutions, were still in the future. If the Ionian thinkers had pupils, the number of these will have been small. There was as yet no market for philosophy. Its earliest practitioners worked for their own self-satisfaction.

By the time of Plato (427–347 BC) philosophy had become a recognized profession. In Aristophanes' wicked satire of Socrates in the *Clouds*, men pay money to attend Socrates' 'Thinking-shop' at Athens, with the object of learning 'how to make the worse appear the better cause'. Socrates, as caricatured in the comedy, combines the speculative interests of Ionian philosophy with the rhetorical skills of a Sophist. Neither of these has anything to tell us about the historical Socrates, but collectively they show what philosophy connoted for a 5th-century Athenian. As a serious scientific activity it was, and always remained, an esoteric interest of a tiny minority. In a more diffused sense, however, it became a significant element in the wider cultural life when men such as Gorgias and Protagoras, travelling about in the 5th century, offered training in rhetorical argument to those who could afford to pay for attendance at their lectures. Thus philosophy impinged directly on politics, a connection which the small size of Greek city-states could foster in a variety of ways. Before the end of the 6th century Pythagoras had founded a community in southern Italy where he became a powerful and, if the tradition is credible, controversial political figure. In Sicily, a little later, Empedocles acquired fame as a healer, wonder-worker, and populist political leader. At Athens in about 445 BC Anaxagoras was successfully prosecuted for (allegedly) claiming that the sun is red-hot metal. Philosophers might include the most honoured members of the community (the Athenians commissioned Protagoras to draft the laws of their new colony of Thurii), and men who could be suspected, like Socrates, of corrupting the youth and of teaching impiety.

Periclean Athens, as the cultural centre of the Greek-speaking world, attracted philosophers from outlying regions. The tradition that the Ionian Anaxagoras taught the Athenian tragedian Euripides shows how purely speculative philosophy was beginning to affect the general intellectual life. Powerful thinkers were attracting a following, a fact most fully documented in the life of Socrates. After his trial and death, his chief adherents split up, founding their own schools which derived inspiration from his teaching. The most famous of these was Plato's Academy at Athens, where formal instruction was given in mathematics. (What other subjects were formally taught, and to how many, is not known.) Plato's pupils certainly included upper-class young men, some of whom will have had political ambitions. Philosophy had not become a state organization. But it was now a recognized institution within the state.

According to Plato, whose account is the most authoritative, Socrates' interests were primarily ethical. Disclaiming certainty himself, Socrates devoted his life to questioning and testing people's opinions on how one should live. In this way he sought to expose false conceits of knowledge, and to convince his interlocutors that the supreme values are rational consistency and spiritual well-being. He conceived himself to have a divine mission as the 'gadfly' of Athens.

This points to a rapid development from the Ionian origins. Predominantly, however, the individualistic, disinterested impulses of the founding fathers remained. Plato had hopes of educating philosopher rulers. But his principal activity, like that of his predecessors, was rational inquiry into the nature of things. Those who could follow him in this, as I have already said, were only a few. What they wrote and thought had little bearing upon everyday life at Athens. Only modern idealizations of the Greeks represent their philosophy as a widespread activity. Its success was due not to the numbers of its practitioners, but to their intensity and open-mindedness, qualities which generated the unprecedented burst of corporate research initiated first by Plato and then by Aristotle.

Atoms and morals

Since even a potted account of Greek philosophy from Thales to Aristotle would be quite impossible here, I have decided to make cosmology my main theme, taking this to include successive attempts to discover the basic constituents of the world. This has three principal advantages. Cosmology describes the questions which characterize Greek philosophy and science in their earliest stages when innovative thought is at its freshest and most perspicuous. Secondly, the first approaches to cosmology generated problems in (what would later be called) metaphysics and epistemology, which shape the concepts and inquiries of philosophers as far as Plato. So we may glimpse something of the way Greek thinkers responded to one another. Finally, cosmology allows something to be said about ethics and theories of human nature, since Plato's pictures of the world were decisively coloured by his interest in discovering the foundations of goodness. Having insufficient space to say much about the forms of argument and justification of theories created by Greek philosophers, I propose to begin by sketching some general characteristics of their enterprise.

The history of Greek philosophy has often been presented as if it were an evolutionary phenomenon, starting with the bold but naive speculations of Thales and his successors in 6th-century BC Miletus, arriving at full efflorescence in the systematic theorizing of Plato and Aristotle, and then declining into a narrow dogmatism chiefly represented by Stoic and Epicurean philosophers, with a final turning towards religiosity and mysticism in the revived Platonism of the early Christian period. Such a portrayal is correct in only one respect, and that explains its beguiling simplifications. Plato and Aristotle, among philosophers of any time, must be judged pre-eminent in their creative intelligence. What preceded and followed them lacks the range and sustained powers of argument to be found in their writings which, it should be emphasized, have been transmitted to us, unlike the books composed by nearly all other Greek philosophers. But the evolutionary model of intellectual history conceals far more than it reveals. Greek thought did not progress and regress in a linear development like the growth and withering of a plant. We are entitled to judge certain of its phases as more interesting or productive than others. But to regard Greek philosophy as a series of evolving stages towards a determinate goal misrepresents the nature of philosophy itself. It would be more correct to view the history of Greek thought as a complex sequence of lines which have no fixed terminus, but many intersections, parallels, convergences and divergences.

This point can be exemplified by the mutations of ancient atomism. In the latter part of the 5th century BC, Leucippus and Democritus identified the basic constituents of the world with an infinite number of indivisible bodies (atoms), and 'emptiness', which provides the necessary condition of the atoms' incessant movement. This theory, as will be seen later, was a direct rejoinder to problems about the nature of the world which had been pointedly raised by Parmenides some fifty years previously; and it was an answer to Parmenides, alternative to, if more compelling than, theories advanced by Empedocles and Anaxagoras. Isolated from its dialectical context the first formulation of the atomic structure of the world could seem a random hypothesis. Within that context it emerges as an extremely powerful theory which seeks to solve some of the most pressing conceptual problems of philosophy at that time. Its historical and intrinsic interest has little or nothing to do with any anticipations of modern physics. Ancient atomism may look superficially closer to modern physical theory than does the Platonic or Aristotelian universe. But that does not, in itself, make ancient atomism a better theory. The adequacy of ancient atomism, as a theory, has to be evaluated by reference to its explanatory power as an answer to the problems of 5th-century philosophy.

During the 4th century, atomism continued to be defended outside Athens by thinkers who are little more than names to us, overshadowed by the dominance of the Athenian schools of philosophy under Plato and Aristotle. But it was revived and bolstered by Epicurus, after the death of Aristotle, by arguments which not only reinforced those of Democritus, but also answered Platonic and Aristotelian objections to it. As developed by Epicurus, atomism is largely a new theory, differing in many details from its earlier version, and designed to support a moral philosophy which sought to remove fears of death and divine intervention in the world. Once again, it is the immediate intellectual context which provides the framework for assessing the significance of Epicurean physics, and not its relationship to the truth, as a modern scientist might conceive this.

Two lessons can be drawn from this example, which are crucial to the interpretation of Greek philosophy. First, its dialectical character: Greek philosophy is primarily a dialogue or argumentative encounter, not only between contemporaries, but also and perhaps more interestingly, with thinkers of the immediately preceding generation. The questions which a philoso-

Boys learning music and writing, from a Red Figure cup of the 5th century BC. Greek education was the reverse of doctrinaire. A whole class of young men grew up eager to discuss, to listen to arguments and to question received ideas.

pher tries to answer are typically raised by his dissatisfaction with theories that are currently on offer. Aristotle's philosophy is in large measure a critical response to some of Plato's most ambitious theories. In order to assess the interest of Aristotle's ethics or metaphysics, we need to consider both his arguments and the dialectical context in which they are placed. Aristotle himself makes this very plain, but it is a point that applies no less strongly to other Greek philosophers whose work is less well preserved. As summarized in ancient or modern handbooks the cut and thrust of philosophical argument, responding to real or imaginary opponents, too easily turns into a catalogue of doctrines – Plato's theory of Forms, Aristotle's doctrine of the Unmoved Mover, and so forth. The significance of these doctrines is only apparent when we engage with the questions the philosopher himself is asking, questions that trouble him because they arise out of the tradition he inherits.

The second lesson exemplified by ancient atomism is different, but equally damaging to the straightforward evolutionary interpretation of Greek philosophy. Nothing debars us from finding in Epicurus or Heraclitus, let us say, insights which are absent from Aristotle. Heraclitus does not philosophize in the manner of Aristotle. He writes in a riddling, epigrammatic style which is totally different from Aristotle's painstaking and comprehensive treatment of problems. Yet Heraclitus deserves the closest study for his own sake, and not as a rudimentary stage of pre-Aristotelian thought. A similar point may be made concerning conflicting theories of different philosophers. Plato advanced a sequence of arguments to prove the immortality of the soul. Several generations later, Epicurus undertook to prove the soul's mortality. Here there is neither progress nor regression. The question remains an open one, and it is up to us to decide which set of arguments is the better, quite irrespective of their temporal relationship to one another.

From the one to the many

For the beginnings of Greek philosophy or science we possess only tantalizing scraps of information, much of it in the form, 'Thales said (or thought that) ... the earth floats on water'. Little is known about the arguments or supporting reasons the earliest thinkers offered for their general statements about the world. Yet the record of these, though often difficult to interpret, is sufficient to prove that what Edward Hussey has called 'a revolution in thought' occurred during the 6th century BC in the trading city of Miletus, on the western coast of modern Turkey. Athens was destined to become the centre of Greek philosophy, but not before the 4th century. The first philosophers were inhabitants of the eastern or western fringes of the

Greek-speaking community, the cities of Ionia or of Sicily and southern Italy. Much has been written, which is inevitably conjectural, on the question of why these were the places where philosophy and science began. Let us pass over that subject, fascinating though it is, and try to see what precisely did begin at Miletus, and in what way it represents a revolution in thought.

Thales, and the two Milesian thinkers who followed him in time, Anaximander and Anaximenes, were the first cosmologists. They were interested in a large number of specific questions, such as the stability of the earth, the nature of the heavenly bodies, and the explanations of meteorological phenomena. The range of the questions becomes significant in the light of the answers given to them. Without recourse to myth or traditional religion, the Milesian philosophers sought to explain problematical features of the world by reference to familiar processes and powers – for instance, hot and cold, expansion and contraction. A concept of 'nature' was in the making, a recognition that the world has a structure which is open to reasoned and impartial investigation. Many of the Greek gods were regarded as controlling particular regions of the world, so that thunder indicated the anger of Zeus, or a storm at sea the wrath of Posidon. When Anaximander explained thunder as 'wind bursting out of a cloud', his distance from the anger of Zeus is obvious. Wind is an intelligible phenomenon which offers an explanation for thunder compatible with what can be observed closer at hand. We have a theory, available to critical scrutiny, and an assumption of primary importance: the physical world is regular and law-like in its processes. Thunder does not belong to a special divine domain. It is an event which can be supposed to conform to principles whose application throughout the world is quite general and free from arbitrariness.

In identifying the kind of questions mentioned above, and in treating them as amenable to uniformly 'natural' explanations, the Milesians initiated cosmology, the study of the world on scientific and empirical foundations. But behind their particular investigations, and the new concepts which they embody, there appears to have lain a more basic question, which is their chief claim to count as the originators of western thought. Expressed in Aristotle's terminology (*Metaphysics*, Alpha, 983b 6), Thales founded that kind of philosophy which looks for some 'material' stuff as the 'foundation' and 'source' of all the particular contents of the world. According to Thales this was water, Anaximenes identified it with air, but Anaximander nominated 'the indefinite', a foundational principle which generates such powers as 'hot' and 'cold' but cannot be observed in the manner of water or air.

Underlying this 'material monism' are two questions of great interest, and one extremely important assumption. The questions can be formulated as first, 'What does the observable world originate from?', and secondly, 'What is it made of?' The first question has its roots in very ancient Near-Eastern mythology; the Greeks were given their own mythological answer to it in Hesiod's *Theogony*, some two hundred years earlier than Thales. Details of those mythological explanations have left their mark on Milesian cosmogony, most notably in the notion that the present complexity of the world is a product of something simple and relatively formless. But in myth the world is generated through the emergence and reproductions of gods; the stages of this process are not articulated in abstract or impersonal terms. In the second question, 'What is the world made of?', the Milesian break with tradition is still more evident. This question treats the observable world, in all its diversity, as ultimately reducible to a single specifiable nature or material. That nature or material, moreover, is identified with the original source of the world. So the two questions can be given a single answer of startling economy, for instance: the world originates from and is now, in its most basic structure, air. All particular phenomena, in the system of Anaximenes, were explained as modifications, by rarefaction and condensation, of the single material, air. Stones are air at its most solid, with ice, water, vapour and fire as phases of its increasing rarefaction.

Implicit in such monistic accounts of the world is the assumption that a unitary explanation should be preferred to a diversity of foundational principles. The modern search for quarks by physicists was sparked off by the assumption that the discovered range of elementary particles was too great for these to be still regarded as the ultimate entities: so quarks were hypothesized as the world's foundational ingredients. Economy of explanation has proved to be an essential feature of scientific inquiry.

In seeking for a single material principle the Milesians were also assuming that the world, at its most basic, is different from the world as it appears to perception. The world is not obviously water or air; these appear to be merely some of its constituents. 'The indefinite' of Anaximander is a still bolder theory, since it is something essentially unobservable, a stuff of quite unspecific nature, which reason postulates as the controlling foundation of observable phenomena. Thus Milesian cosmology, through its novel approach to the origin and present structure of the world, raised further questions of a fundamental conceptual kind which were to preoccupy philosophers over the next two hundred years. How could a pre-existing single material generate a world consisting apparently of many different things? If a single material underlies the diverse appearances of things, what is the relationship between the underlying material and the observable things which it constitutes? Are they the same thing under different descriptions, or have the cosmologists introduced two worlds, two orders of reality, foundational principles on the one hand, and changing appearances on the other?

That the Milesian philosophers prompted such questions is a measure of the fertility of their thought.

Their cosmologies were audacious speculations, which prepared the ground for metaphysical and epistemological problems of the sort just indicated. For the purpose of this essay I have briefly tried to show how their cosmology introduced new methods of thought, focusing attention on the basic constituents of the world. More detailed study would reveal their continuing dependence on pre-scientific conceptions. They probably gave little explicit argument for their largest claims. But it does not seem to be anachronistic to credit them with revolutionizing thought in the manner I have been sketching.

Cosmic flux and everlasting stability

If we think of philosophy as a subject which analyses concepts as expressed through language, the Milesian thinkers would be better described as early scientists. Their theories were not arrived at by reflection upon how we talk about things. But within a generation or so, Heraclitus of Ephesus and Parmenides of Elea (in southern Italy) were offering accounts of the world which are astonishingly precocious in their attention to language and to patterns of thought as revealed in language. Any interpretation of their philosophy is controversial, and that applies to its bearing upon Milesian cosmology. I shall take the view that Heraclitus and Parmenides, in their quite different ways, were critics of the Milesians, and that they perceived conceptual difficulties (as suggested above) in Milesian cosmology. The question of the world's basic constituents remains paramount, but as understood by Parmenides and Heraclitus it becomes a very different question.

Like the Milesians, Heraclitus explained the world by reference to a single material principle, but his statement of this thesis already implies a criticism of his predecessors: 'This ordered world no god or man has made, but it always was and is and will be, ever living fire, kindled in measures and going out in measures' (fr. 30). For Heraclitus, the question 'What does the world originate from?' does not arise. That problem is by-passed by assuming that the world exists for ever. The 'measured' changes of fire explain the law-like regularity of natural processes. This thought recalls Anaximander's notion of cosmic 'justice' as the self-regulating principle which ensures balanced interactions between the primary opposing powers in the world, the hot and the cold etc. But Heraclitus identified justice with strife (fr. 80), and on closer inspection his whole philosophy reads like a radical recasting of Milesian cosmology.

Contrary to prevailing ancient interpretations, Heraclitus probably did not regard fire as something out of which other things are made. Fire in his philosophy is analogous rather to a determinate energizing principle, the 'measure of change'. 'All things are an exchange for fire, and fire for all things, like goods for gold and gold for goods' (fr. 90). The metaphor of exchange suggests that the destructive and

Anaximander of Miletus, one of the earliest of the Ionian philosophers, was mainly interested in understanding natural phenomena (he is seen in this Roman mosaic holding a sundial which he is credited with having invented). But he also speculated on the origins and ultimate foundations of the world, and recognized that the ancestors of human beings must have been creatures of a very different kind.

creative activity of fire is a standard for evaluating all the other things in the world. For Heraclitus fire names or symbolizes the fundamental constituent of reality, but that constituent is more like an everlasting source and process of change than a 'material' in the Milesians' sense. From other Heraclitean statements we are justified in attributing directive power and divine intelligence to fire. That was equally true of the Milesians' foundational principles, but its meaning for Heraclitus has to be inferred from such cryptic utterances as: 'God – day night, winter summer, war peace, excess want – and he changes as fire, when it is mixed with fumes of incense, is named according to each man's pleasure' (fr. 67). Heraclitus appears to be saying, first, that apparent opposites are unities when viewed as components of god; and secondly, that the different names we assign to changing phenomena are all changes of a single thing, god analogous to fire. Remembering the 'measures' which fire's behaviour keeps to, we may conjecture that Heraclitus saw the underlying structure of the world not as an aggregate of relatively durable things, but as a sequence of processes or events, changes or exchanges between opposites, whose regularity is a manifestation of the controlling fire or divinity.

Such stability as the observable world contains is due to the balance between opposites. Heraclitus saw this exemplified in the dynamic equilibrium of a strung bow or lyre (fr. 51), where the effectiveness of these artefacts depends upon the opposing impulses of the string and the frame. But, as interpreted by Plato (*Cratylus*, 402A), Heraclitus supposed all things to be really in constant motion, and this radically dynamic account of the world (though some modern scholars disagree) seems to suit the tenor of his thought. He delights in obscurities and paradoxes. The world, in his philosophy, is orderly, but the order consists in balanced tension or interchange between constituents. What persists for ever is the source and embodiment of regulated change, the divine fire, aptly compared by David Wiggins in *Language and Logos* to modern notions of the conservation of energy.

This sketch of a most arresting philosopher cannot do justice to the effect of his language, where the balance and antitheses of the sentence structure mirror the new theory of the world. But I have tried to indicate the challenge he issues to any thinker who believes that a stable being or set of beings underlies the world's apparent changes. Heraclitus seems to regard appearances as deceptively persistent, in contrast with the unseen struggle between opposites which underlies them.

The consequences of his philosophy, suggestive rather than systematic, are evident throughout much of later Greek thought. He himself was not a sceptic, but his work acted as a catalyst for those who questioned the possibility of objective knowledge and those who wished to remove such doubts. A world of unremitting change might seem to provide no facts of unchanging truth value for knowledge to take as its objects. Heraclitus' expression of the conjunction of opposites could be taken to imply that something can both be and not be in the same respect at the same time. (Aristotle classed the Heracliteans among those who break the principle of non-contradiction (*Metaphysics*, Gamma, 1010a 10), and so make rational discourse impossible.) Heraclitus describes sea as 'most pure and most polluted water' on the strength of its being salutary for fish and destructive for men (fr. 61). This was the kind of material the Greek Sceptics later used in proposing that we have to suspend judgment about the real or underlying nature of things.

The philosopher who reflected most critically and creatively on Heraclitus was Plato. But Plato's responses were importantly shaped by Parmenides, whose whole thought can be read, in Edward Hussey's words, as 'a reaction against Heraclitean paradox, an attempt to see what can be said that will not involve the speaker in self-contradiction'. Parmenides was roughly contemporary with Heraclitus, and there is no biographical evidence to prove that he knew the latter's work. Although Parmenides' arguments are quite general in their scope, their upshot is a conception of the world which rejects any rational conciliation between the stable unity of reality and the plurality of

changing appearances. Heraclitus and all earlier philosophy must be regarded as Parmenides' prime target.

Parmenides, unlike the Milesians and Heraclitus, used verse, the hexameter form of Homeric epic, as the medium of his philosophy. But in what he said he was preeminently innovative. His methods of argument are completely open to inspection in long surviving passages, and there was almost certainly nothing like them before. Heraclitus wrote in an oracular vein, revealing signs which indicate, without analysis, the way things are. We can only guess at the style of Milesian reasoning, but it will hardly have been formal, in a manner that shows a clear recognition of the progression from a premise to a conclusion. The main surviving fragment of Parmenides' poem, 'The Way of Truth', is an extremely concentrated exercise in abstract reasoning. He sets up two contradictory premises, termed 'roads of inquiry', 'It is and it cannot not be', and 'It is not and it must not be' (fr. 2). The second premise is eliminated on the ground that 'what is not' is unknowable and unspeakable. The first premise is then left as the only true road of inquiry: 'What can be spoken of and thought of must be; for it can be, but nothing cannot' (fr. 6).

Parmenides' philosophy can be interestingly compared with that of Descartes. Descartes discovered that he could consistently doubt everything except his own existence as a *thinking* being, and developed his arguments from this foundation. Parmenides begins from no assumption about ordinary experience. His procedure is to discover the world by pure reflection on thinking and its object. He takes it as self-evident or indubitable that we can speak and think of something. Since nothing cannot be, what we can speak and think of *must* be. An exact interpretation of his inference here will not be attempted. What is certain is his elimination of 'what is not' and his leaving 'what is' as the only viable object of rational discourse.

At this stage of his argument Parmenides does not characterize the subject of 'is' beyond its rational intelligibility, nor does he define the sense of 'is'. As his reasoning develops, however, its disturbing novelty becomes manifest. The characteristics of 'what is' are ruthlessly deduced from the complete and unqualified rejection of 'what is not'. It (the subject of 'is') is invariant in time and in place. To suppose that it could begin or cease to be, or that it 'was' or 'will be', is excluded by the completeness of its 'being *now*'. Give 'it' a beginning or an end, a past or a future, and then there would be a time with respect to which 'it is not'. But that 'way' has been eliminated as unspeakable and unknowable. The uniformity of 'what is' excludes all possibility of change or differentiation: 'nor is it divisible, since it is all alike. Not is there more of it here, to prevent it from holding together, nor less of it, but it is all full of what is. Therefore it is all continuous. For what is keeps close to what is' (fr. 8.22–25).

This extract can serve to exemplify Parmenides' logic, with absence of division, or continuity, deduced from the homogeneity of 'what is'. The passage also indicates the conclusion to which his whole argument is tending, the unqualified 'unity' of that which can truly be spoken of and known. He compares it to 'a well-rounded sphere, equally balanced in every direction' (fr. 8.43–4), but the image scarcely recalls the physical world of Milesian cosmology. By purely abstract reasoning Parmenides has conceived of a reality which lacks all the properties of the world as revealed to sense perception. The senses reveal a world of diversity and change. Acceptance of these as properties of 'what is' marks the basic error of ordinary thinking, according to Parmenides, 'taking to be and not to be as the same and not the same' (fr. 6.8–9). He acknowledges that his unqualified 'is' does not describe the world as it appears to the senses. Appearances are therefore wholly deceptive and provide no access to 'what is'. Parmenides offers no explanation of the relationship, if any, between reality and appearances. He is content to assign confidence in appearances to the erroneous acceptance of duality as the foundation of the world (fr. 8.53–4).

The consequences of this extraordinary argument were both immediate and far-reaching. It conceives of the world's unity in a quite different way from the balanced flux and conjunctions of opposites which constitute the objects of Heraclitus' cosmos. No less directly it rules Milesian cosmology out of court, since a unitary being, as presented by Parmenides, could not generate change and plurality. More generally, by the sheer power of his logic, Parmenides posed problems for theory of knowledge and metaphysics (which he can justly be said to have invented) that persist throughout the history of Greek philosophy. If the only proper object of rational thought or knowledge must be an unqualified 'being' (or truths that hold for all time), can the physical world be described and understood in any sense? That question dominated Plato's thought; but before considering his complex response to Parmenides, something must be said about the more immediate reactions.

Reality and appearances

Parmenides, I observed, offered no explanation of the relationship between reality and appearance, but his conception of 'what is' raises that question in a most acute form. Are appearances simply illusions, or can they be accounted for as objective manifestations of a reality analogous, in at least some respects, to that which he deduced *must* be? Any serious attempt to reconcile Parmenides' reasoning with the reality of empirical phenomena was obliged to abandon certain of the attributes of being that he had deduced. The first to go was unqualified unity and uniformity.

Empedocles, another Western Greek, from Sicily, accepted the prescription that 'what is' must be everlasting and that there can strictly be no change into or out of 'what is not'. But instead of being a homogeneous unity the world of Empedocles consists of four everlasting and distinct elements (which he

Some philosophers maintained that matter was reducible to a single element, though they disagreed about what that was. Empedocles postulated four: air, fire, earth and water. His formula was destined to become the orthodoxy of the next millennium. These personifications from a manuscript of about AD 1200 are distantly derived from classical sources.

called 'roots'), earth, air, fire, and water, and two everlasting motive powers, Love and Strife, which generate and destroy empirical phenomena by respectively combining and separating the elements. The world as a whole is a cyclical process, oscillating between a state of unity under the control of Love and a state of plurality under the control of Strife. This theory builds diversity and motion into the basic constituents of the world, and thus far departs completely from Parmenides. Yet it retains a recognizable allegiance to his ban on 'what is not'. In Empedocles, change is explained as the mixture and separation of everlasting elements. Living creatures, and indeed the present state of the world as a whole, are things which have a beginning and an end. But viewed in terms of their constituents they do not involve the inadmissible combination of 'what is' with 'what is not'.

Empedocles' system accounts for the diversity of the phenomenal world by the changing combinations of changeless elements. Underlying and constituting the complex differences of phenomena is an everlasting order of elements any one of which has the homogeneity of Parmenides' 'being'. At the level of logic this response to Parmenides is evasive since Empedocles offers no argument to show how 'what is' can range over qualitatively different elements: earth 'is not' the same as fire, and Parmenides had explicitly stigmatized the naming of 'two distinct forms' as the basic error of ordinary thinking (fr. 8.53–4). (Plato was the first philosopher to grapple formally with Parmenides' logic when he showed, in the *Sophist*, that 'is not', as an indication that X is different from Y, does not import 'non-being' in the unqualified sense repudiated by Parmenides.) But this does not seriously detract from Empedocles' achievements. His concept of elements was a discovery of the greatest influence and importance. It laid the foundations for most physical theories over the next two thousand years. In its historical context it provided clear means of distinguishing complex substances (living things etc.) from their basic constituents, while at the same time it showed how these basic constituents could furnish a complete explanation for the properties and identity of complex substances. Empedocles could claim to have closed Parmenides' disturbing gap between reality and appearances.

It remains true, however, that Empedocles' elements, in their simplicity, are markedly different from the immense variety of qualities found in the phenomenal world. His near contemporary, Anaxagoras (who came from Clazomenae, an Ionian city), signalled his chief reaction to Parmenides by a much more radical rejection of the homogeneity of 'what is'. 'Everything has a share of everything' (fr. 6). According to this remarkable thesis, the stuff of which any substance consists is irreducibly multiform and infinitely divisible. All the qualitative differences between perceptible objects are due to different proportions of the *same* qualities or ingredients everlastingly present in the material which constitutes the world. Black as well as white is a constituent of snow; but snow appears white since white is a predominant ingredient in that segment of material.

For Anaxagoras, it is merely an accident of perception that the food which generates living tissue appears wholly different from the hair or flesh that it nourishes: 'How could hair come from what is not hair or flesh from what is not flesh?' (fr. 10). There is no *real* difference, in other words, between the microscopic structure of a substance's underlying material and its phenomenal properties. As Aristotle stated the theory, 'since it is impossible for things to be generated from what is not, they supposed that ... they must be generated from what is, namely what is already present, but imperceptible to us owing to the smallness of their bulk' (*Physics* 1.187a 33). Anaxagoras' doctrine reduces 'coming to be' to the manifestation of what is already present, and thus far he sticks closer to Parmenides'

ontology that does Empedocles. But in order to reconcile appearance and underlying reality he makes the latter infinitely divisible and heterogeneous, so abandoning fundamental features of Parmenides' being.

The unity and changelessness of reality, as Parmenides had conceived it, were reinforced by near contemporaries of Empedocles and Anaxagoras, Zeno of Elea and Melissus of Samos. Zeno, in his justly famous paradoxes, tried to undermine both plurality and motion by arguing that neither of these can be posited without self-contradiction. His reasoning, which is too complex to be discussed in a few sentences, focuses particularly on the problem of understanding finite magnitudes, since any one of these seems open, in theory at least, to an infinite division which turns each putative unit into an infinite number. Melissus stated explicitly that the 'fullness' of the Parmenidean reality excluded the possibility of its movement, assuming that something can only move if there are empty places in the world for a moving body to occupy.

I single out these points because of their relevance to the Atomists' responses to Parmenides. As already mentioned, Leucippus and Democritus identified the fundamental constituents of the world with an infinite number of indivisible bodies which are incessantly moving in an infinite 'void'. Against Zeno they held that there can be a set of physical units which are not collapsible into diminishingly smaller parts; and they posited 'void' as a form of 'non-being' which is not equivalent to unqualified nothing. Infinite multiplicity and infinite void were startling departures from Parmenides' static monism. Yet the characteristics of the Atomists' 'beings' reveal the continuing respect paid to Parmenides' arguments. Like his 'one' being, each atom is ungenerated, indestructible, everlasting, full, indivisible, and changeless. Unlike his 'one', as interpreted at least by Melissus, the atoms are bodies, and as such they possess size and shape, but no other sensible properties except perhaps weight. The phenomenal world is formed by the collisions and entanglements of atoms whose sizes and shapes are assumed to be so various that they can explain all the other perceived qualities of things, qualities which are not characteristics of the atoms themselves but of the way we perceive the world, when atoms interact with our sense organs.

This last point is of great significance, and reflection on it will enable us to take stock of cosmological speculation at the end of the 5th century BC. Like the systems of Empedocles and Anaxagoras, the Atomists undertook to rescue the phenomenal world from the limbo to which Parmenides had banished it. The main thrust of their theory was to provide a reasoned explanation of ordinary objects through the hypothesis that they are constructs of atoms. Yet in admitting that ordinary objects are perceived to have qualities which are not attributes of these primary bodies, the Atomists opened a gap between underlying reality and ap-

*Plato taught in a garden dedicated to the Greek hero Academus –
hence the word Academy. A mosaic from a villa near Pompeii has
been thought to commemorate the scene, with Plato third from the
left holding a stick.*

pearance which Empedocles evaded and Anaxagoras
explicitly denied. Democritus is credited with gloomy
remarks about the inexactitude of perception, and he
sharply contrasted the 'reality' of atoms and void with
the 'conventionality' (perhaps meaning non-
objectivity) of such qualities as hot and cold, and
colours (fr. 9). This 'dualist' trend in his thought could
be taken to imply that the phenomenal world is real

only in a relative sense; and that implication would gain
support from a distinction he appears to have drawn
between 'genuine knowledge' whose objects would be
underlying reality, and 'obscure knowledge' assigned
to sense-perception (fr. 11). That contrast foreshadows
Plato; but to introduce his philosophy, we need a brief
review of his predecessors' thinking on cosmic order.

The goodness of cosmic order: Plato

Cosmic order is a pleonasm; the Greek word *kosmos*
means order. Early Greek philosophy is nothing less
than the discovery of 'the cosmos', the realization that
the world as a whole has a structure which will reveal

itself to rational inquiry. Speculations about the world's basic constituents, which I have been describing, were attempts to formulate the causes of cosmic order. Apart from the Eleatics (Parmenides and his followers), it was common ground that physical entities of some kind provide the building blocks of this structure, and that assumption has persisted up to the present day. But are physical entities such as fire sufficient, without further characterization, to account for cosmic order? If the world is intelligible, and conforms to a rational plan, must it not in some sense be the product of intelligence or rational direction?

The Atomists were the only early philosophers who answered this question negatively, and thereby earned castigation from Plato and the traditions he established. In atomism life and intelligence are by-products of atoms and their movements. The atoms themselves are inanimate bodies, and the order which they constitute arises purely mechanically. We cannot fail to wonder at the boldness of such an hypothesis at a time when Greek speculative thought was no more than a hundred and fifty years old; the gods are discharged from all duties in the Atomists' world. In the other systems of thought, however, directive power and divinity are either assigned to the underlying materials, or, as in the philosophy of Anaxagoras, a divine Mind, somehow detached from other things, is responsible for initiating the movements of matter which give rise to the phenomenal world. The idea that intelligible order requires intelligent direction was explicitly stated by Diogenes of Apollonia (fr. 3), perhaps under the influence of Anaxagoras: he adumbrated the 'argument from design' when he said that 'all phenomena are organized in the best possible way', finding in this the reason for postulating a divine intelligence.

Without supporting argument, the introduction of divine intelligence could seem to beg questions or to be a reversion to mythology. It should be viewed rather as the beginnings of rational theology and a reasoned belief that matter devoid of intelligence is not sufficient to explain cosmic order. The debate on that question is still with us. I pass now to consider Plato's contribution to it.

Plato's philosophy does not respond to easy summary. The open-endedness of his discussions, and his own development and self-criticism, warn against trying to derive a single picture of the world from writings spread over about fifty years. Plato's followers, in later antiquity, developed certain tendencies in his work into an elaborate metaphysical and theological system which frequently runs counter to the exploratory character of his writings. His dialogues are inexhaustibly resourceful investigations deploying a vast range of conceptual problems and different strategies for solving these. Certain questions, however, engaged Plato throughout his career, and the central one of these has part of its background in the quite divergent philosophies of Heraclitus and Parmenides. How to bring being and becoming into an intelligible relationship, to accommodate the one and the many was an issue which stimulated Plato's thoroughly original thinking on knowledge and logic as well as metaphysics. But in his greatest dialogues, the question of the world's structure and intelligibility becomes a challenge to define a rational order in a far more ambitious way than anything that had been previously entertained.

What chiefly distinguishes Plato from his predecessors is the inspiration he derived from the life and teaching of Socrates. The philosophy of Socrates is difficult to isolate from Plato, since Plato is our principal record of Socratic discussions. But it would be generally agreed today that Socrates, as an historical figure, is chiefly represented in what appear to be Plato's earliest dialogues. These display Socrates in argument with one or more friends whose ethical beliefs become the starting-point for critical scrutiny of the incoherence of conventional morality. Socrates, though he claims to be ignorant, and unable to answer such questions as 'What is piety?', is credited with knowing how this type of question should be examined, and also with certain general moral convictions which answers to it would have to satisfy. His methodology is dialectical or elenctic, seeking to refute propositions endorsed by his interlocutor through showing that they conflict with other propositions which the interlocutor agrees to accept. The resulting impasse generally leaves the question 'What is F?' unresolved. But Socrates usually succeeds in showing what kind of answer would be necessary.

First, it would need to be a proposition which identified or defined that characteristic which must be present in all instances of piety (let us say) to justify their sharing piety as their common feature, no matter how they differ in other respects: given that X, Y, and Z are all F, we need to know what this 'common form' F is, if we are to understand what it is about X that makes it F. Secondly, Socrates was a passionate critic of popular morality, believing that such principles as 'help your friends and injure your enemies', or the equation of virtue with worldly success, were fundamentally at odds with the essential nature of man and the basis of human happiness. 'Virtue is knowledge', 'No-one does wrong willingly', 'It is better to suffer injustice than to do it', are Socratic doctrines which not only conflicted with popular morality, but also indicated his total rejection of moral scepticism and the amoral teachings associated with some of the contemporary thinkers we group together as 'Sophists'.

In their historical setting, Socrates' moral principles created an autonomous moral order which was no less revolutionary, as a philosophy of conduct, than the earlier Greek contributions to the origins of cosmology and science. Socrates himself eschewed speculation on the nature of the physical world. He saw his life as a divine mission to his fellow citizens, with the task of provoking self-examination founded on a view of human nature which picked out the 'soul', and not the body, as that 'part' of a man which chiefly requires cultivation. As the body is improved by healthy exercise, so the soul is benefited by morally right behaviour and ruined by its opposite (*Crito* 47d). *Psyche*, the word translated as 'soul', had been traditionally regarded as the source of life without any ethical colouring. As used by Socrates it primarily denotes what we might call the intellectual and moral personality (though this should not be taken to distinguish intellectual from moral). The essence of Socratic morality is 'love of wisdom' (the literal meaning of 'philosophy'), treating rationality as that which is truly desirable and not being swayed from its dictates by the body's appetites.

It was the example and teaching of Socrates which made Plato a philosopher. But in the full confidence of his middle period (*Phaedo, The Republic, The Symposium, Phaedrus*), Plato provided foundations for the Socratic moral order in a range of theories concerning the rational structure of the world at large. In this he had been anticipated to some extent by doctrines associated with the name of Pythagoras. What these amounted to, in Plato's lifetime, is difficult to state with any precision. They can be assumed to have embraced at least the following three theses: the human soul is immortal and the reluctant inhabitant of a mortal body; abstention from wrong-doing in this life will help to purge the soul of its bodily accretions and improve its prospects of a final disembodied existence; the world is a rational order of numbers and harmonious numerical relationships. The connection between these doctrines was probably founded on the belief that the soul itself is a harmony which needs to be brought into concordance with the numerical proportions of the cosmos.

Pythagorean number theory is a mysterious subject, which had too tenuous a connection with phenomena to provide an exact expression of physical laws. But in the absence of any tradition of experimental science it offered a model for understanding cosmic order which, in its precision and rationality, was far more attractive to Plato than a world constituted out of purely material ingredients. The movements of the heavenly bodies provided visible evidence of the workings of harmony and numerical proportion. Still more important for Plato, the truths of mathematics seemed to show the existence of an intelligible order of reality, quite separate from the phenomenal world, and comparable to Parmenides' 'being' in its eternity and changelessness. Plato acknowledged the force of Heraclitean flux as a description of phenomena, and concluded that the ultimate constituents of reality must be purely intelligible objects, analogous to the ideal numbers of Pythagoreanism. Perception reveals things as one and as many, depending upon the relativities of time and place, but the numbers of mathematical study are stable and self-identical. What holds for the countable features of ordinary objects, Plato reasoned, was equally true of all their other attributes. There are no persisting unities or self-identical entities in the phenomenal world.

Pythagoras was primarily a religious leader, who taught the immortality and transmigration of souls. His later followers developed theories of cosmic harmony, based upon the doctrine that numbers are the foundation of everything. On this coin from Samos, his birthplace, he is shown touching a globe on a column.

Every nameable object is multiple and changeable, large in one respect or time, small in another, beautiful from one viewpoint, and ugly from another. Phenomenal substances and attributes cannot be said 'to be' in an unqualified sense. They combine 'being' and 'not-being', or are describable as 'becoming', too deficient in stable reality to satisfy the requirements of knowledge and truth.

Yet knowledge must be possible. This was Plato's deepest conviction; and he was totally committed to Socrates' insistence on knowledge as the soul's health and the foundation of the good life. Socrates, as we noticed, had looked for knowledge through definitions, specifications of the attributes which are common and essential to every member of a class denoted by the same general term. He probably did not develop a formal theory of predication, but his interest in the relationship between multiple instances and that which they are instances of was probably the main stimulus to Plato's 'theory of Forms'. Somewhat baldly stated, this theory maintains that all particular substances or qualities or relations are 'reflections' or 'images' of eternally existing Forms which stand to the particulars as originals to copies.

To put it another way, beauty is not just the name for that characteristic which all beautiful things have in common. What they have in common is the same relationship to a real entity, Beauty Itself, which exists quite apart from individual beautiful things. All general terms such as 'beauty' name Forms, suprasensible realities, which are 'reflected' by multiple instances in the phenomenal world.

I used the term 'reflected' because it is one of Plato's characteristic ways of indicating the relationship between the intelligible Forms and the phenomena whose reality, as measured against that of the Forms, is derivative and shadowy. This sharp distinction between the thought-world of Forms and the objects of everyday experience is Plato's most famous doctrine. Its force, as a way of looking at the world, has been constantly acknowledged in poetry and religion as well as speculative philosophy. With his immensely powerful image of the Cave, in *The Republic*, Plato likens belief in the full reality of ordinary objects to the state of mind of an underground prisoner who has never experienced the world outside illuminated by the sun. The task of the lover of wisdom is to turn within, towards the light of intelligence, so that he may recognize those ultimate realities which are the true explanations of the order and excellence of the world.

So brief an account of Plato's philosophy at the time when he wrote *The Republic* can hardly begin to indicate its imaginative and conceptual vision. The point I will try to develop a little is the range of problems which he hoped to solve by his theory of Forms. A leading modern Platonist, Harold Cherniss, has referred to its 'economy', and that is completely right, since the Forms offered answers to basic problems in ethics, epistemology, and cosmology. Looking, as Socrates had looked, for absolute moral standards, Plato's hypothesis of Justice or Beauty as 'things in themselves', discoverable to rational inquiry, was a powerful rejoinder to moral conventionalism or scepticism. As the basis of Plato's theory of knowledge, the Forms were not liable to the change and confusion of their similarly named reflections in the phenomenal world. If Beauty Itself exists as a changeless reality, then true statements about beauty could be made, regardless of the absence of anything comparable among phenomena. But phenomena require explanation, and Plato offered his Forms as a 'logical' account of the nature and characteristics of perceptible objects. Phenomena 'participate in' or 'imitate' Forms, and this relationship (though Plato himself, in the *Parmenides*, recognized the difficulties it poses) was his answer to the problem of reconciling unity and plurality, or being and becoming. The Forms are paradigmatic unities – the Form of Beauty is beauty pure and simple. Perceptible objects are always a changeable aggregate of different properties; but their multiplicity and instability require the assumption that unitary and stable beings are the intelligible source of plurality and change.

Accompanying and crucially determining this picture of the world was Plato's dualistic account of human nature. Following the Pythagoreans, and giving substance to Socratic values, he associated a disembodied soul with the best condition for a living being, treating the soul as essentially akin to the Forms and assigning all that disturbs its moral excellence and understanding to the body (or the 'irrational' parts of the soul) and the distractions of sense-perception. Yet the dialogues which affirm this doctrine most insistently (*Phaedo, The Republic, The Symposium, Phaedrus*),

his greatest literary productions, show, as Bernard Williams has pointed out, 'a constant and vivid contrast between Plato's world-denying theories and his literary presentation of them'. The abstract world of Forms, and cognizance of them, are described in images of haunting beauty, which confirm the sensuous and the erotic perceptions even as they seek to transcend them.

The emotional or aesthetic attractions of transcendent Forms are less evident in Plato's later writings. His *Parmenides* is an extraordinarily honest exercise in self-criticism, indicating the difficulties of setting a single Form over many particulars if the Form is predicable of itself. In the *Sophist* he uses the Forms as a kind of logical grammar, to explain the basis of true and false statements about ordinary objects, and to solve problems about negation, in both cases overcoming difficulties in the unitary sense of the verb 'to be' which had beguiled Parmenides and his successors. He also gave much attention to the explanation of motion, proposing that this has its source in a cosmic soul or mind. Thus the notion of an 'efficient cause' was introduced, distinct from the changeless Forms, while using them as the intelligible models for constructing phenomena. Such dialogues as *Philebus*, *Politicus*, *Timaeus*, and the *Laws* all differ from one another in the precise details of how cosmic intelligence works. But Plato was convinced that such a being exists and that phenomena, for all their instability, show it working as a craftsman of the best possible world.

'Nature does nothing in vain' – Aristotle

Analytical investigation of the external world, and reflection on the necessary conditions of knowledge and reasoning, were mutually supportive in Greek philosophy. With hindsight we can see that this interaction between experience and reason was more productive for conceptual understanding than for observational science. Plato's philosophy reveals the tensions which arise if the knower and the known are taken to be fundamentally similar. He rejected Democritean materialism out of hand, since it made mindless bodies prior to mind, and failed to satisfy his deepest convictions about cosmic order: the world must be organized by principles which function analogously to our own thoughts, as expressed in language; there must be purposiveness in nature if reason finds it intolerable to deny this.

The Greeks were too ready to build theories on purely abstract reasoning, explaining complex phenomena by concepts which satisfied intellectual intuitions but were often inadequately grounded in exact observation and empirical testing. Thus, to put the point very generally, the Greek contribution to philosophy, as we understand that subject today, was more fruitful than their efforts in the specialist sciences. Which is not in the least to depreciate the latter. The point I wish to emphasize is the Greek tendency to see a connection between the way the world works and patterns of thought as revealed in everyday language,

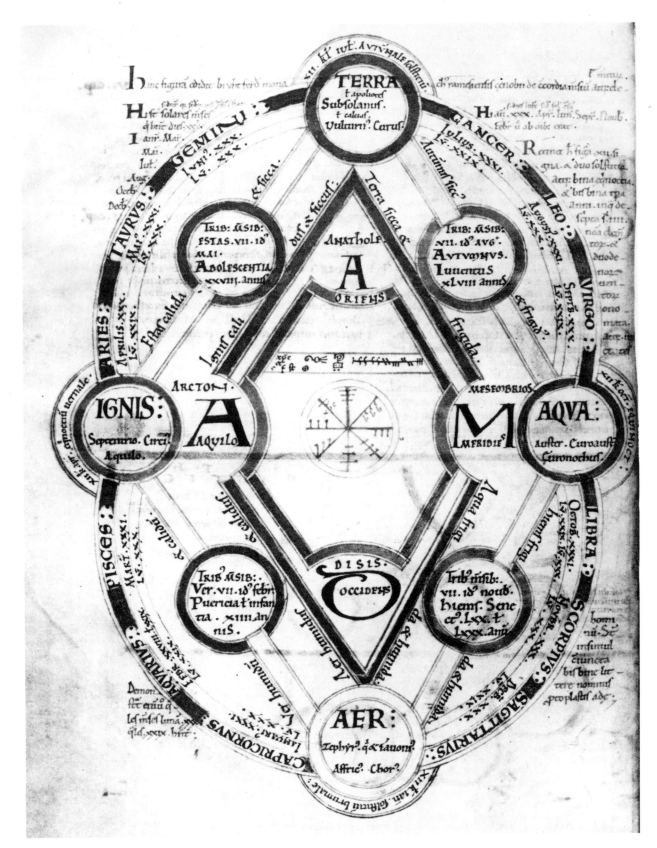

Medieval Europe's picture of reality derived from a Platonist and Christian interpretation of Aristotle. This provided support for a complex web of correspondences between microcosm and macrocosm, man and the universe: four elements, four 'humours', four cardinal directions, four seasons, four ages of man. This diagram was made in England in the early 12th century AD.

modified only by the introduction of a few technical terms.

These remarks are offered both as an epilogue to the chapter and also as a context for reviewing a few features of Aristotle's encyclopaedic researches. In comparison with Plato, his principal teacher and constant starting-point, Aristotle's work appears empirically oriented and dispassionate. There are few

113

traces of Plato's other-worldliness and mysticism, few expressions of yearning for a cosmic goodness transcending the physical world. In a whole range of studies, most notably biology, Aristotle directed systematic collections of data which would provide the material for a scientific understanding of natural phenomena. His classifications of animal genera and species, and his inquiries into animals' parts and their functions, are two examples of the care and energy he devoted to subjects which formed no part of Plato's educational curriculum. Aristotle completely rejected Plato's insistence on innate knowledge and transcendent Forms. He took the 'primary substances' to be particular men, horses etc.: there is no universal Man existing apart from men taken individually, and it is by induction from the particular that we arrive at the general truths which the philosopher can organize into a framework of scientific knowledge.

Nor was Aristotle troubled by Plato's difficulties over accommodating being and becoming, reason and sense-perception. He formulated a series of technical concepts to overcome the Presocratic problems with which Plato had wrestled. His distinctions between form and matter, and potentiality and actuality, provided solutions to questions about identity and change: a substance could remain what it is (a man, say) while undergoing change in respects which do not alter its being a man. His methodology, combining formal reasoning with factual observations and critical scrutiny of accepted opinions, is a model of how to ask and answer questions.

Yet Aristotle's universe retains many characteristics of Platonism. He was no more willing than Plato had been to reduce explanations to mechanical processes. Of the many answers to the question, 'Why?', which Aristotle thought one should ask, the most informative, in his view, was teleological – to show what something is for, the 'end' or purpose of anything, be it a substance or a natural process or an artefact. His teleology affects, sometimes adversely, his answers to particular problems in natural science. It colours his picture of the world as a whole.

For Aristotle the phenomenal world is not the physical copy of an intelligible original. It should be viewed rather as a work of 'art' which has nature as its indwelling artist. As such the world manifests design or purposiveness, but its purposiveness is not the direct intervention of a creative mind; teleology or nature refers to the collective tendency of all things in the world to achieve their specific ends. The end of the child is to grow into the man, and that final end supposedly explains the antecedent processes from infancy to maturity. So does the world as a whole have an end or purpose? Aristotle's cosmology takes this to be certain. There must be an ultimate cause of motion, he argued, to account for the movements of the heavenly bodies, and for the cycle of terrestrial life and change. This cause is god, an everlasting, incorporeal mind, whose eternal activity of contemplation is the best of all possible states for the world. Desire to resemble this state, to the greatest degree possible, motivates the eternal circular movements of the heavenly bodies. The everlasting reproductive cycle of animal species is explicable as the way nature, at the terrestrial level, has the divine Unmoved Mover as its final cause.

Aristotle's conviction that 'nature does nothing in vain' produced a cosmology which shaped western thought up to the 16th century and beyond. It was a magnificent construction by the speculative intellect, finding a 'natural' place for everything, and incorporating acute analyses of time and motion, just to mention two topics where his work has an enduring interest. Without supreme confidence in the heuristic powers of reason, none of this could have been achieved. Yet this cosmology rested on an utterly false theory of dynamics, which supposed the heavenly bodies to move around a stationary earth in perfect circles, and invented the 'aether' as their special element, on the principal ground that circular motion is not 'natural' to any of the terrestrial elements and must therefore be natural to something else. In his approach to cosmic order, Aristotle no less than Plato was influenced by value judgements, and these helped to create his theory of the fifth element which is 'more divine' than earthly bodies. Rational contemplation is the 'best' of all activities, and *therefore* it must characterize the final cause of the world. The 'ends' of natural processes are conceived of as perfections, like the goals of human aspiration. Unjustified assumptions intrude into his biology, such as the superiority of right to left, up to down, male to female.

Such points should scarcely occasion surprise. The Greeks would not have discovered the cosmos unless they had sensed an analogy between human order and rationality, and natural events. They sometimes pressed the analogy too far. Teleology was more edifying than outright mechanism; it made for a more homely universe than atoms moving in the void. The Democritean hypothesis, revived by Epicurus, was a heroic vote for a quite different cosmology, but it failed to dislodge the mind-directed worlds of Plato, Aristotle, and the Stoics. These were the philosophers whose image of the cosmos, for all its superficial differences from modern scientific thinking, has exerted the most compelling influence on our own cultural tradition.

III·CREATION

T IS HARDLY POSSIBLE to exaggerate the importance of art and literature in determining both our image of the Greeks and the place that we give them in history. With every other people of the ancient world – until at least 300 BC – we must painstakingly reassemble their social structure, beliefs and characteristics from archaeological research, the decipherment of inscriptions and the uncertain memory of tradition. The Greeks, by contrast, speak directly to us through poetry, drama and prose, through painting, architecture and sculpture. They are uniquely, startlingly, modern.

How far should we yield to these seductive images? How literally can we take works of imagination as documents? To what degree ought we to see the Greeks as they saw themselves?

Certainly there are snares and temptations. Because most of the literature is Athenian, for instance, we tend to exalt Athens at the expense of other cities (who is on Sparta's side in the Peloponnesian War?) Because in art archaic rigidity matured into classic freedom, it is easy to see Greek society doing the same. And because the Greeks had a healthy contempt for most of their neighbours, we are inclined to dismiss non-Greeks as of no account.

And yet, with every allowance made, the Greeks' claim (explicit or implicit) to be the originators and custodians of all that we value most in civilization must substantially be conceded as true. By some inexplicable genius, they not only invented most of the genres and disciplines that we take for granted in artistic or intellectual discourse, but brought each one to a perfection which later ages have found it impossible to surpass. At the outset of Greek culture stand the two great epics of Homer, emerging from an obscure oral past but coinciding in their present written form with the first figured vases. With the 5th century BC comes the creation of tragedy, comedy, historical writing and philosophy, and at the same time the evolution of the orders of architecture and a complete mastery of sculpture in relief and in the round. In every one of these areas, the Greek example was to shape the course of future civilization in the west.

Of that future, only a small part was to remain centred on Greece. The Greek cultural heritage passed first to the Hellenized kingdoms of the Near East, then to the empire of Rome, through Rome to Byzantium and the Christian Middle Ages. Greek influence percolated into Islam, and flowered luxuriantly in the Italian Renaissance. In the late 18th and early 19th centuries, when Greek architecture was accurately surveyed and understood, Athens itself seemed to rise again in cities all over Europe and North America from St Petersburg to Philadelphia.

During this long span of centuries, Greek art and poetry called up no echo in their native land, though the bare idea of Greek nationhood, somehow tenuously connected with the achievements of its Golden Age, never died. In the final chapter of this book we shall see how that idea, fertilized from the living classical tradition of the west, gave birth to a new Greece that could at last lay claim to its ancient inheritance.

The lying-in-state
(Greek *prothesis*) depicted on this huge figured amphora is dated towards 750 BC. The vase itself, found broken and reconstructed from fragments, was used as a grave-marker and hollow altar in the Dipylon cemetery, Athens. Most of its surface is covered with abstract patterns whose function is hardly more than decorative; this picture shows the central figurative scene. The corpse lies on a bier, the top half of its body shown frontally but the lower half in profile; the chequered area above is the shroud. Two mourners, skirted and therefore probably women, sit on the ground; two others sit on stools. The nearest of kin, one of them a child, touch the bier. Others on either side beat their heads or tear their hair. All this conforms to what we hear of funerals in Homer. (1)

Life and death

During the 8th century Attic vase-painters began to explore animal forms and human activities. Their art is confined to essentials, highly stylized but precise in its renderings.

A funerary procession from another huge Athenian vase (*above*). Body, shroud and bier are carried on a cart drawn by two horses. To the left, a row of mourning women. (2)

Files of chariots and warriors on foot encircle an Athenian Late Geometric amphora, *c.*725 BC. The style of drawing is becoming freer, conveying a sense of movement and life. (6)

The distinctive styles of individual masters now begin to be recognizable. One of them is the Analatos Painter, whose artistic development can be followed in some detail. He experimented in both animal and human forms. *Left:* a hydria in Athens from the place now called Analatos. *Above:* neck of the same vase. *Right:* vase-lid in the British Museum, London. (3, 4, 5)

Myth was present in the minds of
vase-painters and their customers.
The painted versions of the legends
sometimes differ from those in
literary sources.

Odysseus puts out the eye of the
Cyclops Polyphemus, a detail from the
neck of a large amphora found at
Eleusis. It is among the earliest
renderings of this subject. (7)

The escape of Odysseus and his
companions (*below*) underneath the
bellies of Polyphemus' sheep appears
on the fragmentary vase known as the
Ram Jug. (8)

Herakles kills the centaur Nessus,
who has attempted to rape his wife
Deianira. Here the centaur pleads for
mercy, stretching out his hands to his
attacker, who has a foot in the small of
his back and is preparing to drive a
sword into his side. (9)

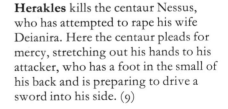

119

The perfection of Black and Red Figure

In the 7th century BC the Orientalizing style developed into Black Figure, which was a most effective medium for the archaic figure style. About 530 BC the technique was reversed to create Red Figure, which gave the painters more scope for foreshortening and interior detail.

Nearly three hundred figures, human and animal, decorate the so-called François crater (*left*), painted by the Athenian Clitias. The scenes on the side shown here concern Achilles and his parents. At the top, the Calydonian boar-hunt and the funeral games of Patroclus; then the wedding of Peleus and Thetis; and the killing of Troilus by Achilles. At the bottom, a battle of pygmies and cranes. (10)

The artists of Corinth liked painting banquet scenes. Here, on the Eurytus crater (*below, left*), Herakles is reclining on a couch and banging the table to attract the attention of his host's daughter, Viola. (11)

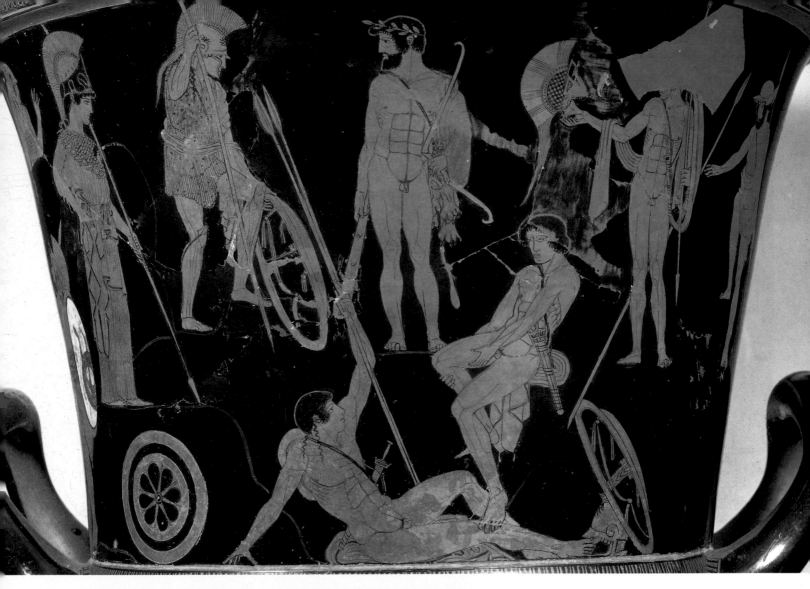

The Niobid Painter, named after this vase (*above*; the Niobid scene is on the other side), flourished towards the middle of the 5th century BC. Here we see Herakles among the Argonauts. They stand on undulating ground marked by faint lines, a trick thought to reflect contemporary wall-painting. (12)

The climax of Black Figure came with Exekias, whose finest surviving work (*left*) is an amphora found at Vulci showing Achilles and Ajax relaxing from the stress of battle and engaged in a game with dice. Achilles (on the left) is saying 'Four' and Ajax 'Three'. (13)

The beginnings of sculpture

Greek sculpture took its initial inspiration from Egypt. By the middle of the 7th century the Greeks were producing large-scale statues in stone (mainly marble). They seem commonly to have been painted.

The Dipylon Head (*above*) is still highly stylized, but many naturalistic touches on archaic statues show close observation of life. (14)

From Didyma near Miletus come smiling marble figures of temple maidens, probably from column-bases. (16)

This lion (*below*), now in Berlin, token guardian of a tomb at Miletus in Asia Minor, has been patiently observed and is very sympathetically portrayed. (15)

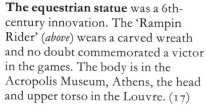

The equestrian statue was a 6th-century innovation. The 'Rampin Rider' (*above*) wears a carved wreath and no doubt commemorated a victor in the games. The body is in the Acropolis Museum, Athens, the head and upper torso in the Louvre. (17)

For the temple at Olympia sculptors of the 460s carved twelve reliefs to be set in the frieze at the ends of the cella, telling the story of the Labours of Herakles in a series of close-ups. *Far left:* Herakles, helped by Athena, carries the heavens for Atlas who is bringing him the apples of the Hesperides. *Left:* the cleansing of the Augean stables, again with Athena standing by. *Right:* Herakles brings the Stymphalian birds to Athena. (20, 21, 22)

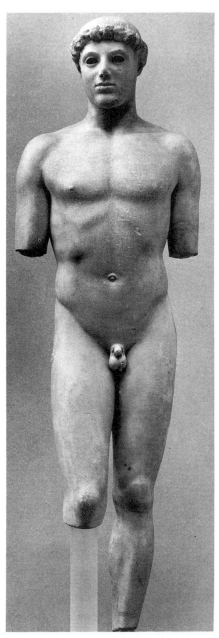

Portraiture as we understand it has no obvious precedent in archaic art. Indeed, portrait statues of the classical era normally had heads with generalized or idealized features. This head, a copy of late Roman date from Ostia which is inscribed with the name Themistocles, is therefore of exceptional interest if the original was a portrait statue of about 460 BC. (23)

Youths and maidens, nude *kouros* and draped *kore*, hover between two worlds – the real and the ideal. The male figure (*right*) is the so-called 'Critian Boy', set up on the Acropolis shortly before the Persians sacked it in 480 BC; the female one (*above*) was set up there at about the end of the 6th century. (18,19)

The theatre of the gods

Drama grew out of religious ritual. Aeschylus, the first dramatist whose works have survived (died 456 BC), is primarily concerned with relations between gods and men. Sophocles and Euripides focus increasingly on human moral and psychological dilemmas.

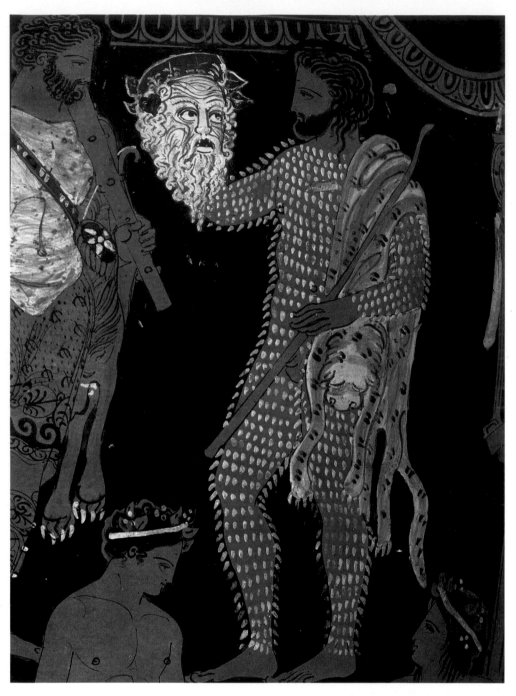

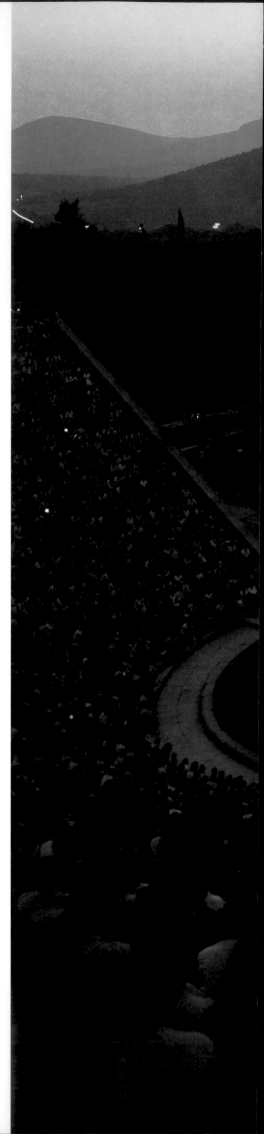

A trilogy of tragic plays was followed on the same day by a short satyr-play. *Right:* A modern performance of Sophocles' *Oedipus* in the ancient theatre at Epidauros. *Above:* Two actors from a satyr-play depicted on a vase. Both are carrying their masks. The one on the left plays Herakles, with lion-skin (the mask shows the lion's head), club and, over his shoulder, a bow and quiver. The right-hand actor is Pappasilenos, the leader of the Chorus. (24, 25)

The sanctuary of Athena

The building of the Parthenon, begun 447 BC, marks the culmination of Athenian imperialism. It also marks a point of balance in the arts, with overall simplicity and great sophistication of detail combining to create norms in architecture, while sculpture was becoming more composed after half a century of rapid progress towards novel solutions.

The imposing eight-column facade of the Parthenon, from the west. (26)

Centaurs fighting Lapiths on the metopes symbolize the forces of barbarism struggling against those of civilization. (27)

At the west end the cavalry are still forming up with the horses and riders shown in a variety of poses. The first picture (*above*) is from Lord Elgin's cast (the original, still on the Parthenon, has lost the man's head). (29)

The gods (at the east end of the frieze) are assembled to watch the procession arriving. *Right:* Hermes, Dionysus, Demeter and Ares. *Far right:* Posidon, Apollo and Artemis. (30, 31)

A cavalryman at the west end of the north frieze shows his agitation as he waits for his companion to have his belt adjusted. (28)

The Acropolis seen between the Doric columns of the temple which used to be called Theseum but is now most commonly recognized as the Hephaisteion. It is contemporary with the Parthenon. (32)

4
Classical Art

the beginning of the European tradition

J. M. COOK

The masterpieces of Greek painting, of which we find
some tantalizing accounts in the literature, are almost
entirely lost, though tombs in Macedonia are at last giving
us some idea of 4th-century pictorial skills. What survive
are Roman copies of works that were often themselves of
Hellenistic date. This fresco from Herculaneum shows
Herakles discovering his son Telephus in the mountains of
Arcadia (personified by the seated female figure). Telephus,
who had been exposed at birth and suckled by a hind, was
the legendary founder of Pergamon. (33)

THE WORLD OF CRETE and Mycenae, as we saw in Chapter 1, had an imaginative pictorial art with a wide range of expression. But in the last phase of the Bronze Age the organic forms that painters reproduced were losing contact with reality. What for instance had been a palm tree or an octopus became a traditional pattern: a knobby stem with decaying fronds and two glaring eyes, or, looked at another way, a creature with a long stem and roots. By about 1100 BC even such quasi-organic forms had disappeared and there remained only the simplest of abstract motifs. This collapse of art-forms was part of a more general collapse of material civilization. It is not a matter of impoverishment but of an all-time low. The slate has been wiped clean; the syntax governing the ornament has vanished, and barely even the most basic elements of vocabulary remain.

In what survives from this era it is the painted vases that carry such art tradition as there was. Here after the 11th century a new spirit had begun to manifest itself. The shapes of the vases became less slack, more tense. One senses a pride in the precision of the craftsman's skill. The decoration is applied sparingly, but it is positioned for effect and acquires a certain intensity. Gradually the field for such decoration expands over larger areas of the vase surfaces and a geometrical motif (the meander) comes to dominate the ornament in increasingly elaborate schemes.

The Geometric world

The art of this period down to about 700 BC is known by the name Geometric. For generations human and animal figures make only the rarest appearances. It is an inorganic world. Towards the middle of the 8th century, however, living forms intrude more insistently; at first they conform to the strict conventions of the Geometric in which freehand drawing is almost taboo. This is a movement which probably began with one artist (the painter of the so-called Prothesis amphora from the Dipylon cemetery in Athens) who was followed by a small number of pupils and imitators. There is nothing in their figured work to suggest that they had any existing art tradition to model themselves on. Some scholars who hold to a sub-Darwinian belief that nothing ever had a beginning look for antecedents in Mycenaean art, but all that can be said is that one occasionally sees forms in archaic Greek art which

could have been inspired by the discovery of some Mycenaean object. Some inspiration from Near Eastern arts can also be surmised; in the generation or so after the Prothesis Painter it manifests itself in creatures such as lions and sphinxes and in elaborate curvilinear ornaments, to such an extent in fact that the period in Greek art which starts towards 700 BC has come to be known by the name 'Orientalizing'. But the high Geometric of the 8th century is completely Greek in its evolution.

Much has been written about the significance of the ornaments painted on these vases, such as swastikas, circles, and wavy lines; some scholars see in them magical symbols, sun standards, sepulchral snakes and so forth. When birds and animals appear they too are given similar values – horses being funerary, carnivorous creatures connoting the gruesomeness of death. Superhuman or demonic powers are conjured up, and Near Eastern symbolism is invoked. But early Greek poetry gives no hint of any such extrasensory and funerary imagery; unlike men, animals eat one another up, says Hesiod, because there is not Justice among them, and the gold headband that Athena made for Pandora to wear on Olympus, with all sorts of strange creatures portrayed on it, was an ornament intended to be worn in heaven, not in the grave. This point needs to be stressed if we are to see straight in early Greek art.

The Prothesis amphora, which was made to be a grave-marker in Athens, is over five feet (one and a half metres) high. On the neck are a couple of shallow bands of animal ornament, but it is the great key meander which commands attention there; the abstract decoration is paramount, with its veritable hierarchy of motifs. The texture of dark and light on these vases is so balanced that the surface has a tapestry-like effect; the bands are graded according to an ordered, rhythmical scheme, and the effect is often one of compression. The main figured scene here is on the body. A corpse lies on p. 117 its bier, head on pillow, the shroud fitted over it, hired (1) mourners on the floor (on some other vases musicians also appear); on either side the extended family beating their heads or tearing their hair, with the nearest of kin touching the shroud or raising a hand to address the dead person. This scene can be matched by the description of the funeral of Hector in the *Iliad* (which is not far removed in time). All night long they mourn; at dawn two men (on the left) wearing swords come from outside to cart the body away.

What happens next is told on the Ekphora crater by a rather less solemn but more circumstantial painter. On a wheeled cart, pulled by two horses, are carpeted p. 118 planks to take the bier, with ropes to secure them; on (2) the bier the dead with the shroud above. The mourners can be 'read' in the way that we can read the human body in Homer's epithets: the broad shoulders, sturdy

The 'Ludovisi Throne', probably once part of a sacred precinct in southern Italy, was carved not long before 450 BC in an old-fashioned style. This detail shows what could be the birth of Aphrodite; the goddess is being raised from the water by two female attendants.

A figured zone from a Late Geometric vase. The warrior in the chariot on the right has a 'Dipylon shield'.

thighs, slender waist and frail neck. It is a literal rendering, not so much of what was seen in real life (the family would be clothed) but of what everyone knew to be there. The different parts are seen in their most typical view, head and legs in profile, the trunk frontal. There is occasional ambiguity (does the cart have two wheels like the chariots, or does it have four?). The whole is carefully articulated; in this we have one of the fundamental principles of Greek art.

The subjects were not confined to funerals. Battle scenes are common, with different schemes of combat which match those described in the epics; there are piles of dead among whom vultures pick, and often ships with oarsmen as well as fighters depicted – rowing being, as Payne remarked, the most Geometric form of exercise. The same principles govern these scenes: forms carefully articulated and detached from one another, and enjoying an almost unlimited freedom of movement.

This could not go on for ever. Painters soon felt the need of more substance for their figures and freedom to depict interior detail within the black silhouettes. Some of course sought solutions in elaborating the traditional modes. But by the late 8th century there were workshops in Athens in which a progressive style was developing and drawing was verging on the freehand.

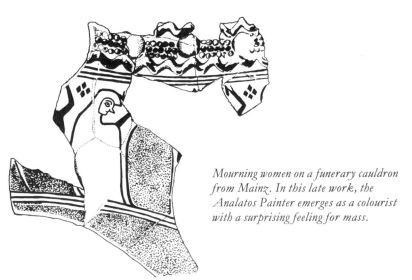

Mourning women on a funerary cauldron from Mainz. In this late work, the Analatos Painter emerges as a colourist with a surprising feeling for mass.

Vase painting and story telling

The first great advance came through the Analatos Painter, whose work – to judge by a dozen and more pieces – spanned a fair working lifetime. If we study the rhythm of his young men's bodies we see the human form becoming an organic whole enclosed in coherent outline: the second basic principle of Greek art. There is also a new swing to the maidens' skirts. The Analatos Painter's name comes from a place outside Athens where one of his early vases was found. An amphora of his in Oxford is more strictly Geometric. In his middle stage his lithe maidens became thicker-waisted matrons; at the end, on a painted funerary cauldron in Mainz, they are hooded crones bending towards the grave. The painter had not only a fine command of line but also an infallible sense of positioning; everything he painted was in perfect order. He invented a range of new forms (the pouched dress and the human and animal faces and schemes, flamingoes and birds in flight, elaborate floral ornaments, and a new rendering of the ship which looks forward to the François crater, see below, p. 136), and he gave them elegance and distinction so that, as Hampe remarks, even his monsters have a civilized look. He also experimented in technique, using touches of white paint and engraved lines to distinguish details on the silhouettes; finally he broke with tradition to the point of using three colours in his old women's mantles. Between the thin angular forms of his earliest work, still in Late Geometric style, and the broad swaying bodies on the Mainz cauldron a very long road has been travelled by this one painter. But he was not a revolutionary. What he did was to transmute the traditional forms that he inherited. A few letters of signature on a fragment of a plaque, elegantly painted by him before the firing, show that he was literate, and we may see in him, as in Homer, an artist of sufficient standing to create norms for succeeding generations. To both the term 'patrician' could be applied.

p. 118 (3,4)

Of his contemporaries in the workshops in Athens none had his vision. But across the Gulf in Corinth also vase painting was becoming an art. A competent but undistinguished Geometric evolved into a fine style in the second half of the 8th century, on vases accurately thrown in refined white clay. Great precision was achieved in the painting also, with Near Eastern motifs incorporated, and a miniature style of considerable elegance came into being in the early 7th century. The middlemen of Aegina cashed in on the artistic talent of Corinth and Athens; it is thanks to them that there survive fragments from some big Protocorinthian cups of near the mid-century which offered space enough to allow free artistic expression. Here coherent outline and articulation of forms are fully harmonized. The technique is simple: black silhouette, fine engraved lines, and occasional patches of an applied red (as on alternating wing quills) – in fact what was later to become prevalent as the Black Figure technique. But the result is the perfection that is met with from time to time in an archaic art.

There are critics who regard Greek vase painting of the 8th and 7th centuries as a minor art. Some look to three-dimensional objects such as bronze figurines as the carriers of the main artistic tradition. But generally these consist of two-dimensional aspects juxtaposed, and more elaborate works such as the Late Geometric stamped gold bands conform precisely to the canons of contemporary vase painting. Similarly, the view that vase painting is a mere reflection of larger-scale painting on flat surfaces is untenable. In fact, archaic terracotta architectural plaques painted in Athens or Corinth later in the 7th century are recognizably the work of the same painters as the vases, as also the Pendeskouphia plaques from Corinth and those painted by Exekias up to a century later. So the vases that we study carried the main stream of Greek and European art.

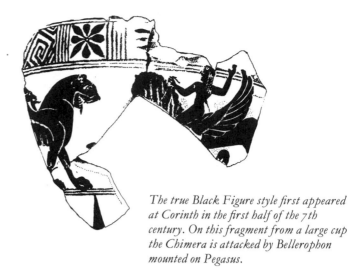

The true Black Figure style first appeared at Corinth in the first half of the 7th century. On this fragment from a large cup the Chimera is attacked by Bellerophon mounted on Pegasus.

Geometric painting was impersonal in the sense that the artists did not have it in their power to depict particular incidents. Their combat scenes – whether thought of as heroic or contemporary, or very possibly a spontaneous blending of the two – were generalized. So it is only very rarely, and probably fortuitously, that scholars can claim to recognize a scene from the Greek legends. But the impact of the Ionic epic on the Greeks of the mainland may have provided inspiration, and the growing skill of the artists themselves made mythological renderings possible by the early 7th century. On the whole, the earliest such scenes are specially distinctive ones: not duels, which would permit too many inter- p. 119 pretations, but those that feature the Cyclops Poly- (7)

This lion (above) and Chimera (right) show with what power the Nessus Painter and his contemporaries could portray animals in a Black Figure style inspired by Corinthian artists.

phemus, for instance, or the Centaur Nessus, who was killed by Herakles, or the monster Chimera – the last of which is immediately recognizable not only in itself but because it is paired with Bellerophon astride his winged horse, Pegasus. Such scenes may have come from a variety of sources, Bellerophon could be inspired by the *Iliad*, where the Chimera is described as 'in front a lion, a snake behind, and in the middle a she-goat'; the *Odyssey* may have suggested the scene of Odysseus' escape from the Cyclops' cave by an Athenian painter where the ram he clutches is 'much the biggest of all the sheep', and a curious portrayal on a large Argive vase of the blinding of Polyphemus, where the giant might be reclining, as Homer says, on the pile of droppings. But the majority of the subjects were ones at home in poems of the epic cycle other than the *Iliad* and *Odyssey*; and of course the painters could draw on mother's-knee or bazaar-singer versions of the tales. Boardman and others have stressed that we should not look for close correspondence with the texts of the epics. One of the fragments from Aegina by the Bellerophon Painter shows a man drawing his sword; he again is distinctive, not (as one might suppose) gazing at the lion, but turning his head away because he is Perseus about to kill the Gorgon.

The manufacture of painted pottery was widespread in the Greek world, and even in Geometric times there were many centres of production. In the 7th century there were short-lived 'schools' in Crete, the islands, Argos, Boeotia, Euboea, and other places. Some of these local fabrics depended on the originality of a single craftsman who may himself have been an immigrant; it is easy to understand that a painter with some talent might make a name for himself locally, but that as he grew older his close vision was impaired, or that his sons or successors lacked the eye for figure painting. Eretria in Euboea is a case in point (for a brief moment there was a painter of some quality there). Sometimes there was more imagination than talent, as in the Aristonophos crater, which was made by a Greek, probably in central Italy. Only in east Greece, where a remarkably homogeneous Orientalizing style – that known as 'Wild Goat', from the most characteristic element in its decorative scheme – was adopted by workshops in a number of different centres, was an on-going tradition established. But this was a decorative art based on the animal-frieze and had little concern with narrative; in the development of painting as an art in Greece the fact is that Athens and Corinth had no serious rivals before the mid-6th century.

Protocorinthian achieved a peak after the middle of the 7th century with the Chigi vase. In Athens, where p. 119 (7) the Polyphemus Painter was the leading figure before the mid-century, vase painting was in something of a ferment; despite what Eva Brann has called his 'easy familiarity with the awesome', the Polyphemus Painter must at times have been amazed when he stood back and saw what he had painted. But order and delicacy p. 119 (8) returned with the painter of the Ram Jug in Aegina,

and the next generation witnessed the installation of a stable, almost monumental style in a sombre Black Figure colouring. Athenian painting was re-aligning itself on the Corinthian model by about 625 BC. By this time the Orientalizing phase of conscious adaptation of Near Eastern forms was long past; the Black Figure technique and the style that went with it were to dominate the vase painting of Athens for the next hundred years.

The steadiest, if not the most exciting, of the pioneers of this Corinthianizing style at Athens was the Nessus Painter, whose figures are so constructed as to act their parts convincingly. His Harpies belt along purposefully, while on the vase from which he takes his p. 119 (9) name the contrast between Herakles' robust, well-jointed limbs and the Centaur's helpless hands and forelegs accentuates the impact. The Nessus Painter still liked to paint on a large scale, with squareish panels that allow room for few figures and so focus attention on the deed – on the body of his vase with the Gorgons there is no room for Perseus! But by the end of the century we are entering a phase where competence (if not circumspection) was the norm and imagination was kept under firm control. Stories can be told, and for good measure they generally travel round the vase in the same fashion as the ubiquitous files of animals.

A Corinthian highlight of this time is the Eurytus p. 120 (11) crater. The scene here is from a disreputable exploit of Herakles who was entertained at Oechalia, killed his host, and carried off the daughter of the house (thus in fact bringing about his own death). The vase has banqueters on couches along the shoulder. The famous hero, however, is not in the centre but at the right end, where he looks up and bangs on the table with the cutlery, to attract the fair Viola's attention when she turns her head away from him.

Sculptural beginnings

To turn to the minor arts, in bronze and terracotta the linear forms that were little more than a silhouette had become almost three-dimensional by the early and middle 7th century. The so-called 'Daedalic' style, which then prevailed, could portray the human head as a triangle against a layered wig of hair – roughly, the crown of the head being the base of a triangle whose point was the chin, and the sides of the face also tending to be oblique. By the later 7th century some rounding of the cheeks modified this angular effect. In the middle of that century, however, a new acquaintance with the monuments of Egypt had led the Greeks to experiment with large-scale sculpture. The islands of the central Aegean (the Cyclades) had good supplies of fine white marble; Naxos in particular became the centre of a new industry that kindled an interest in sculpture and monumental architecture in the principal Greek cities. Technical know-how seems to have been acquired from Egypt, with the result that Greek sculpture had no infancy; the marble lady dedicated by Nikandre on Delos, with its Daedalic features and plank-like body,

Greek figure-sculpture was a legacy from Egypt, and came via the Cyclades and Crete. These three goddesses show its earliest stages. First, impulses from the east give charm to early Cretan sculpture, as on this lintel from the doorway of a shrine at Prinias, second half of the 7th century. Second, a softstone statuette (the 'Auxerre goddess') from the later 7th century, now in the Louvre. Third, the 'Berlin goddess', an Athenian marble statue of about 575 BC, shows a growing feeling for power and a keen interest in the structure of the human face.

must have been one of the very earliest of Greek statues. It was not at all a matter of small beginnings; among other very early marble statues were colossi up to thirty feet (nine or ten metres) high.

The Cyclades did not long maintain a monopoly of this art. To name but some off-shoots, in Crete softer stones were carved in forms that have more volume, in Athens a master of remarkable artistic integrity founded a 'school' or tradition that lived on, and in east Greece an ampler style gradually evolved. Paint was of course used, not only to enliven details like eyes and hair but to cover whole areas; it was applied in a thicker coat on soft-stone sculpture than on translucent marble.

The Athenian master of the so-called 'Sunium Group', which includes the Dipylon head, merits close attention. We see at once that the block of marble has been worked from all four sides with the carving on each relatively shallow. But the outlines are clear cut with a stylization that precludes any notional swelling of the chest to take in air and makes the forehead unnaturally high to emphasize the eyes. Compared with those of the Nessus vase the bodily forms look tentative, the linear modelling of the knee reminding us rather of the Ram Jug, but it is probably not earlier than the Nessus vase – sculpture at this stage was not emancipated from the block, with the result that contemporary paintings look the more advanced. The Dipylon head is over-lifesize. The artist is aware of the problem of what in nature are different substances and handles his surfaces accordingly. The skin stretched tight over the forehead bone lends itself to smooth convex form, and the hollow between brow and eye can be rendered by a concave channel. But the soft flesh of the cheek requires gentler rounding, while the gristly material of the ear needs sharp edging. The hair has to have a strong patterning to suggest a less palpable substance; the desire to give order to what in nature is fortuitous induces a powerful stylization of ear and hair ribbon. The result is not totally realistic but it is high art. A generation or more later not dissimilar qualities appear in the strongly stylized figure of an Athenian goddess in Berlin, whose hands – admirably broad like Penelope's in Homer – create foci in the overall scheme. After this, sculptors were becoming more versatile, and we can detect different approaches to the problem of form. The Master of the Rampin Rider worked in the tradition of the Berlin goddess, exploiting the contrast between smooth convex and concave surfaces and

p. 122 (14)

p. 122 (17)

Detail from the François crater, also shown on p. 120, by the painter Clitias. Priam rises from his seat by a tower, while two Trojan warriors – Hector and Polites – come out of a gateway as reinforcements. Second quarter of the 6th century.

elaborate decorative patterns, but was especially concerned with exploring the structure of the human body under the surface; there were contemporaries of his who took more pleasure in rounded forms. What is noticeable throughout is a semi-conscious advance towards greater naturalism.

In Ionia there was no master capable of creating a Dipylon head. But a distinctive school emerged in the 6th century with Samos and Miletus as its most recognizable centres. Here elementary forms – sphere and cylinder for heads and skirts, and the cube for seated figures – give the initial coherence to the design, whether it be a life-size statue, a perfume flask, or a minutely carved ivory figurine. Repetitive patterns sometimes enliven the composition, but what often surprises the viewer is the pleasure the sculptor took in areas of unadorned, gently curving marble set off by piquant facial features or patterns of folds. Stylized though it is, this is far from being an unrealistic art. The soft body of the seated lady in the Louvre is brilliantly combined and contrasted with the unyielding material of the throne; the guardian statue from a tomb at Miletus shows an unparalleled understanding of the texture and pose of a captive lion.

These sculptures served different purposes. In some cases a statue or a relief stele superseded the now obsolescent vases that had stood as grave markers. A certain number of statues were carved as graven images of deities, and some, like the Rampin Rider, were commemorative. But mostly these figures of youths and maidens were offerings dedicated in sanctuaries by individuals in place of live servants and hand-maidens. The word *agalma*, which in Greek came to be the

ordinary word for statue, meant a 'gladdener' to give pleasure to the god or goddess. An *agalma* became a possession (*ktēma*) of the deity, so dedications were sacred property and could not be thrown away when they were no longer wanted – this accounts for the hoards of offerings that have been found by excavators in ancient sanctuaries, often piously deposited in the filling behind terrace walls or enceintes. To this above all we owe the survival of the archaic sculptures of the Athenian Acropolis.

The climax of Black Figure vase painting

Within the limits of their archaic conventions artists such as the Corinthian who painted the colourful Amphiaraus crater and the Athenian Black Figure painter Clitias had more or less total mastery. The latter had no doubt worked under a venturesome and ostentatious painter named Sophilus, and to this he added a finer touch and unlimited patience. On the François crater, found in a tomb at Chiusi in Tuscany, he painted an array of nearly three hundred human and p. 120 (10) animal figures, scores of men and objects having their names written neatly alongside them. On the shoulder, a subject that had recently become popularized in art, that of the wedding of Peleus and Thetis, runs right round the vase; the bride can be seen in the porch, while the groom stands outside receiving the divine guests. Six other scenes from the Greek legends are depicted, as well as on the foot a battle of pygmies and cranes, a theme taken from a simile in Book 3 of the *Iliad*. One by this time hackneyed Trojan scene, that of Troilus, shows how narrative could be developed at length. With a supporting posse of deities Achilles is crouching in ambush behind a fountain to which Priam's young son Troilus comes with his sister. As Troilus rides away Achilles springs out after him. His sister drops her pitcher and tries to escape. The news is brought to Priam, who rises from his seat at the gate, and already a couple of reinforcements are forcing their way out sideways through the frontal door. Clitias painted with assurance and elegance; he had a command of poses and gestures that almost speak. We are fortunate in having a nearly complete vase which tells us so much.

Clitias was mainly a miniaturist, like many of the Athenian vase painters of the middle decades of the 6th century. But some of his successors aimed at a larger style. By this time the Athenian potteries were producing for buoyant world markets, and thousands of their painted vases have come to light in central Italian tombs. Thanks to Beazley's unremitting, sensitive study through more than half of the present century these Athenian painters are now as well known as the masters of the Quattrocento. We may single out one, Exekias, who achieved a bigger style with a concentration – what Robert Cook has called a 'grave p. 121 (13) inwardness' – that consorts almost more with tragedy than epic. His engraved detail is exquisite, but he could also sense a new pathos in an old story. After his manic attack Ajax had only one course of action left to him; in the lonely dawn light in front of Troy the dishonoured hero with due deliberation plants in the ground the sword on which he will fall. Beazley remarked that Ajax was Exekias' most favoured hero, as Achilles was Clitias'.

Exekias' artistic activity can be dated approximately 550–525 BC. Such precision in dating is not in fact unduly presumptuous. Whereas in dealing with the earlier archaic, scholars have to make questionable assumptions if they are going to posit an absolute date to within a margin of twenty years – as, say, 620 BC for the Nessus vase, we have now reached a time when events recorded by Herodotus, such as the construction of the Siphnian treasury at Delphi, Cambyses' conquest of Egypt and Xerxes' sack of the Acropolis at Athens can be fairly precisely dated and works of later archaic Greek art can be placed in their sequence accordingly.

By this time the Corinthian factories were losing out in the competition. But in fact figure painting was more widespread in the Greek world than ever before. In the Argolid we find an isolated piece that was locally made: an early Black Figure crater from Mycenae gives us an Athenian-looking Gorgon not sure whether to pose as victim or pursuer, but she is tucked away under the handle, and the Argive feeling for first things first is shown by the choice of a boar and piglet for the subject on the front of the vase. Eretrian and Boeotian vases have also yielded good specimens of well fattened livestock. Sparta (Laconia) had a Black Figure 'school' which specialized in painting the tondoes of open drinking cups. One artist with a curious bent must have travelled to Cyrene; he painted King Arcesilas seated

Ajax plants his sword in the ground preparatory to falling on it. In a fit of mad rage after Achilles' panoply was awarded to Odysseus, he slaughtered a flock of sheep, believing them to be his enemies. Exekias conveys the tragedy of the hero's return to sanity.

under an awning supervising the weighing and storing of wool, with talkative workers who take an interest in the local fauna – evidently monarchy wasn't seen as repressive. In east Greece vases were not for the most part carriers of narrative; the painters' repertory had been adjusted to harmonious decoration of the curving vase surfaces. But east Greek artists could work on a larger scale and even paint genre subjects for dynastic patrons under Persian rule. Some of the most vigorous scenes were painted in the west. In southern Italy the so-called 'Chalcidian' ware lasted for a couple of

King Arcesilas of Cyrene supervising the weighing of wool – the inside of a cup painted by a Laconian artist. The king sits under an awning; the wool is being weighed on a balance and stuffed into sacks. This vase was a show piece; note the prominent depiction of the fauna of North Africa.

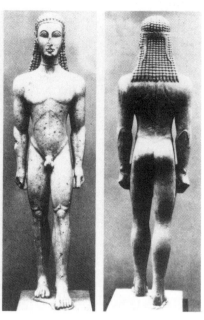

Kouros from Attica, late 7th century. The pose, with one leg advanced, is Egyptian. But though the statue is fully in the round, the principal planes tend to be flat with shallow modelling.

generations as an advanced Black Figure style. At Caere in southern Etruria a one-man-and-boy workshop turned out water jars painted with colourful scenes often drawn from the legends; his individualistic, one-foot-off-the-ground flights of fancy discover humour even among the immortals. Shading off into a derivative Etruscan style, the badly named 'Pontic' vases also display originality. The tombs of Etruscan nobles at Tarquinia and elsewhere were painted in styles that reflect Corinthian painting, the Caeretan master, and finally good Athenian Red Figure; an interest in nature and seascapes adds to their attractiveness.

Athens and Olympia: the new realism

It was in Athens above all that the movement towards naturalism in art broke out of the archaic mould. In sculpture the human form, both the nude male and the p. 123 (18) girl fashionably draped in clothes whose folds in some places hang thick, in others slant or radiate, was rendered to perfection by the end of the 6th century. And in early Red Figure – the Athenian technique that was invented about 530 BC and reversed the Black Figure procedure – costumes, postures, modes and anatomy could be rendered with freedom and facility. This does not mean that the Black Figure style died out. Though lacking the flexibility of Red Figure, it was used to explore a range of interesting genre scenes (as on the Taleides Painter's amphora and on a lekythos in the manner of the very delicate master known as the Amasis Painter), and it continued to present outdoor p. 11 (5) activities – for instance ships at sea, as on the Nicosthenic cylix, women drawing water and the Antimenes

Painter's trim olive-gathering. In such directions Black p. 21 (23) Figure painters could still point the way.

It was, however, with the Red Figure artists that the future lay, for the figures that they painted seem to acquire solidity in the enveloping space. Mythological subjects of course retained all their attraction, though as in the Black Figure there was an increasing interest in more homely or intimate scenes from everyday life in which the newly achieved command of the detail and interaction of parts of the human body was shown to advantage. By the early 5th century the exciting new schemes with torsion of the trunk and foreshortening of limbs had been absorbed in the standard repertory of Red Figure painters (as on the Foundry Painter's cylix); the rendering then became less emphatic and veered rather towards gracefulness with a touch of mannerism (as on Sotades' knucklebone).

After about 480 BC spontaneity was fading. In fact it seems as though a gap was opening between the vase painters in the workshops and artists who were developing a major pictorial style on wall surfaces and panels; of the latter we have only some names and the odd description. Beautiful, delicate paintings are of course to be found on vases of later date, but the general impression is that their painters were no longer the leading artists of their day.

Among the outstanding masters of a couple of generations may be named the Andocides Painter, who was the pioneer of Red Figure, Euphronius and Euthymides, who exploited the possibilities of pose and action, and the powerful Cleophrades Painter, who is now known to have been named Epictetus; of artists who preferred to paint the elegant drinking cups, an earlier Epictetus whose mastery of drawing was unsurpassed, and, impassioned in his earlier work, the Brygos Painter. A facile cylix painter in the earlier 5th century was Douris, whose mastery of line can be seen on p. 65. While painting, sometimes quite ambitious as well as of high quality, carried the Red Figure on into full classical times, a fresh and attractive sideline was the white ground ware, decorated with washes of fugitive colour – a genre in which the Achilles Painter excelled with his funerary lekythoi.

Sculptors also had ceased to be satisfied with the archaic frontality. To stand rigidly is a strain. We find relief in shifting the weight more on to one leg, and this causes asymmetry (one hip not only raised but pushed out, with a consequent curvature of the median line and eventually even a displacement of the shoulders). In Greek art this resulted in a scheme of what we can call 'ponderation'. As factors like this intruded, the artists broke the bounds of the archaic and parted company from all previous art traditions. For the first time a classical art was coming into being.

The 'Critian Boy' is so named because of its close p. 123 (19) resemblance to the statues of the Athenian Tyrannicides of which Roman copies in marble are to be seen in the Naples Museum; the stiff, unresponsive, pigeon-chested torsos, straight-sided faces, and shallow jaw-

The 'Blond Boy', the head from a statue of just before 480 BC; yellow paint on the hair was noticeable at the time of discovery. The statue must have been less symmetrical than the Critian Boy (p. 123, pl. 18) to judge by the tilt of the head.

line provide the connection. The Tyrannicides, we are told, were sculpted (in bronze) by Critius and Nesiotes after the Athenians returned home in 479 BC; the Critian boy had recently been set up on the Acropolis when the Persians sacked Athens in 480. In this original we have a fine example of the art of about 480 – for a more moving head that was also almost brand new then we can turn to the 'Blond Boy' (for all we know this could have been a work of the young Phidias). A new seriousness is appearing in art; the frills and smiling charm of the bespangled Acropolis maidens have faded away – much that was very beautiful went with them.

*Reconstruction of the east front of the Temple of Zeus at Olympia.
The pediment shows the chariot race between Pelops (on the left)
and the old King Oenomaus (on the right). Between them stands
Zeus. The figure of Pelops' seer, here shown beside the left-hand
chariot, should be placed next to the river god with a charioteer to the
right of him.*

The Early Classical ('Severe Style') could be said to
run from the 480s to beyond 450 BC. At the beginning
we have the Berlin Painter, with his powerful spot-lit
figures, and the sculptor Critius. At the end we have
Myron, whose *tour de force*, the Discus-thrower (known
only in copies), is an action figure that is only
superficially more realistic than his Satyr Marsyas
'reculant pour mieux bondir'; and in painting we have
p. 121
(12) vases like the Niobid Painter's which leave us in no
doubt that a major art of painting with perspective of a
sort had arrived (the name that is specially associated
with this development is Polygnotus of Thasos). As
Gisela Richter pointed out, the Early Classical generation was one of experiment. For the most part its faces
are uninteresting; the emphasis was on the effects of
motion and stress on human anatomy and musculature
– in the end this leads to the balanced Polyclitan canon.

But much that is new was attempted, though not always
with success (as for instance the three-quarter view in
the Persepolis 'Penelope' or the knees of Athena in the
Birds metope at Olympia), and there are completely
new ventures: ground lines giving counterfeit depth to
landscape, veristic portraiture (to judge by the copy
named Themistocles, in which an inquiring mind in a p. 123
wise old head is rendered within the plain form- (23)
structure of the Severe Style), and perhaps the female
nude (again in a Roman copy – the Esquiline Venus –
which has some of the austerity of a male body).
Possibly the Olympia sculptures show awareness of the
new pictorial trend.

Copies can be misleading, quite apart from the fact
that they were usually made in marble for Roman
patrons whereas the classical originals had mostly been
cast in bronze. In the study of Greek art much ingenuity
has been devoted over the years to identifying in such
hack-work the statues and groups named by ancient
writers and so staking out claims for the famous
masters. As an example we have an original (Procne and
Itys) that is attested as the work of Alcamenes (one of
the two most famous masters who were junior colleagues of Phidias), but it does not seem to fit
particularly well with the notional artistic personality

that has been conjured up for him. It is perhaps more rewarding at this stage to turn our attention to bodies of original work that survive.

The temple sculptures at Olympia date more or less to the 460s. Though more than one hand may be recognized, a single individual's style seems to be impressed on the twelve metopes and two pediments of which large parts were recovered by excavation. The metopes all showed labours of Herakles. The hero thus appeared a dozen times, and the effect could have been monotonous. But not only is the composition of the action scenes well varied, but Herakles differs in age between the lad who rests exhausted after his struggle with the Nemean lion and the mature man of the Atlas metope, and, as Ashmole has demonstrated, his facial expression varies from absorption in the delicate task of playing Cerberus like an angler to the fierce excitement of battle and to disgust – the pinched nostrils – in the Augean dung-yard near Olympia. The picturesque Stymphalian Birds metope has an almost idyllic flavour; in the Atlas metope, where a less relaxed Athena lends a steadying hand, the giant's huge frame is well brought out at chest level (one is reminded of the 'Atlantean shoulders' of Milton's Satan in *Paradise Lost*).

The east pediment shows the ethos of the Early Classical. The young Pelops has arrived as a suitor for the hand of King Oenomaus' daughter; in the legend he must compete in a chariot race with Oenomaus; all the previous suitors have been overtaken and killed by the king. The venue is no doubt the altar of Zeus at Olympia, but in the pediment it is the god himself who stands there, unseen by the contestants. The first thing we are expected to notice is that the god is twitching his mantle. We turn to the old king, who stands on the god's left (our right), a stiff torso contrasted with the supple young suitor. The king's lips are parted; evidently, as Rodenwaldt pointed out, he is uttering some blasphemy that displeases the god. Pelops and his team are making the first moves to set out. A reclining river god fills the space in either corner: on the left (south) Alpheus flowing in a great sweep, on the right the mountain stream perkily watching, a succession of ripples forming his outline. Next to the latter is a young lad squatting. At first sight his pose does not look convincing, but Ashmole matched it exactly with a newspaper photograph of a young teenage girl waiting her turn in a swimming competition – a waiting position. The two household prophets or seers sit on the ground. Faces here are fairly impassive. But we can read the elation in the seer on Pelops' side from his uplifted head and eyes and the arm that was raised. Oenomaus' balding seer has a different vision of his master's future. Hand to cheek and brow furrowed, he contemplates impending disaster. Thus, static as the figures seem to be, the scene is charged with psychological tension; it is the moment before the storm breaks. As a foil to the old seer, the boy sits by the water's edge, too young to sense the atmosphere; he waits, and for something to do he fiddles with his toe.

p. 123 (20–22)

Above: one of the seers from the east pediment. He is watching his master, Oenomaus. His pose, hand to cheek, and doom-laden expression show that he foresees disaster. The stream god, Kladeos (below), at the right-hand end of the pediment, was matched by a figure in the opposite corner personifying the bigger river Alpheus.

In the more distant parts of the Greek world the archaic values still lingered on with a fugitive grace. In relief especially, figures were deployed with extended curving outlines to fill the space, and close repetitive patterns contrasted with gently modulated plain areas made the surface of the marble a joy to behold. Such old-world reliefs were made in places like Thessaly and the Greek west. A splendid example is the well known p. 130 'Ludovisi Throne', probably not a great deal earlier than 450 BC and possibly from Locri, in the toe of Italy. Presumably intended as a fender for an altar or a sacred pit, it has an apparent counterpart in the 'Boston Throne' but the blend of archaic and Early Classical is different, and the central figure on the Boston piece stands in the new 'ponderation' scheme. With this we must be nearing the time when work on the Parthenon was started.

The age of Pericles

In 448 BC Athens was an imperial power. A treaty had been made with Persia. Thirty years had elapsed since the allies swore not to rebuild the wrecked temples. Pericles unilaterally rescinded the oath, and work on the Parthenon commenced next year under the general direction of Phidias. If we were to believe Xenophon and above all Plato – not to mention later writers – we might suppose that craftsmen like Phidias were of inferior social standing; inscriptions do seem to show sculptors and architects being paid the ordinary wages of artisans or not much more. But Pericles did not look down on Phidias; and we have plenty of evidence from the Analatos Painter onward that leading artists and architects did not feel all that humble. Some will have been prosperous as manufacturers or tradesmen; some will have been successful as what we should call entrepreneurs and taken on fee-paying pupils; and some were evidently affluent as well as socially acceptable. Sculpture and painting in particular often ran in families.

p. 126 (26) The Parthenon was to be the temple of imperial Athena. Its sculptural decoration was lavish (92 metopes, 524 feet (160 metres) of running frieze, and two great pediments); it was completed in no more than fifteen years. The need for sculptors must have been enormous. Calculations like Schuchhardt's of the numbers involved could be misleading because the local or inherited characteristics of an artist's style might be altered by working in a team; but certainly, as the inscribed building accounts seem to confirm, some dozens of sculptors will have been at work, and many must have come to Athens from other parts of the Greek world.

pp. 126–7 (27) The metopes symbolize the struggles of Greek civilization against aggressors and forces of the wild; these were traditional themes. Those of the south side, depicting Lapiths and Centaurs in combat, chance to be in much the best condition. In them we can see the raw material from which Phidias had to form a team. Best preserved is the so-called Critian metope. The forms are

142

The goddess Athena pensively contemplates an upright stele – perhaps a list of Athenians fallen in battle. Despite the rigid folds of the skirt this little relief must date well into the second quarter of the 5th century.

firm and clear. But the tight, barrel-shaped trunk and straight-sided, shallow jaw belong to the tradition of Critius, so the sculptor was working in what by this time was an out-dated style. There are some metopes in which, though the Centaur's face is less mask-like, the carving or the action is inert or feeble: so sculptors of mediocre skill. Others look more advanced. The first metope – still visible on the building in our time – is quite crisply executed; but the head and shoulders of the Centaur show a nobler conception and bolder chiselling – this is where Schweitzer envisaged Phidias coming up to the Parthenon one day and pausing long enough to demonstrate how the marble should be carved.

The rest of the Parthenon sculptures were more directly concerned with the goddess, Athena. The east pediment showed her miraculous birth from the head of Zeus, the west her contest with Posidon for the patronage of Athens. The frieze, which ran along the outer wall of the inner building, depicted what is presumably the birthday procession at the Panathenaic festival in honour of the goddess, beginning with the forming-up in the Kerameikos and ending with the presentation of the new robe in the presence of the Olympians. This is worth closer study.

The carving of the frieze would seem to have started at the west end; Ashmole suggests that an older group of sculptors was at work there than in the east. The central pair of slabs over the west doorway had to be a show-piece. Lord Elgin did not remove the west frieze, and the middle-aged cavalry officer there has since lost p. 126 (29) his head (now known only from the Elgin cast). But whether we regard the vigour of the composition and movement of man and steed, the plastic quality of the bodily forms, the spirit of the horse and creases of its hide, or the swirl of cloth in the wind as the man brings his mount under control, the mastery of carving is unsurpassed. The next slab (to the right), with the bold, big-featured forms of two cantering riders, has a similar grandeur. If we are to look for the style of the Phidias of the 440s there are no more likely examples to be found. The block next on the left is a creditable imitation of this master style. But the neighbouring ones shade off into fuzzier forms and fussy, more timorous carving; here we presumably have pupils or apprentices working alongside a great master.

Towards the left end of the frieze came a different sculptor, perhaps not an Athenian. He had mastered the new ponderation scheme; but it is overdone and given too much air, so the young boy is crowded against the right edge of the slab. Though damaged, however, the p. 126 (28) cavalryman's head has a grandeur of its own; so this seems likely to have been a sculptor of some standing who was capable of being absorbed into the common style. Not so the sculptor of a slab towards the other end of the west frieze. The extended forms flung in sweeping curves and the contrast of smooth surfaces and close-set repetitive patterns might be at home in Ionia or Thessaly, or the world of the Ludovisi Throne. Evocative though they are, these forms are out of place on the Parthenon; since this distinctive fashion does not re-appear, this artist was probably not kept on as work on the Parthenon progressed.

The greater part of the long sides of the frieze is taken up with the cavalcade. Here the massed cavalry ride past with an easy seat, overlapping each other so that they seem to be six or seven deep (colour of course helped to distinguish the horses). Working side by side and helping one another over the transition, the sculptors will have become a team, so we may think of the cavalcade as the anvil on which the Parthenon style was forged. This style proved to be a more relaxed one than the Early Classical, with physical and mental tensions being resolved. At points on the frieze the individualist breaks through. Where the procession was not yet fully

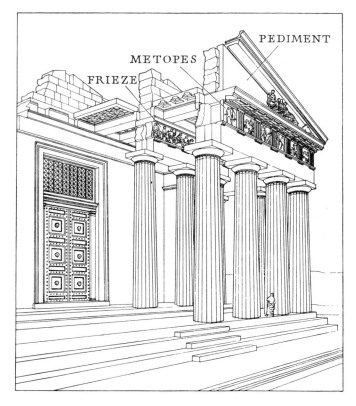

Reconstruction of the east front of the Parthenon, showing the original position of the sculpture. The frieze, high up and badly lit, would have been hard to see even when brightly coloured.

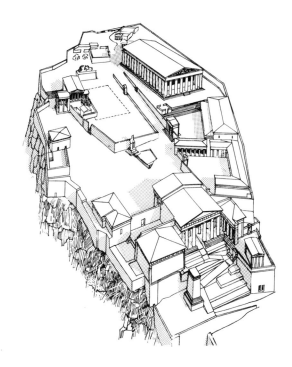

The Acropolis of Athens, with its 5th-century and later cult buildings and monuments. Entering through the Propylaea, the visitor was faced with the great bronze statue of Athena Promachos ('the Defender') by Phidias. Further back were the Erechtheum (left) and the Parthenon (right).

under way a rider is waiting for his companion to have his belt adjusted. He turns back with an agonized expression – others are riding past and they are losing their place; in his frustration he seems to do what only wounded Amazons normally do in Greek sculpture – he scratches his head. At another point a chariot is coming up too fast; a marshal has run out with upraised arm to flag it down, but at the last moment he has to spring back out of the road, revealing a figure that is becoming corpulent.

The central slabs at the east end had the place of honour and were no doubt carved by the most adept sculptors available. Unfortunately, those over the entrance, which showed the climax of the ceremony (the handing over of Athena's new robe – surely not, as some scholars these days imagine, the disposal of the old one), had provided the Turks with target practice before Lord Elgin removed them, and the faces of these supposedly most potent of Christian saints have been shot away. Next to the centre Athena pulls a leg back and presses with her hand on the seat – like Priam on the François crater – as she rises to thank those who are honouring her. The other deities are relatively less damaged. The carving is high-class, and two artistic personalities emerge within the confines of the Parthenon style – one perhaps volatile, the other more majestic.

p. 126 (30) On the slab to the left are four deities. Hermes sits at the end, one foot drawn in (and sun hat on knee), ready to speed on an errand. Beyond an over-familiar Dionysus and an immobile earth-goddess sits the war god, Ares. He is rocking himself with his hands clasped round his knee, his eyes scanning the horizon for battles that might be more to his liking than this birthday p. 126 (31) party. On the other block Posidon sits rather stiffly – a naval man ashore. Apollo turns round easily to make a remark, his face in three-quarter view. Artemis discreetly hitches her dress on her shoulder; and beyond that was Aphrodite reclining more languidly, with her son Eros under his mother's parasol.

These figures are mostly 'classics'. Hermes and Ares are to re-appear in these precise poses in statues perhaps of Lysippus' school. Posidon is a model for grave reliefs of the next generation. The three-quarter face could have inspired the greatest of die-engravers. Praxiteles' statue of Artemis for her Brauronion sanctuary on the Acropolis clipped up her dress on her shoulder, and the seated goddesses helped to provide a model for a long succession of personifications that are familiar down to the present day. Thus the Parthenon style is the classical style par excellence. In the outcome, for better or worse, local styles of sculpture in Greece vanished. With artists now drilled in a common tradition, European art was set on a highway; and from Athens sculptors carried it beyond the limits of the Greek lands.

The Parthenon crowns the Acropolis in a way that no hexastyle (six-column) temple could have done. By having an eight-column façade it sits there broad and ample. It was a headache to its architect Ictinus, who went on modifying his design as the work progressed. Practically every block in it is unique so as to fit the tilts and curvatures. Such extravagance could never be afforded again. Of the other Periclean buildings on the Acropolis, the Propylaea (monumental gateway), whose architect was Mnesicles, has cleaner lines and a stronger accentuation enhanced by courses of dark stone; and the Erechtheum, the joint shrine to Athena and Posidon, which lies to the north of the Parthenon, has its problems solved in the same crisp sort of way. Contemporary with the Parthenon, the 'Theseum', a p. 127 (32) temple on the low brow above the Agora in Athens, has been recognized by Dinsmoor as the work of an architect who also built temples at Sunium and Rhamnus; he was especially interested in making his peristyles lofty, to the point that with each successive temple he had increasing difficulty in finding space for his rafters. In fact Periclean architecture was the work of three or four great masters. The day of the bulbous forms that we enjoy at Corinth, Seilinus, Agrigentum, and Paestum was of course past; the Periclean architects perfected the Doric, and though an excellent scheme of proportions was devised in the 4th century (especially at Epidaurus) the subsequent development of Doric was in the direction of skimpiness. The Ionic order, voluptuous and admitting great diversity in Archaic times, was remodelled by the Periclean architects in an elegant, somewhat prim formulation which the eastern Greeks adopted and played their own variations on in the 4th century. In due course the Corinthian capital was added to the repertory.

Within the limits of a columniate architecture that eschewed the arch and vault classical Athens established the norms that were to be applied not only to temples but to the whole range of buildings that served for public purposes. The models of the Athenian Agora and the Hellenistic upper city of Pergamon give some idea of the versatility – and also the limitations – of this long-lived architectural tradition. The most evident secular form was the long multi-purpose building called the Stoa, which had an ambulatory behind the façade and could have its rear part subdivided for shops or other uses; in the 4th century two-storeyed stoas became common, and Ionic columns came to be used for an inner colonnade or for the upper storey because at that time they could give greater height in relation to their diameter. Various other types of building were designed to meet the different needs of the Greek city: council chambers, courts, theatres and concert halls, altar precincts, gymnasiums and fountains.

After the Parthenon was finished there were many sculptors at large, whose handiwork we see in the beautiful grave reliefs and in carved monuments from the western Peloponnese to Lycia. The most striking development is in drapery which clings to the body and sets up complex decorative patterns with chain-reaction folds. In painting we hear of famous names like Zeuxis and of advances in shading.

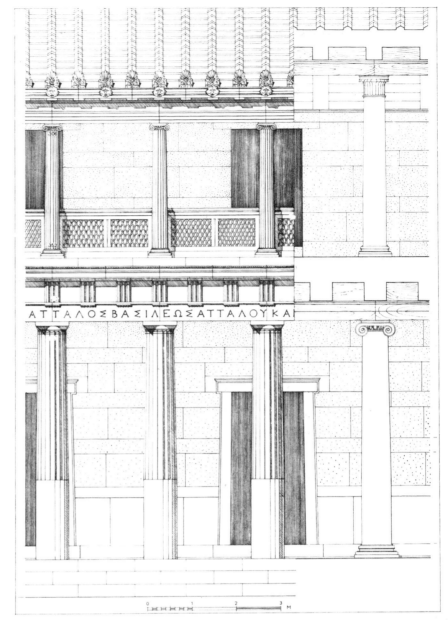

Model and elevation of the stoa of Attalos at Athens. Attalos was a king of Pergamon who died in 138 BC. The stoa, or covered colonnade, that he gave to Athens uses the Doric order on the outside of the lower storey, Ionic within (shown on the right of the cut-away diagram). The upper storey has a smaller Ionic order and one with an unusual Pergamene leaf-capital. The stoa overlooks the Agora.

The 4th century sought a more personal relationship between gods and men. This sorrowing Demeter from Cnidus, with her calm gaze and restless drapery, seems to communicate her pathos to the worshipper.

After the high classical: emotion and realism

By the second quarter of the 4th century creative new modes were appearing in sculpture, allied to closer imitation of nature. With Praxiteles we associate an almost indolent standing pose with a sinuous median line and a less pronounced demarcation of the areas of the trunk which allows a softer and smoother treatment p. 170 of the surface. Praxiteles also set a new fashion with his (3) Aphrodite of Cnidus, the first of a long series of nudes of the goddess in which the female form was studied and understood. His Hermes with the infant Dionysus at Olympia has a dreamy, abstracted look, but other statues of deities of this time seem to show a new rapport with the worshipper, and personifications become more numerous. In contrast to the impassivity of the 5th century, feeling and emotion are often shown in features and pose, especially on grave reliefs. Deep-set, up-straining eyes with a 'bloodhound' look impart a sense of strain which is commonly associated by scholars with the sculptor Scopas. Some of this 4th-century sculpture was superbly executed, witness the so-called 'Aberdeen head' in the British Museum with its exceptional feeling for the texture of the skin, the subtly modelled bronze boy from the sea off Marathon, the Hermes at Olympia just mentioned and a couple of marvellously soft and seductive Praxitelean heads. p. 171 Marble originals such as the so-called Mausolus from (6) Halicarnassus and the Demeter of Cnidus show how stretched and bunched drapery can enhance the expressiveness of a calm but compelling countenance.

The sculptor Lysippus, who worked from the middle decades of the 4th century until almost its end, probably had as much influence on the Hellenistic as Praxiteles. He introduced a new canon for the human figure, making heads smaller and legs longer; and he positioned limbs and head in such a way that, with more space being occupied in the third dimension, his statues present more than a single frontal view and no longer seem quite at rest.

Painting did not lag far behind. To judge by Roman copies such as those after an original showing Perseus and Andromeda which may very reasonably be attributed to Nicias (who also did the painting of Praxiteles' statues), artists by this time could paint figures that look nearly as three-dimensional as statues, arrange them in favoured mythological groups, and give them some architectural or atmospheric setting. Unfortunately, mosaic, which can be durable, had limitations as a medium, and we depend too much for our knowledge of the ancient masterpieces on what are mainly provincial Roman renderings painted on the walls of houses and villas of the skirts of Vesuvius. As regards the great Greek painters who are named in the literature, the style of the most famous master of all, Apelles, is, as Robertson frankly admits, quite lost to us. Individual pieces give some inkling of what Greek

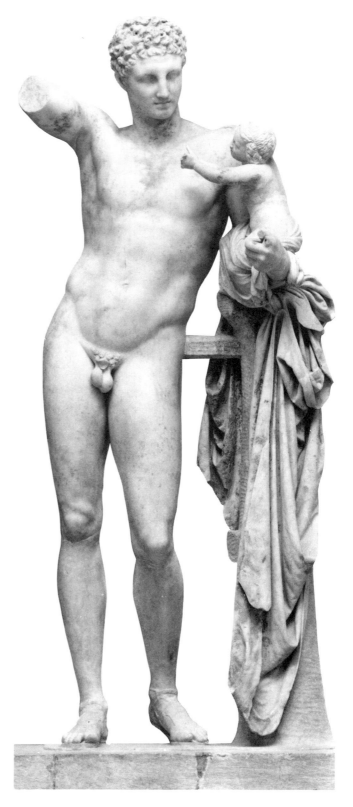

The Hermes of Praxiteles, seen by the traveller Pausanias in the Temple of Hera at Olympia and excavated there in 1877, is thought by some experts to be a Roman copy or a work by a Hellenistic sculptor of the same name. The sinuous pose and the god's absorption in play with the infant Dionysus make the group a study rather than an object of veneration.

147

The so-called 'Aberdeen head', with its exceptionally delicate modelling of the flesh and the impression of fleeting emotion, probably belongs to the Praxitelean tradition.

masters achieved; it is evident that they used chiaroscuro and a sort of perspective. Current discoveries at Vergina in Macedonia should shed fresh light on this.

Christine Havelock has written of the Hellenistic as the first 'modern' art – 'sometimes nostalgic, sometimes revolutionary, at one time austere, at another intimate, comprehending the human tragedy and also the comedy'. This covers a wide range. As a pupil of Rhys Carpenter she would probably not agree with the further formulation that though there is a greater diversity of modes than in the pre-Parthenon era there is now one underlying style – the 'common style' – and thus it is almost impossible to assign works of Hellenistic art to clearly defined epochs.

In sculpture the tradition of Praxiteles and his sons and of Lysippus with his long-limbed athletes continued into the 3rd century. One noticeable advance is the deployment of arms and legs and the turning of bodies so that the figures occupy more space in the third dimension and present different worthwhile views; extreme forms of such torsion are a young satyr turning to inspect his tail, maenads or dancers pirouetting, and Aphrodite trying to scrutinize her behind. Not only do the female nude and semi-nude demand seductive new postures, but children are studied in their own right rather than as diminutive adults – in fact by the late 5th century the podgy toddler was already appearing in funerary art. Sentimentality takes its place with the infant tormenting the family pet, or hermaphrodites, or Cupid and Psyche making innocent love. Much of Hellenistic sculpture is of course wearisome: athletes, benefactors, and civic dignitaries of both sexes who had to be commemorated even if they paid the sculptor's

bill themselves, and, for instance, Muses reinterpreted according to the taste and fashion of the generation.

One of the most striking of the new modes was the brutal realism that appears in genre renderings of dropouts: the bibulous old trot as drained out as the decanter she holds, the hunchback dwarf, the emaciated fisherman, the teetering market woman with her basket, or finally the punch-drunk pugilist. Raddled muscle-bound statues of Herakles after Lysippus almost come into that category. Even portraits of philosophers often have a similar feel – indeed Webster referred to them as 'another kind of Old Derelict'. In the normal way, though the Ostia Themistocles seems to contradict the generalization, classical portraiture had been idealistic (the head of Pericles, for instance, though more or less contemporary, was rendered Olympian-looking to portray the ideal statesman, and the posthumous Sophocles was intended to depict, in Lawrence's phrase, 'the well-fed, well-dressed utterer of dignified platitudes'). Socrates was a more controversial figure to whom rival sects could lay claim; posthumous portraits of him vary from his recorded physiognomy – what we might call Xenophon's Socrates – to the high-brow Academician and the pugnacious Cynic of the statuette in the British Museum. And it has to be admitted that we have only a hazy idea what Alexander the Great looked like. In the middle of the Hellenistic period veristic portraiture seems to have established itself; we have likenesses of some Hellenistic rulers or men of note, as also of Romans later on, that can be thought of as genuinely true to life.

p. 170 (5)

p. 100

The Hellenistic diffusion

Alexandria became the greatest centre of the Hellenistic world. The Muses were the patrons or personifications of literature and learning, and in Alexandria, where the liberal arts were munificently endowed by the Ptolemies, the great cultural centre was called 'Museum'. Scholar-writers and specialists were assembled in one of the biggest brain-drain operations of all time, while literary texts and old masters were collected or copied. This cultural movement was diffused in such a way that the Greek-speaking populace was drawn within its orbit and could see and admire all sorts of works of art and decor. One of the favourite Alexandrian modes was nostalgic – the feeling for the country and the wild (not least satyrs) among people who no longer had roots outside the city.

The age was becoming one of what Gibbon would call 'critics, compilers, and commentators' – people not to be despised, because it is largely to their efforts that we owe western humanism. In the end backward-looking classicism would prevail. But creative vigour was not yet spent, and in the two generations around 200 BC, Hellenistic art in fact reached a climax under the patronage of the Attalids.

The upstart dynasty of Pergamon converted a minor principality into a kingdom after Attalus I defeated the marauding Galatians (Gauls) in a great battle about

*The creative vigour generated by late classical sculptors culminated in
the battle of gods and giants on the main frieze of the Great Altar
at Pergamon, where the familiar theme of civilization versus
barbarism erupts with a new violence. It celebrated the victory of the
Pergamenes over the Gauls and was erected about 180 BC.*

230 BC and made western Asia Minor safe for the Greeks. This victory – a second Marathon – made Pergamon a second Athens and the Attalids before long assumed the appropriate cultural role. Almost certainly the Dying Gaul of the Capitoline is a copy of a statue from a circular monument set up at Pergamon, whose centrepiece was the Ludovisi Gaul (a defeated chieftain killing his wife and then himself). The sculptors' response was equal to the heroic occasion. The human body in action had been studied with attention (as for instance in wrestlers); here a savage grandeur combines with the resources of artistic realism to raise Hellenistic art to a higher plane. To the 'baroque' movement centred on Pergamon we probably owe some of the most vigorous works of which copies survive, such as the Pasquino Group, the flayed satyr Marsyas, the p. 171 Barberini Faun (perhaps an original), and, overstep-
(8) ping the limits of human compassion, the Laocoon.

The capital of the Pergamene kingdom had to have everything: a library rivalling that of Alexandria and presided over by an adaptation of Phidias' Athena Parthenos; a grand theatre for the Dionysiac festivals; a spa or medical school with its own Asklepios (healing god); international games in honour of Athena the Victory-bringer; a piped water-supply feeding not only the city but the high citadel; and an elaborate code of regulations for streets and buildings, fountains and cisterns, and drains and refuse clearance. It had a closed harbour on the coast at Elaea, highways thirty feet wide in the countryside, and an oracular sanctuary of Apollo and repository for treaties at Gryneum down the coast. The minor arts were catered for by industrialized towns – terracotta figurines at Myrina, 'Megarian' relief bowls at Cyme, and finally the new sigillata (red glaze) pottery at Pitane.

The Attalids maintained teams of architects, master craftsmen, and landscape-gardeners; their ambitious projects extended within the Pergamene kingdom and outside it. Individual temples did not now offer the same scope for originality; one no longer feels that, as in the 4th-century Ionic, each building is a work of art in itself. The one famous architect of Ionia in Perga-mene times, Hermogenes, created temples whose design seems too theoretically contrived. But buildings were now being organized in complexes which adapted themselves to contours and different levels without yet creating too self-contained an environment. The upper p. 193 city of Pergamon was a summit of Hellenistic planning.

Pergamon also had to have a historical mythology of its own. Among its known cult figures we can recognize local eponyms, as Halisarna and Teuthras from neighbouring castles, Gyrnus from Gryneum, and the stream Selinus. But the founding hero whom they appropriated was Telephus, in the Greek legends a natural son of Herakles. Exposed in the mountains of Arcadia, Telephus had reputedly been suckled by a hind and in due course discovered by his father – this is depicted in the well known painting found at Her-p. 128 culaneum. Searching for his lost mother, the hero came (33) to Aeolis, where he presently became king; Achilles was also involved in the old myth, so in Telephus the Attalids had a founder with a legend that could carry back to both Herakles and the Trojan War.

The royal library was the greatest glory of Per-gamon. But its most spectacular monument was the Great Altar erected on an intermediate terrace of the upper city. It is generally thought to date after 189 BC. The great external frieze with its battle of gods against giants must symbolize the might of Pergamon embatt-led in defence of Greek civilization. The figures are over-lifesize and in high relief. The frieze ran for 365 feet (111 metres), so deep research by the scholars of Pergamon was needed to discover enough deities and giants with names and appropriate attributes (accord-ing to Erika Simon not only Hesiod's *Theogony* but also Stoic cosmological beliefs were a principal source). The relief is superbly executed, with the repertory of Greek art ransacked for postures, costumes and muscles that can be brought into play. But the effort is too stupendous; only a passionate viewer could rejoice with the victors, or even sympathize with the van-quished giants as we do with the Gauls. As one looks at the serpent-bodied giants it seems appropriate that the battle on what the Apocalypse calls Satan's Seat should terminate in what Milton called a 'dismal universal hiss'.

Rhys Carpenter and his followers have argued that the 2nd century BC witnessed a 'Classic Renaissance' in Greek art comparable to the High Classical of the 5th century. But this involved him in appropriating to it a range of masterpieces that are normally assigned to earlier epochs, some of which are too securely dated by the circumstances of their discovery. This is in fact a timely demonstration of the ineffectuality of stylistic dating in later Greek art. In the main, however, it would seem that the trend in the later Hellenistic was towards classicism. Great technical skill survived; many Greek artists continued to be actively employed; increasingly it was Romans who called the tune. As we look back at it, not the least of the achievements of Greek art was diuturnity coeval with the civilization from which it sprang.

5
The Foundations of Literature
*poetry and prose from Homer
to the gospels*

PETER LEVI

THE EARLY GREEK PROSE and poetry we have are bound to be impressive to us, if only because they show a stage and also a range of human development which are not so well documented anywhere else. The fact that the Greeks learnt to read and write is a cause as well as an effect of that development, and Greek society even as written history and poetry first reveal it was in a headlong process of change. To us the most thrilling thing about Greek literature, even more so than about archaic Latin, is its mere earliness: these writers have become fully articulate and even philosophic when in some ways their thoughts are still primitively forceful, and a preliterate skeleton often underlies their cleverest literary devices. Because of the fact that only written language has a chance of surviving to be rediscovered, and so to influence a new future, most of European literature has been built on these shaky, chance foundations, and the early Greek writers appear to us now haloed with a special purity and originality. Once writing became widespread, writers mulled over what was already written and reproduced it.

But even the *Iliad* and the *Odyssey* mark the closing stages of a long process. Even if they were really the achievement of poets in a single generation in the 8th century BC, none the less they owe their marvellous strength to the unrecorded life of a society in which no one could read or write. Norse and Anglo-Saxon and Serbian and French and central Asian poetry combine to persuade us that simpler Iliads and Odysseys must have been composed in many parts of the world and in many centuries, before the art of writing made these unique poems possible, just when the social changes that go with the art of writing brought the living tradition of heroic poetry to an end in Greece.

Greek literature was always overshadowed by Homer and nourished by the Homeric poems in many ways. Moral philosophy as we understand it appears to begin as a criticism of Homer and his gods, though Homer speaks of the gods by no means without irony. Indeed in his poetry even dawn and dusk are ironic. Socrates redefines Homeric virtue. Tragedy, the greatest literary invention of the Greeks, depends so heavily on Homer that one may be justified in regarding the Greek theatre as a simple substitute for living epic performance, retaining as it does many features of its plot and style. Later Greek and Roman narrative art,

certainly in verse but even in prose as well, was constantly wrestling with Homer's ghost. History was epic in tone before it was theatrical. In order to be great, even Virgil felt he had to be a second Homer, and in some passages of the *Aeneid* was fatally driven by critics of the *Iliad* and the *Odyssey* to try to improve on his original.

And yet there must always have been lyric poets and work-songs and folksongs, even before there was Homer. Epic is already not a pure but rather a mixed form; it contains poetry of many kinds. The Homeric hexameter, the long line with which Greek epic poetry is built, was very likely developed out of lyric verse. The lyrics we have are later than Homer: they seem to us as crisp as untrodden snow, but that is a quality every fresh civilization or language re-invents. It is intimately connected with the freshness of music, but of Greek music we know very little. It is also true that from the first moment we meet it, with Archilochus in the 7th century, Greek lyric poetry is already as supple, as sharp, as dramatic and as fragrant as it will ever become. It has already, as Aristotle says of tragedy, attained its nature. Lyric poetry itself does not seem subject to the laws of evolution, although social evolution affects the conditions of its performance, conscripting it into the ceremonial choir, confining it in the end to theatres and dinner parties, confusing it with experimental music, and making of it a bookish art. But it never quite dies, and modest popular lyrics were still being written in late Greek.

The early Greek lyric poets from Archilochus on (mid-7th century) wrote in strong and sensuously sharp sentences about what most concerned them – the experience of war, quarrels realistically treated, drink, eros and seduction, the dangerous sea, and the refreshment of all the senses. The verses they sang to one another have the shameless straightness of slightly drunken conversation, and must have merged easily with the prolonged celebrations of the warrior class. The simple and confident technique of Alcaeus and Sappho (about 600 BC) gives them a crispness and purity to this day. Songs to the gods are reverent, charming and brief. They lack both Homer's irony and his grandeur. Some of the later, anonymous lyrics show a touch of youthful sentimentality. 'Drink with me, sow wild oats with me, be in love, wear a crown of flowers with me, be crazy when I am, sober when I am.' Yet the metre makes that a touching little poem in Greek, as the music transfigures a German student song. And in its final form, in 6th-century choral narrative and choral religious poetry, and finally in Pindar's work, the Greek lyric created poetry of a formality, variety and sheer power that have seldom been understood or rivalled except by Milton and by Hölderlin. Complexity can be learnt, but inner simplicity is irrecoverable.

The flowering of drama

It is important not to forget that the tragic theatre had its roots in lyric poetry as well as in Homer, and that all three of the great tragic poets of the 5th century were working in lyric as well as in narrative verse. The mysteriously controlled pace and time-scale of tragedy were surely determined by music and by ritual dancing. The greatest writer of tragic lyrics was Aeschylus. His language is bold and powerful; that of Sophocles is intense but often more perplexed; Euripides is more obviously 'lyrical' and all but romantic, yet his lyrics are less memorable, less strong, for all their beauty. It is typical of Browning to be arrested by 'a chorus-ending from Euripides'. The theology, let alone the poetry of Aeschylus is too strong for him, as his translation of the *Agamemnon* shows. The development of tragedy from its first beginnings to the dazzling and bemusing complexity of late Euripides within so brief a period as a hundred years is extraordinary. Aeschylus gives some impression of quite an early stage of tragedy. He saw the democracy of Athens and almost the art of tragedy and its poetry come to birth; he fought at Marathon, and died in 456 BC. Both Sophocles and Euripides lived to be very old; they each experienced most of the years of the 5th century, though we have no play by Sophocles before the forties, and none by Euripides before the thirties.

The most impressive quality of Greek tragedy is its tough and innocent openness of mind, its proverbial wisdom and compassion, and its absolute seriousness.

It was an art of public performance, and very direct in spite of its formalities. Like all theatrical art ever since, it was largely created by the expectations of its audience, for better and for worse. The tension it conveys between men and gods, heroes and their fate, catastrophe and religion, was inherited from Homer, and intensified by unity of action. The theatre is a magnifying glass. When the action of the gods appears in the theatre at Athens, suddenly the gods become subject to severe human judgment. All the same, they remain real and terrifying. Popular wisdom is like that of the tragic chorus: it is not intellectually daring except in the articulation of despair. The heroes who suffer are remote from ordinary humanity. All the same, the phrase of the chorus from *Oedipus the King* 'Call no man fortunate till he is dead' is a message for mankind, a proverb among other proverbs. It is like a liturgical text.

The characters of the tragic heroes are intensely fixed in powerful poetry; many devices of language unite to the same effect. Character hardly shows development during a given play except from an already grave to a blind or a bleeding face. That is because all the persons wear masks. Herakles goes mad or suffers anguish, Hippolytus dies, Oedipus is blinded. Almost all violence happens offstage, presumably because it could hardly be fitted into the formal gestures and acting style that the masks dictated. When violence on the stage does occur, when the crowd turns against Agamemnon's murderers or when Hippolytus dies

The Oresteia tells how Agamemnon, returning from Troy, was murdered by his wife, Clytemnestra; how their daughter Electra remained in mourning while her brother Orestes fled and grew to manhood; how Orestes returned and avenged his father by killing Clytemnestra and her lover Aegisthus; and how he was pursued by the Furies for the sin of matricide. Left: a terracotta plaque showing the return of Orestes to find Electra at her father's grave. Right: the murder of Aegisthus, from a Red Figure vase.

onstage, there is something ballet-like about the scene. When Philoctetes screams from the pain of his wound, he seems to move in and out of his agony to the sound of music. It was a theatre in which only language could show the individuality behind the mask.

> Take no notice of empty dog-barkings.
> You and I hold this house, we shall rule well.

That is a rather literal version of the last words of the *Agamemnon* of Aeschylus, spoken by the murderess Clytemnestra to her lover, Aegisthus. As well as being dramatic, the lines convey something of the murdering queen; they are both arrogant and ominous. They follow on a furious dialogue between Clytemnestra, Aegisthus and the chorus, line piled up on line, that ends with the chorus snarling 'Crow away fighting-cock, crow to your hen'. After the queen's speech the silence tingles. Typically of scholarship, the question has even been raised whether some lines are not missing at the end. But I do not think so. Her character, her mask, has not altered since it was described at the beginning by the dog-like, dogged watchman on the roof, before her first entry. The Latin-rooted word *person*, and the Greek word for it, *prosopon*, both derive from the theatrical mask, the fixed character.

It has often been said that in the achievement of every civilization and language verse comes before prose, as if the skills of written prose are harder to master. This is certainly true of English and Italian and Russian. Montaigne and Clarendon and Machiavelli are complex instrumentalists, they are not the chirp of the first bird. Chekhov and Tolstoy are in debt to Pushkin. The essential skills of poetry are really intuitive; they do not depend on reading and writing. But however bold and majestical some isolated passages of Greek tragic poetry may look to us, the art of Aeschylus is already extremely sophisticated. There is nothing unripe in his work. He can stand back from his problems in a way that Homer hardly could, and his effects are precisely calculated. The *Iliad* shows evidence of huge reshapings of old stories, and of variation in performance, but Aeschylus is a far more deliberate writer. The *Agamemnon* seems to me to show signs of careful revision, like *King Lear*.

Aeschylus differs from Shakespeare, among other ways, in having treated not only mythology and epic material, which he handles with deliberate originality, but also contemporary events. It is interesting to notice that in his *Persians*, the story of the Persian invasion is a Persian tragedy; it is fitted into the form of tragedy by being treated formally from a Persian point of view. His elder contemporary Phrynichus, one of the earliest of all tragic poets (his works have not survived), had already adapted a modern story. When Phrynichus had treated the fall of Miletus to the Persians in tragic form, as the catastrophe of a great city closely allied to Athens, the people fined him for reminding them too sharply of their sorrows. Of course Aeschylus treats the Persian wars also as a glorious Athenian triumph, but all the same not without sympathy for the enemy. Such

155

a sympathy or compassion is directly inherited from epic poetry. The *Iliad* ends with lamentation for the dead Hector, and with his burial. Both sides speak Greek, both sides speak in the same poetry.

Aeschylus in *The Persians* gives an eye-witness account of the naval battle at Salamis, which is scarcely rivalled in Greek prose narrative. It is a remarkable set-piece, a typical messenger's speech; these were a feature of Greek tragedy throughout its development, and the audience loved them, even when the story they told was mere fiction, a lying story reported by one character to deceive another. They were always the eloquent presentation of violent events that had happened offstage. They resembled epic poetry, but with more elaborate syntax and scope for all the actor's arts, in spoken iambic verse instead of the old chanted hexameters. The suppleness and strength of Greek dramatic verse owed something to the use of that same metre by the poet and statesman Solon for real public speeches of national importance a hundred years before the Persian wars.

> And when the light of the sun had perished
> and night came on, the masters of the oar
> and men at arms went down into the ships;
> then line to line the longships passed the word,
> and everyone sailed in commanded line.
> All that night long the captains of the ships
> ordered the seapeople at their stations.
> The night went by, and still the Greek fleet
> gave order for no secret sailing out.
> But when the white horses of the daylight
> took over the whole earth, clear to be seen,
> the first noise was the Greeks shouting with joy,
> like singing, like triumph, and then again
> echoes rebounded from the island rocks.
> The barbarians were afraid, our strategy
> was lost, there was no Greek panic in
> that solemn battle-song they chanted then,
> but battle-hunger, courage of spirit:
> the trumpet's note set everything ablaze.
> Suddenly by command their foaming oars
> beat, beat in the deep of the salt water,
> and all at once they were clear to be seen.
> First the right wing in perfect order leading,
> then the whole fleet followed out after them,
> and one great voice was shouting in our ears:
> 'Sons of the Greeks, go forward, and set free
> your fathers' country and set free your sons,
> your wives, the holy places of your gods,
> the monuments of your own ancestors,
> now is the one battle for everything.'
> Our Persian voices answered roaring out,
> and there was no time left before the clash.
> Ships smashed their bronze beaks into ships, . .
>   . . . One great scream
> filled up all the sea's surface with lament
> until the eye of darkness took it all.

It was worth pondering over Aeschylus and Salamis, if only because of the contrast he offers with the two

great 5th-century historians, Herodotus and Thucydides. But the true business of tragedy was not really historical narrative. A number of the plays have historical resonance of one kind or another. As the shadows fell around Athens towards the end of the century it is not surprising that they could be felt in the theatre. But tragedy was a world of its own. The theatrical achievement of the Athenian democracy is towering, and many of its conceptions still have power over us; there is no stronger tragedy of moral intransigence than Sophocles' *Antigone* to this day. *Oedipus the King* remains the classic tragedy that Aristotle thought it was; Pasolini's Euripides is still thrilling and moving; yet Athenian tragedy had little direct influence on European literature until well after the Renaissance. In its 4th-century revival it produced no work of great interest. It had, as Aristotle says, developed its nature to the full when Athens collapsed. It was born not long before the democracy, and died soon after it. The analogy between the Athenian theatre and other institutions of direct democracy is a compelling one.

I want to reserve some discussion of Euripides for a later page. But in general, tragedy exercised its influence indirectly. Roman tragedy so far as we know it remained an impotent and pedantic minor art, but the tone and shape of tragic writing had entered into history with Thucydides. Being a serious and deep writer, he digested the poets seriously and deeply. Through him, some resonance of the Athenian tragic stage has become part of the way we write about human history. It is not impossible that some indirect reflection, some shadow of tragic form, may underlie the Christian gospels. Certainly Euripides had an influence on the way the lives of first the Jewish and then the Christian martyrs were written. On most popular writers, including historians, tragedy was an influence for the worse. They ranted, they inflated and decorated every speech, drew the last drop of pathos from each event. In a decadent age, every influence becomes a bad one. A superficial writer will use everything superficially. Tragedy reached Renaissance Europe through poets and scholars whose appetites were deeper and sharper than that, but not with full effect until the Greek language was mastered. Aristotle's skeletal discussion of tragedy had a formidable effect on a Europe that had never seen an authentic production. Yet some of the mistakes made were fruitful. Because he had no tradition of tragic unity, Shakespeare could show a world like the sea, and a long moral process where the Greek poets had shown only the machinery of a catastrophe. Now that the masks and the dancing and the music are lost, and with them an irrecoverable style, no authentic production of an ancient tragedy can ever be seen again, although the dramatic orange of the Greeks is not yet sucked dry in English.

A chorus of warriors on horseback, from a 6th-century Athenian vase, evokes Aristophanes' comedy 'The Knights'. It must derive from a similar context, though the date rules it out as an actual illustration of Aristophanes.

Comedy: a mirror to the Greeks

Athenian comedy offers similar difficulties, but its development was far longer; it really does hold a mirror up to the nature of the Greeks in the long process of their history. Through excellent Roman adaptations by Plautus, and imitations by Terence, it had a full-blooded influence on the Renaissance theatre both in Italy and in England. Comedy was far closer to the heart of 5th-century Athenian politics than tragedy was. Today some of its liveliest jokes and most immediate allusions are argued about by scholars in learned footnotes. It was born, or rather was formalized and 'came to town', a little later than tragedy, which it frequently mocked. It was an amalgam of popular jokes, in verse looser than that of tragedy; simple and charming lyrics; a dancing and singing chorus dressed as animals or clouds or wine bottles or whatever seemed unexpected and amusing; bizarre and bold plots; short comic episodes; and a serious interlude when the poet through his chorus leader directly addressed the audience.

Comedy was meant to teach political, moral and social lessons. It even contained literary criticism of tragedy. Its nature was intricately bound up with the conventions of 5th-century Athenian society. Comedy altered as society altered. Unfortunately we have hardly any long fragments of very early comedy, but its humour was clearly vigorous and uninhibited, its comic conceptions were pleasantly wild, and its imaginative language, its poetry, was both rustic and unsophisticated. It belonged in a theatre of hard knocks and a society of very direct speech. Nothing seems so simple as ancient comedy, yet nothing depends on so many complicated conditions of Athenian society. It has strong roots in rustic religious ritual and in country life, it delves even into the world of slaves, and yet it

constantly assumes democratic process, and the values of the city, as year by year the city transforms Athenian life. Its deepest assumption is that human beings can take their own fate into their hands, that the city of Athens had done so. There have not been many such ages of the world. In some ways the theatre of Aristophanes recalls a peasant carnival when the sap of the world was green, in others it resembles the most advanced political cabaret. Brecht is a lesser version of Aristophanes.

Aristophanes as a young man set to work late in the 5th century, in the early twenties, and worked on into the next age; he saw many changes in theatrical style and in music, but his abundance of comic invention never deserted him. The dashing, all-important comic chorus withered away in his lifetime. Political invective more or less ceased with the 5th-century democracy, and social themes mostly took the place of political ones. His early plays had dealt freely with issues of peace and war; no great man in those days was immune from comedy. His last work that we have, *Ploutos*, deals in comic language with the effects of poverty and wealth. It tells in farcical terms the story of the god of Wealth being cured of blindness by holy snakes. This event occurs offstage, and the audience hear it from a messenger, slave to the god of Wealth. The verse is at first glance many miles from Aristophanes' early rumbustious style, though it does retain a few old-fashioned touches of rustic humour, but its poetry is subtle, humorous and perfectly effective.

The theatre of Aristophanes must have had moments of almost uncanny mystery. The revelation of the underworld in his *Frogs*, and the moment early in his *Clouds*, when the goddesses throw off their cloaks, must have been something like transformation scenes in a pantomime for grown-ups:

O everlasting Clouds
let us reveal our dewy glorious selves,
come from Ocean, deep-echoing father,
to the high mountains shaggy with forest,
and gaze on peaks that show in the distance
and all fruits and the watered holy earth
and the loud babble of godlike rivers
and the deep-sounding and the babbling sea;
because the unwearied eye of aether shines
with stony glittering rays.
Shake off the shady drift
of our immortal form and we shall see
all the earth with our distance-gazing eyes.

Comedy soon settled into the moralizing play of characters, or rather types of character – it was still controlled by the mask and its moral conversions have a pantomime quality – and almost into a bourgeois, quotidian world without inner magic, but had it not done so, it could not have been transmitted either to the Romans or to the Renaissance Florentines. In its Greek days, comedy never quite ran out of magic or of religion; the world of later Shakespearean comedy recovers these useful elements or devices. They may be essential in the end to the marriage of comedy and poetry. The gods, or the goddess Chance, or the local patronal god, Pan in his village cave, still preside over the action in Menander's plays, late in the 4th century, and over the comic theatre of the Romans. But when Aristophanes was young, the gods were as visible and solid as their temples.

King of horses, Posidon, whose delight
is in the metal hoof-beats and the neighs
and swift blue-thrusting tribute-bringing ships . . .

As one of Falstaff's hangers-on remarked when the

It is difficult to know how far the comic scenes on vases reflect real performing practice. Among the more naturalistic of such scenes is this fragment of 400–390 BC showing two men carrying a cake.

wicked old man died, 'gone is the fuel that maintained that fire'. One can still feel for the theatre of Aristophanes something closer to love than one can feel for anything in the later history of Athens. It seems that the last charm of the 5th century, distilled into its lyric and comic theatre, seeped somehow downwards into the works of Plato, and into his prose-style. He was a brilliant parodist, and he was nostalgic for an age he hardly knew. The character of Aristophanes as Plato was pleased to recall him in *The Symposium*, which is the account of conversation at a 5th-century dinner party, is as impressive as his comedies. The story Plato has Aristophanes tell to explain the origins of the various kinds of human sexuality is a sparkling comic invention.

If comedy influenced philosophy, it is even clearer that philosophy altered comedy, not only in its less respectable early days, when it was mocked on the stage by Aristophanes among others, but later when it became the intellectual passion of civilized mankind, a process that began with Plato's influence, and continued through many generations. Menander as a young man was accustomed to dictatorship and uninterested in politics. His theatre showed ups and downs and surprising reversals of fortune. He seems to have been the companion during youthful military service of one at least of the new moral philosophers of withdrawal and escape and the defence of limited pleasure. He also appears to have learnt from Theophrastus, a pupil of Aristotle's, a botanist and a geologist and also the author of *The Characters*, a short book of enormous future influence describing the typical behaviour of a range of social and psychological types. Menander's plays draw effectively on that sort of characterization.

The study of man: the first Greek historians

We are accustomed to think that literature above all arts depends on the full emergence of individuality. It used to be said that the daybreak of Greek individuality was the age of lyric poetry in the 7th century and the 6th. But that must be wrong, not only because individuality expressed in words is a common heritage of mankind, possessed as fully by a peasant as by Proust, but also because Homer, when he is examined more closely, turns out to show a full and subtle play of individual art, and on many occasions to portray individuals just for the sake of it. In fact traditional lyric poetry, with its compulsion to joy or to love, and its decorative mythology, is in a way more impersonal than Homer. Our world associates the individual with free moral choice. That state occurs in tragedies and in comedies. There is some difficulty in both cases; in tragedy because of the pressure of the gods and of fate, and passion which is almost a god, and character which is almost a fate, in comedy because of absurdity, and because of the tyranny of psychological and social type-casting.

The whole notion, and the whole survival of humane

THAIS · PHAEDRIA · PARMENO

A certain indirect light on Greek theatre comes from early manuscripts of plays by the Roman dramatist Terence. They date from the 9th–12th centuries AD but they were copied, apparently faithfully, from much older classical manuscripts. Since Terence's plays are Latin adaptations from the Greek New Comedy, we can gain some idea of how a Greek performance might have looked. This scene comes from Terence's comedy 'The Eunuch', based on a play of the same name by Menander. Thais, on the left, is a courtesan; Phaedria, a young Athenian, is in love with her; Parmeno is his wily slave who sets the intrigue going. Parmeno's grotesque mask contrasts with the more naturalistic ones of the others.

literature, depend on the idea of man as free. It may be that he can first be seen to be so in the writing of history. Chronicles are earlier, epic and prose saga are earlier, even the study of mankind as a sort of natural history, in which tribal origins mingle with topography, comes earlier in the 5th century than history does. But with Herodotus and Thucydides we have full-scale history, the attempt to get at the truth of great events by evidence of many kinds, weighed with judgment and written with some degree of fullness and of balance. After astronomy, historical science was perhaps the first science, properly so called, known to mankind. Thucydides likens it to medical research, but one would rely more readily on an ancient historian than on an ancient doctor.

Archaeology and the allied study of inscriptions have now added so much to what is knowable about Greek history, and every inch of the text of Thucydides in particular has been so thoroughly worked over by painstaking and often brilliant, even great, scholars, that I do not feel capable of judging the 5th century historians with any originality in the way they most cry out to be judged, for their professional quality. I can only indicate what has been said, and notice their tone. If one is interested in the Greeks at all, there is no better investment of time than to read these mighty writers. Thucydides is best in the translation by Thomas Hobbes of Malmesbury.

Herodotus was an exile from Halicarnassus, a coastal city once half Carian and half Greek, which the Persians took. At least two other famous writers, Panyassis and Hecataeus, neither of whose works survive now in any quantity, were older members of his family. Herodotus travelled widely. He knew Babylon, the Crimea, Egypt and Cyrenaica and the islands, the lower Dnieper and perhaps the lower Danube. It is typical of the attractions of Athens under Pericles that Herodotus settled there, like Henry James in London. Later he joined the newly founded colony of Thourioi in South Italy, a

project due to Pericles. He was born in the eighties or a little earlier, he was still at work in the thirties and died before 424 BC. The events he covered were mostly those of the generation before his own, from about 540 to 478. Like the mass of epic poetry that he knew, he told the story not of a people but of a war – that of Persia against the Greeks – and so did Thucydides, who knew his work, deliberately rivalled it, and started where Herodotus left off.

History as Herodotus wrote it was critical but still full of marvels. The gods were active, and individual heroes were fully celebrated. He hardly distinguished between written and spoken evidence, but, given his childlike and amiable curiosity, his accuracy, where it can be checked, is amazing; the form and structure of his writing, and the amount of reality he can include, are far more impressive when closely studied than they first appear to be. He uses an intimate speaking style and sometimes a form of folktale, both for better and for worse. He is sophisticated enough to explain a river-gorge as the result of an earthquake and at the same time the work of Posidon, without any obvious sense of contradiction. No ancient and perhaps no modern historian is more entertaining. And yet in his writing fate is rigorous, chance is perverse, and Zeus punishes. The cumulative effect of his treatment of great events, after all his happy meanderings, is like that of a thunderstorm long expected. Yet he ends in triumph.

Thucydides is deeper and his world is more complicated. He had been one of those young men full of fire whom Pericles had led into the great war between Athens and Sparta, and the sadness and defeatism of the last years of Pericles darken his pages. He was born about 455 BC, and died about 400, in Thrace, where he owned land and mines in the goldfield. He was a very deliberate historian and a most deliberate stylist, not without archaisms, but lucid and thoroughly organized. He wrote most of his work in political exile after losing a colony. He was in love with energy, both as a

The Homeric epics were recited by professional performers called 'rhapsodes', one of whom is shown on this Red Figure amphora of about 480 BC.

style, graver, grander and less intimate than the true style of Pericles, so far as we know it. But it remains a full expression of Periclean ideals, and in fact the classic statement of what Athens meant to thinking Athenians of the later mid-5th century. Thucydides follows it at once with a description of the great plague. This is deliberate. His framework is chronological, but only because he means rigorously to trace the machinery of disaster. His syntax is almost awkwardly deliberate, and even the subtlest intrigue, the smallest illustrative anecdote, acquires in his writing an iron mechanism.

But neither had the Corcyraeans any purpose to force entrance by the door, but getting up to the top of the house, uncovered the roof, and threw tiles, and shot arrows at them. They in prison defended themselves as well as they could, but many also slew themselves, with the arrows shot by the enemy, by thrusting them into their throats, and strangled themselves with the cords of certain beds that were in the room, and with ropes made of their own garments rent in pieces. And having continued most part of the night (for night overtook them in the action), partly strangling themselves by all such means as they found, and partly shot at from above, they all perished. When day came, the Corcyraeans laid them one across another in carts, and carried them out of the city. And of their wives, as many as were taken within the fortification, they made bond-women. In this manner were the Corcyraeans that kept the hill brought to destruction by the commons.

The progression of catastrophe is like a drum-beat. Phrases like 'by all such means as they found', and the subordination of the whole anecdote to the simple and clear sentence 'In this manner ...' add power to impersonality. There is a contrast between the violence of the events and the prose in which nothing can get out of hand. The supreme example of this procedure is the last day of the Athenian army in Sicily, where it appears that no individual can act. The account begins when the Athenian general leads out his troops at daybreak, and its impersonality is broken only when he surrenders himself to the Spartan general. No one else is named; the massacre is anonymous. 'The river water was muddied and bloodied but it was struggled for.' Individual deeds of heroism that Thucydides must have known are recorded elsewhere, but not by him. Even his gods are part of the machinery of events. Much of the wide range of thoughts and realities Herodotus used gods to express is closed to Thucydides.

New extremes: rhetoric and the art of Euripides

In the ten years or so that probably separate the work of the two great historians, the Sophists, the first professional teachers of rhetoric and of philosophy, began at Athens to exercise an influence which soon became overwhelming. The speeches in the work of Thucydides, which are so carefully balanced against one another and so exactly structured, owe a lot to that

historian and as a writer. His work shows evidence of painstaking inquiry and of more than one revision. The speeches he records are subtly invented; their fiction is subservient to truth and their themes are often woven seamlessly into the structure of the narrative. The language of individuals is rather fully characterized. Thucydides was praised in late antiquity for 'the originality of his nouns, the variety of his devices, his craggy melody and his rapidity of sense'.

One might almost say that Herodotus studied a war but Thucydides studied a historical process. His history is a study of responsibility and consequences. He was a brilliant analyst of the corruption of the political language of Athens. All the same, he was not as cynical as W. H. Auden about 'the empty, meaningless words important persons speak over an empty grave'. The state funeral speech for the Athenian dead which he gives to Pericles is an exercise in his own monumental influence. The new skill, to make the better argument appear worse and the worse better, was one he had mastered. In the years that followed, the rhetoric they taught was formalized, archaic, delicate and musical. It was less passionate than the rhetoric of poetry or even of the law-courts, but by admixture or by reaction these conscious stylists, the first in European history, transformed literature for at least a thousand years. Some of their rules and procedures have an influence to this day. The conscious cultivation of style and of rhetoric is an effect of literacy; it arises from the availability of diverse written texts, the necessity of choice. The study of style and that of rhetoric and persuasion were inseparable, and they permeated Athenian life from the late 5th century onwards. No one's style was merely personal or merely traditional, and no writer was quite unrhetorical, quite unstylish, ever again. What was new was a self-conscious skill, which could be taught. And one man could write a speech for another: a skill which could be marketed.

In spite of what I have just said about the more passionate rhetoric of poetry, there is a sense in which Euripides, most inventive and experimental of the tragic poets, belongs as much to the history of rhetoric and of the Sophistic movement as he does to that of poetry. That is why he was so popular in later antiquity. His work, which is often of great beauty though it is sometimes slapdash, is full of verbal sparkle and intellectual fireworks. In its final stage it shows a strong tendency towards opera and a taste that can only be called baroque. If one is willing to be pleased, amazed, horrified, if one does not demand the courageous deepness and simple concentration, the sheer economy of means of the early dramatists, if in short one is prepared for a new kind of entertainment which is dazzling, horrifying and surprising, then Euripides deserves his popularity. His tragic conceptions are strong but not pure. Even in his very late play, *The Bacchae*, despite its classic bareness of plot, the role of the chorus, which is almost purely lyrical, and the final scene of revelation, where Agave comes to from her trance holding in her hands her son's head wrenched from his body, hint at musical melodrama. The same play contains also a fire and an earthquake.

Euripides was famous for his sophistries, and for speeches of lamentation, denunciation and many of the passions, including that of unrequited love. His plots play trump card after trump card of surprise and horror, so that at the end of a tragedy his plot and his theology disintegrate together in an explosion of divine action. Medea flies away in a chariot pulled by winged snakes. Hippolytus dies on stage. The end of *The Phoinissai* is so extraordinary that scholars have been unable to believe their eyes; it seems too exaggerated to be genuine, even for Euripides. His ability to wring the last twist of agony or irony out of any situation, and the convincing passion of his arguments, cast a heavy shadow on literature as late as the time of Christianity.

Dying strains: lyric and epigram

One of the recurrent features of 5th-century and even more so of later Greek writing is the habit of returning to older sources. Written pages made it possible to revive and adapt the work of earlier generations. Homer was studied and re-interpreted again and again long after the tradition of unwritten epic that existed only in performance had died away. Even the fresh, early lyric poetry which had faded with its own music was remembered with affection in the theatre of Aristophanes. Later it was revived in a formalized, simplified form in the years around 300 BC. Even the elaborate, formal patterns of rhetoric were only a formalized version of very early prose patterns. Tragic poetry was revived, full of stiffness and archaism, like an old arthritic man wheeled out into the sun. But every revival and adaptation was in a sense a new creation.

We have a mountain of Greek epigrams, short poems in elegiac metre like the dying strains of a self-echoing song. The best are laconic and sensuous, implying much more than they say. Sometimes they recall Japanese *haiku*, sometimes *graffiti* of a ruined city. They imitate one another so constantly that their date and authorship are often problematic. In a way they represent a reaction against long literary works, though the entire collection, *The Palatine Anthology*, really a collection of collections, is enormously long, and mostly in the worst sense literary. But the individual poems often have a freshness.

> Cold water falling out of the split rock,
> and herdmen's carvings of the nymphs,
> rocks of the springs, figures of the virgins,
> water-sprinkled a hundred thousand times;
> Aristokles who came by and washed
> and slaked his thirst has left this offering.

That is by Leonidas of Tarentum, whose quiet modulations of flute-tones and some of whose actual lines were borrowed by Virgil and by Propertius: not a bad way to be remembered. He seems to have lived in the 3rd century BC, but even that is uncertain. Not all epigrams are pastoral of course, but the greatest poets of the age and of later ages learnt a lot of their technique from these short poems, from their sudden stab and their subtle, individual rhythms. Pastoral poetry went on drawing on the vignettes of these epigrams for many centuries. Even when the epigrams were revived, translated and adapted, in the Renaissance, the new Italian Latin epigrams they fathered had a special influence on the new European pastoral poetry.

> Where were ye, Nymphs, when the remorseless deep
> Closed o'er the head of your loved Lycidas?

Milton has been reading the greatest and the earliest surviving pastoral poet, the Alexandrian Theocritus.

> Where were ye, Nymphs, when Daphnis died of love,
> Where were ye?

Daphnis withered away from love; Alexandrian pastoral poetry is erotic, it is about strange or awkward or very simple country lovers and their songs. Although evidently based on a study of real folksong, it is an urban and scholarly poetry, but of wild beauty and strangeness. Because until these last few years country habits remained much the same in remote places, pastoral poetry has not only been revived, it has taken new roots in the soil, in more than one time and place. Neither Shakespeare's *Cymbeline* and *The Winter's Tale* nor Matthew Arnold's 'The Scholar Gipsy' would have been possible without Theocritus. His poetry is both subtler and ranker, smelling more strongly of goat, than the prettier and smoother versions which have given the style a bad name in recent centuries.

In his verses many streams run together. His generation, that of the early 2nd century BC, were the first urban and also the first learned and the first court poets. He draws on the Athenian stage and on dialect poetry, of which very little now remains. The alternative way of treating rustic affairs in his day goes back even further: the *Works and Days* of Hesiod, Homer's contemporary, were meant to teach wisdom, skill and religion to a peasant audience who would learn by heart but never learn to read. This knobbly, didactic style still has a charm, and it was revived in Alexandria as it was in the 18th century in English (John Dyer's *The Fleece* for example), in another of the prose ages of poetry. Long poems were written by the Alexandrians about how to cure snake-bite (illustrated like a snake recognition chart) and about the stars. With the flowering of the Alexandrian world in the 3rd century BC, a new and massive supply of mythical stories became available from the Greek east, and entered literature for the first time, tinging it with exotic sex and a new sort of glamour that urban readers demanded. All the same, what has endured longest from that period has been the love epigram, which gave lyrics to Ben Jonson, and pastoral poetry, which was alive as late as William Barnes and maybe Robert Frost.

Plato: literature in the service of philosophy

The most fertile and powerful single influence on Europe from the purely Greek world has been, I suppose, Plato. It is important not to leave him in the horny hands of our usual professional philosophers; only from a literary point of view, as a wonderful music with the playfulness of the sea full of dolphins, a religious seriousness like that of poetry, constant parody and word-play, and a density of ideas like the stars of heaven, can that extraordinary talent be explained. To abstract his arguments, ignore his tone and all his jokes, and marshal his theories like toy soldiers, is to miss the point. Of course he argues seriously, his intention is serious, it is not only (though it is also) entertainment, and one must take his reasoning seriously. But to do that one must first relax. Charm is one of his weapons, and story-telling, using invented stories as for children but with enigmatic

meanings for philosophers, is one of his favourite solutions.

In Plato, in the 4th century BC, Greek prose reached a ripe perfection that it had never attained in the 5th. For those to whom reading is a serious pleasure, and the most pleasurable form of seriousness, Plato ranks with Montaigne as one of the greatest and most enchanting writers in human history. It may be that truth as well as wisdom is lurking somewhere in that labyrinth. However one may conclude about truth, his enormous intellectual influence has always depended on his victories of prose style. He simply writes so well that one must listen. His mind is complex, multiple, undogmatic, confident, amused. Philosophy is for him the greatest gift not of Zeus but of the Muses. The parliamentary oratory of the Greeks, moving as that sometimes is if one understands its historical context, and vast as its influence was on our own orators, while we still had any, is jejune and rasping by comparison. Plato's manner is captured in this translation, by Francis Cornford, of the closing sentences of *The Republic*:

... if you will believe with me that the soul is immortal and able to endure all good and ill, we shall keep always to the upward way and in all things pursue justice with the help of wisdom. Then we shall be at peace with Heaven and with ourselves, both during our sojourn here and when, like victors in the Games collecting gifts from their friends, we receive the prize of justice; and so, not here only, but in the journey of a thousand years of which I have told you, we shall fare well.

What is compelling is only Plato's tone, his speaking voice, the slow, faultless unfolding of his sentences. They create a space and a leisure around them. In the silence one can listen to him thinking. Never was such intimacy conveyed with such formality. One is compelled, as with Montaigne, or with Diderot or Saint-Simon, to admire the quality of the language itself in their day – echoed in this translation of the conclusion of *The Symposium*:

And when he woke he saw the others had fallen asleep or gone home, and only Agathon and Aristophanes and Socrates were still awake and drinking from an enormous bowl which they were circulating. Socrates was still talking. Aristodemos told me he didn't remember what was said, not having heard the beginning and being drowsy, but the sum of it is, Socrates was compelling them to admit that comedies and tragedies demanded one and the same writer, and that the art of tragic poets made them comic poets. When they were forced to that conclusion, and not following it any too well, they dozed off: Aristophanes shut his eyes first, and when the sky got bright so did Agathon. Socrates, having put them to sleep, rose and left, and went his usual way, off to the gymnasium, and washed, and spent the day like any other, and wandered home to rest in the evening.

Illustration is like translation: it interprets an ancient text for the understanding of another period. Top: a Neoclassical Hesiod – the Age of Gold through the eyes of the English artist Flaxman. Above: Daphnis and Chloe in a woodcut by Maillol, published in 1937. Right: Plato's 'Symposium', an etching in the style of Picasso by Hans Erni.

Fiction and romance

Much of the philosophic writing of later antiquity, both in Greek and Latin, retains some shadow of the charm of Plato's dialogues, and of his deep religious hunger, but never the substance of his writings, never the same combination of the everyday and the wonderful – intellectual argument and the presence of the muses, cleverness and harmony – and never his narrative gift. The Greeks in his time were on the edge of inventing fiction, inventing that form of romance which would lead, with the development of society, to the European novel. Agathon, the tragic poet who stayed awake with Socrates, produced tragedies which, we are told (they have not survived), had a purely invented plot and new characters, instead of re-using the old mythology. That happened in the 5th century. We can spot other hints and traces of fiction in the fringes of historical writing, and of course in 3rd-century poets like Callimachus, who told stories in verse, as he achieved other effects, with a supple finesse in which art concealed art. But the prose romance was late being born.

When it came it owed a lot to comedy, to a world dominated by chance, where the characters led one another blindfold through a complicated dance of intrigues until suddenly everything came right. The god who brought this about was an unconscious projection of the poet or the story-teller, who in fact invented all the complicated adventures and variations. This was a world in which money was hard to come by, war was a natural disaster, piracy a natural force, much like the Mafia and the mosquitoes. Politics being intolerable, and all ambition meaningless or unsafe, private life had become the principal subject of literature, as of philosophy. The star of Aphrodite was dominant. Adventures were love adventures in the end. The saga of star-crossed lovers flourished on dangerous seas.

The best of these narratives is surely *Daphnis and Chloe* (2nd or 3rd century AD), in which a shepherd boy and a country girl fall in love without understanding what love is and without knowing how to set about the act of sex. They are simple islanders, whose gods are Pan and the nymphs. Their faithful love is tested by many picturesque and some thrilling adventures, including a kidnapping by pirates. In the end devotedness has its reward. They are brought together and live happily ever after, as if the story were a pantomime. The tale is told in language of a musical elegance and prettiness, with plenty of irony and humour of various kinds. It will be seen at once that this story is much more cheerfully outspoken than the Arcadian writings of the Renaissance. It is a piece of humorous voyeurism, and it derives from pastoral poetry as well as from comic plotting.

But no one of these stories is quite like another. The Alexandrian kings had been patrons not only of poets but of a great library and of the first professional literary scholars the world had ever seen. It may well be true that scholarship was called into existence by poetry, by the need for poets to understand the past: the first generation of literary scholars and learned librarians were in fact great poets. But scholarship almost at once became a self-sufficient activity, churning up more dust with less genius as each generation succeeded the last, ending in scholarship about scholarship, the compilation of old critics and old commentaries. It is striking that the same pattern can be traced in the Renaissance, from the revival of learning by Petrarch to our miserable modern age. Ancient scholars classified and petrified every branch of literature they could reach: they traced its graph and formulated its rules. Only socially despised forms of writing could remain untreated, unpredictable, alive. Romantic narrative was certainly alive and multiform, and it was popular enough to have survived. It escaped criticism and scholarship.

The most famous of all those writings today are *The Golden Ass* of Apuleius and *The Satyricon* of Petronius; both are in Latin, but both are adaptations of Greek originals. Among their many unexpected qualities, they both show an abundance of material invention and humorous observation. *The Golden Ass* runs to fantasy and its more pretentious pages are almost unreadable to modern taste, but both works offer a wild variety of pleasures, and *The Satyricon*, episodic and fragmentary as it is, can stand comparison with any picaresque novel ever written. It is likely that the first translations of Greek stories into Latin were thin and sour; we hear of a Roman officer under Crassus who carried them to war in his baggage for light amusement, and in that vignette they fulfil their function. And yet *Pericles, Prince of Tyre* is not the only play of Shakespeare's to have its roots in their tradition.

Greek literature at the dawn of Christianity

It would be a mistake to think that Greek literature died with Greek liberty. Menander's marvellous comedies of manners, the plays that, by way of Plautus and Terence, set the first theatrical example for the Renaissance, for Shakespeare and for Molière, were as we have seen the growth of an age politically hopeless. Polybius, through whose history we know that Scipio wept over Carthage destroyed, was a Greek hostage. The historical analysis of Tacitus and of Livy depend on history written by losers, on generations of sarcastic Greeks. Machiavelli rediscovered and transfigured their style, mostly through Tacitus and Livy, and Marx read Machiavelli. Clarendon in his *History of the Great Rebellion* goes back for style to the same ancient historians. Shakespeare transcribes Plutarch's *Lives* at times almost word for word.

The full, rounded conception of a human being as an individual personality is among the last achievements of the ancient Greeks, and one of the first to be revived in 15th-century Italy. The portrait sculpture of the late Roman republic is almost certainly a Greek art. It can be seen in full flower in the portrait heads of the Greek kings who reigned in Afghanistan after Alexander. The equivalent in language is harder to trace. The full sense of individual faces and manners was slow to emerge, although, to read Aristophanes and Plato, one would expect it sooner. Indeed, Plato's Socrates may be the first acceptable example we have of the full drawing of a single person. Certainly by the time of Plutarch (2nd century AD) this sense of individuality, the worthwhileness of one person's story and his portrait, was fully developed. It is significant though that the individual was always a man of action. The prose lives of poets and philosophers are not nearly so convincing, and Plutarch's drawing of great Romans is much more effective than his gallery of Greeks. The Greeks lived longer ago, and he knows less about them. The death of Cicero, the suicide of Cato, and the story of Antony and Cleopatra are written with a brilliant dryness. It was Plutarch's sense of tragedy, not that of the tragic poets, that Shakespeare drank in. Later in time, in modern Greek in Alexandria in the Rue Lepsius, C. P. Cavafy created powerful poetry from the same source. It was Plutarch's and of course Horace's sense of the individual, and Cicero's inherited rags of Greek philosophy, and the mysticism of Plato and Plotinus, that formed the humanism of the Renaissance from which we all derive.

Before the sun set on antiquity – in the late 2nd century AD – one of the last ancient Greek pagan writers that we can still read for their prose style arose as if to prove that Greek was unexhausted. There is something still classic about Lucian. But he is neat rather than grand; he sets out to be amusing, brief, unpretentious. One of his stories is closely related to the original of *The Golden Ass*. He is an admirable companion, a writer on the level of Thomas Love Peacock; his simplicity is deliberate and his sentences are salted. He seems at first sight only one of a number of Greek writers of similar scope, but by some mysterious alchemy, by simple mastery of the language, he is far more readable and memorable than the others. It is almost as if having style one must have nothing else because anything additional would be vulgar; it is as if Lucian is boasting that man can live by style alone.

Untruly of course. The greatest hero of late Greek literature is Jesus Christ. The gospels are in Greek because the entire eastern Mediterranean world in their time had been Hellenized since before Christ, and one of the thrills and shocks of the gospels is that mixture of cultures. In spite of their linguistic awkwardness, or because of it, they are powerful pieces of simple writing such as Greek had never encompassed before. It is hard for anyone of my generation and background to see the gospels simply as a book among other books; in most editions they are not even the same shape or colour as most books. But their seriousness, their wisdom more profound than that of proverbs, and the story itself of the life of Christ, are a reproof to the way literature had gone in the Roman empire.

The seriousness of the gospels is not playful as it is in

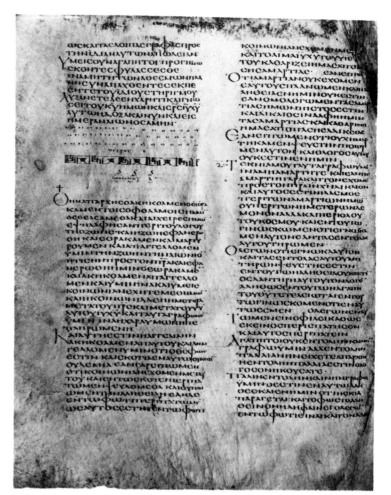

One of the last great works of Greek literature – the gospels. This page from one of the finest ancient copies, the 5th-century Codex Alexandrinus, written on vellum, shows part of the gospel of St John.

the Socratic dialogues; their proverbial teaching is more coherent than Hesiod, more full of light; their simple beauty in passing phrases outdoes Theocritus with fewer means. Only in their tragic sense can the gospels be paralleled, and then one must go back to the *Iliad*. The sense of light and liberation they convey is also to be found here and there in Greek Hermetic and in other gnostic writings, but never with the special simplicity and objectivity of the gospels. Their strength is that they speak to the individual, and appeal profoundly to what is deepest and best in human beings. Still, they have a precise position in the history of feeling, and in the history of literature; Lucian and Plutarch wrote later, but the gospels are the final flower of antiquity.

They are more or less contemporary with the first great scholarly edition of Theocritus, the last Greek writer to be so edited, and with the yearnings and transformation scenes of Virgil and the personal integrity of Horace. Literature had come near to the end of its means. The civilized world was one vast slave farm, washed by an exile-crowded sea. Every new movement of writers was also a scholarly revival. What we call creative was mostly crushed under enormous swags of baroque ornament, or it was sinking into dust, or it was the carving of a cherry-stone.

There is no doubt that Athens in the 5th century BC was happy in the power of its creativity, compared to what followed. But the sources of that creativity were much older; they belonged to a quality of life that had scarcely survived. 5th-century Athens was rushing towards its destruction. A shepherd on the hills who saw the Parthenon freshly built might have known that such a city could not last very long.

But the unfolding of literature did not cease. The work of Plato is a stupendous achievement, though in a way his works read like an appendix to the earlier century. Only with the crossing of cultures, with the rediscovery of older writers (another cross-cultural phenomenon), and the opening up of what was fresh in peasant, serf and slave culture by city poets like Theocritus, did Greek literature have an autumn flowering. History of course continued to be written, largely imitating earlier models. Comedy, even bourgeois city comedy with its happy endings and quotable morality, effectively died with Menander. The big cities of the new age were too big for those subtleties; they were waiting for Petronius. Or they were waiting for the gospels, for the last freshness to be found in their world.

Christians on the other hand were waiting for the whole world to finish. The book called Revelations was intended as a kind of Amen to the history of the world. It was not the only example of such writings. Virgil adapted them and Horace quoted them in full seriousness. At the time of the birth of Christ it was thought an age of the world was ending. The Roman empire was an anticlimax from the beginning, as its writers pointed out. By the time the gospels were written, literature was thought of as something finished and set; it had happened in the past, in Greek, and that was that. It had, as Aristotle said of tragedy, attained its nature. As for the Fathers of the church, on the whole they merely dragged out the decadence of Greek literature at endless length: they were a continuance of literary decadence by other means.

In reality of course, a literature constantly revives with new generations and new twists of human history. In this century the poetry of George Seferis is as great as Lorca's or T. S. Eliot's, perhaps greater. Its profound simplicity and gravity of tone are inseparable from the Greek language, climbing back like the sun out of darkness. The survival and the long, illiterate refreshment of the spoken Greek language ensured a new Greek age of poetry sooner or later, but that took a long time.

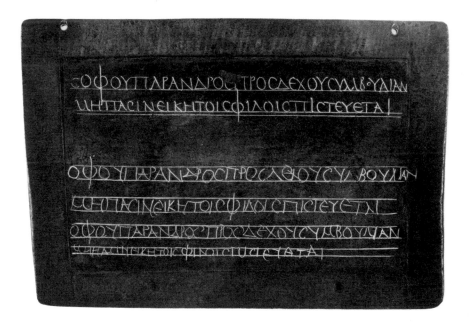

Waxed tablet used as an exercise slate by a Greek schoolboy. Two lines (one of them a quotation from Menander, 'Accept advice from a wise man') have been written by the master at the top and copied twice by the student underneath.

IV·CONQUEST

6
The Age of Kings
*from Alexander
to the Roman conquest*

7
Rome and the Greek East
*imperial rule and
transformation*

ALEXANDER OF MACEDON's rise to the leadership of all the Greek city states between 336 and 334 BC – a rise prepared for and planned by his father Philip – meant the end of one phase of Greek civilization. Although much would continue unchanged, their mutual rivalry, their fertile variety, something of their intellectual ferment, would disappear, submerged by the authoritarian regimes of larger centralized states. But it was the beginning of another phase, scarcely less vital and interesting. For with the fall of the Persian empire, virtually the whole known world was opened up to Greek influence. The Greek language, Greek taste, Greek art, Greek patterns of thought became dominant everywhere.

The Hellenistic age is generally defined as beginning with Alexander's death in 323 BC and leading without a break into the Roman era. It is a complex period, difficult to define. Political power was at first in the hands of Macedonian dynasties – the Ptolemies, the Antigonids, the Seleucids – often at war with each other and often challenged by smaller, local monarchies. They all, however, shared a common culture, and their patronage could be as enlightened as it was lavish. Nor were the cities, whether in Greece itself or in Asia Minor, the Levant and Egypt, either powerless or provincial. In some respects their intellectual life was more brilliant than ever.

Rome eventually inherited most of the empire of Alexander. But Rome itself was in many ways a hellenized or half-hellenized state. Changes brought about by Roman rule were not dramatic or sudden.

The Greek world became part of the Roman empire. The upper classes adopted Roman ways and Roman tastes, and sometimes entered Roman government. In Greece, the cities found themselves divested of even the nominal autonomy that they had enjoyed previously, but in return they were guaranteed peace, a measure of prosperity and considerable esteem.

During the 3rd and 4th centuries AD this flourishing Hellenistic–Roman society was transformed into a Christian society. Most history books represent this as a complete break with the past and the beginning of a new era. Ideologically, of course, it was. But at the cultural level such a clear-cut division can be misleading. Was not Christianity in many ways a Hellenistic mystery religion? Were not the gospels written in Greek? Was not Christ himself, as Peter Levi has argued in an earlier chapter, the last great tragic hero of Greek literature?

Certainly, in founding his new capital Constantine had no thought of repudiating his classical heritage. Its churches were Christian, but it was adorned with the masterpieces of pagan art brought from all over Greece. Literature and philosophy pursued their course barely affected by doctrinal considerations until the reign of Justinian. It was then, rather than two hundred years earlier, that the new religion began to cast its shadow over every aspect of intellectual and cultural life. It may be rewarding for a change, therefore, to look at the whole sweep of history from Alexander to Justinian as one long unbroken sequence.

A new spirit,
fierce, destructive and beautiful, seemed to be released upon the world in the person of Alexander the Great. Even his contemporaries saw him as super-human. To later ages he was a figure of myth, a worker of miracles, a hero to be ranked with the gods. Clearly, he was a man of overwhelming *charisma* (significantly, a Greek word derived from *charis*, grace or charm), who could inspire his followers to feats that they hardly believed possible. Artists too were swept along by that inspiration, although the style we call Hellenistic can be traced back to earlier times and to deeper causes. Their work is filled with a new energy, a rejection of restraint, an ambition to express the inexpressible that differentiates it from the balance and repose of classical art. Pella, in Macedonia, was Alexander's birthplace, and here his successors built a rich palace with floors decorated with mosaics in coloured pebbles. The lion (*opposite*) is typical of this powerful style; the outlines are thin bronze strips. (1)

The language of sculpture

In the world of the Hellenistic kingdoms, the arts found new purposes and a wider range of subject-matter and expression: images of power to glorify the rulers; erotic, realistic and even violent subjects for private patrons.

The human figure remained central to Greek art, but sculptors used it to explore aspects hitherto untouched. *Far left:* a satyr turning to look at his tail, contradicting any single viewpoint. *Left:* a copy (the original is lost) of Praxiteles' Cnidian Aphrodite, the first of a long series of sensuous female nudes, made well before Alexander. (2, 3)

Tenderness and brutality. The head of Aphrodite (*above*) contrasts with the battered features of the old pugilist (*right*), one of the most compelling examples of Hellenistic realism. (4, 5)

Grace, elegance and mystery are all caught in this small bronze of a veiled dancer thought to be from Alexandria. This is now a purely secular art, free from any religious or mythological overtones. (7)

The giant figure of Mausolus, died 353/2 (*above*), adorned his tomb that became one of the wonders of the ancient world, the Mausoleum at Halicarnassus. His features express idealized wisdom. (6)

The Barberini Faun's careless indolence (*below*) would have been unthinkable to a sculptor of the classical age, but fauns were 'inferior' beings, like pugilists, without dignity. (8)

The arts of luxury

Some of the most exquisite craftsmanship of the Hellenistic age went into jewellery, goldwork and decoration for the very rich. Few of these precious objects survived the greed of 2000 years, but in modern times a number have been recovered from undisturbed graves, giving fresh insight into social conditions.

The gilded crater (*opposite*) was found at Derveni in Thessalonica. It stands 3 feet in height (91 cm); the upper part contains miniature figures in three dimensions, the body scenes in repoussé showing Dionysus and Ariadne. This detail is of Dionysus himself seated under a sinuously trailing vine. (10)

A diadem of gold leaves recently came to light at Vergina, in Macedonia. Oak leaves are interspersed with acorns. It was part of a burial which some archaeologists believe was that of Alexander's father, Philip of Macedon. As a symbol of royalty, it encircled the dead man's skull, which was placed in a casket of solid gold. (9)

Alexander's city

Of the many cities that Alexander named after himself, none attained such eminence as that on the edge of the Nile delta in Egypt. Under the Ptolemies Alexandria outshone Athens itself as a centre of learning and its library was by far the largest in the western world.

The face of Alexander soon became idealized and stereotyped. We shall never know how he really looked. This gold medallion from Tarsus dates from the mid-3rd century. (11)

The lighthouse was another wonder, its fame spreading so wide that this representation of it on a glass beaker (*right*) was found as far away as Begram in modern Afghanistan. It stood on an island at the head of the harbour and was said to be 400 feet (92 m) high. (13)

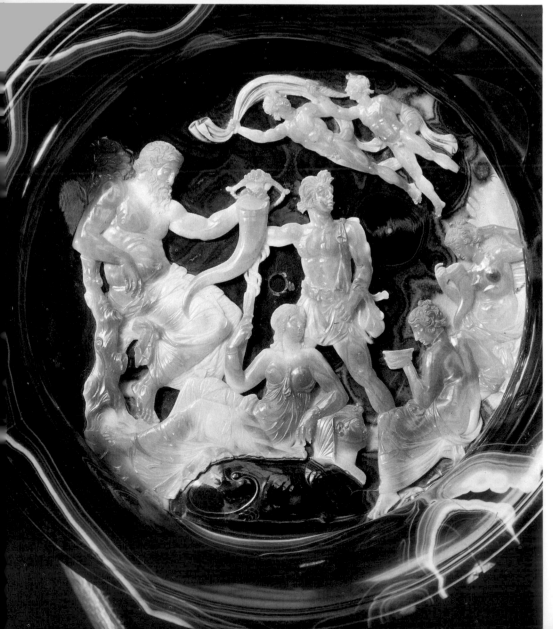

Dynastic propaganda is the theme of the Farnese Cup (*left*), a large cameo dating from about 175 BC. At the bottom Queen Cleopatra I, with the attributes of Isis, sits on a sphinx. The seated figure next to her is Father Nile, holding a cornucopia. Behind the queen stands the next heir, Ptolemy VI, holding in his right hand the handle of a plough. On the right sit personifications of the seasons and overhead fly the winds. The rule of the Ptolemies, says the implicit message, brings blessings and prosperity. (12)

Greece met Africa in the streets of Alexandria. This silver dish personifying the city is crowded with symbols bearing witness to its dual ancestry. The city herself wears an elephant's scalp showing tusks and trunk. The snake in her right hand is the Egyptian *uraeus*; the lion on her shoulder and the bow at her back allude to Herakles, the she-panther to Dionysus. The cornucopia, again, stands for the wealth of Alexandria. *Left:* an Alexandrian official, still Egyptian in stance but with the worried expression of a civil servant throughout the ages. (14, 15)

175

Rome, the inheritor

The cultures that flourished in Asia Minor from the 3rd to the 1st century BC were stimulated by rivalry and local pride. At the end of the 1st century, Rome inherited these cultures, mastering them but also learning from them.

Pergamon was perhaps the most spectacular of all Hellenistic cities, its rulers using architecture and sculpture as a means of dynastic assertion. On a steeply sloping hill were temples, the vast Altar of Zeus now in Berlin and a theatre (*left*) looking on to a long colonnade with at one end a temple of Dionysus. (16)

Sardis attained new prominence under the Seleucids and was taken over by Pergamon in 188 BC. Its main building was another enormous Ionic temple to Artemis (*below left*). Hellenistic architects were fascinated by sheer size. (17)

The kings of Commagene, between the Taurus and Euphrates, claimed descent from both Alexander and Darius; their culture was a suitable amalgam of Hellenistic and Persian elements. Its most impressive remains are at Nimrud Dagh (*below*), where huge heads of gods lie scattered: in the foreground Apollo–Mithras. (18)

176

Athens was one of the Roman emperors' most favoured cities, and many of the buildings we now admire there date from the period of Roman rule. The Temple of Olympian Zeus (*left*) is a palimpsest of the centuries – begun in classical times, continued under Antiochus Epiphanes and completed by Hadrian. Its present form, including the choice of the Corinthian order, is fundamentally Roman. It was the largest temple in Greece. (19)

The Roman vocabulary is distinguished from Greek mainly by increasing elaboration of detail and by the use of the orders decoratively instead of structurally. The Library of Celsus at Ephesus (*below*) was built in the 2nd century AD for a Roman consul. It is typically Roman in its Corinthian order standing over the Ionic and in the way alternate pairs of columns are linked at different levels. (20)

177

Constantine's city: the state

Constantine's intention in founding Constantinople is not altogether clear. His institution of the official Christian church has overshadowed his secular programme. It was called New Rome; its official language was Latin and remained so until Justinian.

Constantine's portrait shows us a statesman rather than a mystic. Although a lavish patron of churches, he was baptized only on his death bed. (21)

The Byzantine official (*right*) is a recognizable successor to the Alexandrian one shown in pl. 15. (22)

Brutal sports continued for two centuries after Constantine. *Below:* detail from a consular diptych of AD 506. (23)

The emperor stood at the apex of a complex but stable system of administration, which brought firm rule and peace, if increasingly strict government control of people's lives. On this silver dish, dated AD 388, Theodosius sits under the arch, flanked by his sons Valentinian and Arcadius. At the sides are bodyguards with spears and large oval shields. (24)

Secular life must have continued largely on the old Hellenistic pattern, though from the surviving literature and art it is easy to overestimate the religious concern. The mosaics of the Great Palace at Constantinople (*left*) are important in this respect. They show a basically classical imagery being used well into the 6th century; here a 'barbarian' head is surrounded by scrolls. (25)

Constantine's city: the church

It was Constantine who presided at the foundation of the Christian church as an official institution. He built major basilicas in the chief cities of his empire and gave power to their hierarchies of priests and bishops. With time this power increased, sometimes to the extent of challenging that of the state.

Justinian's church of Hagia Sophia replaced that of Constantine, destroyed during a riot. An unprecedented masterpiece, it remains basically intact today, though stripped of most of its mosaic and marble decoration. It is essentially a cube covered by a shallow dome. What gives it its miraculous quality of lightness is the fact that the dome is supported on two sides by buttresses invisible from the inside and on the other two by demi- and quarter-domes which have the effect of expanding the space still further. So confident was the engineering that a row of windows was made at the base of the dome itself – over-confident, in fact; the dome collapsed soon after it was built and has had to be repaired several times. (28)

From the ambo, or pulpit, of the great churches Christ's servants proclaimed his message and his dominion. In this manuscript illumination (*below*), a bishop, attended by clergy, holds aloft a reliquary containing part of the True Cross. The setting is thought to be the same as that shown on the Theodosian silver dish (pl.24), the forecourt of a palace called the Magnaura. The pulpit was built between this time and the 10th century. (27)

Authority was now assumed by the church. In this early Constantinopolitan icon of St Peter, the saint occupies the position traditionally taken by a consul, in front of a niche. (26)

Hellenism baptized

Continuity between Hellenistic and Christian ways of thought can be illustrated at many levels. That of iconography is perhaps the most vivid of all, showing very clearly how misleading any theory of a 'clean break' would be.

The Christians saw themselves as uprooting and superseding paganism. This fragment from the Alexandrian World Chronicle (*left*) shows the Patriarch Theophilus standing on the ruins of the Serapeum after it had been destroyed in 391. Far more often, however, Christianity adapted a site or symbol and gave it a new significance. (29)

The fish became a secret sign for Christians during the days of persecution because the letters of the Greek *ichthys* could be read as an acronym of 'Jesus Christ Son of God Saviour'. It was all the safer by being a common classical motif. *Right above:* mosaic from a house on Delos. *Right:* marble panel at Hagia Sophia, Constantinople. (30, 31)

Building types can never be entirely new, and the Christians deliberately exploited the associations of pagan architecture. The church of St George in Thessalonica (*left*) was built as the mausoleum of a pagan emperor. Churches containing martyrs' bones subsequently followed this plan. (33)

Throughout the empire new buildings mirrored the increasing power and status of Christianity. *Right:* three churches of the 5th and 6th centuries. First the basilica of St Paul at Philippi; second, St Sophia at Gortyna, in Crete; third, Kalat Siman, the monastery founded round the pillar of St Simeon Stylites, in Syria. (34, 40, 41)

Constantine's mother, St Helena, is supposed to have founded the church at Katapoliani on the island of Paros, placing it over a secular Roman building containing mosaics of the Labours of Herakles. The cruciform font (*left*) was for baptism by total immersion. (32)

The Good Shepherd, a common metaphor for Christ on Early Christian sarcophaghi, looks back to the ancient image of the calf-bearer. *Right:* archaic Greek figure in Athens, 6th century BC, and its Christian variant, *c.*360, in Rome. (35, 36)

'I am the vine', said Jesus, appealing to an image that lay deep in the Greek consciousness. *Above:* Dionysus in his chariot among vines; a Roman floor mosaic. *Right:* Christ as the source of the eucharistic wine of life, from a silver chalice from Antioch, 4th or 5th century. *Far right:* the vine and the fruit, Christ and the Apostles, from a later Byzantine icon. (37, 38, 39)

6
The Age of Kings
from Alexander to the Roman conquest

MICHEL AUSTIN

The blood of the martyrs was in a sense the seed not only
of the church but of the state. As the emperor had an
ecclesiastical role, so the clergy also had a political function.
A mosaic in St Demetrius, Thessalonica (*opposite*), expresses
this union. Saint, bishop and prefect make a triumvirate that
is in theory indissoluble. The saint, centre, is St Demetrius,
believed to have been martyred in the city under Diocletian,
and after Constantine its patron. The bishop, to the left, is
probably Bishop John, who took part in the defence of the
city against the Slavs in the 7th century, with the Prefect
Leontius on the right. (42)

IN POLITICAL TERMS the Hellenistic period is conventionally reckoned to run from the Macedonian conquest of the Persian empire under Alexander to the overthrow by Rome of the leading Hellenistic states that emerged after that conquest. The process was complete only in 31 BC with the defeat of Cleopatra, the last of the Ptolemaic rulers of Egypt, by Octavian, the future Emperor Augustus, though Rome's dominance in the Hellenistic world, and in the whole of the Mediterranean, had been obvious by the middle of the 2nd century BC. The rise of Rome, however, whatever its significance in political terms, did not mark a fundamental break in the cultural history of the Hellenistic world, and Rome, coming herself under deep Greek influence, never sought to latinize the eastern Mediterranean as she did the western.

The division of history into periods is, of course, an artificial convention of historians; in reality historical periods are never as clear cut as they can be made to appear. What we call the Hellenistic age was not recognized in antiquity as a single unified period, save perhaps in a limited sense, in the application in some sources of the eastern notion of a 'succession of empires': the Persians in Asia had been overthrown by the Macedonians, who were to be replaced in their turn by the Romans. In the 2nd century BC, Polybius, the greatest of the Hellenistic historians, denied any unity to the history of the world before the rise of Rome. The recognition of the Hellenistic age as a period in its own right is due to the 19th-century German historian J. G. Droysen; in his view it was a new period of history, consciously initiated by Alexander the Great, and characterized primarily by the 'fusion' of Greek and eastern cultures. Modern study of this age still owes more to Droysen than just its inception, and the label 'Hellenistic', adapted by Droysen to describe this period as a whole, has come to stay. But nowadays a historian would have to say that, whatever its distinct and novel features, the Hellenistic age was not a completely new beginning, but owed much to previous Greek history – indeed, that it was perhaps less original than once thought; that Alexander was probably less of an innovator, let alone a conscious one, than Droysen and many of his modern successors would have liked to believe; and that the 'fusion' between east and west, which Droysen saw as characteristic of the Hellenistic world at the cultural level, was limited. Rather, the Hellenistic world was notable more for the separateness

and juxtaposition of different cultures, Greek and eastern, than for their fusion.

This shift in perception is not just a matter of scholarly history, but reflects rather an evolution in the history of western Europe. Study of the Hellenistic age, from Droysen onwards, drew much of its inspiration from an analogy, often conscious and explicit, between the Hellenistic world and the world of modern Europe in the age of its colonial empires. The Macedonian conquest of the Persian empire, and the settlement in the east of Greeks forming the ruling class in the new Macedonian kingdoms, were equated (with some plausibility) with the creation centuries later of European colonial empires. The Hellenistic age was presented as the 'modern' period of ancient Greek history. 'No period of Greek history should come home to us like the third century B.C.', wrote W. W. Tarn in 1913. 'It is the only period that we can in the least compare with our own; indeed in some ways it is startlingly modern.' While this approach is not without its justification, it has also had to pay the logical price. The end of the European colonial age, and the reassessment of values this has entailed, have had their inevitable impact on the study of the Hellenistic period, as on other periods of history, encouraging a less positive, but also perhaps less one-sided view of this important age.

The conquest of Asia

The most immediately novel feature of the period was the sudden overthrow of the Persian empire by the Macedonians, opening Asia for Greek immigration and settlement. The wealth of Asia, on the doorstep of impoverished Greece, had long been a temptation. As Xenophon put it, 'the poverty of the Greeks is of their own choosing, since they might see those who live a wretched life in Greece grow rich by coming to Asia'. The idea of a conquest of the Persian empire, or part of it, as a remedy for the social problems of the Greek world, had become a commonplace in the 4th century well before Alexander, openly preached by Greek orators and pamphleteers, notably by the Athenian writer Isocrates. In the end the conquest went much further than anyone could have expected, as far as the Indus. At a stroke the territory open to Greek penetration and influence had been vastly increased. 'We live round the sea like frogs round a pond', Socrates had said in Plato's *Phaedo*. The Greek world had now acquired a new and larger territorial dimension. Except for the Indian gains, resigned within two decades of Alexander's death, the conquests were lasting, if not everywhere to the same degree. Egypt, Syria and Asia Minor were preserved through their subsequent incorporation into the Roman empire. Further east, political control by the kings was finally lost in the 2nd and 1st

A Persian soldier recoils from a Macedonian: a detail from the 'Alexander sarcophagus'. This masterpiece of late 4th-century sculpture was commissioned for Abdalonymus, King of Sidon, to commemorate the conquest of the Persian empire by Alexander.

This magnificent 4th-century pebble mosaic of a stag-hunt is from Pella, capital of Macedonia and Alexander's birthplace (see also p. 169). It is signed 'Gnosis'; the artist had an extraordinary ability to suggest three-dimensional space by means of shading and foreshortening, techniques derived from contemporary painting.

centuries, though Greek presence and influences outlived the passing of the Hellenistic monarchies.

Politically, fragmentation set in from the moment of Alexander's death in 323. The unity of his empire had probably been more apparent than real, and in the absence of any provisions for the succession, the empire

was condemned to divisions that were perhaps unavoidable in any case. A long struggle between the leading Macedonian generals ensued, in which the last descendants of the ruling house of Macedon were eliminated. This struggle was conspicuous for the largely passive role of the newly conquered eastern peoples, and for the inability of the Greek cities to assert successfully their freedom after Alexander's death. In a sense, the struggle was settled, after over a generation of warfare, with the emergence and consolidation of the three leading Macedonian dynasties of the period, the Ptolemies based in Egypt and controlling a maritime empire in the eastern Mediterranean and the Aegean,

Demetrius II Nicator, a Seleucid king of Syria, who spent 10 years as prisoner in Parthia. This coin, minted after his return in 129 BC, shows him in a Parthian beard.

Eucratides, King of Bactria (c.171–155 BC), shown wearing a cavalry helmet. He led numerous aggressive military campaigns.

Philetaerus, the first Attalid ruler of Pergamon (282–263 BC). He was not a king and his coins never bore his image: this superb portrait was used on the coins of his successors.

the Seleucids based in North Syria and Mesopotamia but seeking to rule the whole of Asia from the Hellespont as far as Bactria, and the Antigonids, the last dynasty to establish itself, ruling in Macedon as successors to Alexander's now defunct line and overshadowing the mainland of Greece. In another sense, the conflict remained permanently unresolved until the Romans eliminated it altogether. Conflicts between the Ptolemies and the other two monarchies were endemic, the hold of the Antigonids on the mainland fluctuated, and the Seleucids could not assert a lasting grip on their over-large empire.

Other lesser monarchies emerged in the 3rd century to complicate matters further: native monarchies in Pontus, Bithynia and Cappadocia, which had escaped direct Macedonian conquest, and in the middle of the 3rd century new Greek monarchies, in Asia Minor (the Attalids of Pergamon) and in remote Bactria. The intrusion of peoples from outside the Hellenistic world had further disruptive effects: Celtic tribes created havoc in Macedon in 280–279 and penetrated briefly into central Greece. Repulsed, some settled in Thrace, others in Asia Minor where they stayed, not finally pacified till the Roman conquest (Galatia). Further east, in the middle of the 3rd century, peoples from the steppes penetrated into the Seleucid empire – the origin of the later Parthian kingdom. From the very beginning the Hellenistic world was divided and unstable, and war its normal condition. Hellenistic kings were in the first instance military leaders, and their kingdoms were founded and preserved by victories in war. It was this division which invited and facilitated Roman intervention from the end of the 3rd century. The rise of Macedon under Philip and Alexander had brought peace neither to Greece nor to Asia.

Hellenistic monarchy

The Hellenistic kingdoms differed considerably in size and character, though they shared many common features. The kings ruled over large though fluctuating expanses of territory, and over a diversity of different peoples, Greek and non-Greek. They were kings not of a particular country, nor of a particular people, but of what they could control at any given moment. This type of monarchy has been described as personal in character, based on the military achievements of the founders of the dynasties, and transmitted to their successors as a family inheritance. Only in Macedon had the kingship been based on Macedonian national traditions, though this did little to curtail the ruler's control of all policy decisions. Hellenistic kings were in principle absolute rulers, though their effective power varied considerably. The king's personality, his control over the royal family and over his own governing class, time and distance – these were only some of the limiting factors. The institution of monarchy, however, was not on the whole successfully challenged from within. In the east it survived the decline and disappearance of the

189

Prusias I, King of Bithynia (228–185 BC). His kingdom was hemmed in by stronger powers; he maintained his independence by diplomatic alliances.

major kingdoms. In the west the Roman emperors inherited much from their Hellenistic predecessors.

The monarchies were primarily Greek in character, even though Seleucids and Ptolemies made some outward concessions to native eastern traditions of monarchy. Greek was the language of court and administration. The governing class, the court and the chief military posts were filled from the Greek world. The monarchies brought with them their coinage and the beginnings of a monetary economy, but the royal coinages were self-consciously Greek in style, even in the remote Bactrian kingdom. What is more, the native monarchies of Asia – in Pontus, Bithynia, and Cappadocia – also aped the Greek manners of the major kingdoms, seeking acceptability in the eyes of the Greek world.

The kings and the old Greek cities

One-man rule as such was no novelty to the Greeks, and the 4th century had seen the emergence of powerful individual rulers who in their various ways anticipated features of the Hellenistic kingdoms. Further, the rise of the new monarchies, though it affected considerably the world of the old Greek cities, did not by any means terminate its role. To characterize the Hellenistic age as the age of monarchies, as opposed to the classical age, the age of the cities, is too schematic. Politically the monarchies were dominant, but not totally so. Culturally, their contribution was of great importance, but they did not have a total monopoly of cultural life. In both fields, the old Greek world retained a special status. What is more, the new world in the east was to be in part a world of new Greek cities, promoted by the kings. The relations between king and city were extremely complex, diverse in time and space, and defy easy generalization. The old Greek world was, and would remain, a world of cities: that was an unalterable

fact, taken for granted by king and city alike. Indeed, the kings were anxious to see this world preserved and strengthened. The trend towards the building of larger and stronger units, visible in Greek history intermittently from the late 5th century onwards, was vigorously pursued by the kings, who often imposed on the reluctant communities changes of site, resettlements, enlargements through the addition of new settlers or the merger of several smaller communities into one, to make them stronger and more viable. The kings needed the Greek cities and courted them, for practical and propaganda reasons, and rivalry between the kings stimulated this tendency. With no governing class to start with, the kings had to import their manpower, especially their skilled manpower: governors, officers and administrators, diplomats, soldiers, technicians, craftsmen, men of letters and intellectuals. Philip of Macedon, among other 4th-century rulers, had already shown the way by enlarging the Macedonian governing class with the introduction of Greeks. The world of the cities was a unique reservoir of talent and manpower. This was one of the reasons why all the major monarchies strove to maintain a foothold and influence in the Aegean world on which they depended. More was at stake than practical needs. For the kings, the old Greek world with its traditions was the heart of the civilized world as they knew it, and kings cared for their fame and respectability. The power of public opinion is a Greek invention, and no other people in antiquity had the same ability to impose successfully on others its own criteria. The compulsion on non-Greek rulers to appear philhellenic can be observed as early as the kings of Lydia and Amasis of Egypt who, in the 6th century, was the first non-Greek ruler to be described as a 'philhellene'. The Hellenistic kings were heirs to this long tradition, a tradition they fostered and transmitted to their successors – in the east the native kingdoms that flourished after their own decline, in the west Roman generals then emperors, though the Roman attitude to the Greeks was notoriously ambivalent. Philhellenism was manifested in practical ways: generosity and public munificence were characteristic virtues of the Hellenistic age, inherited from the classical period and magnified. The kings lavished their benefactions on Greek sanctuaries and cities, in the form of civil and religious buildings, gifts of grain, provisions for the performance of religious celebrations, and so forth. Frequently the cities expressed their gratitude by establishing cults of the rulers in return for services and benefactions received or anticipated – a feature of the age, which had started to develop in the late 5th century, but blossomed forth after Alexander, and continued in the Roman empire, Roman emperors taking the place of Hellenistic kings. Royal generosity, however, was not always equally welcome: the acceptance of royal gifts in itself created obligations, a fact both sides were well aware of. Relations between kings and cities were full of ambivalence, and this was particularly true at the political level.

Politically the Greek city did not literally 'die' at the Battle of Chaeroneia (338 BC), though its obituary has frequently been dated too early. It was not till the Chremonidean War of the 260s that Athens finally gave up her attempts to regain an independent role in the Greek world, despite repeated setbacks over a period of two generations. Sparta, in full decline since the Battle of Leuctra in 371, made a remarkable attempt to revive her power in the Peloponnese, abortive under Agis IV (243–241), but very nearly successful under Cleomenes III in the 220s until Macedonian intervention. Political aspirations also asserted themselves in areas of Greece previously little affected by the *polis* spirit, and in new forms. Characteristic of the history of the mainland in the 3rd century was the growth of two independent leagues, the Aetolian and the Achaean, based on the notion of a federal citizenship that could be expanded, a novel experiment, though in practice without future. The two leagues curtailed Macedonian power in Greece, but remained hostile to each other. Furthermore the Achaean leaders took the initiative in appealing to Macedon against the rising power of Cleomenes III of Sparta, contradicting their previous policy. Greek disunity could not be overcome.

In the Aegean a most remarkable development was the rise of Rhodes, not a major Greek state in the classical period, and not unified politically till near the end of the 5th century. Yet Rhodes successfully asserted her independence from the kings in the period after Alexander, to become a powerful, prosperous and stable maritime state, treating with the kings on a basis of near equality, and the recipient of generosities from kings and cities throughout the Hellenistic world. This was an exceptional case, due to a conjunction of unusual circumstances, and the skilful exploitation by the Rhodians of their position between the monarchies and on the major sea route to and from the Levant. The general tendency was for the kings to curtail the political independence of the cities within their sphere of influence, despite the polite language of diplomatic relations, characteristic of a sophisticated world with developed conventions. One device was that of a league of Greek cities, organized under royal control, such as the 'League of Corinth' of Philip and Alexander, grouping the Greek states of the mainland; it lapsed after Alexander's death but was revived briefly by Antigonus the One-Eyed and his son Demetrius in 302, then again in a new and looser form by Antigonus Doson in 224. Another example was the 'League of Islanders', grouping the smaller Aegean islands, founded by Antigonus in 315/314, then taken over by the Ptolemies. The original context for its foundation was Antigonus' proclamation of the 'freedom and autonomy' of the Greeks. Championship of this ideal had a long history before this time: it had been the banner under which Sparta fought Athens in the Peloponnesian War, and great play was made with this theme in the 4th century. Antigonus adapted the slogan to his own uses, to win the goodwill of the Greeks in his struggle against his rivals. Thereafter the 'freedom of the Greeks', or of particular Greek cities, remained a much used, and abused, slogan of Hellenistic politics, used by the Romans against Philip V of Macedon in 196, echoed two and a half centuries later by the Emperor Nero. The persistence of the slogan, and the response it evoked, are indicative of the continued aspirations for a political role by the Greek cities. That such a role was increasingly difficult to achieve may have been true, but it was perhaps less obvious to many Greeks at the time: perception and reality did not move in step. Besides, the very divisions and instability of the Hellenistic world provided opportunities in the interstices of royal power, which was rarely as effective in practice as it may have been absolute in theory. In the long evolution from a world of cities to a world where those cities were incorporated in territorial empires, the Hellenistic age is a time of transition, not the end of the process. It was the coming of the Roman empire, rather than the Hellenistic kings, which finally terminated the political role of the Greek city.

Philip V, King of Macedon (221–179 BC), had his warlike policies curbed by a massive defeat by the Romans in 197 BC. He retained his throne only at the cost of surrendering his conquests in Europe and Asia.

The Greek settlements in Asia

While the rise of Macedon and of the new monarchies constricted the role of the old Greek cities, it also opened a further chapter in the history of the Greek city with the new foundations in the east. The 4th-century trend towards the spread of Greek-style urbanization, visible with Philip in Macedon, or with Mausolus, the hellenized ruler of Caria, thus received a vast new impetus in the east, a model and prefiguration of the Roman empire's urbanization of the west. There were now more Greek cities, and over a much wider area, than there had ever been before. Alexander's own

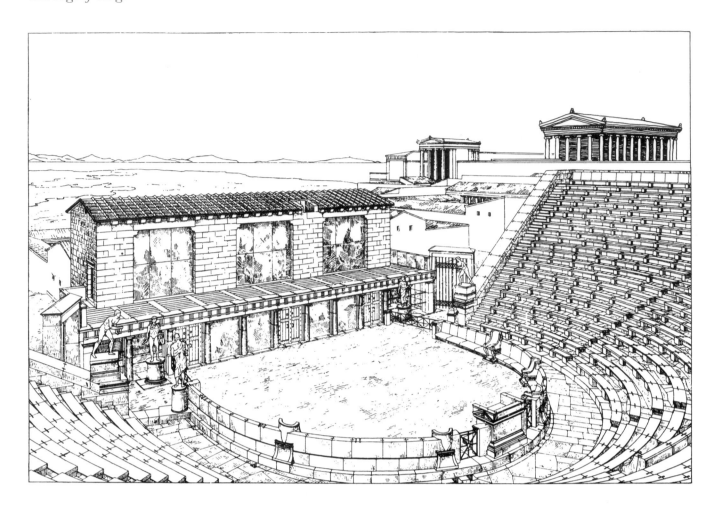

A reconstruction of the Hellenistic theatre at Priene, begun in the 2nd century BC. Drama was immensely popular in the Hellenistic world and every town of any size had its own theatre. The design of theatres had changed since classical times: the skene, the stage building, has moved forward, cutting off part of the orchestra, which is now no longer circular. The audience was interested in the drama alone, its ritual origins largely forgotten.

achievement here was limited by circumstances and the shortness of his reign, but his successors – above all the Seleucids – pursued the process on a very large scale. This was the largest movement of peoples in the history of the Greeks since the archaic age, though it is also one of the least well documented aspects of the Hellenistic world. From scattered evidence it may be inferred that the bulk of the colonists, both original settlers and later reinforcements, came from the Greek world, and probably every part of it, only limited use being made of native peoples. The kings provided the impetus and direction, recruiting colonists sometimes by invitation, sometimes by virtual compulsion; they made land available, and gave dynastic names to their foundations. Not every foundation was that of a Greek-style city; there were also many military colonies, recruiting grounds for the royal armies, which lacked the full trappings of Greek cities, though they might acquire

these in the course of time. The new civic foundations reproduced the institutions and characteristics of the old Greek cities: they had magistrates, a council, an assembly of citizens, temples and civic architecture, theatres and gymnasia. Yet the new cities, founded within the kingdoms and under royal patronage, and without previous traditions, could not aspire to an independent political role. Royal officials were probably a regular presence in them, cooperating with and directing the city magistrates. Tribute and other forms of taxation were common, as throughout the territories under royal control. But except in foreign policy the cities were nominally autonomous, and were regularly treated with outward respect by the rulers – an indication of the strength of civic attitudes and values even in a new and artificial setting.

The foundations were particularly dense in Asia Minor and in Syria, though they were also established in Mesopotamia and further east, as far as Bactria. Egypt was a special case, with only three Greek cities: the old treaty port of Naucratis in the Nile delta, now overshadowed by Alexandria, the prestigious capital developed by the Ptolemies, and Ptolemais in Upper Egypt, founded probably as a counterweight to Egyptian Thebes. This was partly a result of land shortage in Egypt's narrow and peculiar territory, but partly the deliberate policy of the Ptolemies to retain centralized control. By contrast the Seleucids, rich in land, promoted city foundations in their vast empire more than any other dynasty, basing their rule on Greek cities to which they gave a large measure of local autonomy.

Large as the migration may have been (though no figures are available), it remains true that the Greek settlers were a minority within the population of Asia. It had always seemed likely that this was going to be the case, and it had not acted as a serious deterrent against plans of conquest and settlement, though there are indications of initial resistance on the part of some colonists, fearful of the possible loss of Greek identity in distant lands. 'The Macedonians who hold Alexandria in Egypt, who dwell in Seleucia and Babylonia and in other colonies scattered throughout the whole world, have degenerated into Syrians, Parthians, Egyptians.' These words are attributed to a Roman commander in Livy's account of the Roman wars in Asia Minor in the early 2nd century – good rhetoric, but bad history. Greek settlements deep in Asia may have been physically remote from the Aegean world, but they did not allow themselves to become cut off from that world and diluted in a new environment. Mobility had long been a characteristic of the Greek world; a constant stream of travellers of every kind – traders, craftsmen, athletes, men of letters, ambassadors, and so forth –

helped to maintain the cultural unity of the Greek world despite its physical and political fragmentation. The same remained true in the enlarged Hellenistic world, and has received startling archaeological confirmation from as far away as Afghanistan. Intermarriage with natives certainly did take place, at least at the lower social levels, but citizenship in the new cities appears to have been carefully guarded. Intermarriage with Egyptians was prohibited in the Greek cities in Egypt. But it was above all through their culture that the Greeks preserved their sense of identity. The gymnasium, the centre of Greek educational activity, physical and intellectual, became the most distinctive mark of Greekness in Asia, to be found wherever there was a Greek settlement. The Greek cities in the east were thus no ephemeral phenomenon: in fact they outlived the dynasties that had founded them. Alexandria, Antioch, and Pergamon were still there, long after the disappearance of the Ptolemies, Seleucids and Attalids. The non-Greek kingdoms that followed the Seleucids initially observed the same outward relations with the Greek cities as their Seleucid predecessors. A letter in Greek of the Parthian king Artabanus III to the city of Seleucia on the Eulaeus (Susa), dated AD 21, could almost have been written by any Seleucid ruler. In the early 2nd century AD, Tacitus described Seleucia

A model of the acropolis of Pergamon, one of the most splendid cities of Hellenistic times (see also p. 176). We are looking north; the area to the west is occupied by temples and a large theatre; to the east are palaces and houses belonging to important officials. In the right foreground is the agora. The altar of Zeus is slightly to the right of centre.

193

Ptolemy II and his second wife and sister, Arsinoe II. The Egypt he ruled (285–246 BC) was one of the most prosperous Hellenistic kingdoms; his capital, Alexandria, was the largest city in the world and the intellectual centre of the age. On the right is the city's most famous temple, the Serapeum, with the image of Serapis. His cult seems to have been introduced by the Ptolemies perhaps to provide a common religion for Egyptians and Greeks.

on the Tigris (the Seleucid capital for the eastern part of their empire) as 'a powerful city, surrounded by walls, which had not been corrupted by barbarian ways, but preserved the spirit of Seleucus its founder. Three hundred citizens chosen for their wealth or wisdom make up its council, while the popular assembly has its share of power.'

The 'hellenization' of the east

To found Greek settlements in the east and to encourage Greek immigration was not the same as 'hellenizing' the east, whether in intention or in actual result, and there is no reason to believe that this was the policy of the kings. Plutarch, it is true, writing under the Roman empire, does portray Alexander in one work as having intended to, and succeeded in, hellenizing Asia, and from Droysen onwards this has been the starting point for many an idealized conception of the Hellenistic age. Yet the work is rhetorical, perhaps merely a literary exercise, not a reflection of Plutarch's own beliefs, and in any case it reflects a climate of ideas later than the Hellenistic period. Acceptance of native traditions was the normal approach of Hellenistic rulers, with one famous exception, due to very special circumstances – Antiochus IV's attempt in 167 BC to turn Jerusalem into a Greek city and abolish Jewish customs, an attempt which failed in any case. The Ptolemies were officially regarded in Egypt as Pharaohs, and built temples to the native gods they affected to honour. In practice they were Greek rulers, governing in Alexandria with a Greek court and Greek

officials, not in Memphis or Thebes. The Seleucids behaved similarly. Their attitude to Persian traditions is unknown, though it was probably one of aloofness, but they identified themselves with the old Babylonian monarchy and fostered Babylonian cults. In their dynastic marriages they formed links not just with the other Macedonian or Greek dynasties, but with native royal houses as well, as Alexander had done with the Iranians. But the heart of their kingdom lay in their new foundations in north Syria, not further east. Babylon was counterbalanced by Seleucia on the Tigris, and Susa was refounded as a Greek city, Seleucia on the Eulaeus.

Yet the presence of Greek-style monarchies based on Greek immigration and settlement could not but have an impact on the eastern peoples. The Greek language, in the form of the *koine*, the 'common language', derived from Attic, became a world language, used over the entire length and breadth of the Hellenistic world, and adopted by some natives. A few examples may suffice. The Indian king Aśoka (known to the Greeks as Piodasses), on his conversion to Buddhism *c.* 260, set up a series of rock-cut edicts near Kandahar (Afghanistan), in Prakrit, Aramaic, and in a Greek version which shows familiarity with Greek philosophical terminology. The inscriptions also obviously imply the presence of Greeks in the region. He recalls his sending of emissaries to the Greek world, seeking to convert them to Buddhism. During the 3rd century, the Jewish sacred books began to be translated into Greek, for the benefit of Jews in Egypt who had adopted Greek as their language (the Septuagint). Most remarkable is an account of the Exodus written by Ezekiel, an Alexandrian Jew of (perhaps) the 2nd century, and cast in the form and language of a Greek tragedy – the only tragic fragment extant from the Hellenistic age.

Nor was the influence restricted to language, though language was the necessary avenue to cultural influence. The partial urbanization of the east and adoption of a Greek style of urban life were not just a matter of royal policy, but the result also of native imitation and adoption of Greek ways – a process that had started before the Hellenistic age, as in western Asia Minor, but was vastly extended with the conquest of the east. In addition to the attractions of the culture of the dominant people, 'self-hellenization' brought with it the chance of acceptance by the Greek world, and an avenue to higher status and participation. The process may be most clearly seen in Jerusalem in the early 2nd century, as described in I and II Maccabees, though the 'hellenizing movement' here also brought about a decisive traditionalist reaction. Elsewhere, as in the Phoenician cities, the process was seemingly free from stress. The Phoenician cities were accepted as quasi-Greek, while retaining their identity.

Yet hellenization had many limits. Where it occurred, it was above all an upper-class and urban phenomenon, leaving the wide countryside virtually untouched. The evidence for the Hellenistic world is mostly of Greek origin and in Greek, conveying a deceptive impression of a larger hellenized world. From a number of inscriptions relating to land transactions, mostly from western Asia Minor, one may perceive the existence on some large estates of a native peasantry in a status of dependence on their Greek or Macedonian overlords. The institution, inherited from earlier times, was taken for granted by the new rulers of Asia. As far as the new Greek cities are concerned, little is known of the conditions of land tenure or of the relative status of town-dwellers and the country people. Yet it would be justifiable to suppose that they differed fundamentally from what had been the pattern in many classical cities, Athens for example, where there was no division between town and countryside or between citizens and peasants. That division by contrast is manifest in the Hellenistic east, where it is implied by the survival of many native languages despite the spread of Greek (a survival which became obvious in the late Roman empire) as well as by the eventual disappearance of many place and city names imported by the Greeks, despite centuries of settlement and use. Alexandria remained as Iskanderiya in Arabic (though as Rhakoti in Coptic), Antioch as Antakya, but Beroea reverted to Haleb (Aleppo) and Heliopolis to Baalbek, to name but a few. Significantly the Maccabaean movement in Palestine drew its strength from the poorer Jews, a reaction of the countryside against the hellenizing sections of the urban aristocracy. In the sphere of religion the Greeks occasionally adopted eastern gods, though usually in a hellenized form, like the Egyptian Serapis whose cult spread spontaneously in the Greek world, achieving great popularity. There was no corresponding adoption of Greek gods in the east by the natives. Indeed, religion provided a stimulus to resistance against Hellenism, as happened in Judaea, and in Egypt, where a series of native uprisings which started in 217, prompted in the first instance by the incorporation of Egyptian troops into the army of the Ptolemies, was at heart a reaction and protest against

An Indian elephant, shown on the reverse of a coin of Seleucus I, King of Syria. Seleucus' empire stretched as far as India; the coin commemorates a gift to him of 500 war elephants from the Indian king Chandragupta. Seleucus used the elephants with great success in his campaigns.

the foreign occupation and exploitation of Egypt. Little is known of Persia under the Seleucids, but the rise of the neo-Persian empire of the Sassanids centuries later may imply continuous underground ferment within some traditionalist Persian circles. The existence of anti-Greek apocalyptic prophecies which circulated in the Hellenistic age can be inferred from later evidence. The 'hellenization' of the east, and eastern reactions to Hellenism, were complex and diverse processes.

Hellenistic culture and society

By 'Hellenistic culture' is meant here Greek culture in the Hellenistic age, a culture that was largely the work of Greeks, the contribution of hellenized natives being limited in comparison. Most of the leading names in Hellenistic philosophy, literature, art and science are those of men from the world of the old Greek cities, though Zeno of Citium, the founder of the Stoic school of philosophy, was reputed to be of Phoenician origin. In Hellenistic culture, as in political and social history, the complex interplay of monarchy and city may be observed. Patronage of the arts had long been one of the functions of rulers, from the archaic tyrants onwards, and the Hellenistic kings, conscious of their reputation in the Greek world, inherited and pursued that tradition, with greater wealth available to them than to previous Greek rulers. The new royal capitals, Pella, Pergamon, Antioch, and Alexandria, became new centres of culture, rivalling the old Greek cities. Cultural activity tended in any case to concentrate in a few large cities, which enjoyed greater wealth and stability than the many smaller and more vulnerable cities. But the new foundations could not wholly displace the old centres, and remained dependent on the old cities for their recruitment of talent. Besides, royal patronage had its limitations, even its drawbacks. Much depended on the inclination of the individual rulers. Cultural life at the Seleucid court appears to have been limited in comparison with its rivals; Attalid patronage did not emerge effectively till the 2nd century, when the other major dynasties were in decline. Much the most conspicuous and self-advertising, in this field as in others, were the Ptolemies, who made Alexandria the most brilliant centre of the Hellenistic world in the 3rd century. But in the 2nd century Ptolemy VIII, himself a cultured man, quarrelled with the Alexandrian intellectuals and exiled them, to the detriment of Alexandria, but to the benefit of the Greek cities who received them. Furthermore, royal patronage was not equally effective in every field. Where political and social critique was involved, royalty and freedom of thought did not marry happily. Adulation and conformism were among the prices of monarchy.

Philosophy

In one major field, that of philosophy, the contribution of royal patronage was slight, and primacy remained with the old Greek world, or rather with one city, Athens. In the 5th century Athens had become the intellectual capital of the Greek world, attracting the best minds from other cities. Her cultural role and prestige survived her political decline. Athens remained the seat of Plato's Academy and of Aristotle's Lyceum, though these lost their primacy in the 3rd century to the new philosophical schools which also flourished in Athens – the Epicurean school founded by Epicurus of Samos, and the Stoic school (so-called because it met in the *stoa poikile*, the 'painted arcade') founded by Zeno of Citium in Cyprus. The latter was the most influential of the Hellenistic philosophies, and its acceptance by the Roman governing classes ensured its continued vitality into the Roman empire. For all their differences, between schools, and between members of the same school, the Hellenistic philosophies shared a common aim. As Xenocrates, one of Plato's successors at the Academy, put it: 'the reason for discovering philosophy is to allay that which causes disturbance in life'. The objective was thus the attainment of happiness and peace of mind by the individual as an individual. Study of the physical world was pursued, but subordinated to an ethical purpose: happiness was dependent on a correct understanding of the universe. But individual happiness was divorced from any particular political or social context, and in this respect Hellenistic philosophy abandoned preoccupations that had been prominent in the 4th-century thinkers. Speculation and debate over the ideal state were not followed up; Aristotle's *Politics*, the greatest work of political and social analysis in antiquity, had no successor. Under the influence of monarchy, writings on kingship proliferated. Though these have not been preserved directly, their influence may be seen in the 'Letter of Aristeas to Philocrates', a Jewish work of the

2nd century. There is no reason to believe that they contained any deep political critique; they were probably mostly adulatory in character, continuators of Isocrates' monarchical writings.

Nor did Hellenistic philosophy address itself to the issue of wealth and poverty, a recurring theme in the 4th-century thinkers, reflecting the reality and seriousness of the issue. Though eastern emigration probably provided some relief, it did not solve the old problem. One characteristic of the Hellenistic age was the increased dependence of many cities on wealthy benefactors, for their food supply, the celebration of religious festivals, the maintenance of gymnasia and educational institutions, and the erection of public buildings. This, and the increased display of private wealth, probably implies a concentration of wealth at the top. Democracy as it had existed in the classical period in some Greek states was a casualty of the Hellenistic period. The word survived, but increasingly emptied of its original meaning, a trend visible already in the 4th century in the writings of Isocrates. Nor was slavery as an institution the subject of critical inquiry on the part of Hellenistic philosophy. That there had been such a debate, even though only at an attenuated level and within a limited circle, can be seen from Aristotle's *Politics* (Book I) and his attempted justification of the institution. Aristotle's argument was far from flawless. The debate ended, and the institution continued.

It is natural to relate this shift of emphasis in Hellenistic philosophy, away from political and social issues towards individual ethical concerns, with the political evolution of the Greek world after the 4th century. Hellenistic philosophies, it is said, reflect the decline of the city as a framework of Greek life, and its failure to be replaced by other meaningful frameworks: hence the individual was left to himself in his search for happiness in an unstable and frequently violent world. There is truth in this view, yet Hellenistic philosophy cannot be taken as a complete summing up of the many diverse attitudes of the age, if the argument that the life of the Greek cities had not yet been emptied of all political content is correct. Further, the two major Hellenistic philosophies differed in their attitude to political activity. The Epicureans preached total non-involvement in political life, while Stoicism was far from incompatible with it. Indeed there were many links between Stoic philosophers and Hellenistic kings, as in the case of Antigonus Gonatas of Macedon or Cleomenes III of Sparta. Stoic emphasis on steadfast pursuit of duty fitted in well with the exercise of power and provided a sanction for it. No wonder it proved acceptable to the conservatism of the Roman upper classes. More generally, intellectuals and men of letters were to be found at every royal court and were frequently used by the kings, as by cities, for diplomatic missions.

Philology and literature

If Athens remained the chief home of philosophy, Alexandria was the home of philology, and here lay one of its major achievements. The task the Ptolemies set themselves was the collection and preservation of accurate texts of the whole of Greek literature, and non-Greek literature was perhaps included as well. Libraries had existed before in the Greek world, the private collections of some tyrants or of men of learning: Aristotle's library was famous, and was kept together as a collection long after his death. But nothing on this scale had ever been attempted before, and Attalid emulation in the 2nd century could not match the Ptolemaic achievement. Tradition speaks of hundreds of thousands of volumes being gathered, often with great ingenuity and persistence. For instance, every ship reaching Alexandria had its literary texts confiscated for the Library, copies of the originals being returned to the shipowner in compensation. In a world which did not know the printing press, literature was a very perishable commodity: Euripides was one of the most popular authors of the age, yet twelve of his plays had already disappeared by the end of the classical period. The initial inspiration for the Library and its aims probably came from Athens, and from the Aristotelian school's ideal of encyclopaedic learning. In the 330s the Athenians decreed the establishment of official and authentic texts of their three great trage-dians, to be kept in the public archives, for use in performance. The Aristotelian inspiration probably reached Alexandria in the person of Demetrius of Phalerum, an Athenian statesman and philosopher of the Aristotelian school, exiled from Athens in 307 and a refugee at the Ptolemaic court; he may have advised Ptolemy I on the establishment of the Library. Thus the science of philology was founded: authentic texts were established, and commentaries on the best authors written, to serve the purposes of an education based primarily on the study of acknowledged examples of literary excellence – that is to say, on 'classics'. We are still heirs to that Alexandrian tradition.

The literary production of the Hellenistic age was considerable in bulk, yet the majority of it has not survived: hence the difficulty of assessing it fairly. On the whole, the Hellenistic age did not produce literary masterpieces comparable in quantity and quality to those of previous Greek history, and writers had to contend with the popularity of the established classics of the past, which the Hellenistic age did so much to preserve for posterity. The evidence of literary papyri from Graeco-Roman Egypt shows this clearly: with few exceptions the new literary works did not achieve the readership of earlier Greek authors. For instance, the stage enjoyed great popularity throughout the Hellenistic world; every Greek city, however remote, had its theatre, and travelling companies of actors put on performances far and wide. Many new works were written, but could not rival the established tragedians.

This bronze statuette of a philosopher may represent Epicurus, the founder of one of the new schools of philosophy which arose in 3rd-century Athens. For Epicurus, unlike most earlier philosophers, political and scientific interests were subordinated to ethical concerns, primarily the creation of a theory of life that would ensure peace of mind for the individual.

The playwright Menander was among the most popular and influential writers of the Hellenistic age. Above is the colophon of his play 'Dyskolos' ('The Disgruntled Man'), from a papyrus discovered as recently as 1956. The author's name and the title of the play are at the bottom.

Only in comedy did the Hellenistic age contribute one great name, that of the Athenian Menander in the late 4th and early 3rd centuries, much admired in antiquity and influential through his Roman adaptors Plautus and Terence. The evidence of literary papyri from Egypt shows him to have been next in popularity after Homer and Euripides, and it is to papyrological discoveries, some of them in recent years, that we owe the recovery of extensive fragments of lost plays and one virtually complete one, the *Dyskolos* (*The Disgruntled Man*). Menander's comedies were far removed in spirit from the vigorous social and political satire of Old Comedy. They revolved around stock themes and stock characters (young lovers thwarted by a gruff father, reunion of parents with children long believed lost, etc.); elements drawn from real life acquired unreality. The plays provided the happy endings that were missing in real life. Psychological observation, the original use of established themes and delicate use of language were their outstanding qualities, much prized in the Hellenistic age and till the end of antiquity.

Menander's activity was centred on his native Athens, another indication of the limits of royal patronage, to be seen also in historiography. Many royal histories were written, but they soon fell into neglect and eventually disappeared, perhaps deservedly so. Hieronymus of Cardia, author of the principal ancient account of the history of the generation after Alexander, and the ultimate source behind our extant accounts (his own work is lost), is a rare example of a writer who reconciled royal service and historiographical quality. Otherwise the best historical works originated from the world of the old Greek cities, and drew their inspiration in part from civic values and opposition to royalty. Timaeus of Tauromenium in Sicily, the greatest historian of the Greek west, wrote his work in political exile in Athens in the late 4th and early 3rd centuries, unyielding in his hatred of the Sicilian tyrants. In the west, the Greek cities had fallen under one-man rule earlier and more completely than on the mainland, yet civic attitudes survived. Phylarchus, perhaps the most important of the historians of the 3rd century, strongly disliked the Hellenistic courts of his time, idealizing instead the Spartan reformer kings Agis IV and Cleomenes III who sought to revive Spartan power in the Peloponnese. Polybius of Megalopolis, an Achaean statesman, regarded the kings with ambivalence; it was the rise of Rome, not the Hellenistic world itself, that prompted him to write his great work, a history of the Roman expansion between 220 and 146 BC.

The Alexandrian contribution to literature lay in another field, in poetry, not in prose. There were many differences between individual writers, and Alexandrian literature cannot be reduced to a single type. For example, two of its most celebrated names, Callimachus of Cyrene and Apollonius of Rhodes, were involved in a famous quarrel over the supremacy of epic poetry as a literary form. Apollonius, author of a long novel in epic verse, the *Argonautica*, was worsted in the conflict and withdrew to Rhodes. Callimachus preferred shorter works, on which great craftsmanship and care were expended. Common to both, and to all Alexandrian poetry, was a love of erudition for its own sake, in the use of poetic language and in the wealth of mythological allusions, a reflection of the philological interests of the Library. Callimachus himself was one of its librarians. Learning and literature were consciously blended together, for the benefit of a select and sophisticated readership, proud of the sense of superiority derived from its literary pursuits. Characteristic too was the interest in the picturesque, the small-scale observation of daily life and detail, displayed also in the visual arts. The *Idylls* of the Syracusan poet Theocritus, only briefly active at the court of Ptolemy II, show this quality; it was Theocritus who established pastoral (or bucolic) poetry as a popular literary genre, destined to a long history. But it was a town-dweller's view of country life, a style of life he idealized from a distance but had no intention of sharing, very far in spirit from either Hesiod's *Works and Days* or the Attic farmers of Aristophanes. Sophistication and artificiality are characteristic of Hellenistic poetry.

Alexandrian science

Patronage of cultural life involved the sciences as well: mathematics, astronomy, geography, botany and zoology, anatomy and medicine, and in these fields the Alexandrian achievement was considerable. Scientific research had previously been left to individual philosophers – indeed Greek science never completely lost its connections with philosophy. Now for the first time scientific research had at Alexandria the benefit of royal patronage and its resources: in medicine and anatomy, for instance, Herophilus of Calchedon and Erasistratus of Ceos were able to practise dissection, perhaps even vivisection, on the bodies of condemned criminals provided by the Ptolemies, which made possible progress in anatomical knowledge. The achievements of Alexandrian science were many and diverse, and many of the greatest names in Greek science are related to Ptolemaic patronage. Euclid's *Elements* systematized Greek mathematical and geometrical knowledge up to his time (early 3rd century). Aristarchus of Samos, at the same time, propounded the heliocentric theory of the universe, though it did not gain wide support. The polymath Eratosthenes of Cyrene (3rd century), the most versatile intellectual since Aristotle, succeeded in measuring the circumference of the earth by a simple method, by measuring the angle of the sun's rays at two different places, Alexandria and Syene (Aswan) at the same time of the day. Ctesibius of Alexandria (early 3rd century) and subsequent inventors down to Hero of Alexandria (1st century AD) are credited with a number of mechanical inventions, sometimes of considerable ingenuity. Many more examples could be given, yet the modern reader is struck above all by the lack of practical impact all these discoveries and inventions had on the society of their time. The short answer to this problem may be simply that they were not meant to: science was pursued in the first instance for its own sake, as a means of understanding the world, not of changing it. The frequently noticed divorce between what we call pure and applied sciences continued in the Hellenistic age, which in this respect did not differ fundamentally from earlier Greek history. The notion of progress was not by any means unknown. For example, the Hellenistic scientists were well aware how far their own branches of study had progressed since those studies had begun, but there was no general awareness of the possibility and desirability of unlimited material progress through technical means. The sophisticated mechanical devices of some Alexandrian inventors remained merely clever inventions to impress the layman. Knowledge was rated more highly than practice. Plutarch writes of Archimedes, the great 3rd-century Syracusan scientist and inventor, who was active at the court of the Ptolemies as well as in his native Syracuse under Hiero II, that 'he regarded mechanical occupations and every art that ministers to needs as ignoble and vulgar, and so directed his own ambition solely to those studies the beauty and subtlety of which are not tainted by necessity'.

Hellenistic medical and anatomical knowledge made considerable advances under royal patronage. This 4th-century votive relief from Attica shows the oracle god Amphiaros as a doctor treating a patient.

In only one sphere was there any attempt to link research directly to its practical application, that of warfare. War was not just a permanent reality of the Hellenistic world, it was also in a sense the basis of royal power, both ideologically and practically. The monarchies owed their foundation and preservation to continued military success. Their support of research into military technology reflects this. Extant, for instance, are parts of the *Mechanical Handbook* of Philo of Byzantium (*c.* 200 BC), which deal in part with military technology (artillery and siege-craft). War had first emerged as a subject of study in the 5th century with the Sophists, and was pursued in the 4th with the growing specialization of warfare: the Hellenistic kings developed that tradition. Yet even in the field that concerned them most directly, practical efficiency was not the sole concern of the kings. The early Hellenistic age witnessed a most remarkable competition between the kings over the construction of warships, a naval 'arms race' as it has been called. Yet the competition concerned the building of bigger ships, not better ships; the end products were so monstrously unwieldy that the competition defeated itself. In every field, royalty was inseparable from considerations of status, prestige, and display, rather than practical efficiency, and the Roman world inherited these attitudes. The Hellenistic age was notable for the kings' prodigal display of wealth, but consumption of wealth ranked higher than its production. The Ptolemies made great efforts to reclaim land and improve agriculture, but it was for their own benefit, to increase the revenues of their kingdom, not for that of Egypt as a whole. This was not the same as trying to improve the economy of the country, though an earlier generation of historians, of whom M. Rostovtzeff is one of the most distinguished representatives, was inclined to interpret their policy in the light of the planned economy of modern totalitarian states.

The Greeks and the east – a one-sided dialogue?

Because of its geographical position, the history of Greece is, as it were, a long dialogue with the peoples and cultures of the east. The Hellenistic period is one major stage in that dialogue, yet in retrospect, and in comparison with the archaic age with all its borrowings and adaptations by the Greeks from the east, the dialogue was perhaps less productive and less complete than it might have been. For a start, Greeks as a rule did not learn foreign languages. There were exceptions, of course, and there had to be interpreters for the purposes of government. But generally it was up to the foreigners to learn Greek, not the other way round. An interest in non-Greek peoples and customs had been characteristic of earlier Greek history, as exemplified by Herodotus. That interest continued, and Herodotus achieved renewed popularity, but it did not deepen as it might have done. In the early Hellenistic period, histories of Egypt and Babylonia were written in Greek by native priests, Manetho and Berossus respectively. But the Greek public preferred their own preconceived

and inaccurate versions of eastern history; Egyptology and Assyriology are modern, not Greek, creations, though ironically it was a Greek inscription (the Rosetta stone) that made possible the decipherment of hieroglyphs. The Old Testament, translated into Greek, was read by Jews, not by Greeks. The role of the eastern peoples in the running of the Hellenistic monarchies was limited, restricted usually to the lower administrative levels.

Looking at the eastern side a Greek historian might be inclined to suppose that such hellenization as did take place was in itself a positive step. Yet the Macedonian conquest also meant three centuries of warfare, largely at the expense of the east and for the benefit of foreign dynasties. Culturally, the coming of the Greeks provided a stimulus to the eastern peoples to advertise themselves to the Greek world; Manetho and Berossus are examples of this. But in the long run it is not clear that native cultures benefited or were revitalized by their contact with the Greeks. Only the Jews were impelled by their encounter with Hellenism to assert successfully their separate identity.

The history of the Hellenistic age is framed by two military conquests, that of Asia, rapid and deliberate, and the Roman conquest, long drawn and probably not the result of any preconceived imperial plan. The Roman conquest was destructive, in political, human, and economic terms. But the political decline of the Hellenistic world had started even before the Roman intervention, and Rome cannot be made solely responsible for the process. Eventually the coming of Rome brought stability, peace, and political unification, but at the price of loss of political freedom. Culturally, the encounter was of the greatest significance. An imperial people, but without initially a culture of their own to match, the Romans were impelled by their conquest of the Hellenistic world to develop their own cultural personality, in imitation and emulation of the Greeks. It is perhaps ironical that the influence of the Greeks on their Roman conquerors turned out to be more fruitful than it had been on most of the eastern peoples they themselves had conquered.

7
Rome and the Greek East

imperial rule and
transformation

AVERIL CAMERON

UNDERSTANDABLY, Octavian preferred to advertise his victory at Actium in 31 BC as the triumph of Rome over the east rather than as the defeat of a personal rival. Coins emphasized the theme of the conquest of Egypt, and the great triple triumph held in Rome in 29 BC paraded the effigy of the dead Cleopatra as well as her living children. From now on there would be no hindrance to the grip of Rome over the Hellenic world. Symbolized in Greek cities by the appearance of temples to Augustus and the imperial family, the idea of Rome gradually came to seem normal and acceptable. From now on the Greek world had to recognize that Roman rule was to be a permanent reality.

The yoke was relatively easy. Rome required two things: security and revenue. The first was not a problem in Greece itself, part of the Roman province of Achaea, which, as a senatorial and non-military province, required no legions. The same went for the province of Asia – western Turkey – while much of eastern Turkey was at first ruled by client kings. Syria was a different matter, requiring both permanent troops and direct imperial control, as did the troublesome province of Judaea (annexed in AD 6). But most of the Greek cities in mainland Greece and Asia Minor could be left undisturbed without fear of uprising. Taxes, too, though essential to Rome for the upkeep of her large and permanent army, must have been relatively light in the early principate, for the 1st century saw a striking growth in the prosperity of the Greek east which would have been impossible if Rome had demanded significantly more. In any case, Roman rule was invariably conducted in the interests of the rich, and the tax system was no exception. The rural population was the main source of tax revenue, while the well-to-do, living in the cities on the rents and profits of their large estates, were largely able to escape. Very little effort was made to tax the commercial enterprise of the cities. Thus while the general taxes levied on the agricultural population were adequate for Rome's requirements and not beyond the means of the tax-payers, the rich were able to retain most of their income and trade and commerce to expand without hindrance. Roman officials were few and the Roman governor rarely to be seen, except on his rounds of hearing law suits in the major cities of his province. The governor of a province such as Asia typically held office for only a year, having been given his province as a result of a ballot among the senior senators available; he thus had little time to acquaint himself with the province's problems, and equally little opportunity, since there was only a minimum staff. Accordingly, governors in the early empire had two primary concerns – keeping the peace within their province and dealing with law suits involving Roman citizens or disputes between cities. For the most part, the provincials were left to themselves to conduct their own business. As Tacitus said, the price of peace was imperial rule, but the signs indicate that many of the inhabitants of the Greek world thought that a price well worth paying. Even if at this stage there were those who disliked the idea, the first two centuries of the empire saw a remarkable degree of acceptance and even of enthusiasm for the Roman regime from the upper classes in the Greek east – a development which needed little or no direct encouragement from Rome itself.

The Roman peace

At this early date there were still relatively few Roman citizens in the Greek world. Most cities now perhaps had their settlements of Roman traders and the like, and occasional provincials, like St Paul, would have acquired the citizenship through service rendered by themselves or their fathers or grandfathers. There were a few 'colonies' of Roman citizens, like Corinth, refounded in 44 BC after it had been razed to the ground in 146, or like the early colonies of veteran soldiers planted by Augustus at strategic places in the empire. From now on, however, the citizenship was steadily extended more widely, though its real advantages declined. For a few, though, it could be the path to entry into the senate itself, and from the reign of Vespasian on (AD 69–78) we find Greeks entering the senate in significant numbers. The first, naturally, tended to come from cities which were either Roman colonies or where there were actually settlements of Romans. Usually they were members of the local élites, rich men with good connections, for the way to the top was through patronage and favour. It was occasionally possible for someone lower in the social scale to work his way up, but he would have to serve long years in minor military and civil offices before (if he was very lucky) reaching a senior equestrian post or even the senate. Most were content to stay in their own communities and confine their ambition to the local level, for few outsiders indeed succeeded in reaching the top ranks of the imperial administration. One such was the Athenian millionaire, Herodes Atticus, who was consul in AD 143; though quite exceptional for his wealth and culture, a man of this sort was nevertheless more typical of the kind of provincial who moved easily into Roman society than were the small number who succeeded in climbing the social ladder from lower origins.

Constantinople, personified as a female figure carrying a cornucopia, from a 5th-century ivory. Her stiff pose and fixed gaze are typical of late Roman art and herald the non-naturalistic spiritual intensity of the art of the new Christian Hellenic empire.

As the reality of Roman rule percolated into Greek consciousness, so the Greek cities acquired a Roman appearance. Colonnades, temples, baths were built or rebuilt in the Roman style, so that classical cities were to some extent refashioned, alongside entirely new foundations. This was an empire-wide phenomenon: by the middle of the 2nd century one could go from east to west and still feel securely in a Roman environment. The 2nd century, indeed, was the great age of building, done in many cases by individuals at their own expense and commemorated in the inscriptions in which they recorded their benefactions. Again the Roman government profited from their enthusiasm. All over the Greek east wealthy notables vied with each other to spend on gifts, whether buildings to adorn their cities or distributions of food or money to their fellow citizens. They were willing to pay large sums to enter public office, and then to give more than was required in the performance of it. Oil for the gymnasia, expenses for the games, all became the object of rivalry among the rich, who would then boast of the vastness of their generosity. Opramoas of Rhodiapolis in Lycia was one of the greatest givers; others would even on occasion themselves pay the entire poll-tax of their province, as did P. Popillius Python in Macedonia. And these same city benefactors typically held such useful offices in Roman eyes as priest in the imperial cult, or *dekaprotos*, one of the ten in each city responsible for tax collection. Thus local generosity, often termed euergetism from the Greek for 'benefactor', meshed in with service to the imperial government. It would be hard to draw the line at which men like Python (and some women, too, held these offices and gave generously to their cities) began to feel that they were serving Rome rather than their own cities; more probably the distinction, obvious and sharp at the beginning of the empire, had become so blurred as hardly to matter.

The peace and security of the late 1st and early 2nd centuries allowed a flourishing of cultural life in the Greek east. Members of the wealthy urban élites were usually highly educated in rhetoric and sometimes also philosophy, and they had not only the leisure but also the audience to encourage their literary talents. As political strife evaporated in the settled conditions of empire, the dominant product of the rhetoric that still provided the staple of Greek and Latin education came to be the panegyric – the formal speech of praise or congratulation that now accompanied every public ceremony. Since there was usually little that was contentious to discuss, form and style mattered at least as much as content, and care for style now took the form of a passion for archaism and the search for 'attic' Greek – perhaps a half-conscious need to remind Greeks of their past glories now that their public aspirations were inextricably identified with the reality of Rome. Historians wrote in the manner of Herodotus and Thucydides, orators tried to emulate Demosthenes and extremists earned some scathing comments from the satirist Lucian. But this flowering of literature was

neither purely ornamental nor purely local. Men such as Herodes Atticus received acclaim in their own city and elsewhere in the Greek east and then went on to capture the ear and win the favour of the emperor; earlier, Plutarch had been rewarded for his literary talents by being made procurator of Achaea. Aelius Aristides, educated at Pergamon and Athens, travelled throughout the Greek world giving displays of oratory, composed panegyrics on Athens and Smyrna and then on Rome itself. Thus these Greeks brought their Greek culture to the wider world of Rome, while the emperors in turn favoured them with their patronage. The interest of the Emperor Hadrian in all things Greek was a great stimulus to this two-way traffic, and encouraged the process already to some extent under way whereby 2nd-century Rome enthusiastically embraced Greek culture, even to the extent that educated members of the Roman élite were as at home in Greek as in Latin. Marcus Aurelius, for instance, was deeply influenced by the works of Epictetus, and moved to tears by the oration of Aelius Aristides on Smyrna after the earthquake of AD 178. But Hadrian had taken his love of things Greek to the lengths of making three long visits to Athens, himself initiating public works and restoration, building temples, instituting a regular panhellenic assembly and participating in public life; he had even, before his accession, held the archonship, the chief Athenian magistracy. Not many emperors were so visible in the Greek east as Hadrian, but by the mid-2nd century the interrelation of Greek institutions with Roman public life was too well established to falter. At the end of the 2nd and beginning of the 3rd century the historian Cassius Dio from Nicaea in Bithynia exemplified to the fullest degree the assimilation of Greek to Roman styles of life. A senator in Rome for thirty years, he reached the consulship twice, the second time as ordinary consul alongside the Emperor Severus Alexander, governed important western provinces and wrote a history of Rome from the beginning to his own day.

But the early principate, advantageous to the urban élites of the Greek world, whose interests were soon identified with those of Rome, deprived the lower classes of their political rights. As in Rome itself popular assemblies and elections gave way to an elaborate system of patronage operated by the emperors and the élite, so in the Greek cities the once common popular assemblies gradually died out, and the local rich, the so-called decurion class, defined by its wealth alone, were left to run the cities unhindered. Benefactions and distributions to the rest of the citizens perhaps encouraged their acquiescence. By the 2nd century, they were actually at a legal disadvantage: *humiliores*, 'the lower classes', were liable in law to severe and arbitrary penalties from which their betters were at least in theory protected. The extension of Roman citizenship to all in AD 212, whatever its purpose, made no difference to this inequality, which for the first time institutionalized a differential which

Miletus, on the west coast of Asia Minor, as it appeared in Hellenistic times. This detail shows the approach to the vast south agora, which lies to the right of the buildings here. The elaboration of the architecture demonstrates the move away from pure Greek styles towards distinctively Roman forms.

had no doubt often existed in practice, especially in the dealings of Romans with the lower orders. The power of Roman governors to deal with criminals or simply doubtful characters had always been great, as can be seen from their dealings with Christians, but now ordinary people, whether in towns or countryside, could only expect the worst. This was part of a steady decline in the rights and legal position of the free population that led in the 4th century (under the Christian emperor Constantine) to successive governmental attempts to restrain their movements and to reduce the free rural population to virtual enserfment. Even if such attempts were far from successful in practice, it is undeniable that such were the intentions of the Roman government and that the lower classes in the Greek east as elsewhere had fewer legal rights than in the early empire; of political rights they had none at all.

The challenge of Christianity

In fact the *laissez-faire* Roman rule of the early empire had had its darker side too. The Romans might idealize Greek culture but they did not like those who were not cooperative. So the troublesome Jews, never content to adapt themselves to the mechanisms of Roman culture, were in the end ruthlessly suppressed, their Temple destroyed and their ruined capital rebuilt as a Roman colony. The holy places of Christianity and Judaism were therefore equally buried beneath heaps of Roman masonry, which Constantine's workmen in the 320s had to demolish before they had a chance of finding the

tomb of Christ. The Christians themselves invited suspicion as a secret and subversive sect; no more was needed than that for Nero to use them as a scapegoat for the burning of Rome in AD 64, with full approval from all sectors of Roman society. So it became established that for a man to admit to being a Christian was reason enough for execution. Once it became apparent that sincere Christians would not take part in sacrifices to the gods or in the imperial cult, the Romans were confirmed in their suspicions. Probably the numbers of those who perished in the arena during the period of persecution has been exaggerated by Christian writers such as Eusebius, but there were many moving incidents, such as the martyrdom of the aged Polycarp at Smyrna, probably in the 160s. Nevertheless, the church continued to grow, especially in the 3rd century when it acquired the well-based institutional hierarchy on which Constantine was later able to build. This growth, together with a general increase in religious sensitivity stimulated by the empire's troubles, inspired more determined persecution organized by the state itself, and in the early years of the 4th century, in the so-called 'Great Persecution', many of the Christian clergy in the eastern provinces were called upon to hand over the Scriptures as a sign of compliance; if they refused they were often mutilated and sent to the mines in Egypt. Many others however must have acquiesced, for when persecution ended the treatment of such *lapsi* was one of the church's major problems. It is hardly possible to estimate the proportion of Christians in the empire by this time, but they were probably still only a small minority, concentrated in the towns, and no doubt more numerous in the Greek provinces that were the object of the first missionary journeys of St Paul. Even so, the tight organization of the Christian communities, with their chain of authority from lay members to bishop, gave the Christian emperors an ideal basis on which to build; imperial patronage and direct political favour enabled the church to win many more converts in the early 4th century, especially among the educated urban upper classes, the bearers of the dominant culture.

By then however Christianity had long been under the influence of Hellenism. It was at the beginning a religion not merely of the *chora* (the countryside), of the village rather than the town, but also of clear semitic origins. But shortly after the death of Jesus, the decision was taken by his followers that the message was to be universal, not confined to Jews. In the context of the eastern Mediterranean that meant first and foremost that it would be preached to Greeks. The Pauline letters to Corinth and Ephesus would reach a mixed community of Greeks and Jews or Judaizers; in Athens Paul tempered his gospel to the tastes of Greek philosophy. In the next century Clement of Alexandria was already evolving a fusion of Christian and Hellenic thought. Educated Christians could not be expected to reject the whole of their classical culture. When Origen wrote his refutation of the pagan Celsus in the 3rd century he could suggest that the unification of the empire by Augustus was a necessary part of God's plan for the furtherance of Christianity – and the part of the empire which above all was the first home of gentile Christianity was the Greek world.

The 3rd century saw, besides the steady growth of Christianity even under persecution, many troubles for the empire as a whole and for the Greek east. Athens itself was attacked and severely damaged by the Heruls, a Germanic tribe which had swept down from the Danube; its defence was organized by the historian Dexippus, who also wrote about it. Antioch was sacked by Shahpuhr I, second monarch in the new and aggressive Sassanian dynasty. Like the west, the Greek world felt the effects of political instability, and the collapse of the financial system, though it was perhaps more cushioned than the west by its long history of urban prosperity, and seems to have been able to recover more quickly and more completely. It is a matter of dispute how serious a general crisis there actually was in the 3rd century, and it is true that in many areas, especially the remoter ones, life probably went on without too much disruption, if only because they had always been relatively immune from the central government. But we should not underestimate the changes which took place during and as a result of this period. In the Greek cities, for instance, the private generosity so typical of the early empire came almost to a stop. It ceased to be so desirable, and was frequently becoming a burden, to be a member of a town council. Under Constantine repeated laws show that many were

trying to evade their municipal responsibilities, not least by joining the Christian clergy, who were now granted immunity. When stability was restored in the reign of Diocletian (AD 284–305), a drastic reorganization of the government was thought necessary. The old easy prosperity had gone, and Diocletian attempted to control the economy by several measures, among them a fierce law fixing maximum prices, of which several copies inscribed on stone have been identified, all from the Greek east. It is unlikely that measures such as this made much difference; but by the end of the reign of Constantine (who died in AD 337) both the army and the administration had been significantly increased, and the tone of government changed from the *laissez-faire* to the deliberately interventionist.

Constantine and the new empire

One aspect of this intervention by the state was Constantine's adoption of Christianity, traditionally dated from his defeat of Maxentius at Rome in AD 312. He did not outlaw paganism, but he used the Christian church in secular matters and strengthened its position by many favours, not hesitating to intervene personally in church disputes or to spend public money on lavish church building. Above all, he founded a new capital in the eastern empire and named it Constantinople after himself. This was to be an overtly Christian city. Even though the population of the existing city on the site, Byzantium, was presumably mostly pagan, and though pagan authors claim that he built temples there, the public space of the new city was occupied conspicuously by Christian churches, of which the greatest were those of St Sophia and the Holy Apostles, where Constantine himself was to lie. The city was decorated with the best works of art from the classical world, including the Tripod from Delphi, the Serpent Column, the Lindian Athena and scores of others. Greece was plundered to adorn Constantinople. Many temples, even if they remained open, lost their precious treasures, which Constantine did not hesitate to appropriate. By this foundation, however, Constantine did not only create a Christian capital, but a Greek one. It is unlikely that he intended it at the time to rival Rome, though a writer of the late 4th century claims that he did; but in time New Rome, as Constantinople came to be called, was not only to rival but to outlast Rome, and to preserve a Greek empire for another thousand years. It was to be an empire both Hellenic and Christian, even though its citizens called themselves 'Romans' (*Rhomaioi*). Whatever Constantine's actual intentions (which are so overlaid by bias in the literary sources that we can hardly recover them), the foundation of Constantinople was to guarantee the survival of Greek culture even when the Roman empire in the west collapsed. It was both the continuation of Roman tradition and, though Constantine could not have foreseen it, the beginning of a new empire.

We are badly informed, however, about the development of Constantinople during the 4th century,

The emperor in triumph: a gold medallion of Constantius II (337–61). Booty is displayed beneath the horses' hooves and goddesses of victory hold out garlands. The nimbus which surrounds the emperor's head (a symbol of the sun, not of sainthood) and the elaborate decoration of the horses' trappings suggest Persian influence.

and it was not until AD 395 that there was a formal division between the eastern and western halves of the empire, and thus a beginning of independence for the east. Nevertheless, the administrative and military changes that came in during the reigns of Diocletian and Constantine, together with the very positive favour shown towards Christianity by Constantine and all his successors except Julian (AD 361–3) provided the foundation for a new start. It is often argued that the Late Empire (beginning with Diocletian) was an overloaded economy whose government turned to repression and autocracy in its efforts to keep the empire going and pay for the vastly increased army and administration – the so-called 'idle mouths'. It has thus been adversely contrasted with the supposedly mild and cultivated style of government that prevailed during the first two centuries AD, and especially in the 2nd. Edward Gibbon begins his history with a famous passage in praise of the 2nd-century regime, according to him the happiest and most civilized in the whole of history, after which there was only room for decline. And there is certainly something in this view, at least insofar as it points to the continual laws by which the 4th-century emperors tried to regulate and restrict the lives of their subjects. The free peasants, the *coloni*, could be chained up if found trying to escape their obligations; all trades were made hereditary; town councillors were now compelled to stay in their cities

and perform the duties for which their wealth qualified them. The tone of government utterances is indeed far more authoritarian and interventionist, and even if it did not always succeed in its efforts, its aim was undoubtedly to control the movements of its people. In a system where the means of enforcement of these laws were extremely limited, corruption inevitably grew rife.

Paganism at bay

All the same, there are grounds for supposing that the east developed in a different way under these conditions than the west. It had always been more urbanized than the west, and because of this, and its long established economic superiority, it had been able to weather the storms of the 3rd century more successfully. With the return of stability came some degree of growth. In some areas, such as North Syria and Palestine, the population grew as olive culture and irrigation brought increased prosperity. Many towns in Asia Minor, like Aphrodisias, flourished in the 4th century and were able to support an active cultural life. At Antioch the pagan rhetor Libanius taught and wrote in the second half of the century. At Berytus (Beirut) a great law school developed to which, until its destruction by earthquake in AD 551, many easterners went for the legal education that was one of the pathways to a post in the imperial administration. Higher education, rhetorical, legal or philosophical, was much in demand in the late 4th and 5th centuries, and centres of learning at the major cities of Athens, Alexandria and Constantinople came to resemble modern universities in the cosmopolitanism of their students, though the restricted subjects on offer made them also very different. Perhaps the disruption of the 3rd century had halted the process of Romanization; at any rate, the intellectual culture of the east in the 4th and 5th centuries was a virtual Greek renaissance. There were indeed a few literary men who made their way to Rome and wrote in Latin, such as the poet Claudian from Alexandria and the historian Ammianus Marcellinus from Antioch. But the 5th century in particular saw an astonishing revival in Greek poetry; the elaborately learned style of the Egyptian Nonnus was copied by many imitators, some of whom were able to hire out their services as writers of panegyrics for cities or great men, and to travel round the Greek world, living by their talent for verse. Increasingly, the Greek inscriptions from this period were written in verse – itself an indicator of the market for literary talent and the capacity of the cities to provide a level of education high enough to produce the composers of these epigrams. Many of them were far from perfect – perhaps the lowest level was reached in the wretched effusions of Dioscorus of Aphrodito in Upper Egypt who was still composing such verse in the later 6th century – but they are witness to a self-conscious pride in literary accomplishment fostered by the continuance of urban life in the Greek east. It was no easy matter to compose stylized verses when spoken Greek had long departed from the classical norm, and the notable flowering in this period of this élite accomplishment indicates the prosperity of many areas in the Greek east.

At Athens, in particular, philosophy flourished, with its centre in the Academy, the school originally founded by Plato himself. The Academy had been through many vicissitudes, but now it reached a new peak in the 5th century AD as one of the main centres of pagan philosophical opposition to the Christian empire. Especially with the teachings of Plotinus, who found an audience among the Roman aristocracy in the 3rd century, and his pupil Porphyry, author himself of an attack on Christianity, Platonism had taken on a new and more nearly a religious form. Neoplatonism, as this later version is called, made of Platonic philosophy a sect and a semi-mystical faith to which many intellectuals were attracted – including the Emperor Julian and the young Augustine – as a real alternative to Christianity. The most serious counter to Christian teaching in fact came from this source, and Christian writers in their turn found themselves either arguing specifically against Neoplatonism or, whether consciously or not, attempting some kind of synthesis. Augustine in the west never lost the influence of Neoplatonic thought, though he rejected its tenets. One who attempted a synthesis between Neoplatonism and Christianity in the early 5th century was Synesius, who ended his life as bishop of Ptolemais in North

Africa. A native of Greek-speaking Cyrene, he came from well-to-do pagan gentry stock and naturally went to Alexandria for his further education. There he studied under the remarkable Neoplatonist Hypatia who had succeeded her father Theon as head of the school. Hypatia was to be martyred by fanatical Christians fearful of her success, but Synesius carried with him through his life the impress of those days. His Neoplatonism was of a religious kind: philosophy had its mysteries and its initiates like any cult. A later stay in Christian Constantinople led him however to see that the future lay with Christianity, preferably with a type of Christianity that could enshrine the best of Hellenic culture. A man of his kind naturally disliked the extremes of Christian asceticism and identified them as un-Hellenic. Ultimately he himself, after considerable hesitation, some of it still concerned with the problems inherent in trying to align Neoplatonism with Christian teaching, agreed to accept ordination and became a bishop. Synesius's intellectual struggles were however also on a wider scale, concerned with bigger issues than simply Neoplatonism itself. He was, like many others, trying to find a way of adopting Christianity without destroying the ideals of Hellenism. But it was significant that Synesius ended his career as a Christian bishop. In the previous generation another pagan, Themistius, had attained great honour at the court of Constantinople, going on many embassies and holding the offices of proconsul and city prefect. He found it possible to adapt Greek philosophical tradition to the Christian status quo, and did so without ceasing to be a pagan. In turn successive emperors gave him their support, no doubt partly in order to conciliate thereby the still pagan upper classes of the Greek cities to the new Christian capital. Themistius was thus a Hellene who found a way of accommodation to the Christian empire. But when he became city prefect in AD 384 he was severely criticized by pagans of a more traditional kind; it was not the philosopher's role, in their view, to consort with kings, and of course especially not with Christian monarchs. Synesius's way was easier to understand – to adapt Hellenism by arriving at a fuller compromise with Christianity. But many 5th-century pagans could follow neither Themistius nor Synesius, and some of them went to the lengths of open and intransigent opposition to the Christian rulers.

Such was the case with the philosophers of Athens. Under its heads Syrianus and Proclus in the 5th century the Athenian Academy became not merely a focus of Neoplatonism but also of paganism. Increasingly the leading philosophers intermarried and, with their pupils, regarded themselves as a special sect set apart. As in Athens itself during this period temples were beginning to give way to or be converted into Christian churches, a sense of being under siege contributed to their self-awareness as a group. Sometimes they were themselves in danger from public opinion, and had to retreat for a while, as happened to the great Proclus. But by and large Neoplatonic philosophy was able to hold its own as a minority but powerful belief in intellectual circles. When the more determined Christian policies of Justinian in AD 529 dictated a law forbidding pagans to teach, the Academy was still functioning strongly. But if it did not entirely cease to exist after this law, as has usually been supposed, and as has been concluded on the basis of archeological evidence, it never recovered from the blow. Seven teachers, including Damascius and Simplicius, the greatest Neoplatonists of their day, left Athens and journeyed to Persia in the hope that the new Shah Chosroes might be a genuine lover of philosophy.

Disappointed in this romantic idea (though he did have some Platonic dialogues translated into Persian), they returned to Byzantine territory where they continued to write, though necessarily keeping a low profile and perhaps not returning to Athens itself. Yet in the minds of many educated Christians of the day, the Athenian Academy stood for the best in Hellenic philosophy, and its last philosophers found admiration as well as religious opposition. By contrast the School at Alexandria adapted itself to the Christian regime by concentrating on an Aristotelianism that was easier to reconcile with Christianity. One of its later teachers, John Philoponus, in the mid-6th century, was himself a Christian and conducted a debate on the standard polemical topic of the eternity of the world with the Athenian Simplicius. This Christian Aristotelianism continued into the 7th century with Stephanus. Thus the Alexandrian School survived until the Arab conquest of Egypt, and became instrumental in passing on the Aristotelian tradition to the Arabs.

Athens and Alexandria were not however the only centres of philosophy and Greek letters. In the 5th century many of the cities of the Greek east still retained teachers of rhetoric, and a classical education was possible in many centres. It was common, however, for a young man to travel in search of higher learning to one of the bigger places. Many leading Christian clerics from St Basil and his brother Gregory of Nyssa to Severus of Antioch, who studied rhetoric in Alexandria and law at Berytus, received a standard classical education in this way, and in a significant number of cases it deeply marked their writings. Philosophers also travelled, like Damascius and Asclepiodotus, but their paganism kept them out of official circles. In some ways the openness and cosmopolitanism of the Greek east in this period recalls the Hellenic revival of the 2nd century AD; now however the divide between paganism and Christianity caused an underlying and sometimes an open tension between the differing types of intellectual.

Ascetics, pilgrims and monks

Another factor making for division was the tremendous growth in popularity of extreme asceticism and its frequent association with non-Greek culture. Simultaneously with the ending of persecution came the rise of asceticism and its corollary, monasticism. Many of the

St Symeon Stylites resisting the snake of temptation. Symeon lived on his pillar at Kalat Siman in Syria from 423 to 459. His public asceticism won him many followers; when he died, a monastery and a sanctuary were erected around his pillar, the base of which still survives (see p. 183, pl. 40).

desert fathers, however, were hostile to secular learning, and often the holy men who now rise to prominence in Syria and Egypt spoke no Greek. It would be a mistake to suppose that they did not influence the members of the educated élites. Indeed, St Daniel the Stylite and others were the recipients of favour and interest from the highest quarters. Educated aristocrats themselves also turned to the simple life and abandoned the outward signs of culture. Admittedly monks were the objects of extreme hostility from pagans as well as respect from Christians; their opponents took pleasure in drawing attention to their occasional lapses and drew the conclusion that they were mostly hypocrites. But the monastic life flourished none the less, and the more striking the ascetic practices of individuals, the more they became centres of attention and objects of pilgrimage. To some extent they represented the common man, who had never been reached by the élitist education of the classical world. But the members of the aristocracy and of the court were among the first to show their enthusiasm for the stylite or the ascetic. The Empress Eudocia, supposedly herself the daughter of a pagan Athenian philosopher and a supporter of the arts and letters, as well as a poet in her own right, settled in the Holy Land in 443 and

*The sumptuous mosaics beneath the dome of St George,
Thessalonica, are midway between Hellenistic and Byzantine styles.
Richly dressed martyrs stand in front of fancifully elaborate
architectural backdrops. Erected c.400, these mosaics are among the
earliest masterpieces of Christian art.*

was a correspondent of St Symeon Stylites. Meanwhile
her rival, Theodosius II's pious sister Pulcheria, had
turned the palace at Constantinople into a virtual
monastery. This is not, then, an upsurge of popular
values, but a real change in the ideas of some of the most
pious members of the educated classes. The Empress
Eudocia, before she left Constantinople for the Holy
Land, had been the patron of another who interestingly
exemplifies the change: Cyrus of Panopolis, praetorian
prefect, builder of the walls of Constantinople, poet,
suspected pagan, dedicator of a church to the Virgin,

exiled from Constantinople to be bishop of Cotyaeum –
and devotee of St Daniel the Stylite, who cured his
daughter of demon-possession.

The departure of Eudocia for the Holy Land, for
whatever real reason, symbolizes the enthusiasm for the
holy places that characterized the post-Constantinian
period. Jerusalem became the centre of a tourist trade,
as swarms of pilgrims, high and low, carried back
souvenirs of their visit in the form of ampullae of holy
oil or water from the Jordan. Gregory of Nyssa
protested at the hustle and bustle which was a distrac-
tion to true faith, and unnecessary for salvation – yet in
his younger days he had made the journey himself. It
was all part of the cosmopolitan atmosphere of the
Greek east in Late Antiquity, for many of the visitors
were westerners, like the Spanish nun Aetheria who did
a tour of the holy places and the sites of early

Christianity at the turn of the 4th and 5th centuries, or like the aristocratic Roman women who followed St Jerome to his retreat in Bethlehem.

The establishment of Christianity played a large part in reshaping life in the eastern provinces in this period. Great churches arose in the major cities, along with many lesser ones, while bishops came to play a central role in secular organization. The churches organized alms to the increasing numbers of poor, and life for rich and poor alike was structured by the weekly sermon and the repetition of the yearly festivals of the church. And it is likely that the growing number of monasteries had a practical as well as a spiritual effect: in some areas, notably in Palestine, they acted as centres of minor production, working the land and influencing the productive capacity of the area. At the end of the period, when urban life was beginning to decline, it was often the monasteries that organized the food supply in times of drought or pestilence, and it was to them that the local people naturally turned. Not only did they provide an alternative medicine, holy men constantly receiving petitions to cure the physically and mentally sick, but they were the focus of every kind of practical help. In the cities the bishops survived as the local governors when civil administration decayed; but the monasteries were more intimate and more familiar sources of aid to the majority of the population in both town and country.

Art for a Christian world

The gradual Christianization of the Greek world brought with it also the need for a new kind of art and architecture. Until the end of persecution and the conversion of Constantine churches remained on the whole modest and Christian art severely limited. But once Christianity gained imperial support great edifices were built, at first very much on the pattern of secular public buildings; the basilical church, for instance, with its nave and rounded apse, was simply adapted from the standard public audience hall or court room, for unlike pagan temples, the new churches needed public space to accommodate their congregations. Soon these churches were felt to need pictorial decoration, not only for its own sake but to act as a means of instruction to the uneducated. Scriptural scenes balanced by symbolic compositions or crosses could now be found in the churches of most Greek cities, for the benefit, as St Nilus of Sinai and others claimed, of the illiterate who could not read the Holy Scriptures for themselves. Whereas the Emperor Constantine had decorated the new city of Constantinople with hundreds of classical statues, many of them of pagan gods and goddesses, his successors preferred more specifically Christian images. Leo I, for instance, commemorated the arrival of relics of the Virgin in Constantinople in the 5th century by building a special chapel at the Blachernai church and setting up a mosaic depicting himself and his family together with the Virgin. Public Christian art was matched by a growing taste, despite the objections of

the stricter clergy, for holy pictures which could be kept in the home or carried about. It was even common to wear clothing decorated with embroidered panels showing the saints. These centuries saw the development of pictorial depiction of Christian figures, and laid the foundation for the enormous growth in popularity of icons of all kinds which was especially strong in the 6th century. The visual experience of town-dweller and countryman alike was changed by the official adoption of Christianity in the empire. Temples, while still open in the 4th century – and later in some places – had lost many of their most precious treasures, if we are to believe the Christian claims; certainly the dominant role which they had previously enjoyed in the towns was rapidly giving way to an increase in church building and church decoration.

Christians were both conscious and proud of this development, and many literary descriptions survive of the notable churches built during this period. Again classical literary forms were turned to Christian use, and the renaissance in Greek verse which we have already noted found some of its themes here. All this increase in Christian art gave rise to debate over the theology of representation of the divine; but most Christians accepted the new development with enthusiasm.

Certain other changes in the style of public life took place during this period. For one thing, all public occasions were now invested with an elaborate ceremonial. Similar ceremonial might even accompany Christian and secular occasions – processions of citizens wearing white, carrying candles or lighted torches, waving palm fronds. Usually, if the occasion was appropriate, there were acclamations – of the emperor, of the city, of the particular official. Like panegyrics, which also usually accompanied public events, often in multiple (it was common to have not one but a series of panegyrics delivered, sometimes in both Latin and Greek), acclamation belongs to an authoritarian society in which the populace is asked to assent rather than debate. That sometimes petitions were included in the shouts of praise is a further indicator that the people were not now expected to express opinions but might on occasion hope to receive favours from their rulers. Such popular opinion as was expressed was to be found not on official occasions or in political assemblies but at the theatre or in the hippodrome, both of which by the end of the period became focuses for any kind of public feeling. As gladiatorial contests gradually, though only slowly, faded out under Christian opposition, and the Greek athletic contests declined with the decline of the old classical way of life of the Greek city, they were replaced in many of the cities of the Greek east by the chariot racing that was so much the vogue in Constantinople, where the emperors showed themselves to their people chiefly from their box in the hippodrome – a secular ceremony which thus curiously balanced the frequent appearances of the emperors in liturgical ritual. In the other cities of the Greek world too, passions were now polarized round the contests of the two chariot teams, the Blues and Greens. This was neither a Greek nor a Roman phenomenon; extreme faction rivalry, often amounting to violence, was specifically a product of the Christian empire, and, what is more, of the latest phase of the Christian empire before it was to be seriously diminished by the Islamic conquests. The chariot races, and the popular excitement that accompanied them, flourished most when the old social patterns of the Greek city were beginning to break down and when the empire itself was coming under threat.

Threat and recovery: the age of Justinian

Since the 3rd century, barbarian incursions had been a serious danger. After AD 395, when each half of the empire was ruled by its own emperor, they were still more serious. The eastern empire, however, was in a stronger position than the western, in that it was able to buy off a succession of invading tribes from its greater resources. Even so, the payments were high, and the Huns, for instance, overran Thrace and penetrated as far as Thermopylae. But the eastern government of the 5th century was able to avoid the fate of the west, where weak emperors yielded power to barbarian generals and where, in AD 476, the last Roman ruler was deposed. Germanic kingdoms replaced the western Roman empire; the emperor in Constantinople was left as the representative of Rome, and to him in some sense the Germanic kings of the Ostrogoths and the Merovingians owed a symbolic allegiance. The loss of the west did not go unmarked in the east, though there was no outcry at the time. Two expeditions were sent to try to recover the province of Africa, lost to a handful of Arian Vandals, but both proved disastrous. When the western empire actually came to an end the east was preoccupied with internal problems – the deposition of the Emperor Zeno – and with barbarian dangers of its own. There were Vandals in Greece and Ostrogoths in Thrace, while a great fire in Constantinople destroyed the library at the Basilica, founded by the Emperor Julian, and many of Constantine's classical statues, including the Lindian Athena and the Cnidian Aphrodite. Nevertheless, stable government was eventually restored and the dangerous Ostrogoths diverted to the west at great financial cost. For much of the later 5th century Thrace and Illyria were in constant danger and even Constantinople was more than once under threat. Nor did the danger end when Theodoric led his band to the conquest of Italy; the Ostrogoths were merely replaced by a new threat from a people we can identify as the earliest Bulgars. But for a time in the early 6th century, the eastern empire enjoyed something of a respite, until new waves of invaders in the late 6th century – Huns, Avars and Slavs – proved a more serious matter.

The waning of the barbarian threat was indeed such that the Emperor Justinian (AD 527–65) could actually contemplate – and in large part achieve, even if it was not to last – the reconquest of the western provinces,

and that simultaneously with major hostilities in the Persian front. Justinian was an ambitious ruler intent on reform and restoration, and some of the measures necessitated by the enormous financial requirements of his military plans were deeply unpopular, especially as they were combined with a forceful ecclesiastical policy. But the achievements of the reign were spectacular. North Africa was reconquered in a short campaign; parts of Spain were won and held; Italy took much longer, but was in Byzantine hands by AD 554. The eastern wars were hard, the enemy powerful and determined under the Shah Chosroes I; many border cities such as Apamea, Beroea and Edessa found the Persians more than once at their gates, while in AD 540 the great city of Antioch was sacked. Yet peace was made in 561. Along with these military actions came massive building activity in the provinces aimed mainly at strengthening them against further attack. Justinian's public panegyrist but secret enemy, Procopius, probably exaggerates the amount of building actually carried out in this reign, but even if Justinian was in several instances only continuing and consolidating work begun by his predecessor Anastasius, the middle years of the century saw a striking increase in fortifications, especially in the north. At home Justinian codified the whole of Roman law in the Digest. The language of the law and the army was still Latin and there were many in Constantinople who spoke Latin, although when Justinian began issuing his own laws, he did so in Greek. Attempts were made to strengthen the administration of the towns, and serious decline does not seem to have set in yet. One of Justinian's other main preoccupations was the effort to reunite the church, to bring together the easterners, who increasingly veered towards monophysitism (which emphasized the divinity at the expense of the humanity of Christ), and the westerners, who were again coming within the sphere of the empire after up to a century of barbarian rule. The great Fifth Ecumenical Council of AD 553 purported to settle the issue, but like others relied too heavily on active persuasion. In the eastern provinces Monophysitism was already acquiring an institutional organization with its own alternative clergy and bishops. This was to prove a major factor in the failure of those provinces to withstand Islamic attacks in the 7th century.

These efforts at restoration were far too costly, however, in terms of manpower and resources. The eastern empire could hardly sustain war on so many fronts simultaneously for very long, and we soon encounter complaints that the soldiers are not being paid and that their numbers are falling below the minimum necessary for security. It seems that the forces sent on the wars of reconquest were often very small; Justinian kept his generals chronically short of reinforcements, partly for political reasons, but also because the men were hard to find. His successors had the same problems, and even under Justinian himself the burden that fell on a newly conquered province was

An imperial procession in Constantinople, shown on a 5th- or 6th-century ivory reliquary case. At the door of the church, still under construction, the emperor is greeted by a patriarch. He hands over his candle as he prepares to venerate the relic of the Cross which the patriarch carries. At the rear are two ecclesiastics in a carriage, holding a relic casket. In the background are the buildings of the Great Palace.

very great, as we can see from the case of North Africa. The building and defensive work in other parts of the empire had to be paid for at high cost too. It is clear that the border areas of Syria and Mesopotamia were already denuded of troops, except in the major fortresses, for the Persians were able simply to bypass these and penetrate at will deep into Byzantine territory. Instead the empire relied on a complex and not always reliable system of alliances with local peoples, all along the eastern border from the Black Sea to Arabia.

For a short time in the reign of Justinian, however, there was a restored sense of unity in the empire, and it could be felt that Roman rule (as contemporaries saw it) extended from east to west. Justinian himself was a Latin-speaker, and Latin enjoyed something of a revival under the circumstances of his court, especially when many westerners found themselves in Constantinople, either as political refugees or as proponents of a particular ecclesiastical policy. Even Latin poetry could be appreciated in Constantinople. Conversely, Greek-speaking administrators were sent to the western provinces, and North Africa, for instance, came to feel

some eastern influences; indeed, in the 7th century, and perhaps before, Greek was used as the language of public occasions there without apparent difficulty. In a smaller degree, the Justinianic reconquest brought westwards the influence of Greek culture, in opposite tendency to the earlier Romanization of the Greek east.

Retreat and transition

But the hold over the west could not be maintained for long, and was won only with great suffering. In AD 542 Constantinople experienced a shattering onslaught of bubonic plague, part of an epidemic felt all over the Greek east, and which, recurring as bubonic plague does, finally reached the shores even of Britain. There is no doubt that the mortality from this attack was one of the major factors in retarding Justinian's conquest of Italy and in causing the difficulties experienced later in the reign and during the reigns of his successors. It must also have had a devastating effect on individual Greek cities. Where exact or nearly exact dating is possible from archeological evidence, the decline in use of public buildings – indicating shrinkage of population – seems to start in the middle of the 6th century. Certainly the end of the century sees frequent signs of urban decline, at Anemurium (Anamur, on the south coast of Asia Minor), for instance. The church historian Evagrius tells us of the terrible effects of the plague on Antioch, where many members of his own family succumbed to successive waves of the disease. The government in Constantinople reacted quickly with legislation attempting to preserve the tax revenue it lost when people died in such numbers, but there must have been much more serious effects on the revenues and prosperity of the eastern provinces as a whole, and it is unlikely that the damage will have been completely repaired before the Persian invasions into Asia Minor in the early 7th century, followed so closely by the first Arab successes. Together with the strain of Justinian's wars of reconquest, the 6th-century plague destroyed the buoyancy of the Greek cities. Athens, for example, could not withstand the Slav incursions of the 580s; in 559 the Huns were driven only with difficulty from Constantinople itself, while in the 7th century the Persians were able to move with impunity from one city of Asia Minor to the next, dealing a fatal blow to urban civilization there.

It was at this point that the empire retreated in on itself and became self-consciously Hellenic rather than 'Roman'. But with that withdrawal Greece itself became for centuries little more than a provincial backwater.

For many centuries Greece and the Greek east had shared the fate of the Roman empire. They had first adapted themselves to a Roman way of life, and accepted Roman citizenship while promoting and enjoying a revival of Greek culture. With the Christian empire they had seen a new capital arise in the east which tipped the balance back again and stimulated both a revaluation of Hellenism in Christian terms and a strongly philosophical pagan opposition. This Christian capital was to survive, even if with a much weakened sphere of rule, and to preserve a Greek Christian imperial culture into the medieval world. So the Roman domination of Greece was only temporary, even if lengthy, and the culture of Byzantium was based on a Christianity that had been Hellenized from its earliest days, long before it was moulded by the Councils of Nicaea, Ephesus and Chalcedon into a specifically Byzantine form.

The continuing feature in this long period is the Greek city, not Constantinople itself, which was always *sui generis*, but the countless Greek cities, some of them very small, which had existed all over the eastern provinces since Hellenistic times. Once peace was established under the Roman empire they flourished. Still more, they set their stamp on the nature of Roman rule, and were the showplace and the means of the revival of Greek culture and its assimilation by Rome. The cities survived the 3rd century and adapted themselves anew to Christianity. In some areas, notably in Syria and the Holy Land, the Christianization of the cities meant a change in their very being, and the church and the bishops moved to the fore, and Christian charity replaced the old style of euergetism. Splendid, and often extravagant, churches were built everywhere, and as their property gradually grew, so did their influence in the local milieu. In the eastern empire under Justinian the cities were still the backbone of provincial organization, but certain changes were becoming apparent, which manifested themselves in the physical configuration of the cities. The public spaces characteristic of the classical city – wide streets, market places, baths – were, in city after city, built over and gradually superseded by narrow 'oriental' alleys with shops huddled together. Nor was it merely a matter of economic decline, for these changes often took place simultaneously with the building of grand churches on a sumptuous scale. Later in the 6th century, and still more in the early 7th, came other strains which hastened the process: the major plague, and consequent loss of population, and the threat of invasion, which caused hasty fortification and the retreat to a strong acropolis, often the bishop's residence. Once this change had begun, the days of the classical city were numbered, and indeed the look and feel of the Greek world in the Middle Ages was to be very different.

Nevertheless, the Greek *polis* in a necessarily transformed but recognizable form characterized the Greek world for many centuries of Roman rule, and transferred many of its values into the cultural inheritance of Byzantium. The city, not the *chora*, remained the acme of culture, the height of a civilized man's aspiration. That the Greek city should have shown such powers of survival for so long is one of the great success stories of Greek history.

V·TRANSFORMATION

THE DEATH OF JUSTINIAN was followed by turmoil in the empire and a long period of disturbance for Greece. Slav invaders advanced from the north, forcing many Greeks to scatter over the Mediterranean. But slowly Constantinople regained a secure hold over the Balkan peninsula; the Slavs were converted to Christianity and gradually became absorbed into Hellenic culture. Some Greek communities returned from exile.

From the 9th to the 12th century Greece prospered as a province of Byzantium. Imperial and ecclesiastical patronage encouraged the economy; great monasteries were founded; Christian missions were launched into the Balkans; Arab scholars purchased and translated Greek texts; architecture, art and craftsmanship flourished. The structure of Greek society changed radically: villages replaced the city-centred life of Late Antiquity and wealthy new families rose to eminence, occasionally marrying into the imperial house itself.

The catastrophe of the Fourth Crusade (1204) delivered Greece into the hands of western overlords. After the recapture of Constantinople by Byzantine forces from Nicaea in 1261, imperial authority was rapidly re-established in northern Greece, but a French and an Italian presence remained. In the Peloponnese, the Despotate of the Morea and its capital, Mistra, witnessed the last flowering of Byzantine culture in Greece before the empire was swept away for ever by the Ottomans in 1453.

Greece's years under Byzantine rule had seen the fostering of a sense of Hellenic tradition, encouraged by the preservation of the language and literature of the ancients and by the development of literature in the vernacular. It was this sense that helped to preserve a distinctively Greek culture throughout the years of Ottoman rule and to bring about the resurgence of nationalism in the early 19th century. The Byzantine legacy was enduring and dynamic.

'The Queen of cities, Empress...'
were titles given to Constantinople by the Byzantines. For ten centuries she preserved much of the literary and artistic heritage of the ancient Greek world, as well as being the proud centre of a new Christian Hellenic civilization. This personification of the city is a detail from an 11th-century silk tapestry; she is handing a diadem crowned with peacock's feathers to an emperor on horseback – probably Basil II, who celebrated a great victory over the Bulgars in 1017 with a double triumph in Athens and Constantinople.

The silk demonstrates the colourful opulence of much Byzantine art, of which this is a comparatively rare secular example. It was given to Bishop Gunther of Bamberg in 1065, probably as an imperial gift for the Holy Roman Emperor Henry IV. The bishop died on his return journey from Constantinople and the silk was used as his shroud. (1)

The viceroys of God

The Byzantine emperor was both God's representative on earth and the envoy of his people to God. He was a sacred figure, surrounded by solemn ritual, his power in theory absolute. In reality he could not do without the support of his army, the church or the vast Byzantine civil service, but in the art of the empire he stands alone in his sanctity and majesty.

Christ and the Emperor are figures of equal size in this ivory plaque of *c*.945 (*left*); Christ stands only a little higher. The emperor is Constantine VII Porphyrogenitos and the plaque celebrates his accession to sole sovereignty (although emperor since childhood, he had only recently disposed of his co-rulers). (2)

Emperors shared the widespread Byzantine delight in theological argument. The manuscript illumination *below* is from a copy of the theological works of the Emperor John VI Kantakouzenos, made between 1370 and 1375. He is depicted as emperor and as the monk, Joasaph, that he became. Joasaph in one hand holds his first *Apologia Against the Moslems* and with the other points to the the three angels who visited Abraham (a type of the Trinity). (3)

The emperor's authority over the church was all but total, despite attempts by various patriarchs of Constantinople to assert themselves against it. In this depiction of an ecclesiastical council (*right*), the emperor (John VI Kantakouzenos again) towers larger than life over the assembled patriarchs and metropolitans. (4)

Imperial art disseminated powerful images of the emperor's might: *above*, Basil II Bulgaroktonos ('the Bulgarslayer') in military garb gazes grimly over the prostrate Bulgars while angels support his crown and lance and Christ holds a heavenly diadem over him: a painting from a psalter of about the same date as the silk in pl.1. (5)

The compassionate emperor: Theophilos, *right*, listens to a widow's complaint outside the Blachernai church, Constantinople. (6)

The armies of God

'We tread them down by the might of Christ, who gives to us the power to trample upon the adder and the scorpion' wrote one Byzantine of the empire's enemies. The favour of God, conveyed through the church, was the guarantee of the success of the imperial armies.

The wealth and prestige of Orthodox Christianity in Greece at its apogee is embodied in this 13th-century Exultat roll from the monastery of St John on Patmos. It shows St Basil and two deacons. (7)

Frankish soldiers appear in this icon from Cyprus (*below*), which shows scenes from the life of the Virgin. The artist was Italian, working in a Byzantine style. The Frankish conquest of Greece was a severe, but temporary, set-back to imperial military self-confidence. (8)

'The Cross has conquered' was the Byzantine war-cry and death on the battlefield was often regarded as martyrdom. This spirit is embodied in literature (the Epic of Digenes Akritas, a frontier soldier) and in art, in the images of the 'soldier saints' that decorate many Byzantine churches: *right:* St Mercury, a wall-painting from Ohrid. Mercury was reputedly a soldier who, despite gaining the emperor's favour for his heroism on the battlefield, was executed for refusing to sacrifice to Artemis. (9)

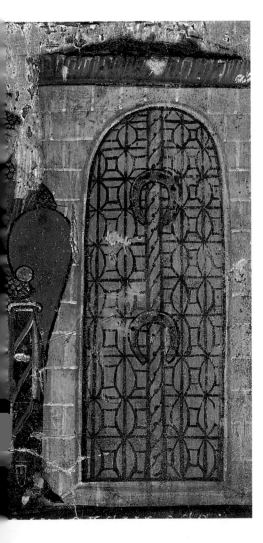

Daily life in the province

Secular life in Greece under Byzantine rule is hard to reconstruct, for much of the physical evidence of it was swept away during the Ottoman rule. One of our main sources of information is the tradition of vivid manuscript illumination.

Work and relaxation: *right*, masons use a pulley to raise a column up scaffolding; *far right*, a scene of feasting: an illustration to the Book of Job, probably painted at Mistra in the 14th century. In the Christian empire of Byzantium even secular artefacts – like the set of weights on the *left* – were decorated with religious symbols. (10, 11, 12)

Science and technology: Byzantine science was essentially practical and based almost entirely on the achievements of classical and Hellenistic thinkers. Botanical knowledge, for instance, was largely valued for its medical use: *right*, the gathering of herbs which will be used for treating the sick couple on the left, while labourers at the right of the picture work in the fields. *Far right*, ship building – an industry encouraged by the Byzantines because of the importance of defence and maritime trade to the empire. (13, 14)

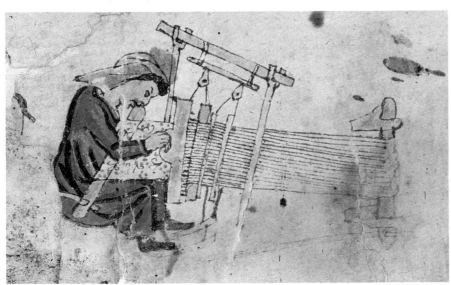

Agriculture and craftsmanship: life
for the small farmer in Greece and the
Balkans changed little between
Byzantine times and the 20th century.
Far left: dairy farming and bee-
keeping. Silk farms were numerous
(the medieval name for the
Peloponnese 'Morea' is derived from
'mulberry tree') and the export of silk
was central to the economic life of
Greece. *Left*, a silk weaver at
work. (15, 16)

223

The artifice of eternity

Byzantine art is essentially religious. Whether the medium is mosaic or fresco, gold or enamel, the artist has one over-riding purpose: to mediate between God and humanity.

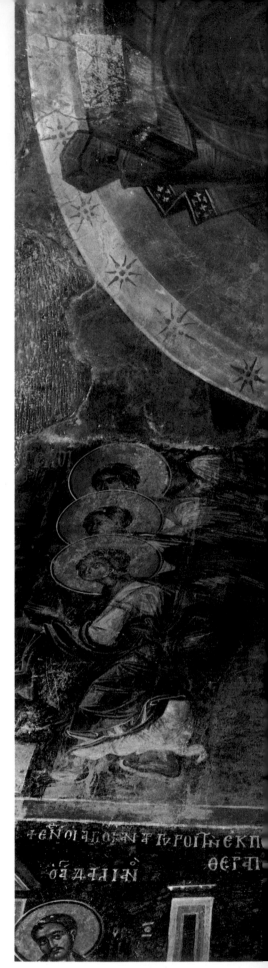

Enamellers had an astonishing ability to suggest tone and modelling with only flat enamel and gold. This tiny, beautifully detailed figure of Christ is from the 10th-century outer case of a reliquary of the True Cross. (17)

Mosaicists achieved some of their greatest masterpieces in the 11th century, when this mosaic of Kings David and Solomon was made for the new monastery of Nea Moni on Chios. The severe, static appearance is tempered by the glittering play of light on the glass tesserae. (18)

Goldsmiths worked with enamellers to produce works of astonishing virtuosity. This 11th-century icon of St Michael (*above*) was probably loot from the Fourth Crusade; it is now in the Treasury of St Mark's, Venice. (20)

Painters created a new style in the late 14th century, in which the monumental forms of earlier art were softened by a sophisticated and often tender realism. Among the greatest achievements of this last renaissance of Byzantine art are the wall-paintings in the churches at Mistra. This example, from the Metropolitan church, shows the Preparation of the Throne for the Last Judgment. (19)

The legacy of architecture

Architecture is the most enduring memorial to Byzantium. Rarely spectacular in size, but always subtle, the medieval churches of Greece are often buildings of great emotional impact.

A donor offers his church to Christ. This portrait of the Bulgarian Sebastokrator Kaloyan was painted on a wall of his church at Boyana, near Sofia, in 1259. (21)

Simple, massive, but superbly proportioned, the church of the Panaghia at Skripou (*above*) is dated by an inscription on the apse to 873/4, a period of increasing building activity in Greece, as the empire re-asserted her hold on a province over-run by the Slavs. (22)

During the Frankish conquest of Greece, building in Byzantine styles was limited to the empire's succession states. The church of Arta, the capital of the Despotate of Epirus, was built 1282–9 (*above*). The dome (*opposite, top*), with its original mosaic of Christ, is supported by re-used antique columns on a primitive cantilever system. The beautiful 14th-century church of the Hodeghetria, Mistra (*left*), shows the small-scale complexity of Byzantine architecture in its last phase. The focal point of the interior of a Byzantine church is the iconostasis (*right*, an example from the Great Meteora monastery), the icon-covered screen which separates nave and sanctuary. (23–26)

The monastic environment

Christian monasticism began in the eastern provinces of the empire. It rapidly established itself in Greece, where several monasteries have preserved an unbroken tradition from early medieval times to the present day.

The bizarre landscape of the Meteora, in Thessaly (*left*), has sheltered monastic communities since the 14th century. They have now declined; the 15th-century monastery of Ayias Triades, shown in the picture, today houses only one monk. In contrast, the 17 Greek monasteries on Mount Athos (*below*, the monastery of Dionysiou) still flourish: cut off from the world, on a spectacularly beautiful peninsula in the Aegean, they remain the spiritual centre of the Orthodox church. The first was founded *c*.963. Hosios Lukas, *above*, begun in 961, is one of the largest and most sumptuously decorated monasteries of the Greek mainland. (27, 28, 29)

The Greek influence

The cultures of the Moslem and Slav peoples came under Byzantine influence in the 9th century. The Arabs absorbed many aspects of Greek intellectual life into their own civilization, while rejecting everything with religious connections; the Slavs, in contrast, were totally transformed by the acceptance of the central feature of Byzantine life: Orthodox Christianity.

Envoys to Russia. Constantine IX sends ambassadors to Vladimir, who ascended the throne of Kiev *c.*978. Russia became so Byzantinized that after the fall of Constantinople Moscow was claimed by the Russian church as 'the Third Rome'. (30)

The missionary saints Cyril and Methodius were responsible for the conversion of the Moravians in the 9th century. They even created a new script, so that the scriptures could be written down in Slavic languages (a

couple of lines are visible in the manuscript above). This illumination shows the baptism (by immersion) of Bulgarians *c.*865, watched by their king, Boris, and his queen. (31)

Art, as well as religion, was sent by Byzantium to the Slavs. This enamel is the central plaque of a crown presented to Hungary in the 11th century, probably as a gift to the queen. It shows the Emperor Constantine IX Monomachos. (32)

λατεθδιωαϊπιπ̅πολλά ὁ ιοταυμαιϑεταιμαολέιαρ̣εωμαϊων · καὶ τοτοωλλοε ϑρωνγροσεκ
τηιϲετα · τροϲεπιδδιωκαὶχριοϊοὐκενΤηνγάρια τεϲϲαράκοντα ·
ὁ αμερ̅μοϋ̅δενικϲ Ϊω̅ϲεϋϊκϲ Ϊω̅ϲεϋϊκε ολθιοϋδεϊ

The interest of Arabs in Greek civilization was limited largely to the translation of philosophical and scientific texts into Arabic – a complex undertaking. The emperor (*above*) exchanges letters with the caliph. A popular Greek text for Arabs was the *Materia Medica* of Dioscorides of Anazarbus, an account of the medical properties of about 600 plants: *left, top*, an Arab portrait of the author, *below left*, an illustration of Agrimony, glossed in Arabic. The miniature *below* shows the most often translated author, Aristotle, with his translator Ibn Bokhtisho on the left. (33–36)

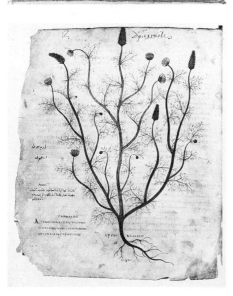

8
A Christian Millennium
Greece in Byzantium

JUDITH HERRIN

The ruined city of Mistra, in the Peloponnese, is often described as the Byzantine Pompeii. It is grouped around a fortress founded by the Franks and conquered by the Byzantines, who in 1349 made the city the capital of the Despotate of the Morea. After the downfall of the despotate in 1460, Mistra was governed by Turks and Venetians before being abandoned in the 18th century. 14th- and 15th-century buildings line the narrow streets leading up to the fortress, which is visible at the top of the hill in this view from the lower town. In the middle distance is the Palace of the Despots, a rare example of a surviving Byzantine civic building; its pointed arches show western influence. Several of the numerous churches contain splendid frescos (see, for example, pl.19), which testify to the importance of Mistra as a cultural centre. The Platonic philosopher Gemistos Plethon taught here, and it was visited by Cardinal Bessarion. Both men carried Greek scholarship to Renaissance Italy when the empire collapsed. (37)

At the turn of the 6th and 7th centuries AD, the history of Greece enters a period which is perhaps the least well documented since the development of Greek script and written records. The early medieval period has been aptly characterized as the 'Great Breach' in Greek history. For the first time historical documents are almost completely lacking; archaeological evidence is also sparse; outside sources present little information. While a similar trend is clear throughout the Mediterranean world from the late 6th to the late 8th centuries, giving rise to the epithet 'The Dark Ages', the label does not assist our understanding of developments in Greece. For what is witnessed during this period is the very slow and uncertain shift from a society organized according to the principles of the ancient world – a world of half-autonomous cities – to one dominated by a peculiarly medieval concept of empire, the Christian Roman empire of Byzantium.

Precarious survival

During the first half of the 7th century the great empire built up by Justinian was subjected to a series of devastating blows from which it barely recovered. Among the newly reconquered lands in western Europe, south-east Spain and much of Italy succumbed to the Visigoths and the Lombards. From the 580s onwards, the Slavs from across the Danube swept through the Balkans, reaching as far south as the Peloponnese and sailing to Crete. Finally, in the east, no sooner had the threat of the Persian invasion been removed by Heraclius (628) than it was replaced by the far more irresistible advance of Islam, which deprived Byzantium of its Near Eastern provinces – Syria, Palestine and Egypt – in one decade (634).

The effect of these upheavals, combined with the changes already underway within the empire, was traumatic. The first evidence of fundamental change is the marked decline of urban life: there was a radical break with the traditions of the ancient Greek *polis* and an increasing ruralization of areas previously dominated by cities. The second, related, aspect lies in the movements of population which forced Greeks away from their cities, scattering them to Sicily, southern Italy, small Greek islands and fortified refuges in the eastern Peloponnese, while newcomers from the north settled in the fertile agricultural areas. The Slavonic tribes who raided, plundered and finally occupied parts of the Balkan peninsula from the late 6th century onwards undoubtedly contributed to these upheavals.

The monasteries of the Meteora. This 19th-century engraving gives a vivid impression of a great Byzantine monastic centre at the height of its activity. Ladders enable the monks to scramble up to their monasteries perched on the high outcrops of rock; pulleys are used to send provisions up to them. See also pp. 228–9.

Major sites such as Athens, Corinth and Thessalonica shrank to smaller areas within defensible walls, reflecting this process of adaptation. Similarly, ancient cities often associated with riverine trade were replaced by settlements on inaccessible mountain peaks. Among the Greeks, withdrawal, circumspection and self-protection imposed themselves in place of outgoing contacts, open access and confident self-assertion.

For many years during this breach, numerous Greek communities existed sometimes in self-imposed exile, sometimes in enforced flight. They were directed by their elders and religious leaders, in isolation, beyond the authority of any ruler. But many survived and in due course returned to their regions, as Arethas, bishop of Caesarea (in Cappadocia) describes. His ancestors had sailed from Patras to avoid the incursions of non-Christian 'barbarians'. They settled in Calabria, where many generations had lived until his own grandparents learnt that the emperor in Constantinople could guarantee their safety. Then they returned to repopulate the city of Patras in the early 9th century.

Such turbulent uprooting, resettlement and mobility of population was indeed characteristic of the entire Byzantine empire at this time. From Palestine, Egypt and Syria large numbers of Christians fled the Persian and Islamic invaders of the early and mid-7th century to occupy safer lands behind the natural frontier of the Taurus mountains; island populations harried by Arab pirates similarly sought refuge elsewhere. Through these movements the inhabitants of Sicily and Syria were brought into much closer contact than usual; Greek colonies once again dotted the Italian landscape, reinforced by refugees from North Africa. But in the east Mediterranean these political changes were accompanied by a total eclipse of Greek culture; Arabic gradually replaced even Syriac, the *lingua franca* of a vast area in northern Syria, and endowed some of the Christian communities that remained behind with a new language for their worship. The Coptic churches of Egypt and the Greek monasteries near Jerusalem succeeded in maintaining their own identity but had progressively less and less influence over the Islamic environment in which they survived. Knowledge of Greek and observance of Christianity remained the preserve of a tiny minority; in general the dominance of Islam became undisputed.

In contrast, the Slavonic invaders of the Balkan peninsula failed to preserve their own distinct identity. They may have disrupted the political and military control of Constantinople for many years, but they could not dislodge the Greek tongue or the Christian faith. Instead, the Slavs gradually embraced both, adopting in addition the medieval Byzantine style of city life (as cities slowly revived), of coinage, trading organization, ecclesiastical structure and Hellenic culture. So while the 'Great Breach' divided ancient from medieval Greek, it did not involve a fundamental linguistic loss. Certainly changes occurred in the Greek tongue between the 6th and 9th centuries, but the process of 'hellenization' predominated: the newcomers were converted to Christianity and inducted into Hellenic culture to become the not-always obedient subjects of the Byzantine emperors.

Stability restored

During the late 7th and 8th centuries the Byzantine state slowly imposed its authority upon nearly all the Slav tribes which had crossed the Danube. This process will be described in more detail in a later section; it was not finally complete until 1018. By about 800, too, what seemed to be a reliable defence system against Islam had been established in the east.

For the next 400 years, from *c.* 800 to 1204, the Greek world was governed by the emperors of Constantinople, who extended their own political system throughout the east Mediterranean and as far west as Palermo. Administered through a series of large provinces (called *themata*, singular *thema*) embracing Cyprus, the Aegean islands, the northern Balkans, Thrace and the mainland, Greece was subordinated to the needs of the imperial capital in the same way as the rest of the empire. Thus it was expected to provide naval and military forces, manpower for the industries of the capital, taxation in kind and coinage, as well as to act as a place of exile for dissidents. These duties were balanced by an imperial responsibility for the wellbeing of provincial inhabitants, not only in the form of an often rhetorical philanthropy, but sometimes in direct assistance. When the people of Tenedos, Imbros and Samothrace were taken prisoner by Slavs, Constantine V (741–75) ransomed 2500 by sending an embassy laden with silk clothing. The internal development and organization of Greece, however, were geared to that of an empire, whose centre lay on the Bosphorus, on the site of a colony established by Greeks from Megara in the 7th century BC.

It is no exaggeration of the conflict between centre and periphery to say that an element of competitiveness governed the relationships between Constantinople and all its provinces. And everywhere the tedium of provincial life was contrasted, unfavourably, with life in the metropolis – the Queen of cities, Empress, as Constantinople was called. This reflected both the fact that Constantinople had remained a great urban centre, while other famous cities had declined, and also an extreme centralization which had concentrated power and influence in the capital. Provincial inhabitants understandably looked to it as if to a city whose streets were paved with gold. One, the future Basil I (867–886), even made good that dream, in a career from 'stable-boy' to emperor, assisted by his wealthy patron, the widow Danelis from Patras. Another, Rendakis, rose to be a senator, and married his daughter to the heir presumptive in the early 10th century.

Metropolitan disdain for provincial life, however, should not be allowed to obscure the fact that the Greek provinces became relatively prosperous in the 11th and 12th centuries. This development was related both to the decline of imperial power in Anatolia, and to the inherent resources of Greece. A clear demographic increase accompanied greater economic activity; there was a more rapid circulation of coinage and local products, which included silk spun in central Greece on mulberry farms established by Justinian. While internal demand accounts for some of the expansion, the role of Italian merchants in stimulating greater production may be significant. There can be no doubt that the appearance of Venetian, Amalfitan and Genoese traders in the ports of Methone, Korone, Nauplion, Thebes, Corinth, Almyros and of many islands attracted additional commerce. They took a larger share of Byzantine foreign trade than the Greek merchants of the time. And their presence was to be formally recognized by treaties which gave them a privileged position in Byzantine commerce – for example, the charters of 1084, 1126 or 1147. They established landing stages in many harbours and set up warehouses, depots and offices. Eventually, by the mid-12th century, there were Italian residential quarters in several major export centres, each patterned on the extensive communities of Constantinople, which were strung along the Golden Horn and in Pera (Galata), the Genoese enclave.

The penetration of Byzantine commercial life by western merchants was paralleled by a military threat from the west. While it may not have been as dangerous as the challenge from the east, posed by the Seljuk Turks, it was still a constant worry. For many years the Normans had threatened Byzantine possessions in southern Italy; from the late 11th century they extended their attention to Greece. Ports on the Adriatic littoral and round the Peloponnese – Dyrrachion, Korone, and Methone – were attacked. Although the Norman naval force of 1147 was beaten off by Monemvasia, it proceeded to sack both Corinth and Thebes, carrying off as booty their skilled artisan populations as well as much woven cloth and embroidered silk. In 1185 the great city of Thessalonica succumbed to a Norman attack. Imperial military and naval weakness (and reliance on Italian mercenary forces) were partly to blame for this increasing Norman presence in the empire, but it was also part of a continuous western push to establish states in the east, on the model of the kingdom of Jerusalem, set up after the First Crusade (1098–9).

In both a military and an economic sense, therefore, western activities in Greece during the 12th century foreshadowed the occupation which followed the Fourth Crusade of 1201–4. This ill-fated attempt to recover the holy places from Islamic control, preached by Pope Innocent III and accompanied by many pilgrims and feudal princes of the west, also brought the Venetians permanently into the eastern empire.

Perhaps the only beneficial result of the sack of Constantinople by the crusaders in 1204 was that some of the treasures they looted were thereby accidentally preserved for posterity. Had they been left, they would probably not have survived the Ottoman conquest 250 years later. The booty included this 11th-century chalice, one of thirty-two Byzantine chalices now in the treasury of St Mark's, Venice. It is made of gold and semi-precious stone and decorated with exquisite cloisonné enamel plaques.

Under the combination of military challenge and economic rivalry Byzantium collapsed.

The disaster of the Fourth Crusade

Some powers in Constantinople had no doubt hoped to use the crusade for their own, more local, concerns: ever since the first expedition of westerners it had been Byzantine policy to assist crusading troops on the march further east while forcing them to participate in imperial campaigns of reconquest, unrelated to the holy places. This tactic had caused bad feeling in the past. When it appeared to be surfacing again in 1203 – as Alexios III refused to honour the terms of an agreement made with the Venetians – the crusaders quickly decided to assist the Doge in taking revenge, and captured and plundered Constantinople. The Byzantine court and many metropolitan inhabitants fled to Asia,

some to Trebizond, others to Nicaea, where they gradually regrouped under the leadership of Theodore Laskaris (son-in-law of Alexios III and emperor 1204–22). The sack of Constantinople in April 1204, which lasted for twelve days and denuded the city of many of its finest antiquities (the four gilded bronze horses now at S. Marco, Venice, for example), set a new precedent in crusader brutality towards Christians. Possession of the city then permitted Doge Andrea Dandolo and the crusaders to implement their planned division of the empire; Baldwin of Flanders was elected Latin Emperor of Constantinople, while all the possessions of the Orthodox patriarch were assigned to Venice. Booty was divided and lands allotted to the crusader knights, who set out eagerly to conquer them.

Mainland Greece and the islands thus became the preserve of a variety of Western rulers, most of them

Emperor Michael VIII Palaiologos, leader of the Greek forces from Nicaea that recaptured Constantinople from the Franks in 1261. His diplomatic skills helped to restore the empire and to preserve it against western aggression for the next twenty years; his ecclesiastical policy of union with Rome was never widely accepted in Byzantium.

feudal vassals of the Latin emperor, or of the Lombard Boniface of Montferrat (who had married the Emperor Isaac II's widow and became stepfather to the young Byzantine prince Manuel). Opposition to the crusaders was led by local Greek *archontes*, Leon Sgouros in Corinth and Nauplion, and the chief families of cities like Monemvasia in the far south. Only in Epirus, however, was an independent Greek state established

by Michael Komnenos Doukas, cousin of the Emperors Alexios III and Isaac II. In the Peloponnese the Burgundians Guillaume de Champlitte and Geoffroi de Villehardouin succeeded in imposing their own authority, forming the principality of Achaea in an area which had been given to Venice in the partition plan. The Venetians concentrated initially on gaining firm possession of those ports and harbours in the Ionian and Aegean seas which would guarantee their commercial dominance. Most importantly, Marco Sanudo assumed the title 'duke of the Archipelago', and set up his own Venetian authority in the Aegean, from which west/east shipping could be regulated.

At a gathering held in Ravennika in 1209 the occupying forces reviewed their position and reaffirmed their loyalty to the Latin emperor, Henri de Hainault (1206–16). Boniface was already dead, killed in a battle with the Bulgars (1207); control in the Thessalonica region remained tenuous rather than firm and would be largely destroyed in 1224 when Theodore, despot of Epirus, recaptured it. But in central and southern Greece, Othon de la Roche, Nicolas de St Omer (a newcomer) and Geoffroi de Villehardouin had established principalities which would endure through most of the 14th century. In Thebes, Athens and Clermont (the site chosen by Geoffroi for the capital of Achaea) crusader culture intermingled with that of the occupied Greeks to form a flourishing hybrid, aware and relatively tolerant of the differences between Greek and Latin, Orthodox and Catholic, eastern imperial and western feudal traditions.

The scene was thus set for a complex development of political, military and economic rivalry, with crusader princes, Byzantine emperors and despots and Venetian dukes as the main protagonists. In 1261 Constantinople was recaptured by Michael Palaiologos (emperor 1259–82), thus effectively removing the claims of Epirus to represent Byzantium. Imperial authority was quickly established in northern Greece, Thessalonica again serving as the administrative centre, and in 1263 Michael VIII sent his brother Constantine to recapture several fortresses in Achaea (Morea). The Greek residents, of Monemvasia in particular, assisted in this reoccupation of parts of the Peloponnese, which resulted in the Byzantine province (later despotate) of Mistra. Meanwhile, to counter Venetian domination in the east Mediterranean, the emperor granted extensive privileges to the Genoese, who effectively monopolized Black Sea trade from their important base in Pera/Galata (Constantinople).

Venice, however, remained entrenched in Greece and even extended its authority during the 14th century – taking Pteleon in 1323, Cerigo (Kythera) in 1363, Argos, Nauplion and Corfu in the 1380s, and Tinos and Mykonos from 1390. (Cyprus was added in 1489.) In some of these colonies Venetian control was still exercised in the 18th century – Cerigo and Corfu only becoming briefly part of the Ottoman empire in 1797.

The final act

The Turkish advance had been felt in mainland Greece centuries before, as Moslem pirates from Anatolia harassed mercantile activity, raided coastal towns and took prisoners amongst the local Greek population. Acre, the last stronghold of the Latin kingdom of Jerusalem, was stormed by the Mamluk Sultan, al-Asraf, in 1291. And twenty-five years later (1326), the Ottoman Turks captured Bursa in western Asia Minor and made it their capital. The Byzantine empire was therefore much less extensive in the late 13th century than in the 12th century, and was progressively reduced in the east, regular contact with the independent empire of Trebizond being lost by the Turkish conquests.

From 1353, when they crossed the Dardanelles and captured Gallipoli, the Turks of Bursa had a European centre from which to direct their conquest of the Balkans and Greece. Leaving Constantinople in an isolated position, Murad I, the first Ottoman ruler to use the title Sultan (1359–89) pursued a westward thrust into Thrace against both Byzantine and Serbian authorities. He forced the Byzantine emperor, John V, to campaign with him. His son Bayezid I accomplished the conquest both of other Turkish principalities in Anatolia and of Bulgaria (1393), but when the Mongol forces of Timur (Tamerlane) advanced from Samarkand and defeated Bayezid at Ankara (1402), Ottoman authority in Anatolia was destroyed, making the European capital at Adrianople (Edirne) a city of great significance.

It was from this base that the final Turkish assault on Byzantium was launched, the campaign which resulted eventually in the fall of Constantinople (1453) and the conversion of Hagia Sophia into a mosque. All those who had a stake in the empire had long realized that they had to fight or come to terms with the forces of Islam. Encouraged by Pope Eugenius IV, a crusading movement had sailed from Venice in June 1444, only to be crushingly defeated by Murad II. Venice itself made peace and offered tribute in order to preserve at least some colonies in the east, but the rest of Greece remained open to the conqueror.

In 1446 Murad embarked on this campaign, breaching the newly fortified defences at the Isthmus of Corinth and forcing the two despots of Mistra and Patras – Demetrios and Constantine – to flee. All of central Greece, including Corinth and Patras, was subjected in this attack. A revolt against Turkish authority in Albania, led by George Castriota (Iskender Bey or 'Skanderbeg') was successful for a brief period and was supported by dissident Greeks in the Morea. But the momentum of the Ottoman advance was not to be checked. Despite Genoese assistance, the Byzantine capital was taken (1453) and the Albanian revolt suppressed. The last despots of Mistra (Thomas and Demetrios, brothers of Constantine IX, the final Byzantine emperor) were effectively tributaries of the Sultan, then vassals and, finally, were forced into exile

(1460). Apart from a few Venetian colonies, the whole world of Greece had been incorporated into the Ottoman empire.

This brief sketch must suffice as an outline of Byzantine history from the death of Justinian in 565 to the fall of Constantinople in 1453. To offer any meaningful generalization on the political and religious structure, the culture and thought of a period of nearly 900 years is not easy, but in the pages that follow the nature of the Byzantine state as a whole will be discussed, concentrating specifically on the story of Greece during the vital period when it was laboriously and painfully restored to the Byzantine world, and concluding with a necessarily condensed account of some of the larger issues – economic, social and cultural – that affected Greece in common with the rest of the empire.

Byzantium – a medieval theocracy

As heir to both ancient Greece and Rome, the Byzantine empire preserved the Hellenic culture of the former and the imperial organization – military, legal and administrative – of the latter. In addition, however, by promoting the Christian faith to an absolute dominance within Byzantine society, these ancient traditions were further transformed to serve a medieval purpose. Under the leadership of 'the most pious, Christ-loving emperors' (as they were styled), pagans, Jews, non-believers, schismatics and heretics were all subjected to the full weight of official attempts to impose uniformity of belief. Although patriarchs claimed an independent control in the ecclesiastical domain, emperors continued to intervene in church affairs, debating theological problems, defining dogma, presiding over oecumenical councils and deposing and appointing clergy at will. So while secular rulers ceded the ritual functions of *pontifex maximus* to ecclesiastics (normally the patriarchs of Constantinople), they retained nearly all the authority implied by the ancient title. Only in matters relating to moral standards and the application of canon law could the church overrule an emperor, as Nicolas Mystikos (Patriarch, 901–7) tried to do over Leo VI's fourth marriage. And even then he was unsuccessful.

Church and state were therefore intimately connected through their dual administration and hierarchies, which culminated in the patriarchal chancellery and imperial court. A double network of control spreading outwards from Constantinople established representatives of each throughout the empire – metropolitans in charge of ecclesiastical dioceses, military and civilian officials with responsibility for provincial administration. Normally the two collaborated to ensure that central policy was thoroughly enforced. But there were always grey areas and local elements which escaped such rigorous control – in the form of pirates, bandits, soothsayers or holy men, who maintained a limited independence. Their activities occasionally led to open revolt – as in the case of Thomas the Slav, whose ascent to the throne had been predicted by an Anatolian monk

– but usually they co-existed under nominal imperial rule, a thorn in the flesh of local bishops and administrators. Naturally the network was most efficient in the capital, where the presence of crack troops (the *tagmata*) and police (under the city prefect, the *eparch*) deterred opposition, and grew progressively weaker as the distance from Constantinople increased. In frontier areas this structural weakness permitted adventurers as well as heretics to flourish, as the epic stories of Digenis Akritas reveal.

Greece reclaimed for Byzantium

In Greece itself this frontier mentality remained a permanent feature of certain mountainous areas even after imperial rule was re-established: the northern Rhodopes (straddling the border with medieval Bulgaria), parts of the Pindos settled by Vlachs, and areas of the Taygetos range in the southern Peloponnese, where Slavonic tribes maintained their separate identity into the 10th century. But from the reign of Nikephoros I (802–11) onwards, the pattern of dual control was enshrined, with the clear aim of maintaining uniformity of administration and belief. It had taken an exceptionally long time to win back the provinces of Greece, because Slavonic tribes continued to move south during the 7th and 8th centuries, filling every void in imperial authority, sometimes in alliance with other antagonistic forces – Arab, Bulgar or internal rebel.

The first stage of reconquest involved limited military actions against specific targets, often Slav settlements in Thrace and Macedonia. In 657/8 Constans II campaigned in this region. Five years later he successfully marched a considerable imperial force through Thessalonica, Athens (where they wintered in 662/3) and Patras, where the emperor embarked for Sicily in his ill-fated attempt to move the imperial capital back to the west. (He was murdered in his bath in the palace at Syracuse in 668.) His son, Constantine IV, also attempted to check the ravages of Bulgar tribes in Thrace, an important grain-producing area of increasing significance to Constantinople as supplies from Egypt declined (due to the Arab occupation of the 640s). A further campaign in 688 by Justinian II succeeded in clearing the main route from Constantinople to the west (the Via Egnatia) of Slavonic settlements. The emperor was welcomed into Thessalonica in triumph and celebrated by granting privileges to the city and its churches. The success was only partial, however, for the western sector of the Via Egnatia, which ran through the Balkans to Dyrrachion on the Adriatic and had formerly provided the chief method of communication with Italy, had passed irretrievably out of imperial control. For many centuries Slavonic settlements would render this route unusable.

The second stage of reconquest developed from the campaigns of the first, as permanent forces of occupation were established under Byzantine control. Thrace was the first of the European *themata* – it is recorded together with the four Asian ones in a letter of Justinian II to Pope John V sent in 687. Probably created after the Bulgarian incursions of 679, which routed the Byzantine cavalry and caused serious damage, it became the major base for operations against these hostile forces to the north, for instance during Justinian II's campaign of 706.

Hellas was the next *thema* to be set up; it comprised the area of central Greece and Thessaly. The first mention of its *strategos* (military governor) occurs in 695. Some military and naval forces were attached to the new province, for in 727 Agallianos, a subordinate officer (*tourmarches*), led a detachment of local people (*Helladikoi*) in an unsuccessful attempt to replace Leo III by their own imperial candidate. The civilian aspect of provincial administration in Hellas may be deduced from the existence of seals belonging to the officials responsible: for example, that of a *protonotarios*, Nikephoros (dated to the 8th or 9th century). The *protonotarios* supervised the surveys of land and population on which tax returns were based. The seals of customs and excise officers (*kommerkiarioi*) may not reflect provincial administration, but certainly imply an imperial presence in the region. *Thema* administration was probably facilitated by a policy of Constantine V introduced in the 750s. Constantinople, like Greece, had been attacked by an outbreak of plague and its population reduced. To increase the number of inhabitants, people from the islands, Hellas and the *katotika mere* (Peloponnese) were moved to the capital. Ten years later the decision to restore the major aqueduct of the metropolis involved a similar procedure: construction workers were summoned from all parts of the empire, including 500 potters from Hellas and the islands and 5000 workmen and 200 ceramic craftsmen from Hellas and Thrace. Such directions could not have been implemented had not there been a definite degree of imperial control in the European provinces. A further indication of such control may be deduced from the fact that both Thessalonica and Kephalonia served as places of exile in the early 8th century.

The empire of the church

The process of restoring imperial control in Greece was also assisted by a reorganization of the church. Until the early 8th century the ecclesiastical diocese of East Illyricum, which included the entire Balkan peninsula, the Aegean islands, Crete, Sicily and southern Italy, had formed part of the territory of the west and fell under Roman control. Popes maintained their own vicars in Thessalonica (normally metropolitans of that city) and exercised certain rights of jurisdiction within the diocese. In 668, for instance, the bishop of Lappa (Crete) appealed to Pope Vitalian against his deposition by a local synod. The pope judged the decision uncanonical and ordered the metropolitan, Paul of Gortyna, to reinstate the bishop and to hand back two monasteries wrongly removed from his control. Similarly, disputes over the see of Larissa and among its suffragan clergy were resolved by appeal to Rome.

Under Leo III (717–41) this somewhat anomalous situation was altered by the emperor's unilateral decision to place the diocese of East Illyricum under Constantinople. Church leaders were thereby brought into much closer contact with the capital, and the patriarch gained a firmer say in the ecclesiastical organization of Greece – both in elections and in disputes; appeals were henceforth directed to Constantinople not Rome. Later popes, notably Nicholas I (858–67), greatly resented this imperial coup, which deprived them of a good deal of revenue from church patrimonies, as well as the right, for example, to nominate the metropolitans of Syracuse. In Greece, however, the change stimulated a rapid growth of episcopal sees, from about 18 bishops (recorded in the late 7th century) to the 46 who attended the Council of 787. This not only increased the Christian presence, especially important at inland sites previously occupied by Slavs, but also involved greater communication between the metropolis and provincial cities.

A further significant bond was established in 768 by the marriage of Irene, a member of the Sarandapechys family of Athens, to the son of Constantine V, the future Leo IV (775–80); this united a prominent Hellas family with the ruling dynasty. Although Irene is most renowned for the restoration of icon veneration by the Second Council of Nicaea (787), her attention to Greece was of equal importance. Members of her family were favoured with imperial appointments and involved in the detention and blinding of political rivals held in exile in Greece. In 783 her general, Staurakios, was sent on the first major expedition against Slav communities in the Peloponnese. His victory was celebrated in a ceremonial triumph at Constantinople and an imperial tour in the following year to Berroia in Thrace (Stara Zagora). In classical fashion the city was renamed Irenopolis after the empress, who observed the Byzantine reconquest from her litter. Macedonia

became a separate *thema* between 789 and 802. The return of imperial authority was commemorated in the rebuilding of S. Sophia, Thessalonica, which Irene and her son, Constantine VI, endowed with new mosaics. Finally, at the empress's insistence, Athens was raised to metropolitan status and thus given the same rank as Thessalonica and Corinth, the two established archiepiscopal sees in Greece.

Although Irene's successor, Nikephoros I (802–11), is not known to have shared her personal commitment, he did continue the work of pacification in the Peloponnese. When Patras was threatened, the emperor sent imperial forces under a *strategos* to relieve the city. It was rebuilt, repopulated and promoted to a metropolitan see. The *thema* administration of the Peloponnese probably dates from his reign. Greek communities then returned from southern Italy and Sicily to the region – the family of Athanasios, later bishop of Methone, moved back to Patras in about 826. Greek-speaking Christians from other parts of the empire were also transplanted to the *Sklaviniai* (Slav settlements in Greece) and the Peloponnese to support the process of 'byzantinization'. This forced movement of population was another imperial method of consolidating control. With imperial aid the churches of Lacedaemonia were reconstructed and bishoprics were established in Lacedaemonia, Korone and Methone.

An integrated state

Nikephoros also adopted a novel method designed to integrate the Slavs into Byzantine society. After their defeat at Patras in about 807, he issued a *chrysobull* (golden charter) setting out the conditions for their continued residence in Patras. All their property, wealth and children were given in perpetuity to the cathedral church of the city, dedicated to its patron, St Andrew. As servants of the saint, the Slavs were to maintain the governor's residence (where imperial agents, distinguished visitors and envoys from abroad might stay). While the metropolitans of Patras were forbidden to interfere in these arrangements, their 10th-century successors clearly did, and Leo VI (886–912) had to issue another charter specifying the duties and the autonomy of the cathedral servants.

Similar methods were used by Michael III (843–67) after the Slav revolt of 840–2, in which two tribes in the southern Peloponnese played a prominent part. The Melingoi and Ezeritai were forced to pay an annual tribute of 60 and 300 gold coins (*nomismata*) respectively. And 80 years later, when they began to act in a thoroughly independent fashion, refusing to obey the governor, to perform military or other public duties, or to pay the tribute, another campaign was launched. After a decisive Byzantine victory by the *strategos*, Krinites Arotras, in *c.* 921, 600 *nomismata* each was fixed as a new level of payment. But on their appeal to Romanos I (920–44) the old sums were restored and confirmed in a new *chrysobull*. One reason for the apparent climb-down by imperial officials was that an incursion of Bulgars in 922 threatened the Peloponnese, and it was deemed essential to prevent any alliance between the newcomers and the Melingoi and Ezeritai. So even in the 10th century imperial authority was regularly disturbed. None the less, the arrangements set out in the charters appear to have been largely successful; they permitted the gradual incorporation of the Slavs into imperial society.

Less official but equally effective methods of integration arose from the trading contacts between the Slavs and the indigenous population. In the 4th century such activity across the Danube frontier had familiarized the Visigoths with Roman customs and Christian beliefs. During the 'Dark Ages' it once again became a factor of importance, as the Slavs settled to agricultural occupations and sought to exchange their crops for objects of Byzantine manufacture. In the course of one of the many sieges of Thessalonica which occurred in the 7th century, the inhabitants sent an embassy to a Slav tribe in Thessaly, and successfully purchased corn from them. Similarly, at the end of the 9th century John Kameniates describes the relations between Greeks and Slavs near Thessalonica. Around Berroia Slavs traded with local inhabitants and brought fish to sell in Thessalonica. They made profits and cooperated with the city people. Some lived in mixed villages such as those which were already established near Patras prior to the great siege of *c.* 807. But in contrast to the Slavs of the Peloponnese, the Slavonic tribes had all adopted Christianity by John's time. Yet he insists that it was through commercial activity that Greek and Slav became familiar and learned to live in the same villages.

Not all economic activity was purely spontaneous, however. From the 8th century onwards emperors appointed *kommerkiarioi* to collect the customs and excise dues on the sale and transport of goods. Bronze coinage was also struck by imperial mints at Thessalonica, Corinth, and possibly another in central Greece, at Patras, Thebes or Athens. Archaeological finds tend to confirm the impression that imperial coinage circulated more widely in Greece from the reign of Theophilos (829–42). In this way local exchange was regulated and long-distance commerce taxed by imperial agents while the Slavs were gradually drawn into a commercial network based on a monetary economy and an urban way of life. Increasing supplies of silver and bronze coins satisfied the economic expansion of the 11th and 12th centuries, some of the smaller denominations being produced for central Greece probably at Thebes. Gold tended to be restricted to a cyclical movement through the Byzantine provinces: it went out in the form of soldiers' pay and was returned to the capital as taxation (such as the tribute paid by the Melingoi and Ezeritai). Only when hoarded for a particular purpose (marriage dowry, for instance) does any quantity of gold appear in provincial finds.

The chief means of incorporation, however, was neither political nor economic but religious. It was through a combination of official and unofficial missionary work that the Slavs were converted to Christianity – a development which probably did more than anything else to transform them into Byzantine citizens. The construction of numerous new churches, frequently at sites apparently unconnected with episcopal activity, confirms the spontaneous and local initiative behind such building. Ecclesiastical complexes grew up around monastic retreats and tombs of holy men such as St Nikon of Lacedaemonia or Hosios Lukas (Holy Luke) of Steiris (near Delphi). In the case of one particularly fine monument, the great domed church of the Virgin at Skripou (near Lamia, see p. 226), Leo the *protospatharios*, a military official, is known as patron. He probably served in the *thema* administration in central Greece, for which he was rewarded with lands near Lake Kopais. These formed the basis of his local property, on which his church and attached monastery were built in 873/4. Perhaps like many officials with sufficient means he wished to retire to the monastic community when his active military service ended.

While private foundations of this type account for a good deal of Byzantine ecclesiastical building, at both Skripou and Steiris a quite exceptional initiative in both architecture and decoration is observable. The earlier church was adorned with specially fine sculptures which appear to indicate the existence of a team of skilled local carvers. Their work can be traced in later monuments, extending as far west as Corfu, and including the twin churches at Steiris. At these 11th-century foundations, however, expertise in stone sculpture is matched by unusual decoration in carved tiles, fresco and mosaic. These monuments established a distinctive school of Middle Byzantine architecture, responsible for many important churches of the 11th to 13th centuries (see pp. 226–7). Those at Daphni (near Athens), in the Argolid, Messenia, Epirus and at Kastoria reflect the wide dissemination and develop-

A detail of the south wall of the 11th-century Katholikon, the main church of the monastery of Hosios Lukas. Its richly textured surface, achieved by carvings (probably reused from earlier buildings) and a mixture of brick, stone and carved tiles in the masonry, demonstrates Byzantine architects' new interest in exterior decoration.

ment of this independent style in Byzantine art. And it was in these magnificent surroundings that the hellenized Slavs and medieval Greeks forgot their origins in a common devotion to their faith.

From the reign of Nikephoros I, therefore, *thema* administration appears to have been securely established in parts of Greece and would cover the entire region by the end of the 9th century. Dyrrachion and Kephalonia became separate provinces by 809; Thessalonica between 796 and 824; the Aegean and Samos (both specifically naval units) in 843 and 899 respectively; Nicopolis and Strymon are also first mentioned in 899. Ecclesiastical control was similarly extended, with a large number of new sees being created in remoter inland sites – Bolaina, Zemaina and Maina in the Peloponnese, Stagoi, Loidorikion, Ezeros and Trikkis in Thessaly, for example. Other bishoprics were established on islands such as Corfu, Zakynthos, Leukas, Skopelos and Aigina. Through a number of mechanisms the mixed population of Greece was being integrated and unified.

These achievements did not remove the threat of revolt, whether by Slavs subjected to imperial rule, by Bulgars and Arabs from beyond the frontiers, or by disaffected sectors of the local population. In the 790s the sons of Constantine V, banished to central Greece for conspiring against their nephew, the young Emperor Constantine VI, received support from Greeks as well as from the Slavs of Belzetia in their unsuccessful revolt. Arab pirates were active in at least one attack on Patras (*c.* 807) and became a menace to the entire Aegean after their capture of Crete in 827. Two years later the population of Aigina was forced to flee; at the end of the century Demetrias, on the Gulf of Volos, was captured and occupied (897–902), and in 904 Thessalonica was sacked. This hostility was subsequently contained by Byzantine campaigns to recapture Crete, which finally succeeded in 961.

Throughout the 10th century, however, Bulgar inroads disturbed the empire. In 917/18 Tsar Symeon raided as far south as the Isthmus of Corinth, after inflicting a serious defeat on imperial forces near Anchialos, on the Black Sea. He even besieged Constantinople (without success). Another raid into central Greece in 943 made it necessary for Holy Luke to leave his ascetic retreat for a more inaccessible one. And in the 980s Larissa, a well-fortified stronghold, was plundered by Tsar Samuel, who removed the precious relics of St Achilleos.

To put an end to this continuous instability, Basil II (998–1025) directed several campaigns against the Bulgars with the aim of incorporating their independent state within the empire. His victories and reprisals earned him the nickname *Boulgaroktonos*, 'the Bulgar-slayer'. After a long struggle Byzantine forces defeated Samuel's in the Struma Valley (1014) and imposed a terrible punishment on the vanquished: 99 out of every 100 survivors were blinded; the last retained the sight of one eye to guide the rest back home. The arrival of this unseeing procession is said to have caused the tsar's death. Basil reorganized imperial administration in

Life on the land in medieval Greece, three miniatures from an 11th-century manuscript. Top to bottom: a goatherd playing a flute; a herdsman whittling a stick; a farmer pruning his trees.

Kastoria, Serbia and Berroia, creating three small *themata* to protect the western approaches to Thessalonica, and established direct rule in Bulgaria proper. After the final victory in 1016 he made a special pilgrimage to Athens, to give thanks in the church of the Virgin on the Acropolis (the converted Parthenon). He endowed it with new plate and ecclesiastical decorations and confirmed its privileges as a metropolitan see. The spectacular silk hanging (now known as the Gunther silk because it was used as the shroud of Bishop Gunther of Bamberg in the 11th century) may have been woven to commemorate this visit. It depicts a mounted horseman flanked by the symbolic representations of cities – Constantinople and Athens – in female form (see p. 217).

This was the last direct military intervention by a Byzantine emperor in the provinces of Greece. Subsequent revolts were dealt with by governors or generals despatched from the capital. But it was by no means the last instance of imperial patronage, which had already created many major monuments of Byzantine art in Greece. For later in the 11th century

244

Constantine IX Monomachos constructed an enormous new basilica over the holy spring at Nea Moni, on Chios. The Nea Moni mosaics (see p. 224) brought to the Aegean islands that style of metropolitan art then being exported to Kiev, Jerusalem, Venice, Torcello, Palermo and Cefalù (to name only the most important sites graced with Byzantine mosaics). Throughout the 12th century imperial patronage consolidated the monastic foundations of Mount Athos, extending their properties and privileges in charters. The same pattern of endowment encouraged the later Byzantine communities of Meteora, Mistra and Monemvasia, while provincial officials and local notables emulated the imperial style of patronage in their own churches and monasteries. The well-documented monastic complex at Bačkovo (northern Macedonia), established by the Georgian aristocrat, Pakourianos, illustrates the wealth which might be transferred to ecclesiastical institutions in this way. Similarly, 13th-century Serbian and Bulgar princes commemorated their own Christian faith in foundations such as Mileševo (King Vladislav, 1235) and Boiana (Tsar Kaloyan, 1259; see p. 226). Metropolitan artists or local artists trained in the style of the capital were employed to execute the fine frescos that adorned these churches. In their thoroughly Byzantine celebration of orthodoxy, the erstwhile enemies of the empire revealed what a complete integration had taken place over the centuries. As in so many other cases (Russia, Venice, the south Italian trading communities, for instance), the Hellenic culture of medieval Byzantium won allies and devotees through its artistic skills.

Byzantine economy and society

The material base for this flourishing provincial society lay in the village communities of Greece, which developed during the poorly documented period from AD 600–900. As in Roman times, rural and agricultural property continued to be the most significant source of personal wealth, but its distribution was completely altered by the breakdown of traditional patterns of cultivation. The villas and extensive private estates, typical of Late Antiquity, began to collapse under the impact of Slavonic incursions and the failure of Justinianic administration, and were replaced by smaller and more collective forms of agriculture. From the Farmers' Law (late 7th or early 8th century) and the fragmentary tax-rolls of Thebes and Athens (late 11th and 12th centuries) it is possible to reconstruct the new village system that developed.

The organization of the village, as reflected in the Farmers' Law, was structured round a collective responsibility for the total land tax paid to the central treasury. Villagers farmed the surrounding land in strip cultivation. Individual members owned strips (on which their tax contribution was assessed); rented land from their neighbours or in turn rented out their land to others; all shared in the communal grazing and facilities like watermills, ovens and wine and olive presses.

Stringent regulations governed situations which might cause friction between members, such as the straying of flocks into vineyards or cornfields, or the killing of a sheep dog. This possibly idealized picture of rural life is not identified with any particular area; the Farmers' Law is ubiquitous and universal, and probably sprang from an experience common to all parts of the empire. Because the village combined two essential functions, cultivation and self-government, this form of settlement was used to establish foreigners (such as the Mardaites from Syria), prisoners-of-war and populations transplanted to different provinces. Such villages were later incorporated into *thema* institutions, although their autonomy was sometimes threatened by the centralized control of government agents.

None the less, after three or four centuries the tax-rolls of Thebes and Athens confirm the persistence of scattered land ownership and strip cultivation. As these are basically fiscal records, revised every twenty-five years to list the taxes due on each strip, they provide evidence of each owner's resources: his titles, family, property, and livestock. They thus indicate changes in land ownership through inheritance, sale, gift or exchange, which in turn make it possible to trace variations in family fortunes. While one might prosper and acquire additional land, another could find itself unable to cultivate its strips and forced to sell them. Gradually, such differences resulted in extremes of poverty and wealth – creating the opposition between poor and rich well known to Byzantines. The Theban records, in particular, reveal the economic base of richer families: from increased land ownership and rents they were able to move from a village to a town, where they built houses and obtained posts in local administration. Samuel Gerontas commanded a small detachment of the local militia as *drouggarios* and lived in Thebes, although his strips were far away. Similarly, a member of the Pothos family had become a monk in Euripos. In contrast, one of the villagers had become so poor that he was qualified as *ptochos* (destitute) and was probably unable to pay any taxes. Such a process of differentiation lies behind the emergence of identifiable local families such as the Sarandapechys, from whose ranks Irene rose to be empress, or the Pardos and Chalkoutzes, who had been settled in central Greece for many years. The source of their power stemmed from their considerable control of landed property.

Emperors, however, tried repeatedly to check the domination of these families (called *dynatoi*, powerful) by legislation designed to protect the less powerful and to maintain a more equitable distribution of village lands. But they were unsuccessful. A combination of factors, not least the imperial use of land grants as a reward for military service, permitted certain families to form a provincial aristocracy. The Xeros family of Lacedaemonia, the Kamateroi of central Greece or Choirosphaktoi of Thessaly were part of an indigenous nobility, which then intermarried with representatives of the Anatolian *dynatoi* settled in the west, the

Tornikai, Kantakouzenoi and Branades, for instance. By the time of the Fourth Crusade the countryside was divided up between such families (who enjoyed tax exemptions and other privileges) while the surviving village communities were expected to bear an increasing tax burden.

Imperial concern for the weaker members of village communities was not a purely philanthropic matter, whatever rhetoric might be used in the preamble of such laws; it sprang from the need to maintain a tax-paying capacity throughout the empire. Since local notables frequently obtained imperial titles and administrative positions which carried an immunity from certain taxes, it was essential to preserve the village communities who remained collectively responsible for the basic one – the direct tax on land. They were also forced to make contributions towards the upkeep of public services – castles, roads, bridges, etc. – as well as payments for military defence and the governor's expenses (a much abused privilege). During the 11th century, when a number of such taxes in kind and *corvées* (in the form of labour services or the provision of food and transport animals for the governor) were commuted to money payments, the entire population of Epiros (the *thema* of Nicopolis) rose in revolt. Their antagonism was directed especially against John Kontzomytes the *praktor* (chief tax collector) whose method of commutation had resulted in excessive sums, harshly extracted. A generation later, in 1066, even the Vlachs (transhumant shepherds of the Pindos range) joined in a more serious rebellion against a new tax. Nikoulitzas, a local leader, was elected to represent the Thessalians at court and obtained a remission, whereupon a deputation of Vlachs and inhabitants of Larissa accompanied him to Constantinople to express their appreciation. Such extreme opposition to treasury demands heralds a new phase in the underlying hostility between capital and province. It also reveals the degree of autonomy exercised by individual officials, which might well border on an intolerable degree of exploitation.

That these changes sprang from an economic crisis at the heart of the empire is clear from the accompanying devaluation of the gold coinage. For close on 700 years the Constantinian gold *solidus* (in Greek, *nomisma*) had maintained its dominance. As a reliable currency, it exercised a profound influence in the medieval west, draining gold from all available sources and leaving silver as the supreme precious metal there. The power of Byzantine gold can be traced through hoards excavated over a wide area of European Russia, Scandinavia and throughout the west. Many had found their way to such findspots as pay packets for mercenary soldiers, notably the Varangians (Norsemen from Scandinavia who travelled to Byzantium through Kievan Russia and served as a special imperial bodyguard). From the reign of Constantine IX (1042–55) this gold coinage was debased by the introduction of silver alloys which reduced both its value and fineness. As a measure intended to spare the treasury much needed funds for the increasing demands of military activity against the Turks in Asia Minor, devaluation may have been temporarily successful. But in the long term it had disastrous results, which eventually permitted the new gold currencies of Italian city states to replace the Byzantine *nomisma* as the most acceptable trading coin.

The overall economic crisis of the 11th century arose from a series of pressures, military, political and economic, that placed enormous strains on the imperial system. In an empire which ran most industry as a state monopoly and kept a tight control over all commercial transactions, urban resources could never compete with rural ones. Employment in the imperial administration and the purchase of court sinecures might enable the wealthy to reside in the capital, but ownership of land provided the essential base. So it is hardly surprising that the empire found itself in financial difficulties when its land base began to be eroded. Military failures to maintain the expanded eastern frontier were matched by a rapid Seljuk advance into Anatolia after the Battle of Mantzikert (1071). Simultaneously, more of the remaining agricultural land passed out of imperial and village control into the hands of tax-exempt individuals.

Such a reduction in rural resources might have been balanced by an increase in urban profits from trade, for Byzantine cities recovered and prospered from the 10th century onwards. But the restrictive nature of imperial control of commerce effectively prevented this. An urban bourgeoisie comparable to the Islamic and Jewish middle classes of medieval cities of the east Mediterranean was inconceivable in Byzantium. Instead, strict regulations over all guild activity in the capital (recorded in the 10th-century *Book of the Eparch*) stifled economic initiatives. In particular, the production of luxury goods exported or presented as diplomatic gifts to foreign potentates, especially silk, remained a state preserve. In Greece the results of this imperial stranglehold can be seen in different fields. As silk was one of the prestige manufactures of Greece, the cultivation of mulberries and weaving of cloth played an important part in the local economy, for instance, in Stagoi (in Thessaly). Regrettably, very little is known of the organization of this crop, though documents from southern Italy may be typical of provincial silk production. Carpets and other woven materials, some embroidered with gold thread, appear to have constituted a second valuable sector of Greek production. Such activity implies increased trade and prosperity for the region, which was reflected in the annual fairs held on local saints' days, for example of St Spiridon at Corfu, and St Demetrios at Thessalonica. From accounts preserved by 12th-century travellers, such as the anonymous Cappadocian author who visited Thessalonica and described local events in the *Timarion*, or the diary of Benjamin of Tudela, it is clear that Greece was prosperous. To some observers, however, the central administration appeared to drain local wealth away from the provinces to the metropolis. As Michael Choniates, bishop of Athens (1182–1205), complained:

What do you (in Constantinople) lack? Not the wheat-bearing plains of Macedonia, Thrace and Thessaly, which are farmed by us; nor the wine of Ptelion, Chios and Rhodes, pressed by us; nor the fine garments woven by our Theban and Corinthian fingers, nor all our wealth, which flows, as many rivers flow into one sea, to the Queen City.

This policy of extraction, combined with a traditional determination to manage all aspects of the economy, impoverished and limited provincial life. It was also consonant with the imperial habit of balancing the budget through currency manipulation and tax reform. By these methods the 12th-century dynasties of Komnenos and Angelos attempted to tap the growing wealth of Greece.

Their efforts were hampered by local opposition which increasingly took the form of separatist movements, led by local notables such as Leo Sgouros in Corinth in 1203. Other prominent families (*archontes*) or castle inhabitants (*kastrenoi*) participated in revolts to establish independent principalities. This splintering prefigured the post-1205 division of Greece among crusader knights, in the same way that growing social stratification among the rural population prepared it for feudal relations. Although the distinction between rich and poor had arisen from entirely different processes, it produced a strange effect when taken in conjunction with the distintegration of imperial control and appearance of local rulers: the poorer inhabitants of Greece had been assimilated to a position similar to that of western medieval serfs.

The mixed crusading society documented by the 14th-century *Assizes of Romania* reveals how western social relations had been introduced to the Morea. But in Thrace and Macedonia apparently similar institutions developed within the imperial framework. Village communities continued to exist as before but many of their members sought the patronage and protection of aristocratic landowners or large monasteries. As dependent labourers (*paroikoi*) they then paid their taxes to the state via intermediary *dynatoi*. These changes were a natural consequence of the pressure of the powerful and the imperial failure to preserve a free peasantry.

During the civil war of 1341–7 the anti-aristocratic faction of Zealots seized control of Thessalonica, proclaimed its independence and opened a campaign against the local nobility. Although the commune of Thessalonica drew on popular peasant support in a rare example of political democracy in Byzantium, it was destined to fail. A firmly aristocratic administration was re-established by the coronation of John VI Kantakouzenos (1347) as emperor and regent for John V Palaiologos (reigned 1354–91). For the peasantry, however, the civil war, Zealot commune and resulting expansion of Serbian domination in the Balkans brought little change. They remained the serfs of feudal landowners, chiefly monastic. A similar dependence on ecclesiastical patronage is clearly visible throughout Greece. The monasteries of Meteora in Thessaly, constructed from the 14th century onwards, and of Mistra and Mega Spelaion in the Peloponnese, occupied a privileged place in Late Byzantine society. And it was these ecclesiastical institutions, now strengthened by the patronage of Russian, Georgian Serbian and other non-Greek Orthodox, which survived the Ottoman conquest.

Byzantine culture

Throughout the Byzantine world, intellectual activities declined during the 7th and early 8th centuries. In education even the schools of Constantinople failed to provide an adequate training and students sought out the few individuals who maintained the old traditions. One of these, Tychikos, gave instructions in Trebizond; another (unnamed) on the island of Andros. It was to the latter that Leo 'the Mathematician' turned for lessons in rhetoric, philosophy and arithmetic in the early 9th century. And when he had mastered the principles of these disciplines, Leo pursued his interest in ancient wisdom in the monasteries of Andros (and in mainland Greece, probably). Classical manuscripts, therefore, were to be found in religious communities, an indication of the shift of intellectual work into the ecclesiastical domain. Despite the church's hostility to aspects of ancient learning, such manuscripts continued to be copied, studied and annotated by clerics to the end of the empire and beyond.

During the 'Dark Ages', however, there is little evidence of manuscript production, profane or spiritual. Threatened by the rapid expansion of Islam, both empire and church fought to survive. And it was in the struggle with the Moslems (who observed the prohibition of graven images) that the rejection of icons attained a popular support and an imperial champion in the person of Leo III (717–41). Iconoclasm developed in reaction to the veneration of these pictures of divine and saintly figures, which had assumed a central position in Christian worship. While the iconoclast party felt that only the removal and destruction of icons would prevent idolatry and return the church to the observance of Old Testament law, the iconophiles justified the cult as a long-established Christian tradition. Because Leo III came from the eastern frontier region and Empress Irene, who restored icon veneration in 787, was a native of Greece, a polarity between the iconoclast east and iconophile west has often been assumed. But there is insufficient evidence to justify this dichotomy; supporters and detractors of icons can be found in most parts. A more interesting aspect of the iconoclast debate lies in the stimulus it provided for intellectual work and for closer relations between the iconophile party and the church of Rome. Both sides plundered the Bible and patristic writings for arguments in favour of their views; they travelled (often illicitly) between isolated communities to give en-

Ezekiel's vision of the four animals that later became symbols of the Evangelists (on the right, the lion of St Mark): a 6th-century mosaic in the apse of the church of Hosios David, Thessalonica. It was covered up during the iconoclast controversy and so escaped destruction at a time when most Greek churches lost their figural decoration.

couragement, and composed tracts against each other. In the journeys of St Gregory the Dekapolite and the correspondence of St Theodore of the Stoudios monastery in Constantinople, an iconophile network stretches beyond the empire (evidence for a comparable iconoclast organization was destroyed after 843). The Byzantine cursive script (minuscule), which evolved at the turn of the 8th–9th centuries, was a lasting result.

In Greece itself indirect evidence for iconophile sympathies is found in Thessalonica, where the 6th-century mosaic of Ezekiel's Vision in the apse of Hosios David was boarded up for protection. When other figural representations were destroyed, this one was saved and still exists today. Official iconoclasm in the same city is marked by traces of a monumental cross in the apse of S. Sophia. Thessalonica was obviously a centre of intellectual aspiration for it was here that Constantine (later St Cyril) and his brother Methodios received their elementary schooling and knowledge of the Slavonic vernacular. Still, Constantine had to go to the capital for a training in grammar and philosophy, which prepared him for his life's work as the 'Apostle of the Slavs'. Before 862, when he and Methodios left Constantinople for Moravia at the invitation of Prince Rastislav, they had already devised a script (Glagolitic, later replaced by Cyrillic) and were able to make translations of the Greek liturgy, lectionary and Bible.

The Moravians, thus presented with the possibility of worshipping in their own language, turned against the Frankish missionaries (who employed Latin) and rejected Roman authority. Through the use of the new alphabets large areas of central Europe and Russia were converted to Christianity and Byzantine influence enormously extended.

This attention to Slavonic needs was not matched by a comparable concern to render the Greek liturgy more easily comprehensible. Apart from the relatively uncomplex congregational responses and some of the older hymns, ecclesiastical Greek conformed to the sophisticated Attic employed in intellectual circles. From the early 9th century onwards this official language was enriched and developed by scholars such as Leo the Mathematician, who taught the traditional trivium and quadrivium in the Magnaura School in the 850s. The achievements of these early humanists can be illustrated by the career of Photios, twice patriarch of Constantinople, polymath and bibliophile extraordinary. His sermons, for instance, full of classical allusions, rhetorical devices and ancient techniques, must have been hard for any but the most educated to understand. They established models (in addition to ancient exercises) for the Greek taught in institutions of higher education for centuries, and thus shaped the language used by historians like Anna Komnene (daughter of Alexios I), lawyers and administrators.

Photios also demonstrates the tendency for intellectual work to be combined with a clerical career. While secular education continued and the civilian administrators provided posts of high status for laymen, a great number of scholars entered the church. Many became monks, like Constantine, who took the name Cyril shortly before his death in Rome – he was buried in the church of S. Clemente in 869. Others assumed leading positions as bishops, like Arethas of Patras, for instance, who was appointed to the foremost metropolitan see of Caesarea in 902/3. But he had already acquired an interest in classical learning before taking orders. In 888 he commissioned a copy of Euclid's works (the manuscript survives in the Bodleian Library at Oxford, d'Orville 301), the first of many ancient authors he studied and wrote about in important marginal notes (*scholia*). Aristotle, Plato, Aelius Aristides, Lucian, the Chaldaic oracles, Pausanias and many others followed. Arethas probably received a regular classical training, partly in Patras, partly in Constantinople. But even in the alternative schools, run by monasteries (notably the Stoudios foundation in the capital), the same essentially secular lessons were taught.

With this foundation of humanist study, 10th-century Byzantium witnessed an artistic and cultural revival (known as the 'Macedonian Renaissance'). Constantine VII Porphyrogenitos' personal interests and patronage were responsible for some of the finest artefacts produced, the gold reliquary of the True Cross now in Limburg, for example, and for new standards of historical research and encyclopaedic scholarship. While the resources of the capital and the imperial workshops ensured the employment of precious metals, jewels, ivory, enamel and silk, a similar spirit inspired less extravagant products made far from the capital. It was not only a case of manuscripts copied in Constantinople being decorated with motifs taken directly from their classical ancestors: in provincial *scriptoria* the same rediscovery of ancient art took place.

In addition to its Hellenistic inspiration, 10th-century art is characterized by a reduced scale. The change in dimension constitutes a major transformation of ecclesiastical architecture, from Late Antique basilicas to Middle Byzantine cross-in-square churches. Churches were increasingly built as private chapels for family use. Even in vast public churches like Hagia Sophia, the liturgy was often celebrated in side chapels. Icons also encouraged an individual style of devotion, a more personal form of worship. Such features resulted in a plethora of smaller foundations, for instance in Kastoria or Cappadocia, which were lavishly decorated, often with portraits of their donors. In northern Greece a quite distinctive style of brick, stone and tile construction developed, with domes raised on high drums and ornate carved decoration. In Cappadocia the rock-cut churches permitted few architectural features but a complex programme of internal frescoes. Their small scale and provincial origin does not, however, imply a 'provincial' style in the pejorative sense, one inevitably inferior to the higher metropolitan style of the capital. For these individual styles were to develop into a number of particular schools which produced the frescoes of Asinou and Lagoudera (Cyprus), and of Nerezi (Macedonia), the mosaics of Hosios Lukas and Daphni, and the finely proportioned churches of the Chalkoprateia at Thessalonica and Porta Panaghia at Arta (see pp. 226–7). These are without doubt some of the masterpieces of Byzantine art and stand comparison with the greatest monuments of Constantinople constructed at the same time.

Nor should the degree of interaction between different parts of the empire be overlooked, even if it frequently took the form of a rivalry between metropolis and province. During the 11th and 12th centuries the cultural life of Greece was greatly influenced by some of the ecclesiastics appointed to its bishoprics. They brought not only theological expertise but also intellectual interests and artistic concepts. Theophylact of Ochrid was distinguished by his observations of the Bulgarian people; Eustathios of Thessalonica by his commentaries on Homer; Demetrios Chomatianos by his concern for canon law. In addition, they all expressed themselves to their friends and ecclesiastical colleagues in letters which form a fascinating branch of Byzantine literature. Of course, their letters carry complaints about the unsophisticated conditions of provincial life, but they also reveal a concern to correct injustice, to train the local clergy and supervise the copying of manuscripts. Through the work of these

A detail from a manuscript of Euclid's works commissioned by Bishop Arethas in 888. Arethas was an important classical scholar, whose career demonstrates the fascination secular Greek learning had for Byzantine ecclesiastics – a fascination that laid the foundations for a renaissance of art and scholarship in 10th-century Byzantium. The manuscript is written in a pure form of minuscule, the Byzantine cursive script, which evolved at the turn of the 8th and 9th centuries AD.

bishops a wide range of religious experiences could be shared between all levels of society – the 1054 schism with Rome (a political decision taken in the capital) as well as the growth of religious confraternities, such as the one in central Greece centred on the 'Naupaktiotissa' icon of the Virgin (an indigenous expression of devotion).

Bishops none the less constituted a literary élite in a largely non-literate world and employed the stylized Attic Greek of ruling circles for their correspondence. It was very rare for a general like Kekaumenos (11th century) to master the skill of writing, and even more unusual for a military official to record his memoirs in a simpler form of Greek. The dichotomy between official and spoken language became more marked from the 12th century, when a written vernacular developed. The introduction of new literary forms – satire, romance and verse histories – in a demotic Greek readily understood by one and all made a profound change. Whether this literature was stimulated by a new audience, the growing numbers of urban dwellers, or by new patrons, the western princesses who had difficulty in mastering classical Greek, it found a broad popular response. In Frankish Morea, particularly, the new medium was put to use to record the conquest and history of the crusaders. The *Chronicle of Morea* survives in vernacular Greek, French, Italian and Spanish versions, which were declaimed at feasts in castles throughout the Mediterranean. Like the earlier Greek epic of Digenes Akritas (the eastern border hero) it combined accessibility and contemporary relevance. While it never removed the dominance of official Greek, the new demotic encouraged romances like *Kallimachos and Chrysorhoe*, satirical tales by Theodore Prodromos and the development of different vernaculars – for example, the Cypriot dialect used in the chronicles of Leontios Makhairas and George Boustronios. And through these literary works demotic Greek established its own history, so that when the battle with *katharevousa* (pure) Greek was joined in the modern period it could draw on a rich tradition.

While the events of 1204 brought eastern and western cultures together in a stimulating fashion in parts of the Morea, elsewhere an ingrained hostility was merely confirmed. From the schism of 1054 onwards, the Byzantine church was very torn, one party striving for unity with Rome while another clung to independence. The custom of holding theological debates at court, if necessary with translators for the western representatives, encouraged both factions but induced a feverish agitation in the reign of Michael VIII (1259–82). Largely for political and military reasons the emperor negotiated with the papacy for reunion, which was finally achieved in 1274 at the Council of Lyons, but immediately repudiated by significant sections of the Byzantine clergy and laity. Although diplomatically advantageous, the union never commanded popular support.

In Greece an uneasy symbiosis had developed. The Byzantine clergy maintained their church in exile while a Latin hierarchy was established: Cistercians took over Daphni, for instance, and William of Moerbecke assumed the archbishopric of Corinth (1278–?86). In contrast to the Holy Land and Cyprus, however, no Gothic cathedrals were built; western influence is far more visible in the castles of the Peloponnese. Byzantine art flourished under both Latin and Greek patrons and is especially evident in the city of Mistra, capital of the Byzantine despotate (see pp. 225, 226 and 232).

The Late Byzantine period was marked by a renewed concern for spiritual values and a vigorous interest in Neoplatonist philosophy. Both contributed to the development of Byzantine mysticism, which bore fruit in the Hesychast movement of contemplation and silent prayer. The work of scholars such as George Pachymeres and Maximos Planudes at Nicaea (1204–61) and later at Constantinople established a pattern of outstanding scholarship. For the first time major works of western thought in Latin were translated, including parts of St Augustine. Planudes also prepared new editions of classical authors, notably Plutarch, and revived Byzantine interest in ancient epigrams. Under Manuel II (1391–1425), who was himself a gifted humanist, Demetrios Kydones of Thessalonica was encouraged to prepare a Greek edition of Aquinas' *Summa Theologiae*, a project related to the effort to renew union with Rome. But the philosophical interest in Neoplatonism was most characteristic of the period, and culminated in the work of Gemistos Plethon, who established a Platonic Academy in Mistra. Ancient Greek philosophy, as well as religion, brought Byzantine intellectuals into close contact with Italian Renaissance scholars and transmitted much eastern learning to the west even before the fall of Constantinople.

The Byzantine legacy

Because of its long history spanning the ancient and early modern worlds, Byzantium was bound to influence neighbouring states. This influence – with its Hellenistic component – can be traced particularly in those that adopted an imperial form. In 10th-century Germany, for instance, the court of the Holy Roman Empire adopted Byzantine ceremonial and political ideology with the encouragement of the Empress Theophano. As the niece of John I Tzimiskes (969–76),

she was married to Otto II in a diplomatic alliance and brought up her son, Otto III, in the traditions of a Byzantine prince. Under Theophano's tutelage he tried to rebuild an empire in the west following the Byzantine model. Although this project failed, it left an important tradition which lived on into the days of Frederick II and Charles V.

A more profound adaptation of imperial ideals occurred in the Slavonic lands converted to Orthodoxy by Byzantine missionaries. In medieval Bulgaria and Serbia, but especially in Russia, theocratic systems proved long-lasting. The roles of prince and *tsar* (itself a corruption of the Latin, *caesar*, which had passed into Byzantium as the official term for a co-emperor) drew upon ancient types. State hierarchies of both honorary and active positions emulated the Byzantine system and were similarly distinguished by special costumes made from materials reserved for the ruler.

The greatest contribution of Byzantium to the world, however, lies in its legal, literary, devotional and, above all, artistic traditions. By conservation, interpretation and commentary, the Byzantines elaborated the inheritance of Roman law. The systematic edition made by Constantine Harmenopoulos of Thessalonica in 1345, the *Hexabiblos*, was widely used in eastern Europe during the late medieval period and into modern times. Similarly, the *Syntagma* (Constitution) of Matthew Blastares (1335), which consisted of secular and ecclesiastical rulings arranged in alphabetic order, was translated into Serbian at Stephan Dušan's order. The Byzantine liturgy also played a decisive role not solely in the Orthodox churches of the east but also in literary culture. Traditions of icon painting, fresco decoration and architecture formed another common inheritance, as many 16th- and 17th-century monuments of purely Byzantine character testify.

In Greece particularly, the Byzantine domination bequeathed a rich heritage to the Hellenic world. Through many of its distinctive features, aspects of ancient and classical learning were preserved and transmitted together with a particular medieval contribution to the modern era. In the mid-14th century, for instance, a cleric of the Orthodox bishop of Athens, then under Catalan domination, could copy and illustrate a medical manuscript of ancient origin for a local doctor (this is preserved in the Bibliothèque Nationale, Paris). By maintaining the language and literature of ancient Hellas, and encouraging the development of a lively written vernacular, the medieval inhabitants of Greece ensured a continuity in their own history. Byzantine forms of intellectual, artistic and religious expression added invaluable strength to this tradition. And when it was put to test by the Turkish occupation, it was not found wanting.

9
The Impact of Hellenism

*Greek culture in the
Moslem and Slav
worlds*

SPEROS VRYONIS, Jr

كرويا

كروسا

الشِّبِثّ بابيشو اذا اطبخ جشدشه وشرب ادرّ البول واللبن وسكّن
المغص والنفخ وانطلاق البطن والقى والفواق لكنه يظلم البصر ويضعف
الباه واطبخه يجلس في الست الاوجاع ارحامهن وبزره اذا احرق
وذرّعلي تعفّن الملتهبة ويواتيها بسها نفع وقلع ذلك ولم

٤١٤

With the extinction of the Roman empire in the west, the establishment of Constantinople as the heir of the classical world and the rise of Islam as a dominant force in the east, the history of Greek civilization enters a new phase. No longer confined to the areas where Greek is spoken, it begins to penetrate cultures that are quite distinct in their origins – that of the Slavs to the north and of Islam in the south and east. Its impact was so strong that those 'host' cultures were in many ways radically transformed.

Such transformations have happened many times in the past and are still happening today, and the process by which they occur is an important subject for historical research. They raise a number of general questions. What are the elements in the dominant culture that are available for transmission to another culture (i.e. the whole problem of translation and what is translatable)? What are the minimal essential conditions in a host culture that enable the transmission to take place? Who actually brings about the transmission? Who translates and what is translated? Finally, what is the lasting effect on the host culture likely to be, and to what extent may it stimulate a new creative process? Partial answers to all these questions emerge when we look at the specific topic with which I shall concern myself here – the transmission and diffusion of Greek literature, through the study and translation of texts originally written in Greek, over large parts of the Slavic and Islamic worlds.

But first, what did 'Greek literature' consist of in the 6th century AD, just before the rise of Islam and the Slav invasions? Most importantly, there was the body of works that had come down from the classical period: poetry (Homer, Hesiod, the lyric and elegiac poets), drama (tragedy and comedy), history and philosophy. There were also scientific and medical texts.

Clustering round the great masterpieces of the past there was the accumulating body of work by scholiasts and exegetists. This is the most characteristic product of the Hellenistic age, when a centralized and powerful imperial government had replaced the classical city state, when philosophers turned from the problems facing man as a political animal to study the inner life of the individual, and strove to produce 'good' citizens rather than efficient citizens and when commentary and classification were encouraged more than original creation. Parallel with this tendency was the ambition to synthesize and reconcile all knowledge and theory

Islamic culture was heavily dependent upon Greek sources, but was highly selective in what it chose to assimilate. Science was eagerly studied, anything with theological implications rejected. This page is from an 11th-century Arabic translation of Dioscorides, a Greek writer on medicinal herbs who lived in the 1st century AD.

rather than to divide and analyse. Thus religion evolved from the particular to the universal, towards a kind of abstract monotheism as embodied in Neoplatonism. Aristotelian psychology, as expounded by Alexander of Aphrodisias, evolved a theory of the mind (*nous*) that lent itself to the Neoplatonic concept of the prime mover. Medicine and the sciences continued to be studied, particularly in Alexandria, the intellectual centre of late Hellenism, though after Galen there was little original speculation.

In the realm of literature and language, the admired style was neo-Attic, in which the goal was to imitate what was in fact a dead language (5th-century BC Greek) as closely as possible, and to use it to express both scientific and literary concepts. Thus the classical texts came to be studied not for their content but for their grammar, rhetorical techniques and vocabulary. Even obscurity became a recognized means of achieving eloquence. Every branch of writing – philosophy, science, medicine, rhetoric – was subjected to the same discipline and emerged as something very different from what it had been in the classical period. This was not because writers and thinkers of the first Christian centuries failed to understand their predecessors. They used their work to meet the needs of their own day and so maintained the current of a living and developing tradition.

The triumph of Christianity was a second major factor in the situation. Yet, as W. Jaeger has said, 'the Christianization of the Greek-speaking world involved the partial Hellenization of Christianity'. The language of the Christian church was Greek, (even though the earliest Palestinian Christians may have used Aramaic). This entailed the automatic adoption of a technical and philosophical vocabulary that to some extent moulded its doctrine. Clement and Origen of Alexandria and the Cappadocian fathers presented much of their argument and scholarship within the forms that their contemporary pagan neighbours could understand. They and their pagan opponents employed a system of logic, ultimately derived from Aristotle through Porphyry, which was not Christian. Neoplatonic presuppositions formed a common background for theological disputation and for mystical experience. Even pagan literature could be used by the student as a model of style and sound grammar, said the 4th-century theologian Basil, and those passages where there were to be found sentiments acceptable to Christianity were to be employed for the illumination of the young. On the other hand, the new religion also produced a body of literature of its own which was different from that of the pagan past: the Christian chronicles, the lives of saints, the liturgy and its accompanying poetry, canon law and much else.

Thus Greek culture in the 6th century had a double

اهذهالصفه لايشتهيالطعاماوزكانت قوتهتحلوصفته على

heritage or tradition; that of the evolved pagan cultural forms – that is, forms that had been developing over the centuries and which, though they had been reshaped, were nevertheless identifiable with those of an earlier period – and also the new Christianized cultural forms. Though these two elements were often at war with each other, there were circumstances which contributed both to their mutual accommodation and to their separate and independent development.

For the period between the 6th and 9th centuries – the so-called Byzantine Dark Ages – we are poorly informed on the availability of Greek manuscripts in the empire and the extent to which middle and higher education were maintained. Probably both were at a low ebb. The copying of manuscripts seems to have declined drastically, and higher education may well have ceased to exist. In the reign of Leo V (813–20) an imperial library in the palace is mentioned, and slightly earlier (later 8th century) an increase in demand for manuscripts has been inferred from the fact that the new minuscule script seems to have come into use at this time, a script that was quicker to write, cheaper to produce and easier to read than the old uncial. Monastic *scriptoria* developed as centres for copying and book production; evidently the older style of education had not disappeared at the lower and middle levels. Two of the patriarchs (Tarasius, 784–806, and Nicephorus, 806–15) have been shown to have had a good grounding in the classics, philosophy and Aristotelian logic. Their successor, the iconoclast John Grammaticus, had received a good education, had taught in a school of higher education, and had a reputation for dabbling in what might be called experimental science. The so-called renaissance of classical learning, or what has been termed the First Byzantine Humanism, comes into historical focus only with the personalities of Leo the Mathematician and Photius, both of whom dominate the field of letters in 9th-century Byzantium. Leo, in part an autodidact, who had gone to the island of Andros to find a teacher, went on to study manuscripts on his own in the monasteries. He is said to have been sought, on loan, by the Caliph al-Mamun, and served thereafter for a short spell as metropolitan of the city of Thessalonica. Earlier he had taught in Constantinople, privately at first, and then on a stipend from the state. When Caesar Bardas, who was much concerned with pagan learning, founded the school of the Magnaura perhaps sometime before 855, he appointed Leo as its head with the task of providing instruction in philosophy. Others were appointed to preside over departments of geometry, astronomy and grammar. Thereafter, and particularly in the persons of Photius and Arethas, the copying, study, and interpretation of the ancient Greek texts were firmly established, or reestablished, in the Greek-speaking lands.

The diffusion of Greek culture in the Islamic world

It was just at this time, in the reign of al-Mamun, that Islamic society turned to the massive collection, translation and study of a large number of ancient Greek texts. Al-Nadim, a 10th-century Arab scholar, in his famous *Fihrist*, a descriptive analysis of the formation and content of Islamic intellectual history, presents what his contemporaries believed to have been the inspiration for this startling new development.

'Mention of the Reason why Books on Philosophy and other Ancient Sciences Became Plentiful in This Country'

One of the reasons for this was that al-Ma'mūn [al-Mamun] saw in a dream the likeness of a man white in color, with a ruddy complexion, broad forehead, joined eyebrows, bald head, bloodshot eyes, and good qualities sitting on his bed. Al-Ma'mūn related, 'It was as though I was in front of him, filled with fear of him. Then I said, 'Who are you?' He replied, 'I am Aristotle.' Then I was delighted with him and said, 'Oh sage, may I ask you a question?' He said, 'Ask it.' Then I asked, 'What is good?' He replied, 'What is good in the mind.' I said again, 'Then what is next?' He answered, 'What is good in the law.' I said, 'Then what next?' He replied, 'What is good with the public.' I said, 'Then what more?' He answered 'More? There is no more.'

This dream was one of the most definite reasons for the output of books. (al-Nadīm, Dodge, II, 583–4.)

Is there any connection between this diffusion of Greek texts in the lands of the caliphate and the renaissance of Greek studies that we saw emerging in Byzantium? As mentioned above, one Byzantine source relates that the Caliph al-Mamun (813–33), hearing of the brilliance and knowledge of Leo the Mathematician, tried to tempt him to his court, promising him wealth and fame in return. He even wrote to the Emperor Theophilos offering peace terms and 2000 pounds of gold if he would persuade Leo to settle in Baghdad. However, says the same source, Theophilos refused to allow a man who would bring such renown to his empire to go over to his foe.

Al-Nadim reports an anecdote which again points to connections between Byzantium and the caliphate in regard to Greek texts.

Between al-Ma'mūn and the Byzantine emperor there was correspondence . . . Then he wrote to the Byzantine emperor asking his permission to obtain a selection of old scientific [manuscripts], stored and treasured in the Byzantine country. After first refusing, he complied with this. Accordingly, al-Ma'mūn sent forth a group of men, among whom were al-Ḥajjāj ibn Maṭar; Ibn al-Baṭrīq; Salmān, the director of the Bayt al-Ḥikmah; and others besides them. They brought the books selected from what they had found. Upon bringing them to him [al-Ma'mūn], he ordered them to translate [the manuscripts] . . . (al-Nadīm, Dodge, II, 584.)

There is reference even to a later expedition to retrieve Greek manuscripts from Byzantine libraries, an expedition financed by the family of al-Munajjim and which included as a member of the expedition the most famous of the translators, Hunayn ibn Ishaq.

These spectacular exchanges between Baghdad and Constantinople concerning classical philology seem to have been the effect rather than the cause of the rise of interest in ancient Greek learning in the Islamic world. The interest itself, and the tradition to which it belonged, had never died out in those lands of the Near East which, after the 7th century, came to constitute the territory of the caliphate. Further, the basic consideration seems to have been pragmatic. Al-Mamun had found that the texts and the learning they contained had

a practical application, especially in the field of medicine. And since the medical texts (predominantly of the school of Galen) were based on a philosophical structure, the study of medicine entailed the study of philosophy too. The sudden expansion of the Islamic empire had brought the Arabs into contact with largely unknown lands and peoples, and made geography a matter of practical interest. The sciences and mathematics likewise had practical application. As we shall see, the basis of selectivity as to which texts and authors would be translated thus had in the beginning, and throughout, a very heavily pragmatic orientation.

The conditions of the host society, the Islamic world, were sufficiently receptive to allow this new intellectual tradition to take deep root, with the result that it had long-term effects on many aspects of Islamic intellectual and scientific life. The caliphate included peoples and lands that had enjoyed an unbroken tradition of organized schools, teaching and intellectual, religious, and medico-scientific preoccupations. These traditions had not been erased by the spread of Islamic political control, and as Islam began to crystallize as a civilization and society it came into contact with these non-Moslem components within its own empire. Their specializations were often useful or indeed necessary to the conquerors. Even among those who converted, many retained a memory of such traditions and schooling.

Perhaps the most spectacular example is the old school of Djundeshapur, founded by the Sassanids. This nurtured a lively tradition in Greek medicine, and its graduates, especially the Nestorian family of the Bokhtishu, furnished the court physicians of the caliphs in Baghdad. (Nestorians were a sect who believed that Christ's nature was predominantly human.) Thus the Moslems, in this symbiosis with their conquered subjects, were exposed to many aspects of the older civilizations of the region, and could select the Greek texts that they wished to study according to their immediate needs. We therefore find the borrowings and translations confined mainly to philosophy, geography, music, mathematics and medicine.

In theology, of course, the case was different. Islamic religious thinkers might be stimulated in certain ways by contact with Syrian Christians, especially by their training in philosophy and logic, but they could not allow themselves to be influenced too deeply. The same considerations cut them off from sharing in imaginative literature. The dichotomy between science and literature was virtually absolute. Both the Moslems and the Christian translators were conscious of this and made choices quite deliberately. The most important of these translator-scholars, the Syrian Nestorian Hunayn ibn Ishaq wrote:

If the reader finds a remark in classical works beginning with the words 'Galen (or Plato, Aristotle, etc.) says', and it turns out to be a strictly scientific discussion of the subject under investigation, he should study it carefully and try to understand it. If, on the other hand, it concerns questions of belief and opinion, he must take no further notice of it, since such remarks were made only in order to win people over to the ideas expressed in them or because they concern old, deeply rooted views. (Quoted by F. Rosenthal in *The Classical Heritage in Islam*, p. 27.)

Thus texts of a pagan nature (which includes all Greek creative literature) would be excluded, as well as works of a specifically Christian character. A further barrier was that of aesthetics, specifically in regard to poetry. Al-Jahiz was clearly aware of this:

Poems do not lend themselves to translation and ought not to be translated. When they are translated, their poetic structure is rent; the metre is no longer correct; poetic beauty disappears and nothing worthy of admiration remains in the poems. It is different with prose. (ibid., p. 18)

There are further indications that even the most gifted of the translators, Hunayn ibn Ishaq, found the language of Aristophanes beyond his command of Greek. Finally, none of the ancient historians was translated into Arabic; Moslem readers had little interest in what happened before the advent of the Prophet.

Problems of translation

Who were the translators of the Greek texts? Al-Nadim presents us with a catalogue, which though not complete, gives the names of forty-seven translators active in translating texts from Greek into Syriac and Arabic. Of these, far and away the majority were Syriac speakers and only a very few were Greeks; all were Christians. Of the later great Islamic philosophers it is interesting to note that none seems to have known Greek. The edifice of Islamic philosophy and the utilization of Greek expertise by Moslems in other domains, such as science, geography, mathematics and medicine, seem to have rested by and large on the translations for a knowledge of Greek learning in these fields. Thus the importance of the translators is crucial.

It is of further significance that the bulk of the translations was made not by Greeks themselves but rather by Syriac speakers who were largely Nestorians and to a much lesser degree Monophysites (members of a sect which emphasized the divinity at the expense of the humanity of Christ). This observation, common knowledge to all those who concern themselves with the topic, brings us back to the general condition of Near Eastern society during the first Islamic centuries and helps explain why the so-called 'renaissance' of Greek studies was possible in the 9th and 10th centuries at a time when such studies had long vanished in western Europe.

One scholar in speaking of the Syriac speakers of Late Antiquity and the early Middle Ages has coined the felicitous phrase, 'the Syrian version of Hellenism'. The expansion of Hellenism under Alexander the Great had resulted in the partial Hellenization of

the life of Mesopotamia, Syria and Palestine, the regions inhabited by these people. To speak of the Hellenism of Syriac speakers may sound like a contradiction in terms, but actually it is not. Many of the intellectuals of this cultural group were familiar enough with Greek and with the tempo of Hellenism's intellectual life to appropriate substantial parts of the Hellenic heritage, dress it in Syriac garb and introduce it into the Syriac school curricula. Ibas (d. 457) made a Syriac translation of Porphyry's *Eisagoge*, the introduction to the study of Aristotle's *Organon*. Perhaps the most active of all the Syriac Hellenists was Sergius of Ras al-Ayn (d. 536) who translated much of Galen and made versions of the *Eisagoge* and the *Categories*. He wrote on astronomy, logic, the soul and other subjects, and his writings were regarded as authoritative by both Monophysites and Nestorians. To him is attributed the foundation of the Syriac school of medicine that ultimately gave birth to Arab medicine. The other Monophysite contemporary of Sergius, Ahudemmeh, arranged the commentaries of John Philoponus for the Monophysites. The theological school at Nisibis was dissolved when the city was conquered by the Persians in 363. But after the condemnation of Nestorius in 431, his followers fled to Persia and re-established the school of Nisibis, which now continued in a foreign land. The Monophysites established their centre at the monastery of Qeneshrin on the Euphrates river where their leading scholar, Severus Sebokt, just prior to the Arab conquests, wrote commentaries on Aristotle. Thus the Syriac-speaking Christians, though alienated and often expelled from the Byzantine empire, were nevertheless sufficiently Hellenized to be the bearers of a living tradition of the study and translation of Aristotle, Galen and of other Greek scientific authors. They applied this knowledge in the realms of education, medicine and theological and intellectual discourse. It was these living traditions which the Islamic patrons of the Christian translators encountered in the early 9th century. The Syriac speakers thus brought to them precisely that part of the Greek cultural tradition which was current among themselves and in the form which it had attained in the 6th century, primarily in Alexandria. Thus we have a double paradox. Greek culture was conveyed to the Near East by Syriac speakers, not by Greeks, men who were persecuted for their religion and who preferred to use their own language in the liturgy rather than Greek. This Syrian version of Greek intellectual materials was therefore a living tradition when the Arabs began to receive it via translations from Syriac into Arabic. It should be noted that many of the translations were first made into Syriac for Syriac-speakers in the 9th century, in response to a revival of interest among Syriac-speaking Christians. What is of importance is the fact that once the texts had been translated into Arabic the great Arab scholars such as al-Kindi (d. c. 870), al-Farabi (d. 950), and al-Biruni (d. 1051) surpassed both the Syriac and the Byzantine Christians in their creative use of this ancient material

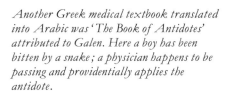

Another Greek medical textbook translated into Arabic was 'The Book of Antidotes' attributed to Galen. Here a boy has been bitten by a snake; a physician happens to be passing and providentially applies the antidote.

and in turn passed on a portion of it to western Europe.

A brief examination of how the work of translation was financed and who provided the patronage will tell us more about the way it was regarded in Baghdad. First and foremost was the Caliph al-Mamun himself, followed closely by important men in the court. A powerful patron was Abu'l Hasan 'Ali ibn Yaha (d. 888), son of al-Mamun's astronomer. Hunayn ibn Ishaq mentions Arab versions of ten of the works of Galen that he and colleagues prepared at his instigation. Muhammad ibn 'Abd al-Malik al-Zayyat, vizir of al-Mutasim, very heavily financed this work, whereas the Banu Musa (an important family in court circles) seem to have been the principal supporters of Hunayn ibn Ishaq and his circle. The translators worked also for Abu'l Hasan Ahmad ibn Muhammad ibn al-Mudabbir, the governor of Egypt. Even the chief of the Baghdad police, Ishaq ibn Ibrahim al-Tahiri, commissioned Hunayn ibn Ishaq to translate Galen's *De viribus alimentorum* for him. Thus the principle patrons of the translations into Arabic were public figures, themselves Moslem. In contrast, the translations into Syriac were intended for the most part for Syriac Christians in the field of medicine or else for colleagues of the translators. These included the famous physicians of the caliphs, the Bokhtisho family of Djundeshapur. Obviously such a large-scale enterprise, which called for the services of skilled individuals, expensive trips, massive purchases of manuscripts, and in some cases the provision of buildings, entailed large expenditures. These seem to have been forthcoming. The Bayt al-Hikma was founded by the caliph al-Mamun and financially supported so that it had a regular staff and library (it does not seem to have survived the reign of the Caliph al-Mutawakkil, 847–61). There was, apparently, at least one other circle concerned with translation, that of Hunayn ibn Ishaq, who was largely supported by the Banu Musa, according to al-Nadim:

... the sons of al-Munajjim [Banu Musa] supported a group of translators, among whom there were Ḥunayn ibn Isḥāq,

Hubaysh ibn al-Ḥasan, Thābit ibn Qurrah, and others besides them. Each month the translation and maintenance amounted to about five hundred gold coins. (al-Nadīm, Dodge, II, 585.)

Al-Mutasim's vizir, Muhammad ibn 'Abd al-Malik al-Zayyat, is alleged to have spent up to 2000 dinars per month for the translating services of Hubaysh, Ibn Masawaih, Bokhtisho and Hunayn. The intense interest of these highly placed and wealthy personalities soon created a very expensive market in Greek manuscripts and their translations. One scholar involved in the enterprise, Abu Zakariya Yahya ibn Adi, relates that he was looking for works of Alexander of Aphrodisias:

The two expositions [i.e. commentaries of Alexander on Aristotle's *Physica Auscultatio* and his *Analytica Posteriora*] were offered to me for sale for one hundred and twenty gold coins. I went to fetch the coins and upon returning found that the people had sold the two expositions along with other books to a man from Khurasan for three thousand gold coins. (ibid., 608–9.)

His luck was no better when he sought to purchase works of Aristotle:

... he offered fifty gold coins to Ibrāhīm ibn 'Abd Allāh for a copy of the *Sophistici* [*Elenchi*], a copy of the *Oratory* [*Rhetorica*] and a copy of the *Poetry* [*Poetica*] as translated by Isḥāq, but he would not sell them. (ibid., 609.)

Contemporaries tell us about the methods of these scholar-translators, who for about a century played such an important role in the intellectual life of Baghdad:

The translators use two methods of translation. One of them is that of Yuḥannā b. al-Biṭrīq ... According to this method, the translator studies each individual Greek word and its meaning, chooses an Arabic word of corresponding meaning and uses it. Then he turns to the next word and proceeds in the same manner until in the end he has rendered into Arabic the text he wishes to translate. This method is bad for two reasons. First it is impossible to find Arabic expressions corresponding to all Greek words and, therefore, through this method many Greek words remain untranslated. Second, certain syntactical combinations in the one language do not always necessarily correspond to similar combinations in the other; besides, the use of metaphors, which are frequent in every language, causes additional mistakes.

The second method is that of Ḥunain b. Isḥāq ... here the translator considers a whole sentence, ascertains its full meaning and then expresses it in Arabic with a sentence identical in meaning, without concern for the correspondence of individual words. This method is superior, and hence there is no need to improve the works of Ḥunain b. Isḥāq. The exception is those dealing with the mathematical sciences, which he had not mastered, in contrast with works on medicine, logic, natural science and metaphysics whose Arabic translations require no corrections at all. (Quoted by F. Rosenthal, op. cit., pp. 17–18.)

Hunayn ibn Ishaq, in his own writings (discussed by M. Meyerhof in *Isis*, VIII), tells us how he often worked on these texts, particularly in his monumental work on Galen. First he had to find Greek texts, and in the case of Galen's *De Demonstratione* he sought it in Mesopotamia, Syria, Palestine and Egypt, finding only about half of the Greek text in Damascus. His short note accompanying the entry under Galen's *De Sectis* is revealing of a rigorous philological method:

I translated it when I was a young man ... from a very defective Greek manuscript. Later on, when I was about forty years old, my pupil Hubaish asked me to correct it after having collected a certain number of Greek manuscripts. Thereon I collated these so as to produce one correct manuscript, and I compared this manuscript with the Syriac text and corrected it. I am in the habit of proceeding thus in all my translation work. Some years later I translated it into Arabic for Abu Ia'far Muhammad ibn Musa. (Trans. M. Meyerhof, *Isis*, VIII (1926), 690–91.)

Further techniques in emending and correction of bad texts are described in his entry under Galen's *Methodus Medendi*:

Sergios [Sergius] translated this book into Syriac, the first six parts when he was yet weak and inexperienced in translation work. He translated the remaining eight parts when he had acquired experience so that he did this version better than that of the first six parts. Salmawaih urged me to correct the second half for him believing that this would be easier than to make a new version. So he collated with me a part of the seventh section, he holding in his hand the Syriac version while I held the Greek text, he reading the Syriac and I telling him of any variations from the Greek text and suggesting corrections. At last the work became troublesome to him ... so he asked me to translate these parts, and I translated them completely. (Trans. M. Meyerhof, op. cit., 692–3.)

This particular work had a further history. As Hunayn ibn Ishaq's translation was destroyed by fire, he proceeded to a new edition on the basis of a defective

Greek manuscript. When he found a second manuscript he made yet one more collation and a second edition expressing the hope that he might find a third manuscript and further improve his edition in the future. But he realized that his hopes were not well founded for 'The manuscripts of this book in Greek are not numerous because it was not one of those which were read at the Alexandrian School.' (Trans. M. Meyerhof, op. cit., 693.) He was thus aware of the syllabus in Late Antiquity and of the dominance of Alexandria in setting it.

The new learning

Which texts and authors did these Syriac translators render into Syriac and Arabic during this period of extraordinary translation? Basically they took what had been canonized in the intellectual centres of Late Antiquity in the form in which they had been picked up by the Syriac schools. They of course went beyond the Syriac schools and eventually expanded the number of texts that were offered to the intellectuals of the 9th to 11th centuries. Two groups of texts in particular dominate the corpus of translated Greek works: practically the entirety of Aristotle's works (with the exception of the *Politics*, the *Eudemian Ethics* and the *Magna Moralia*) were translated, as was a vast number of Galen's works. Of Plato we know that the *Timaeus, Republic, Laws* and the *Crito* were rendered into Arabic (also part of Proclus' commentary on the *Phaedo*, and there are quotations from the *Symposium* and the *Phaedo*). Though the titles of other dialogues attributed to Plato were known it is not yet determined how large a portion of the Platonic corpus was translated. In any case, Moslem scholars considered Plato less important than Aristotle. Greek philosophy generally was read in the light of the commentators of Late Antique and early Byzantine times; that is, primarily according to Neoplatonic theory. It was also conceived as a totally consistent body of doctrine, with Plato and Aristotle forming part of a unified whole. As we have seen, translations also included works on mathematics, geometry, astronomy, astrology, music and geography.

The large-scale incorporation of this rich material had profound effects on the development of Islamic civilization. Most obvious are the effects in the realm of science and scientific literature: Islamic medicine, optics and pharmacology took the Greek texts as a basis and then developed further each of these sciences. Similar progress can be seen in geography, mathematics and astronomy. The development of medicine in particular must be ranked among the highest achievements of Islamic civilization.

Greek philosophical texts, on the other hand, posed the problem, also confronted in early Byzantium, of the conflict between the authority of divinely revealed truth and that of truth arrived at by the exercise of human reason alone. Islamic philosophers and theologians had somehow to reconcile human reason and revelation. Philosophers such as al-Kindi and al-Farabi

Omurtag, prince of the Bulgarians, receiving Byzantine ambassadors in his tent. Omurtag, who ruled in the early 9th century, represents a period when the Slavs and the Bulgars, people without writing or any sophisticated institutions, were becoming aware of Byzantine superiority in these respects. This led to their acceptance of Christianity some fifty years later.

attempted to separate human logic and revelation and to assign to each separate and discrete lines of development. Therefore they might coexist without the one interfering with the other. Al-Razi took a predominantly secular view: he gave preeminence to philosophy and reason and left less room for prophecy and religion. The Mutazilites, too, sought to discuss Islamic dogma within a framework of the ideas of Greek philosophy. Al-Ashari (d. 935) moved in the reverse direction, positing the superiority of revelation to reason. Al-Ghazzali (d. 1111) went a step further in this final subordination of philosophy to religion by utilizing the Aristotelian syllogism to buttress religion. Thus Moslem 'dalliance' with Greek philosophy, which in the beginning had possibilities for the creation of a type of religious humanism, drawing together the spiritual and intellectual life, ended with the assertion of the revelational strand of Islam and the subordination of philosophy, which was assigned a merely supportive role as defender of the faith. It was, in the mainstream of Islamic civilization, reduced to a type of scholasticism. Nevertheless, the process of adjustment provoked by the impact of philosophy is reflected in many aspects of the intellectual life of Islam. Indeed the total effect of this Hellenism of Late Antiquity and of the early Middle Ages was, according to Carl Becker, to give important elements of similarity to the Islamic world, the Byzantine world and the world of the Latin west.

The diffusion of Greek culture in the Slavic world

When we come to the world of south-eastern and eastern Europe at roughly the same time, we are confronted again with the phenomenon of the diffusion of Greek culture, but with a number of marked differences. Like Syria, Palestine and western Mesopotamia, the Balkan peninsula had been an integral part of the Byzantine empire in Late Antiquity, and like the Levant a substantial portion of it had been lost by Byzantium to new peoples, Slavs and Bulgars, who conquered it by force. These peoples were in a state of comparatively low social and cultural development, and their conquests and settlements largely deracinated the culture, society and languages that had predominated in these areas before. Thus by the 7th century Christianity and Graeco-Latin culture had largely disappeared from the northern and central portions of the Balkan peninsula, and peoples without an alphabet, in a state of paganism and tribalism, replaced the earlier inhabitants. But by the 9th century they had become settled, and were exposed to the political, economic and cultural force of Constantinople and Thessalonica. Their rulers became aware of the need to adopt more advanced institutions. This culminated in the religious conversion of the Bulgarians (now largely Slavic-speaking) to Byzantine Christianity, first in 864 and then definitively in 870. Essentially a political move, it had none the less the most significant consequences for the South Slavs and eventually the Russians and Rumanians as well. By adopting Byzantine Christianity they thereby adopted Byzantine culture and ideology as well, giving a new cohesion and centralization to their social structure and helping to overcome the ethnic and tribal divisions still surviving in their society.

This diffusion of Greek culture among the Bulgars (though not among the Serbs, Russians and

Rumanians) owed much to the efforts of Byzantine missionaries, of whom the first and most famous were Saints Cyril and Methodius. Called to be missionaries in Moravia by the Slavic prince Svatopluk, they translated the Gospels into Slavonic and invented an alphabet, the Glagolitic, in which to write it. It was the beginning of Slavic literacy and literature.

Now Cyril and Methodius, by birth, education and career, were ideally suited for their task. Greeks born in the city of Thessalonica, they received the finest education that could be had at that period in Byzantium and were equally versed in sacred and secular Greek letters and learning. Just as important was the fact that they were bilingual. Having grown up in a city and province (Macedonia) where Greeks and Slavic-speakers lived side by side, they spoke both languages, and they adopted the Slavic spoken in Macedonia, related to today's Bulgarian and Macedonian tongues, as the literary language for the first Slavic literature. Equally predictably, the Slavic literature they created was based upon the religious tradition of medieval Greek culture and was functional in terms of the religious need of the new converts. They also initiated a programme for the translation into what has come to be known as Old Church Slavonic of the Greek liturgical texts essential for the functioning of the Christian church, including the Gospels, Psalter, Acts of the Apostles, collections of prayers and hymns, and a calendar of saints' lives.

Methodius died in 885. Soon afterwards his disciples were expelled from Moravia, and it seemed as though the whole Cyrillo-Methodian edifice of Slavic Christianity might crumble into ruin. However, the recently converted Bulgarian prince Boris received them into his country. The disciples seem now to have been all Slavs, though familiar with Greek culture. Here, with state support, they extended the work begun in Moravia. One of them, Naum, was put in charge of the new monastery, St Panteleimon, near the capital city of Preslav in the north. Another, Clement, was sent to the district of Kutmichevitsa in the south. This district, which included Ohrid, Glavinitsa and Devol, was in Macedonia, where Clement himself had been born. Here Clement busied himself until his death (916) organizing the training of priests who, equipped with the new learning, would go out to convert the populace. He is said to have produced some 3500 priests, deacons, readers and other ecclesiastics. Clement's school became the cradle of Slavic Christianity in the Balkans.

By the time Symeon succeeded his father Boris on the Bulgarian throne (893) the Slavic apostles had found secure bases for their work in Bulgaria (at Preslav) and in Macedonia (at Ohrid) and from these two foci they began to expand their work. The reign of Symeon was decisive in the spread of Byzantine culture, especially its literary and religious aspects, to the Bulgars. Boris had been a warrior. Rough and brutal in his methods, he had pushed through the conversion of his followers and

ruthlessly suppressed any pagan reactions. Symeon, though no less energetic and ruthless, was a different personality. Sent early to Constantinople by his father to be trained as a clergyman so as to take over the direction of the new Bulgarian church, he was deeply immersed in medieval Greek culture. As well as studying the ecclesiastical texts, he was also devoted to secular and pagan Greek literature, displaying a special propensity for Demosthenes and Aristotle, i.e. rhetoric and philosophy. When he was suddenly called upon to take over the throne Symeon did so as a fully Byzantinized ruler, Byzantinized both in his political ideology and in his taste for all of Greek literature, Christian and pagan. Under his direction the schools of Preslav and Ohrid continued their activities. Clement, now a bishop, presided over the school of Ohrid, which continued with the use of the original, or Glagolitic, alphabet. Since the new Bulgarian clergy had little or no knowledge of the type of Greek in which ecclesiastical literature was written, Clement prepared a series of panegyrics, hymns, prayers and homilies for church feasts in Old Church Slavonic and translated from Greek the *Triodion* (hymns for the period from Easter to Pentecost). His work eventually penetrated into Serbia, Bosnia and Croatia.

A Christian literature

But it was the school of Preslav, under the direct inspiration of Symeon, and therefore much more directly exposed to Constantinopolitan influence, which took the lead both in the work of translation from the Greek and in literary creation. In so doing, it adopted a modified form of the Slavic alphabet, the Cyrillic. Symeon himself selected many of the texts and took part in the work of translation. Such was the case in the translations from John Chrysostom and others which he had put together in the *Zlatostruj* (an anthology of homilies for liturgical use) and in the selection of translations from the church Fathers, Choeroboscus and others in the *Izbornik* or *Miscellany* of 1073. A later Slavic prince, Sviatoslav of Kiev (quoted by G. Soulis, p. 32), referred to him as 'the new Ptolemy, who, like the industrious bee, gathers the juice of the flowers'. More important than his own participation was the sponsorship of a group of translators and authors at Preslav who created the golden age of Bulgarian literature. These included most notably Constantine Presbyter, a disciple of Methodius, who composed the *Didactic Gospel* (*Učitelnoe Evangelie*) and the *Alphabetical Prayer* (*Azbučnaja Molitva*) and who translated in 907 the sermons of Athanasius against the Arians and the short chronicle of the Greek patriarch Nicephorus, bringing it down to the year 894. Important also was John Exarch who translated St John of Damascus' *Exposition of the Orthodox Faith* and who composed the *Hexameron* or *Šestodnev*, a work which he based on St Basil and to which he added translations of certain of the writings of the church Fathers and others. These and a few more authors and translators are known to us by name. Many others, however, remain anonymous. The works they produced were re-creations in Slavonic of Byzantine prototypes, and were mostly of a liturgical and theological character, with a preference for the church Fathers of the 4th and 5th centuries. Works by John Climacus and John Moschus, hagiographical texts and even apocryphal literature were also translated. One finds many fewer translations from secular literature, but there are some examples – the popular romances of Barlaam and Josaphat, the Alexander legend, *Stephanites and Ichnelates* (a Sanskrit work which had been translated into Greek in the 11th century) and, at a later date, Aesop's fables. None of the Byzantine historians was translated and only certain chronicles (John Malalas, George Syncellus, Patriarch Nicephorus) and certain semi- or pseudo-scientific texts, such as astrological treatises and the *Physiologus* (a descriptive catalogue of animals).

The logic behind this selective process is easy to see. The Slavs were relatively unsophisticated, without a literary tradition and without scholarship. Conse-quently – despite Symeon's classical education – both Byzantine learning and the whole of Greek classical literature were by and large ignored. These texts would have been incomprehensible to the new Christians. Nevertheless, the great achievement of translation and transmission had a profound effect on the Balkan Slavs. The formal aspects of their lives were thoroughly Byzantinized through the adoption of at least the religious half of the medieval Greek heritage. Their language, their alphabet, their forms of thought all followed the model of that culture, which was a one-sided reflection of the intellectual world of Byzantium with its two roots, classical and Christian. In Bulgaria this cross-fertilization resulted in the golden age of Bulgarian literature, a literature that was Bulgarian in form but basically Greek in content. The Bulgarians in turn became the purveyors and transmitters of this part of Byzantine culture to other Slavic peoples, just as the Syriac-speaking Christians passed on their Greek cul-tural inheritance to the Islamic world first through Syriac and then by direct translation from the Greek itself into Arabic.

The next phase in the expansion of Byzantine Christianity brings us to Kievan Russia and the rising Serbian state under the first members of the Nemanjid dynasty in the late 12th and 13th century. The emergence of Mount Athos as the principal monastic centre of the Orthodox world was of particular signific-ance in this process. The Slavs and Rumanians came to have close ties with the Holy Mountain, in whose religious and literary movements they shared. The so-called Palaeologan renaissance, or the last phase of Byzantine cultural creativity, reinforced the Byzantine cultural influence in this larger world. With the rise of Hesychasm, a 14th-century quietist doctrine, and the creation of what has been termed the aristocratic monastic milieu, South Slav religious and secular circles were once more brought into close contact with

Saints Cyril and Methodius were revered not only as evangelists to the Slavs but as the originators of Slavonic literature and letters. This copper engraving was made as late as 1867 in the Serbian monastery of Khilandarion on Mount Athos. Its purpose was as much political as religious; an assertion of Bulgarian independence, it was widely circulated throughout Bulgarian lands.

Byzantine culture. Though the Serbian component in this last phase of cultural activity was important, the centre of activity seems to have been Bulgaria. The monastic foundations of Paroria and Kilifarevo trained a number of outstanding South Slavic clergymen in a tradition that was now dominated by Hesychastic teaching. Under the patronage of two Bulgarian mon-archs, Ivan Alexander (1331–71) and Ivan Šišman (1371–93), the state threw its full support behind the work of translation and composition, as Trnovo became the South Slavic centre of cultural life in its more formal manifestations. The Hesychast Bulgarian patriarch, Euthymius, inaugurated an important re-form of ecclesiastical books. Heresy, he maintained, was the result of ignorance and the best way to cure it was to strengthen and improve education. One urgent priority was the correction of erroneously translated texts. In this way, the foundations of a Slavonic scholarship based on Greek models were laid.

The destruction of the Bulgarian state at the end of the 14th century put an end to the cultural life of

Trnovo, the new Tsargrad (i.e. Constantinople) as the Bulgarians had come to call it, but the scholars assembled there then dispersed to other lands, taking with them manuscripts and the new learned tradition. Though the character of this so-called Second South Slavic Influence has been heavily debated, and though allowance must be made for the fact that neither the Serbs nor the Russians were passive partners in this diffusion of Byzantine culture in its Slavic form, nevertheless it is undeniable that the scholars of Bulgaria moved into Serbia, the Rumanian regions and into Russia. Constantine of Kostenecki became active in the last refuge of Slavic letters among the South Slavs, the court of the Serbian despot Stephen Lazarević (1389–1427), a patron of Christian literature and art. Constantine compared him to Ptolemy II, the supposed translator of the Old Testament, Cyrus, Manassas and Symeon the Bulgar. He glorified Belgrade as the New Jerusalem, the city of divine wisdom, and tried to relate Stephen's genealogy to Nemanja, Licinius, and Constantine the Great. Thus the Serbian court participated actively and creatively in this last South Slavic cultural flowering through patronage of translations, composition, and copying activities. Those who argue strongly for the Serbian contribution to the Second South Slavic Influence in Russia point to the fact that stylistic traits which appear in Bulgarian literature during the 14th century are found earlier in Serbian, and they also stress the importance of the Serbian biographical genre.

In the one non-Slavic area, the Rumanian regions, the Second South Slavic Influence was apparently decisive at the level of formal literary and religious culture. The courts at Arges (Wallachia), and Suceava (Moldavia) fostered this new tradition as a number of South Slavic churchmen made their way there, including the Serb Nicodemus and the Bulgarian Gregory Camblak. The Rumanian monasteries preserved and reproduced the manuscripts of the Euthymian circle of Trnovo, and Rumanian Christianity was essentially South Slavic, as indicated by the literary and state language, which was a form of Slavic.

In the case of Russia, the weight to be given to the Second South Slavic Influence has been much disputed. Some historians regard it as crucial, others as negligible. All agree, however, that many features of what was to become Muscovite culture go back to Byzantium, though the exact process of transmission is not clear. Similar doubts have been raised about the importance of the marriage of Ivan III to the Palaiologan princess Sophia and of the letter of Filofei, abbot of the monastery at Pskov, enunciating the theory of Moscow as the Third Rome.

Thus Byzantine influence on the Balkan and Russian worlds continued to be exercised, not only in the greater days from the 9th to the 11th century but even thereafter. Despite the drastic decline of Byzantium's political fortunes, the South Slavs, Rumanians and Russians continued to derive constructive elements from this culture, which they then readapted according to their own genius and needs.

We have examined the way in which a rich and complex tradition, the Greek, was transmitted to two quite alien cultures, the Islamic and the Slav. There are significant parallels and significant differences between the two. In both cases the transmission began during the 9th and 10th centuries, so the options available to both were theoretically the same. In both cases, too, the transmitters or translators were for the most part non-Greeks: Syriac Christians for one and Slavo-Bulgarians for the other. Here, however, the similarities cease. The process of selection was radically different, indeed totally opposite. Islamic society, heir to the cultural traditions of the old Middle East, maintained and then revitalized this inheritance by adopting Greek philosophy, science, mathematics, medicine and geography and putting it into Arabic. It possessed the sophistication and expertise for such a venture, placing on it at the same time the religious and aesthetic limits of the Moslem faith and the Arabic language. Specifically Christian elements, in other words, were automatically excluded. In the Balkans and eastern Europe exactly the contrary conditions prevailed. Christianity was accepted, but society was just emerging from tribalism and groping for the civilized forms of statecraft, religion and education. It had neither a literary tradition nor an advanced religion. It therefore opted, to use Ibn Khaldun's language, for the necessities and not the luxuries. Consequently it adopted Byzantine political and religious institutions and the religious half of medieval Greek literary culture. When, much later, the Slavic world eventually acquired the classical tradition, it was as a result of importation not from Byzantium but from the post-Renaissance west.

VI · REVIVAL

THE END OF THE BYZANTINE EMPIRE
left the Greeks stripped of political power and
administered by a people whose language,
culture and religion were all alien. Even the Christian
church survived only on sufferance. These three-and-
a-half centuries of subjugation have until recently been
the most neglected in Greek history but they are not
the least fascinating. When Greece eventually emerged
from under the Ottoman shadow, it was a new nation.
How had the transformation come about? What were
its links, if any, with the past?

After the Ottoman conquest, Greeks found
themselves enjoying certain advantages over the other
subject Christian peoples. The Turks chose to
categorize these peoples by religion rather than by
ethnic origins. Since the Orthodox church was always
Greek-dominated, Greeks acquired a degree of
administrative power over Orthodox Christians
within the empire that was out of proportion to their
numbers. They used that power to promote trade,
thereby acquiring economic power as well. By the 17th
and 18th centuries, with the decline of the Ottoman
state, the Greek community further improved its
position, until by 1800 it was fully aware of itself as a
distinct entity and as a potential nation.

War broke out in 1821, but the Greeks were
motivated by varying – often irreconcilable – aims,
and found it difficult to cooperate in a common cause.
The struggle was complicated, though strengthened,
by the intervention of westerners like Lord Byron,
whose concern was often historical and idealistic.
It was finally the refusal of the Greeks to submit and
the grudging support of Britain, France and Russia,
based on political expediency, which in the end
defeated the Turks and made Greek independence
possible.

By 1833 Greece was a monarchy, restricted in
territory, ruled by a Bavarian and dominated by the
foreigners who had 'guaranteed' its existence. A
constitution came in 1843. In 1862 the Bavarian
dynasty was replaced by a Danish, followed by a more
democratic constitution in 1864. By 1913 the frontiers
had expanded to include nearly all Greek-speaking
areas in the Balkans, though never Constantinople.
But economic progress was slow. Many Greeks
emigrated, principally to America.

During the First World War the dilemma about
which side to join split the country. The subsequent
attempt to annex part of Turkey in 1919 prompted a
Turkish back-lash which led to a horrifying loss of
Greek lives and the uprooting of populations. The
1920s and 30s were times of unrest and political chaos,
with Greece lurching from monarchy to republic and
back to monarchy and then dictatorship.

From 1941 to 1944, Greece was occupied by Fascist
powers. The political antagonisms of the interwar
period were reflected in the resistance movement, with
the result that when the Germans were finally expelled
a full-scale civil war between the Communists and
their opponents was soon under way. This ended in
1949 with the defeat of the Communists, following
massive American aid.

The thirty-five years since then have been notable
for two things. One is the gradual achievement of
political stability under a democratic system, a process
only temporarily reversed during the seven-year
period of the Colonels' regime, an extreme right wing
military dictatorship (1967–74). The second is a sharp
rise in material prosperity, a rise that has brought
benefits but also new problems. Although Greece has
entered the EEC, one might argue that culturally the
new nation has still to find itself.

The shock
of the fall of Constantinople was felt through all
the western world. In Greece it was felt through all its
subsequent history. Tuesday, the day of the week when it
happened, is still an unlucky day. Between 1836 and 1839 a
modest icon painter, Panagiotis Zographos, did a series of
narrative paintings under the supervision of General
Makriyannis portraying the War of Independence. In this
detail from the first picture we see Sultan Mehmet the
Conqueror exulting over Constantinople. In front of him a
row of submissive Greeks is put under the yoke. (1)

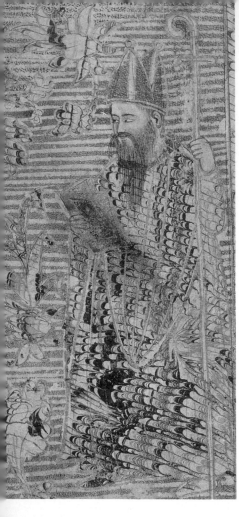

Greece under the Ottomans

As the years of subjection to Turkish overlords passed, the Greeks adapted themselves to their situation and some managed to attain a high standard of living. For a few, indeed, national independence threatened to diminish rather than enhance their wealth and privileges.

The Orthodox Church, by an ironic paradox, found itself strengthened rather than weakened under Ottoman domination. Its patriarchs and higher clergy, who were invariably Greek, acquired authority both ecclesiastical and civil over the other Christian denominations. *Left:* an unusual Turkish painting of an Orthodox bishop, 17th century. (2)

Greek merchants too came to dominate the commerce of the Ottoman empire and could use their position to their own advantage. *Right:* a merchant, dressed in Turkish style, from a German 16th-century album. *Below:* part of a wall-painting showing Constantinople, from the house of a rich Greek merchant of 1798. (3, 4)

The Ionian Islands, off the west coast of Greece, escaped Ottoman rule. For several centuries they were ruled by Venice. In the early 19th century they came under British protection, a situation that prevailed until 1864. In this view of Zante in about 1820 (*above*) the British presence is clearly in evidence. (5)

Athens in the early 19th century had
many features of a typical town in
Turkey. It had a bazaar (*left*) with a
minaret at the end of the street. The
Acropolis, in the distance, was
surrounded by a ring of fortifications,
and a mosque (*above*) had been built in
the ruins of the Parthenon, which had
been severely damaged by a Venetian
bombardment in 1687. (6, 7)

Greek customs, the Greek language and the Greek way of
life continued with little change under Turkish rule. In 300
years the two peoples never achieved assimilation in Greece
and there were few converts from Christianity to Islam. A
French engraving of about 1800 (*right*) gives a charming
picture of a Greek wedding, the bride dressed in almost
Byzantine finery. (8)

Hellas reborn

The War of Greek Independence captured the imagination of western Europeans. Although they mostly had a highly romanticized view of it, their moral and material support helped to ensure Greek victory.

War began in March 1821. The Greeks soon lost their initial advantage through internal quarrels, and the struggle degenerated into a series of minor but ferocious clashes. *Right:* a revolutionary flag bearing the portrait of one of the War's heroes, Markos Botsaris, who commanded the forces defending Missolonghi in 1823. He corresponded with Lord Byron, but before the latter's arrival was tragically killed in the hour of victory at the battle of Karpenisi. *Below:* the battle of the Piraeus. The Greek commander was Andreas Miaoulis, the admiral who led the Greek navy for most of the war. (9, 10)

The first king, Otto, arrives in his kingdom. For four years, 1827–31, Greece was a republic under an elected president, Count Capodistrias. In October 1831 Capodistrias was assassinated, and the great powers (Britain, France and Russia) now imposed a monarchy of their own choosing. The king was Otto of Wittelsbach, the son of King Ludwig of Bavaria. This painting, by a German artist in his entourage, shows him landing at Nauplion in 1833. For the next year Nauplion was the seat of government and capital of Greece. (11)

269

Images of Independence

A new Greek mythology was born with the War of Independence. The upsurge of romantic nationalism produced memorable images of the struggle – idealized, of course, but strongly conveying the spirit of optimism that followed liberation.

'The Friendly Society', Philiki Etairia, was a secret society (founded in 1814) whose aim was Greek independence. One of its banners is shown *left*. The standard of revolt is raised: Germanos, Archbishop of Patras and a leader of the Society, blesses the Greek flag (*below*). This event, on 25 March 1821 at the Aghia Lavra monastery near Kalavrita, is traditionally regarded as the beginning of the war. (12, 13)

The oath at Missolonghi. The participation of western enthusiasts for the Greek cause transformed the war into the great romantic crusade of the early 19th century. No foreign fighter was more famous than Lord Byron: in the picture *above* he is shown at Missolonghi swearing an oath of loyalty to Greece on the tomb of Markos Botsaris (see pl. 9). (14)

'In Gratitude' by Theodoros Vryzakis expresses the debt which Greece owed to her liberators. Greek heroes kneel in the foreground; Greece, freed from her chains, blesses them. (15)

271

272

The new Athens

In 1830 Athens was no more than a village (the modern Plaka) nestling at the foot of the Acropolis, but the prestige of its classical past made it an appropriate choice as the capital of the new state. The first architects were German and Danish, but by the 1870s Greeks too were designing large public buildings in the Neoclassical style.

A triangle of streets was laid out to the north of the Acropolis. In this photograph (*left*), taken in about 1865, many projects are under way, and the city is spreading out towards the base of Mount Lykabettos. The Royal Palace, on the extreme right of the old photograph, faced the main public open space of the new city, Syntagma (Constitution) Square. In an exactly contemporary painting (*above*) we are looking from the square towards the Acropolis. (16, 19)

The monumental group of University, National Library and Academy makes Athens one of the most notable Neoclassical cities in the world. Built by Danish architects (Christian and Theophil von Hansen) between 1839 and 1891, they utilize sculpture and polychromy to recreate a vision of the classical past. *Far left:* the entrance to the Academy, flanked by figures of Socrates and Plato. *Left:* portico of the Old Parliament. *Right:* allegorical painting above the main door of the University, showing King Otto with the Sciences. (17, 18, 20)

Diaspora

Greek communities took root in the Near East, in Russia, in the Balkans and in Central Europe from the 16th century onwards, their members acting as middlemen in countries which lacked a merchant class of their own. By the beginning of the 20th century this role had largely disappeared. Greeks retained their commercial flair but now tended to be integrated into their host societies.

Alexander Ionides, a second generation immigrant to Britain, made his fortune in Victorian Manchester and became a leading patron of the arts. What is interesting in this family group (*right*) is that two of the children have been given Greek national dress. (22)

Cardinal Bessarion was a major figure in the intellectual diaspora from Byzantium to the west. Giovanni Bellini's portrait of him (*above*) shows the Byzantine reliquary he presented to the Scuola della Carità, Venice. (21)

Vienna had an old-established Greek colony. *Right:* the 'Greek coffee-house' in 1824. (23)

The mobility and versatility of Greece's merchant marine enabled it to survive the decline of the Diaspora communities and flourish to the present day. Aristotle Onassis (*above*) was the most famous of modern Greek shipping magnates. (24)

In New York (*left*) the Greek district of Astoria is one of several areas where immigrants live their own lives, speak their own language and eat their own food. But many other Greeks have become totally Americanized, to be identified only by their names, religion and consciousness of their origin. (25)

Melbourne (*right*) now has one of the largest expatriate Greek communities in the world, largely of post-war origin. (26)

Greek art today

For contemporary artists, the crucial issue is how to reconcile their heritage of ancient, Byzantine and popular art with influences from outside Greece. Most Greek artists have received their training or have lived and worked abroad for substantial periods.

Yannis Tsarouchis was born in 1910, spends considerable time in Paris and has worked as a stage-designer in the great opera-houses of the world. *The Dance – with the sculpture of Eros* (1971), a frieze-like painting a metre in length of soldiers and sailors (*above*), touches upon a perennial Greek theme – admiration for manliness. The Bacchanalian dance of one sailor, the classical urn, the figure of Eros – are all echoes, though muted and transformed, from the past. (27)

Ghika (born 1906) is well-known in London, Paris and New York. A cubistic landscape such as *Hydra* (*left*), reminiscent of Byzantine pictorial space, with its concentration on light, water and the integration of man and nature, could be paralleled as far back as the art of ancient Crete. (28)

Jannis Kounellis (born 1936) is an artist of the post-war modernist era. For him the classical heritage seems to pose, in certain works, an explicit challenge; he has lived in Rome since 1956, helping to originate there the style known as *arte povera*. Sometimes he incorporates classical fragments combined in unexpected ways. This work (*right*) uses a cast of a 2nd-century BC head of Athena in the National Museum of Athens. (29)

A century of upheaval

In the last hundred years Greece has endured the devastating effect of two world wars, each with a bitter aftermath – the disastrous expedition into Turkey and the Civil War – as well as seven years of repressive military dictatorship.

Democracy returns to the land of its birth: the Debating Hall of the Old Parliament in the late 19th century (*above*). The system was never stable: between 1864, when a revised constitution was promulgated, and 1910, there were 21 general elections and 70 separate administrations. (30)

Territorial triumphs: Venizelos announces the terms of the Treaty of Bucharest to the Greek Parliament. Eleftherios Venizelos was the most dynamic and charismatic politician of modern Greek history. His skilful leadership during the Balkan Wars in 1912–13, when Balkan states combined against the Turks, ensured territorial gains for Greece – including Thessalonica, Macedonia and southern Epirus – at the expense of the moribund Ottoman empire. The Treaty of Bucharest brought the Balkan Wars to an end. (31)

German occupation (*left*) was as traumatic for Greece as for the rest of Europe. National resistance was largely Communist controlled. Liberation in 1944 brought it into conflict with British forces. The internal rivalries of Greece became part of a wider political struggle. (32)

After two years of uneasy peace and the restoration of the king, civil war got under way in 1946. Substantial American aid ensured the defeat of the Communists. *Above:* mountain guerilla fighters who fought for the Communist leader, Markos Vaphiadis, are rounded up by government troops. *Right:* a trial of alleged Communist spies in Thessalonica in 1948. (33, 34)

The king and the colonels. Conflict between Constantine II and his prime minister, George Papandreou, paved the way for a military *coup d'état* in April 1967. The king fled five months later after a failed counter-*coup*, but the new regime, seeking the appearance of legitimacy, preserved the monarchy: the souvenirs *below* were on sale during the dictatorship. The brutal – if often incompetent – rule of the colonels led to widespread internal and international opposition. The student sit-in at the Athens Polytechnic (*right*), in November 1973, was crushed by tanks, leaving 34 dead. Even many senior army officers were turned against the colonels by this event. (35, 36)

The collapse of the regime was brought about by its disastrous attempt to provoke the Cyprus *coup*, which led to the Turkish invasion of the island. The elder statesman of Greek politics, Constantine Karamanlis (*right, above*), was summoned from France to form a new democratic government. He is watched by the last of the old order, General Gizikis , as he takes an oath of leadership. *Right:* Andreas Papandreou, son of the former prime minister, and a left-wing leader, returns from exile in 1974. (37, 38)

Towards Nationhood
the survival of the Hellenic spirit

NIKOS SVORONOS

Economic growth is no less important to the history of modern Greece than political upheaval. Industry has boomed and tourism increases annually: many millions are drawn to Greece each year, attracted by the climate, the landscape, the antiquities and art. This growth has brought problems which have attracted international concern: pollution and the influx of visitors harm the archaeological sites and the countryside. At Megalopolis (*left*), the ruins of the great theatre, the largest in Greece, are overlooked by the smoking chimneys of a power station. Greeks have often felt overburdened by their glorious heritage. Now, many seek ways in which that heritage will be neither neglected nor excessively dwelt upon, but reconciled with the needs of a 20th-century industrialized European nation. The four-thousand-year-old drama of Greek history seems set to enter a new phase. (39)

By the time of the Roman conquest one can already speak of a 'Greek world' in the sense of a coherent, unified culture made up of peoples who shared a common civilization, a common language and a common education. In origin purely Greek, this culture had been extended and enriched by the Hellenized peoples of the east. Although not a nation as we should define it today, it was a community conscious of its identity and its historical continuity.

To belong to this Greek world within the Roman empire was to belong to a privileged élite. The Romans recognized that the central element of the common culture of the empire was Greek. Indeed, so deeply did Rome become Hellenized that when, after the crises of the 3rd century, the western part of the empire began to decay and finally to disintegrate under the impact of the barbarian invasions, the eastern part continued as a second Rome in the form of the Byzantine empire.

It would certainly be going too far to say that Byzantium was simply the Greek nation Christianized and Romanized. Yet the continuity is there. In the spectrum of peoples that made up the Byzantine empire, the Greek element was always the most vigorous, though not always the largest. From Constantinople and the other large cities, the Greeks began to dominate the whole empire. Vital areas such as Thrace and central Asia Minor became Greek lands.

Although Latin continued, until the 6th century, to be the official language of the state, in practice Greek had become established throughout the empire and soon became the language of the state and of the church. Administrative terminology was translated into Greek; Roman law, which had been enriched by Greek law, and is thus rightly called Graeco-Roman, was formulated by Justinian in Greek and Latin, and from the 7th century legislation was in Greek only; it was continuously enriched by new elements of local law, adjusting itself, in the new imperial legislation, to the needs of Byzantine economy and society; and, in its new Hellenized form, it was applied more thoroughly throughout the empire. The rulers of the Byzantine world considered themselves to be continuing the traditions and practice of Rome, but it would not be a mistake, I believe, to maintain that unconsciously what they were continuing was the tradition of the Hellenistic kingdoms of the east. This is equally true, whether we are looking at administration or agriculture, the economy or the social system. Everywhere the Greek presence plays the most prominent role.

The rapprochement between the Christian church and the Hellenic tradition comes through particularly clearly in iconography. This manuscript illumination of David composing the Psalms, from a Psalter of about 900, is obviously a Christianized version of Orpheus charming the beasts. Note the Muse behind David.

How far may we see in this Greek predominance a foreshadowing of Greek nationhood? The answer is a paradox. Half the Greek history leads away from nationhood, the other half towards it. The progress of Greek culture lies in two opposite directions – first away from the Hellenic ideal, culminating in medieval Byzantium; then a return to it, leading finally to the realization of a national state.

Hellenism, Rome and Christianity

In the movement away from the Hellenic ideal, Rome was the first step and Christianity the second. Under Byzantine rule the Hellenic concept of the individual citizen as the bearer of political authority gives way to that of the absolute monarch, the sole bearer of collective authority. In the same way the notion of distinct ethnic units (though it does not disappear completely) gives way to the broader concept of universal empire. Hellenic identity is replaced by imperial identity, and in the end the Greeks call themselves Romans.

This process – the merging of the individual into the ecumenical community – was taken to its ultimate extreme by the total victory of Christianity. The Greeks were now at their farthest remove from the Hellenic intellectual tradition. True, the early Fathers of the church made heroic and creative efforts to reconcile their Christian faith with their Hellenic culture. But these efforts ceased with the formulation of Christian dogma and the imposition of orthodoxy. Freedom of thought, the essence of Hellenism, was now branded as heresy.

This process can be analysed as several distinct stages. In the first, between the conversion of Constantine and the 6th century, the term Greek (or Hellene) lost its national connotation and kept only its cultural meaning, though with strong religious overtones, i.e. adherent of pagan Greek culture. In the second stage, from the 6th to the 11th century, the religious meaning took over entirely: Hellenic now simply meant pagan or idolatrous. Ioannes Moschos talks of 'a Hellenic Saracen'; Photios speaking of the Russians before they had been Christianized says that they had 'Hellenic and atheist beliefs'; Psellos asserts that the Chinese were 'Hellenes in their beliefs'. The old Roman empire became the orthodox Christian state. Christian and Roman become identical notions, the concepts of the Roman empire and of Christian orthodoxy the main elements in the official ideology of the supra-ethnic Byzantine empire.

The historical continuity of Hellenism was further eroded, first by a social and then by a linguistic split. The old Greek democracy had already disappeared by the Hellenistic period, and with it that relatively wide participation in political and cultural life by people from varying social levels that had given ancient Greek civilization its unity. In the Byzantine empire, education and cultural pursuits were confined to the aristocracy, the great landowners, the higher officials and military officers and the higher clergy. Two cultural trends were thus created, one élitist, the other popular.

This cultural split was reflected in the most explicit way by a linguistic split. The official language was still Attic Greek of the classical age, which Byzantine scholars imitated as best they could. Spoken Greek, however, was continually developing further and further from this standard, until in the end most of the population could not understand the official language. Futhermore, those Hellenic elements that were retained in the official Christian culture of Byzantium were extremely limited and specialized: the language itself; rhetoric; dialectical analysis; logic; and some remnants of Aristotelian, Platonic and Neoplatonic philosophy. This was not the stuff by which the consciousness of Hellenism could be perpetuated.

Against this must be set the fact that ethnic distinctions among the peoples who constituted the Byzantine empire never died out. Examples of such distinctions abound in the work of Byzantine writers. Whereas 'Roman' is applied to all the citizens of the empire, 'Greek' (*Graikos*) very early came into use to indicate Greek nationality and to distinguish it from other ethnic constituents of the empire. Priskos, in the 5th century, uses it to describe someone who speaks Greek and is 'Greek by birth'. Procopius (6th century) uses it interchangeably with 'Hellenic' to refer to the inhabitants of Greece. Constantine Porphyrogenitos calls the inhabitants of Patras '*Graikoi*', but when he comes to those of Mani he says that they are descended 'from the most ancient Romans' and that they are called 'Hellenes' by the locals because they were in the past idolators 'like the Hellenes of old'. Similarly, the coastal towns of Sinope, Amasia, Teion and Amisos are singled out by Constantine from other Paphlagonian towns as 'Greek cities' and their inhabitants called 'Greek colonists'; the *thema* (province) of Chaldia and the city of Trebizond are likewise designated 'Greek colonies'.

The turn of the tide

By about the 10th century we can trace the beginning of that reversal to which I referred earlier. It coincided with the end of iconoclasm, when scholars began to re-establish contact with the Hellenic tradition. Again, one can distinguish several phases.

Up to the 11th century, the terms 'Hellene' and 'Hellenic', though still mainly implying idolatry, started to re-acquire their cultural overtones. Gradually the cultural meaning prevailed, and eventually came to stand for the core of Greek education. This is already clear in the works of Leo the Mathematician, Photios and Arethas. With the humanists of the 11th century, notably Psellos, it becomes clearer. There is a continuous effort to rehabilitate the previously rejected Hellenic culture and to bring out those elements that

did not contradict the Christian world-view and even in some way seemed to anticipate it. John Mavropous prays to Christ to save the souls of Plato and Plutarch, whose lives and thoughts so closely approached Christian ideals.

It was still not possible, however, to adopt the whole classical tradition as part of the Christian Greek heritage. Byzantine scholars were obliged to maintain a certain distance from that tradition, since the educated class consisted largely of the Orthodox clergy. Leo, Photios and Psellos were all at one time or another accused of paganism and witchcraft. They were forced to recant, to acknowledge the gulf separating Christian from ancient Greek philosophy and to endorse the superiority of Christan culture, based on truth, over Hellenic culture, based on error. We find these ideas expressed in some of Psellos's panegyrics. In the one addressed to Constantine Monomachos he says: 'the words of the ancient sages were of great power, but they were establishing that which is insubstantial and supporting that which is without foundation'. Psellos has this to say about Homer: 'Leaving aside the impressive style and the variety of metre and rhythm used by Homer in the *Iliad*, the whole work is nothing more than the story of Paris abducting a girl and the war that broke out as a result. The rest is simply myth, fiction and lies.' Michael Choniates, who had a classical education, writes as follows of his brother Niketas: 'His exposition of the Old and New Scriptures, and his close intimacy with them added to the treasure of his theoretical knowledge. But the "currency" of both the old and the new Hellenism he denounced as brilliant fakes. When a really skilful goldsmith submits them to the test, they turn out to be merely copper instead of gold.'

Social and political changes, however, encouraged the shift in values noted earlier. As the empire grew weaker and less centralized, the temptation to identify with the past grew stronger. More specifically, the Hellenic element within the empire was learning to see itself as the direct heir of ancient Greece. It was the beginning of a process that was eventually to lead to conscious nationalism.

What, then, were the historical factors that loosened the ties that bound the various ethnic groups into a single state? Some were internal, particularly the desire of the great landowners for local autonomy. Some were external: military attack from the east (after the Battle of Manzikert, in 1071, a large part of Asia Minor was lost to the Seljuk Turks), and confrontation – economic, ideological and political – with the Catholic west, culminating in the Schism of 1054. Norman invasions of southern Italy in the 11th century and of the Balkan provinces in the 12th were preludes to the disaster of the Fourth Crusade (1204). Finally, in the period between about 1040 and the end of the 12th century, a number of non-Greek peoples managed to secede from the empire, from the Armenians in the east to the Serbs and Bulgarians in the north.

In all these upheavals, the only constant element in the empire was the Greeks. Isolated and driven in upon themselves, the Greeks naturally looked back to the days of their classical greatness. That which had been rejected was now accepted with pride. Anna Comnena, writing about the school established in Constantinople by her father, Alexius Comnenus, remarks that 'here one could see Latins being educated and Scythians [Bulgarians] being Hellenized, Romans reading Greek literature and unlettered Greeks learning to express themselves with Hellenic purity'. Niketas Choniates brings his *History* to an end with the fall of Constantinople since, as he says, one cannot write history, the most beautiful invention of the Greeks, about the actions of barbarians.

Furthermore, Byzantine intellectuals began trying, over and above simple imitation of Hellenic forms of expression, to absorb Hellenic thinking. This was what was attempted by Psellos, John Italos and their students. Although their thought was still dependent on theology, it showed, at the same time, the beginning of a certain independent attitude which confronted philosophical problems on the basis of human reason. The sort of problems which were posed then were analogous to those which were posed in the west at about the same time: Platonism and Aristotelianism, realism and nominalism. During this period a tendency to bridge the gap between official and popular cultures can also be observed. Psellos examines popular traditions, sometimes using a fairly rational method, sometimes looking on them as allegories. It was then that for the first time the language of the people began to be used more widely by literary writers. To this period belong the poems of Ptochoprodromos and perhaps the earliest version of the Epic of Digenes Akritas.

Finally, the official church itself, in spite of its resistance to these new tendencies, began to lose its ecumenical character and was transformed, especially after its final break with the western church, into a specifically eastern church based on Greek tradition.

A beleaguered culture

As the years passed, the Greeks found themselves increasingly isolated and therefore increasingly thrown back on their own cultural resources. It was a question of Greeks against Franks, against Turks, against Bulgarians. The cause of Hellenism and the cause of the Byzantine empire were the same.

This attitude finds classic expression in the words of Theodore II Laskaris of Nicaea. 'Our enemies are numerous', he wrote, 'and who will come to our aid? How can the Turks help us? How can the Latins help us? Both are raging against us. Or the Bulgarians, clearly our enemies? Or the Serbians, who never do anything except under duress? Or can we believe that help will come from someone who seems to be on our side, but is really against us? [Theodore means Michael II of Epirus.] Only the Greeks can help themselves, relying upon their own resources.'

Post-1204 Nicaea, Epirus and later the Despotate of the Morea can be seen as the first neo-Hellenic states. Their national character comes across in their internal organization and in the way they relied on local forces to combat invaders. In particular, the efforts of the Nicaean emperors both to develop a self-contained economy independent of the west and to protect the interests of the lower and middle classes in order to achieve real national cohesion were of extreme significance in the evolution of the new Greek consciousness. It is not, therefore, without significance that this state was called by contemporary scholars a 'Hellenic state' and that its inhabitants, headed by the Emperor John III Vatatzes, who was canonized as a saint by the Orthodox church, thought of themselves as 'descendants of the Hellenes'.

The restoration of the empire after Constantinople had been recovered from the Franks did not retard this awakening national consciousness. Michael Palaiologos, it is true, tried to revive the old ecumenical spirit and to make the empire once again a world power, but he failed. The landed aristocrats became more and more independent of the central government. They owned the largest part of the land and received most of the state income; they increased their 'concessions' (fiefs) in the provinces, they added to their hereditary holdings of 'privileged land', and they occupied many of the higher administrative positions. This was the first time that legal jurisdiction and the rights of property were concentrated in the same hands.

The movement towards decentralization was facilitated by the fact that the nation was being torn apart by foreign conquest. Around the end of the 13th century whole sections of the empire became totally isolated. Politically, Hellenism had no existence. It survived largely under the foreign domination of Franks, Serbs, Bulgarians and Turks. Those areas where it could still enjoy Greek administration were divided between Constantinople and the various despotates and local authorities of Epirus, Thessaly, the Peloponnese and, for a short period, Asia Minor. Even when these regions gave theoretical recognition to the authority of Constantinople, in practice they were independent. Constantinople was no longer the unique political centre of Hellenism.

The new centres in Thessalonica, Jannina, Arta and Mistra saw social and political innovations that were to have decisive importance in the development of Greek society. Beside the traditional aristocracy of the landowners a new class was coming into being: that of the merchants, entrepreneurs and artisans who, freed from the restrictions of central government, controlled their own economy and dealt directly with their Italian opposite numbers. Some of the aristocracy were themselves members of this class, either because they owned local industries or because they had foreign mercantile interests. Such a new mixed class was open to influences from the Italian cities. More politically educated, they demanded more political participation. And there was no central authority to stop them. It is no accident, therefore, that from the 11th century onwards we find the first embryonic forms of self-government emerging in the 'communes' of Thessalonica, Jannina and Monemvasia and the first successful challenges by the middle classes (with wide public support) to the power of the landed aristocracy. Such challenges typically occurred during periods of political crisis and dynastic conflict, e.g. when Andronicus II was in dispute with Andronicus III Palaiologos, or John VI Kantakouzenos with John V Palaiologos.

As the empire faded, the mixed class we have described came to be the repository of the Hellenic idea and the predecessor of the Hellenic nation. There is a certain irony in the fact that although it had come into existence through the weakening of the central authority, it came eventually to constitute one of the chief bulwarks of that authority. In the quarrel between John VI Kantakouzenos, a representative of the landed aristocracy, and the legal emperor, John V Palaiologos (1341–7), the Zealots of Thessalonica and the Thracian towns supported the latter. It was also the middle and lower classes who resisted the Serbs when they threatened Thessalonica, and who in Epirus opposed the separatist tendencies of the local leaders, insisting upon submission to the legal authority of Constantinople. And it was popular reaction that obliged the despot Theodore to abandon his plan for delivering the Peloponnese to the Knights of Rhodes in 1400.

This growth of a national ideology in social and political terms is also reflected in the cultural field. The church no longer stood in the way of a re-connection with the Hellenic past. The study of ancient Greek civilization became more widespread, and the 'Greek idea' steadily gained ground, even in conservative circles, until it became a factor common to the whole spectrum of opinion on basic issues. It was, for instance, as important to the die-hard defenders of Orthodoxy (for whom Catholicism was as deadly an enemy as the Ottomans) as it was to the rationalists and westernizers who advocated union with the Catholic church. One finds frequent references to ancient Greece and ancient Greek models in the writings of scholars. The Byzantine emperors are compared to and equated with the great names of antiquity, the Turks being referred to as 'Persians'. John VIII Palaiologos, for example, was called the 'Sun King of Greece'. One could quote many similar expressions. Constantine Palaiologos, the last emperor, called Constantinople 'the refuge of Christians, the hope and joy of all Greeks'. It was the lover of antique Hellenism, Georgios Gemistos Plethon, who gave this ideal its most vivid expression. His recipe for Greek nationhood followed principles very close to those underlying the new nations that were emerging in the west after the dissolution of medieval feudalism: a national currency, taxation based on income, and firm central government headed by a monarch advised by upright and expert counsellors drawn from the middle class. Gemistos also defined the geographical and ethnic foundations of a Greek nation of this kind, which for him would consist of the purely Greek areas. He placed his faith in the despot of his native Mistra, Manuel Palaiologos: 'We, therefore, whose leader and king you are, are Greeks, as our language and our ancestral culture attest.' It was from the Despotate of Mistra that Constantine Palaiologos, just before the final fall of the empire, launched his last attempt to re-unite the Greeks as a nation.

One sign of the rapprochement with classical culture was (paradoxically) a flowering of demotic Greek. Intellectuals began to look afresh at popular art and literature. The result was a series of notable achievements, such as verse romances combining Hellenic tradition with influences from the west. The spoken language was elevated into a literary form; popular imagery took on the sophistication of high art; and as part of the same 'renaissance' spirit we find the first awkward efforts at scientific thinking.

How did the Greeks now see themselves and their history? The idea of Byzantium being the offspring of Rome, a powerful thought for a thousand years, was weakening. The name 'Roman' still retained its political if not its ethnic connotation, but it was now being used by many writers to refer to the western supporters of the Catholic church. Demetrios Kydonis, for instance, hardly ever uses 'Roman' for anyone but westerners; Greeks he calls *Graikoi*. One finds the same usage in the minutes of the Council of Florence (1439). Other writers take a middle course; for them the Byzantines were descended equally from Romans and Hellenes and united the cultures of both. John VI Kantakouzenos (1347–54), for example, sometimes reserves the word Hellene for the inhabitants of Hellenic mini-states outside the frontiers of the empire; at other times, addressing his troops, he calls them 'descendants of the ancient Romans'.

Laonikos Chalkokondyles, a student of Gemistos Plethon, rejected these confusions and compromises. For him Hellenism was the mainstream of Greek history. The Byzantine people and especially their emperors, he maintains (perhaps with a certain irony), had been 'in error' in forgetting their Hellenic nature and calling themselves Romans. And he prophesied that one day the Greek nation would rise again.

Everything points to the conclusion that by the time of the fall of Constantinople and the destruction of the empire by the Ottomans, the idea of Greek nationhood had already been born and that it was this idea that would sustain the Greeks through their long years of Turkish and Frankish occupation. Eventually it would crystallize into the will to achieve identity and independence, and the concept of the new nation would include elements from every phase of its history, the Roman and the Christian as well as the Hellenic. The story of how that destiny was fulfilled is the subject of the last chapter of this book.

II
Beyond the Frontiers
the Greek Diaspora

GEORGE YANNOULOPOULOS

THE TERM 'Greek Diaspora' implies a dispersal of Greeks from their country. But this rather simple and seemingly uncontroversial definition raises a number of questions. The meaning of the term 'Greek', for example, has often been altered and modified throughout the centuries and the boundaries of Greece as a geographical entity have similarly fluctuated. Even more problematic is the time-scale to be applied. Should we include the whole of Greek history as covered in this book? If not, when does the 'Greek Diaspora' begin?

There is a way out of these difficulties – and a very tempting one – the conception of a certain kind of continuity based on a timeless definition of Greekness, a rather elusive quality consisting of the ability to thrive in unfamiliar surroundings, to adjust quickly and profitably to new circumstances, to manipulate situations, and so on. What better illustration than Odysseus, the archetypal Greek, and what better proof than the numerous Greek colonies that dotted the Mediterranean coast in classical times? This view has the obvious attraction of simplicity and it also manages to flatter those to whom it applies. Not surprisingly then it has been adopted implicitly or explicitly by most Greek historians until recently, and has generally been accepted by the people at large as conventional wisdom. The Greeks who founded Massalia (Marseilles) in 600 BC are seen as imbued with the same spirit that led their descendants to the same (and of course by that time, French) city in the 18th century. The poor Greek who attains fame and fortune in far-away lands has become part of the mythology of modern Greece.

I propose, however, to reject this simple and attractive view and to treat the Greek Diaspora as an essentially modern phenomenon beginning with the fall of Constantinople in 1453. This has the merit not only of bringing the subject into definable limits but also, I hope, of providing an opportunity to place in historical perspective an issue which has played such an important role in shaping the modern Greek state and ideology.

The collapse of the Greek empire: the Diaspora begins

The Ottoman conquest of the Byzantine empire and the extension of Turkish rule throughout the Levant transformed the Greeks from a dominant race in a

The Orthodox church was one of the great unifying factors in the Greek Diaspora, and most European capitals were provided with churches, often designed by non-Greeks in a style approximating to the Byzantine. The Greek church of Vienna (left) was built in 1785, but was given its present façade by Theophil von Hansen in 1860.

politically moribund state into a privileged minority in an expanding empire. The Ottomans differentiated their non-Moslem subjects along strictly religious lines and not on the basis of their ethnic or linguistic identity. Thus the Greek patriarch of Constantinople became not only the spiritual but to some extent also the temporal leader of all the Orthodox population of the empire. The upper clergy were almost exclusively ethnic Greeks, but their cultural outlook, like the language of their liturgy, was supra-national (or Byzantine). The sense of 'Greekness' which became identified with the Orthodox church thus avoided a narrow definition which would have confined it to ethnic Greeks, concentrated mainly in the southern end of the Balkans and the Aegean islands, and opened up possibilities for renewed Greek cultural expansion in the Near East.

These long term advantages, however, were not enough to soften the national trauma caused by the fall of Constantinople. The exodus which had started already as the Ottomans were tightening their grip on the Byzantine empire continued after its demise. Most of the Greeks who fled in the 15th century found refuge in Italy or in Christian-held enclaves in the Levant. Among them were prominent members of the intellectual élite who immediately made their mark in the Italian city states, providing some evidence in support of the exaggerated claim that the Greek refugee scholars were the catalysts for the Renaissance in western Europe. The contribution of Chrysoloras, Bessarion, Laskaris, Mousouros and many others in the revival of classical scholarship was far from negligible, but they failed to create the conditions for a continuation and development of the Greek cultural élite in the west, although they helped to make the university of Padua the main centre of learning open to young Greeks from Ottoman and Venetian-held territories. The threat of conversion to Catholicism, which became more real in 1576 when Pope Gregory VIII founded the Collegio Greco in Rome, persuaded the Greek Orthodox church that the opportunities offered by the Christian west were decidedly a mixed blessing.

The majority of Greeks who crossed the Adriatic after the fall of Constantinople were not intellectuals. They gravitated mainly toward Venice and the southern end of the Italian peninsula. Those who headed for southern Italy and Sicily were to some extent a special case, for they settled in places where there were still residues of Byzantine culture and Greek speech. In a sense they were Greeks returning to Magna Graecia, which by then of course had become predominantly Italian. This is why it is extremely difficult to establish which Greek communities were created in the 15th and 16th centuries and which were simply reinforced by fresh blood from across the sea. Certainly, Greek-speaking communities sprang up in Calabria, Messina and Palermo. In Naples in 1487 there were 5000 Albanians, Epirots and Greeks serving in the army of Ferdinand I. Military service in the kingdom of Naples continued to be an attractive proposition for many mainland Greeks and Albanians, and in the 18th century Charles III formed a separate corps that became known as the Reggimento Reale Macedone. Other Greeks decided to go north; Venetian territories and Venice itself were the obvious choice since the Serenissima maintained a strong presence in the Levant and dominated the east–west trade at that time. The first Greek *scuola* in Venice was founded in 1470 and by 1585 there were 15,000 Greeks living in the city. Other Greek refugees were settled by the Venetians in the Istria region.

There was, however, another kind of Greek community in Italy which is far more interesting for our purpose because it provides one of the first examples of what was to become later the typical Greek settlement of the Diaspora. In 1514 we find Greek merchants from Arta, Jannina and Avlona in the Adriatic port of Ancona, and their presence is also recorded in Livorno, on the other side of the Italian peninsula. The importance of these groups lies not in their numerical strength, though this was far from negligible in the case of Ancona, but in their commercial function. Unlike the Byzantine intellectuals or the other refugees who settled in southern Italy or entered the military service of Naples or Venice, the Greek traders of Ancona and Livorno had not fled; they were merchants active in the trade between the Ottoman empire and the Christian west. The Turkish conquest of the eastern Mediterranean did not signal a decline; trade had already reached its nadir in the first half of the 15th century. On the contrary, the conquest created the impetus for a vigorous Ottoman commercial policy, ambitious in scope, whose implementation changed the terms of trade between east and west to the benefit of the former.

Ottoman expansion, Greek opportunity

The young Ottoman empire created the necessary conditions for the flowering of commerce, both internal and external. The Pax Ottomanica within the boundaries of the state and trade with the west under terms more favourable than before to the Ottoman subjects together acted as a strong stimulus for the Greeks and other national groups. The Greek merchants of Ancona should be seen in this context. At this point we may attempt a preliminary and general definition of the Greek Diaspora: it was the migration of Greeks away from the predominantly Greek-speaking areas of the Ottoman empire in order to participate in local, trans-regional or foreign trade.

A look at the map is enough to show why the Greeks, more than the other Balkan ethnic groups, had to migrate if they wanted to take up such commercial activities. The major trade routes that led to the Adriatic ports and further afield to central Europe

bypassed the southern part of the peninsula, where the bulk of the Greek-speaking population was concentrated. Long-haul trade in those days involved the slow carrying of goods over long distances, and therefore the presence of partners or agents in certain key positions along the route and at the place of destination. The Greek communities in Ancona and Livorno may have been the first such settlements but they were by no means the only ones. Halfway through the 16th century we find Greek merchants in what is today Romania; a little later they are in Antwerp and Poland, and by 1600 Greek mercantile communities begin to multiply along the major trading routes and in the main ports of the northern Balkans, central Europe and Italy.

The movement toward the northern provinces of the Balkans continued throughout the 17th century despite the decline of the Mediterranean as the commercial hub of the world. At first the principal focus of Greek penetration was the provinces north of the Danube, where the local rulers Vasile Lupu and Matthew Basarab not only accepted the presence of Greek merchants but also promoted the use of the Greek language in education and public life. By the end of the century there were printing presses in Jassy and Bucharest that could publish Greek books and a Greek academy in Bucharest. It was the beginning of the Greek cultural ascendancy in Romania that reached its climax at the end of the 18th and the beginning of the 19th centuries, when the main intellectual centres of the whole Greek world, whether Diaspora or mainland Greece, were the Danubian principalities of Moldavia and Wallachia. The Greek element was considerably strengthened in 1711 when the Istanbul Phanariots, a kind of Greek *noblesse de robe* that had slowly emerged at the core of the Ottoman administrative machine, managed to secure for themselves the privilege of being appointed Hospodars or governors of the Danubian principalities; Nikolaos Mavrogordatos, the first Phanariot Hospodar, founded the Academia Grecească and a little later a library in Jassy. It is indicative that the first Greek theatre opened not in Greece itself but in Bucharest in 1817.

The penetration of the northern Balkan provinces and central Europe by Greek merchants gathered momentum after the Treaty of Passarowitz in 1718 between the Habsburg empire and the Porte. A year later the Orientalische Compagnie was established in Austria and trade between south-east and central Europe began to increase by leaps and bounds. The conjuncture was highly favourable to Greek and other Balkan merchants for many reasons. The Austrian economy, although stronger than the Ottoman, was not powerful enough to dominate the Balkan market to the detriment of the local commercial element. Instead the Austrians relied on the help of Greek and other Balkan traders who acted mainly as exporters of commodities like cotton, grain, tobacco, wool, etc., from the Ottoman empire. The international situation

*The Greek community in Venice, already large before the fall of
Constantinople, numbered 15,000 in 1585 and possessed several
churches. This view shows the 16th-century church of St George, with
the adjoining scuola designed by Longhena in the 17th on the left (now
the Hellenic Institute of Byzantine and Post-Byzantine Studies).
Above right: a Greek merchant of the 16th century. Venetian
trading links with the Levant made the city an obvious choice for
Greek mercantile activity.*

also proved very favourable because France and England, whose presence in the Mediterranean had been
very strong, were involved in the War of the Austrian
Succession and the Seven Years War, thus offering the
local mercantile class the opportunity to assert themselves. In particular the Anglo-French struggle allowed
the Greek merchant marine to consolidate and expand
its activities for the first time. A similar situation was to
occur again during the Napoleonic wars when the
Greek shipowners amassed enormous fortunes by
running the continental blockade. It is certainly true
that in the 18th century competition among the foreign
trading nations intensified in the Mediterranean, and
naturally the services that the Greek-speaking merchants and shipowners were willing to offer were highly
prized because of their superior knowledge of local
conditions and the contacts they maintained with the
markets, mainly as buyers of export commodities. Such
knowledge played an important role in the commercial
success of their foreign partners. On their part the local
mercantile class took advantage of the situation in more
ways than one. Under the 'capitulations', i.e. the
bilateral commercial treaties between the Porte and the
major western countries, foreign consulates could issue
'*patentes de protection*' and '*lettres de protection*' to their

local protégés who, in this way, became secure enough
to accumulate the capital necessary for their commercial
activities.

The growing disintegration of the empire weakened
the control that the central organs of state could
exercise and in the second half of the 18th century the
despotic power of the local governors reached new
heights. The protection afforded to the local merchants
by the foreigners was one way of dealing with the
problem. The other solution was emigration and the
massive proportions that the Diaspora assumed before
the Greek War of Independence can be interpreted in
part as an effort by the local commercial bourgeoisie to
evade the arbitrary rule of the Turks and pursue their
interests in states where private property was protected
by law.

The Treaty of Passarowitz, which was confirmed by
the Treaty of Belgrade twenty-one years later, meant
that Greek and other Balkan merchants could settle in
the territories of the Austrian empire in order to
consolidate their position and expand their business as
exporters of commodities from the Ottoman provinces.
In the Austrian port of Fiume there were 7 Greek
families in 1733; by 1787 their number had risen to 82.
In Trieste the growth of the Greek community typified
the general trend, both in terms of its numerical
increase and the organization of its activities. In the
1720s a Greek-speaking consul was appointed by the
Habsburgs and five years later a Greek church was
built, followed by another in 1782. There was also a
school and in 1789 the community financed the publication of a Greek grammar by Venieris, an intellectual
within the mainstream of the Greek enlightenment, a
movement which flourished in the second half of the
18th century, mainly in the Diaspora communities.

291

Greeks, Vlachs, Serbs and Albanians dominated the trade with central Europe and beyond. In some cases, like the villages of Zagora, the infertility of their native land might have prompted the inhabitants to seek their future abroad in Wallachia, Moldavia, Austria, Hungary, Russia, Germany or Holland. But if poverty was a factor it was not always the only or the main one. The merchants of Phillipoupolis, which is situated in the middle of a fertile plateau, showed just as great a zeal for long-haul trade. They settled in Smyrna, Syria, Moldavia, Vienna, Odessa and Moscow, and by 1760 they had reached Calcutta. We are dealing with an ever expanding commercial network. There were offshoots outside the main areas of trading activity, like the Greek community of Port Mahon in Minorca which was created in 1743 (its members numbered 500 in 1755), but the main bodies of the Greek Diaspora communities were concentrated in regions whose geographical position offered the possibility of active involvement in the trade between western and central Europe on the one hand and the less developed countries of what would now be called 'periphery' on the other. The case of Russia is indicative of the process. When Catherine the Great decided to build a new major Black Sea port in Odessa toward the end of the 18th century in order to promote the foreign trade of Russia and provide an outlet for Ukrainian grain, the Greeks were among the first to answer her call. The Greek community in Odessa grew in numbers and influence and in 1817 the Commercial School of Odessa was founded, attracting pupils from the other Diaspora settlements in southern Russia and from mainland Greece. A similar case is Hungary where there were seventeen Greek schools in different towns at the end of the 18th century. The Hungarian word for trader was 'görög' which means 'Greek'. Vienna as the capital of the Austrian empire attracted a large number of Greek-speaking merchants, some of whom amassed enormous fortunes and attained the rank of nobility. At the beginning of the 19th century there were Greek schools, libraries, newspapers and churches, all financed or supported by the Greek merchant community of Vienna.

Secrets of success

Trade between the Ottoman empire and the west was the fundamental enabling condition for the emergence and rise of the Greek Diaspora. For a little over a century after the fall of Constantinople in 1453 the Ottomans had been in a position to dictate their own trade terms to the westerners, a situation that was generally beneficial to the local mercantile class. But the situation changed. By the beginning of the 18th century the balance of power had shifted in favour of the west, and it was the west that now forced the Ottoman empire to play a dependent role in production and trade. Then for almost a century, even before the industrial revolution in the west flooded the Levant markets with cheap manufactures that put the local

handicraft enterprises out of business, the population of the Near East was exploited as producers. Whole areas went over to producing specific cash crops to satisfy the demands of the western nations preparing to enter their industrial phase.

What remains to be explained is why it was the Greeks among all the ethnic groups in the Ottoman empire that played such a prominent part in the east–west trade. It has been suggested by Toynbee that 'any community or class that is penalized politically tends to make itself economically efficient and successful, partly because economic activity is an alternative outlet for repressed energies, and partly because wealth is some offset to the loss of political power ... the Greeks reacted to military and political disaster by bringing into play an economic prowess that had been inhibited under the now defunct East Roman Imperial regime.' The Turkish historian Inalcik remarked that 'The Greek genius for commerce always flourishes in areas where the Greeks are debarred from political power.' There is more than a grain of truth in all that. The defeat and subsequent disfranchisement of the Greeks probably did function as a spur for vigorous commercial activity. But the other Balkan Christian peoples were in a similar position. Why did they not react in the same way? Perhaps they did. Traian Stojanovich has argued that all Balkan merchants were liable to be called Greek because they belonged to the Orthodox church, not because they were ethnically Greeks. This is a complicated problem which is central to the question of the Greek Diaspora. There is no doubt that many Serbs, Vlachs and Albanians did take up trade as a profession and created their own Diaspora communities abroad. Some of them were very successful in their commercial enterprises. The greater and more sustained success of the Greeks should be explained not by their 'genius for commerce', but by the cultural hegemony they managed to impose on their co-religionists in the Balkans.

The most important single factor in this hegemony, at least at the beginning, was the part played by the Greek Orthodox church, because the power of the church was immense and its Greekness undisputed. Its dominant position inevitably led to the spread of its liturgical language, which happened to be the language of one Balkan ethnic group. Another contributing factor was the printed word. The printing of books in Greek characters started in the west in the 16th century and was of course related to the revival of classical studies in the Renaissance. Nevertheless it meant that Greek books preceded books in other Balkan languages by centuries. The first publication in Bulgarian characters did not appear until 1806 and Albanian texts were printed in Greek characters well into the 19th century.

Outside the strictly cultural field the Greeks slowly managed to create a small group of Christian patricians who fitted successfully into the interstices of the Ottoman state machine, rising in power and importance as the Turkish rule declined. The Phanariots that have already been mentioned were a few Greek Istanbul

The suburb of Pera, on the right-hand side of the Golden Horn, was the centre of the Greek community that remained in Constantinople after the Ottoman conquest, though the Patriarch's palace (Patriarchato) and Christian church (S. Pietro) are on the other side. The noblewoman shown here comes from an album of German woodcuts made in the 16th century. Many families had by now risen to wealth and power. As middlemen between east and west, the Greeks were in an ideal position to develop their skills as businessmen and administrators.

families who made themselves useful and increasingly indispensable to the Porte by facilitating contact with westerners at a time when such contact was becoming necessary, and by providing financial services when needed. They became powerful enough to control the patriarchate and eventually to rule the Danubian principalities of Moldavia and Wallachia.

All the above factors go a long way toward explaining the cultural, linguistic and ideological hegemony of the Greeks over their co-religionists in the Balkans. They add up to a specific combination of circumstances under which the Greeks were able to implant their numerous mercantile communities in the northern Balkans from a position of strength and at the same time emigrate in large numbers to various key commercial centres abroad which controlled the trade between the Ottoman empire and the west. Calling all the Balkan merchants 'Greeks' was certainly a mistake, but a mistake made possible by the absence of sharp differentiation in ethnic terms at that time. Before the 'balkanization' of the Balkans, national and linguistic identities were neither strong nor exclusive. A sense of 'natural' language and ethnic self-consciousness were subordinate to religious affiliation and social function. To be

called 'Greek' in the 18th century implied that the person so called was a member of the mercantile bourgeoisie in a part of the world where nationalism was still underdeveloped and certain social activities like trade and culture were conducted under Greek cultural hegemony. According to Tsoukalas this process of hellenization was in effect a process of social differentiation because it provided access to the commercial middle class. We are dealing with a variant of nationalism as we understand the term today, a kind of inclusive nationalism that the Diaspora Greeks could practise as a result and at the same time a condition of their cultural hegemony.

The Diaspora and the revival of nationalism

It was inevitable that the commercial function of the Diaspora communities made many of their members receptive to the ideas of enlightenment which began to dominate west European thinking in the second half of the 18th century. The Greek merchants, as others before them, proved susceptible to the lure of Reason and the secular spirit that was typical of the times. Memories of Turkish rapacity and arbitrariness and church obscurantism were fresh in their mind, so it is hardly surprising that most members of the intellectual élite that sprang up in the Danubian principalities, Odessa, Vienna, Trieste, Amsterdam, Paris, London and Budapest slowly rejected the Byzantine ideals of the Orthodox church. Instead they began to elaborate a new programme which combined some derivative 'progressive' and secular elements with a spirit of Byzantine supra-nationalism. Its effect would have been to translate the Greek ideological hegemony into a resurrected Christian empire in the east, comprising all the different ethnic groups, distinct from each other but

293

all to some extent hellenized. The contradictions of such a Diaspora dream were to become painfully obvious in the course of history, but its importance lies in the fact that for the first time it combined Greek nationalism with the idea of national liberation. Up to then the main support of the Greek identity, the church, had been more than content with the Ottoman state structure, which was after all the source and the guarantee of its power. This explains why it was in the Diaspora communities that the ideals of liberation and independence were born, rather than in Greece itself. Rhigas Pheraios, a native of Thessaly who had emigrated to Austria, was the first to elaborate a plan that envisaged a free Balkan federation. In the 1810s the Philiki Etairia, the secret society which prepared the armed struggle against the Turks, was set up by three Greek merchants of the Diaspora and most of its initial membership came from the Diaspora communities. The first move of the War of Independence was typical of the spirit that pervaded the leadership of the Philiki Etairia and a clear indication of what was to follow the successful conclusion of the armed struggle ten years later: Alexander Ypsilantis, aide-de-camp of the Tsar of Russia and a scion of a distinguished Phanariot family, raised the standard of revolt in the Danubian principalities hoping that the local population would support the Greek struggle for independence and make a reality of the Diaspora dream of a hellenized Balkan federation. His attempt ended in disaster mainly because such support failed to materialize. The real confrontation occurred in the southern end of the Balkan peninsula, where the main body of the Greek-speaking population finally succeeded in creating the first modern Greek state.

The Diaspora communities, having initiated the independence movement and provided its ideological underpinnings, found themselves outside the boundaries of Greece and among foreigners that would soon follow the example of Greek nationalism. Almost inevitably an exclusive and aggressive sense of ethnicity, aggravated by conflicting claims that were bound to be raised in a region so mixed as the Balkans, took the place of the inclusive nationalism made possible by the Greek cultural hegemony at the turn of the century. The emergence of national states in the northern part of the peninsula meant the creation of national middle classes which supplanted in the end the Greek mercantile bourgeoisie. The Diaspora communities were slowly being transformed into dwindling minorities, increasingly insignificant.

After independence: the Diaspora in decline

The coming into being of the first modern Greek state did not, in itself, affect the Diaspora Greeks in any significant way. The liberated area included no major centre of economic activity, with the exception perhaps of the islands Hydra and Spetsai that had played such a prominent role in the development of merchant shipping during the Napoleonic wars. However, the existence of a national base, however weak, did provide the Diaspora Greeks with a certain amount of diplomatic leverage and a potential fall-back position. What did affect them deeply was a major shift in the international balance of economic power that occurred at the beginning of the 19th century. In the 18th century the nature of the trade that linked the Near East with the expanding economies of western and central European states had not in any significant way impeded economic growth in the east. On the contrary, historians, have argued that the export-oriented Levant economy witnessed increased production of raw materials and processed goods, to the benefit of both the local producers and the Diaspora merchants who channelled the exports abroad. This trend, however, was cut short by the industrial revolution which took place in England first and then spread to the rest of western Europe. The terms of trade between the industrialized states and the eastern Mediterranean changed dramatically and the new economic order that emerged through this transformation placed the former in the 'core' and the latter in the 'periphery' of the international economic order.

The function of the Greek Diaspora, which had always been determined by the overall balance of economic power between the Levant and the west, changed accordingly. In western and central Europe it entered a phase of rapid decline. The flow of emigration from Greece ceased and the communities which decided to stay were assimilated or became insignificant minorities. Some of the richest members of the Diaspora were admitted into the ruling class of their adopted country, the Sinas family in Austria being a case in point. In the north Balkans, with the exception of Romania, the emerging national states with their own middle classes and their own brand of exclusive nationalism effectively removed one of the main reasons for the existence of the Greek Diaspora. But the fundamental change was the one that affected the economic relations which linked the Near East with the west European markets. The industrial revolution meant a sharp increase in the imports of cheap manufactured goods, which stifled the local unprotected handicrafts and the exports of unprocessed raw materials. The geographical focus of the east–west trade moved to Egypt and Asia Minor and the Greek Diaspora followed. It was not a mere change of location; the 'conquering Orthodox Balkan merchant' began to assume gradually the features of the comprador.

The only Balkan country where the Diaspora Greeks managed not only to maintain but also to reinforce their position was Romania, despite the unsuccessful revolt of 1821 and the abolition of the Phanariot rule. Serbia and Bulgaria had created their own middle classes imbued with a sharp sense of ethnicity, but the appearance of such a group in Romania was delayed by more than half a century. Indeed, it is very likely that the traditionally strong cultural and commercial presence of the Greeks in that country impeded the emergence of a local bourgeoisie. Not until the 1860s did the Diaspora Greeks in Romania face the first serious challenge to their supremacy and even after that, despite a steady decline in their fortunes, they retained control of the lower Danube and Black Sea trade thanks to the contribution of the Greek merchant marine. At the beginning of the 20th century there were still large concentrations of Greeks in most Romanian cities along the Danube and the coast. According to a conservative estimate of a Romanian historian there were 50,000 Greeks living in Romania in 1915, but Greek historians of the Diaspora in that country suggest a much higher figure.

Outside the Near East, the Diaspora communities in southern Russia were the only other example of Greek presence that continued to grow in the 19th century. As we have seen, these go back to the founding of Odessa at the end of the 18th century. During the next sixty years large numbers of Greeks settled in the cities on or near the Black Sea coast that then were the outlets of the growing grain trade – Taganrog, Kherson, Nikolayev, Kars, Rostov and Marioupol. As in the case of Romania the reason for the vigorous commercial presence of the Greeks in southern Russia, particularly in the export trade, was the absence of a native middle class that would have occupied this social and economic space. Unlike Romania, however, the Russian state was strong and the Diaspora Greeks were denied the opportunity to exercise any kind of cultural or linguistic hegemony. When the Russian commercial bourgeoisie began to emerge after 1860 the decline of the Greek communities again proved inevitable. It gathered pace after the revolution of 1905 and the final blow was the October Revolution in 1917. It must be noted that in Russia the withering away of the Greek Diaspora assumed the form of progressive 'russification' and this probably explains why the estimates of the number of Greeks who lived in Russia in 1920 vary so much. According to a Greek source there were 800,000, but the official Soviet figure for those granted linguistic and ethnic protection was only 213,000.

The growth of Greek communities in Egypt and Asia Minor

The main focus of the Greek Diaspora in the 19th century was the Near East, and in particular Egypt and Turkey, for reasons outlined above. The case of Egypt is perhaps more indicative of the general trends at work. Up to the 1840s the presence of Greeks in Egypt was negligible despite the geographic proximity of the two countries. By the end of the century their number had swelled to 100,000, reaching a peak of 200,000 in the 1920s. The spectacular growth of the Greek Diaspora communities in Egypt was closely linked to the opening of that country's economy to the markets of the west. The main commodity was cotton, which was exported from Egypt in increasing quantities,

In Liverpool, England, the Greek community built one of its grandest churches – a huge domed space carried on Byzantine columns and with an ornate iconostasis at the east end. It was opened in 1870.

especially after the American Civil War. Greek merchants dominated the Egyptian cotton trade in the second half of the 19th century, amassing great fortunes. One of the big Greek commercial firms that specialized in the Upper Egypt trade and at the same time operated a monopoly of transport on the Nile employed a staff of 1000, while Greek capital accounted for 36 per cent of the total capital of all limited companies that were incorporated in Egypt during the first thirty years of this century, an investment calculated at fifteen million pounds. Although British capital controlled the banking and finance sectors, we find Greek directors and major shareholders in practically all the important banks that operated in Egypt at that time. The role of the Greek Diaspora communities in Egypt was not confined to purely economic activities. Together with other groups of western Europeans, mainly the Italians, they provided the bulk of the professional, middle management and skilled labour strata, thus occupying the social space of the national middle class whose inability to perform such a task was prolonged by its exclusion. The Greek communities in Egypt also led

295

The Greek cemetery at Norwood is still used by London Greeks. Classical temples rise among tombstones inscribed in Greek and English.

the way to deeper penetration into black Africa. The principal targets were Sudan, where Greeks fought alongside General Gordon in the defence of Khartoum, and Abyssinia, a country whose strong ties with Greece survived well into the 20th century.

A similar picture emerged in Anatolia, the heartland of the Ottoman state, although in this case there were certain special features that must be taken into consideration. There had always been Greeks living in Asia Minor but their number had declined steadily up to the beginning of the 19th century. Ironically enough, the liberation of Greece did start an immigration movement but not in the direction that one would have expected; the number of Greeks who emigrated to the Ottoman state was much higher than the number of those who chose to make their home in the nascent Kingdom of Greece (this also applies to the Diaspora

Greeks from the communities in the northern Balkans and the Levant). Up to the 1920s, when the Greek irridentist dream ended in the Asia Minor disaster, the number of Greeks in Turkey went on rising. Their presence was particularly strong on the Aegean coast, in Istanbul and along the coast of the Black Sea. Smyrna, the 'infidel Ismir' as the Turks called it, is a good illustration of the general trend: it has been calculated that in 1776 when the total population was about 100,000, there were 21,000 Greeks living there. By 1922 the number of Greeks had risen to 200,000 out of a total of 380,000, a spectacular increase both in absolute and percentage terms. Perhaps the single most important reason for the growth of the Greek communities in Turkey was the changes in the economic and social structure of the Ottoman state introduced during the so called Tanzimat period from 1839 to 1876. It was a period of reform from above and by decree which resulted in the opening of the Turkish market to western investment and exports under conditions that reinforced the unequal relations between Turkey and industrialized Europe. The dependence of the former on the latter became even more pronounced. In practical terms the Tanzimat reforms meant that both foreigners and subjects of the Sultan could engage in economic activities relatively safe in the knowledge that their property would not fall prey to the rapacity of the Ottoman officials.

The rapid growth of the Greek communities in Asia Minor can be seen as a response to the opportunities which opened up when the west conquered Turkey economically, leaving its political structure intact but increasingly ineffective. The indigenous Greek population must have shared in the general upsurge of the Greek presence in Anatolia but it would be wrong to overlook or underestimate the vital role played by the immigrants from the other parts of the Greek world who created another Diaspora in the land which they considered their own by tradition and inheritance. The newcomers of the Diaspora gravitated toward the cities, and together with the Armenians and other minorities they also occupied the 'space' of the lower middle class and spearheaded the advance of the market economy into the depths of Anatolia. Travellers often noticed that there were very few villages without a Greek grocer who was also the local money lender. In Istanbul, Smyrna and the rest of the commercial centres of Turkey it was Greeks and other foreigners who provided the same kind of services on a much greater scale. The assets of certain individual Greek magnates in Turkey, or in Egypt for that matter, were higher than the annual receipts of the Greek state.

The rise of the Greek merchant marine

Since the 18th century the fortunes of the Diaspora communities had been closely linked to the growth of the Greek merchant marine. In calculating the strength of the Greek-owned mercantile fleet during the last two hundred years we encounter insuperable difficulties because, unlike settlements on land which can be identified and counted, shipping activities are more elusive, given the traditional privilege of shipowners to choose the flag under which they sail. The Greeks took advantage of this privilege in the second half of the 18th century when Russian ships secured the right to sail through the straits, thus opening the Black Sea trade to the world market. The subsequent development of the Diaspora communities in southern Russia and the Danube was partly due to the strong presence of Greek shipping in these waters. The sea trade was an integral part of the vast commercial network that the Diaspora communities spread in the eastern Mediterranean and the Black Sea. Despite strong competition from Britain and France the Greeks managed to retain a sizeable share of the market. Investment in shipping allowed capital to be easily liquidated and moved around, and the international character of the Diaspora trading activities was particularly well suited to this kind of operation.

The mobility and versatility of shipping capital meant that the merchant marine of the Diaspora was not significantly affected when the communities in Egypt and Turkey entered the final stage of their decline in the 1920s. In Turkey the end came abruptly in 1922 with the Asia Minor disaster but in Egypt the process lasted for decades and culminated in the exodus of the Greeks in the 1950s. Despite the differences between the two cases, the fall of the Diaspora in the Near East followed the same pattern as in the Balkans a century earlier. The emergence of national middle classes combined with the creation of truly national states based on a sharply defined ethnic identity made it impossible for a large community of foreigners to retain its control over certain vital sectors of the national economy. In the case of Turkey the confrontation assumed such violent form because the Greeks, having infiltrated the economy, threatened to take over the state. The rise and fall of the Diaspora communities, taken together, reveal the real character of the phenomenon under examination: the propensity of the Greeks to emigrate was created both by the conditions prevailing in their own country and the opportunities that existed abroad. But the Diaspora slotted into a system it could only manipulate, never control. Its fortunes, which at times reached great heights, were essentially dependent on the wider international conjunctures. The choice that one community after another finally had to face was whether to return home or be assimilated; the only thing that the Diaspora could not achieve was to remain a diaspora.

The modern Diaspora: Greeks in the USA and Australia

This may sound very strange today when more Greeks live abroad than at any other time in their history. The size of the Greek communities in the USA, Canada, Australia and West Germany seems to suggest that the traditional virtues of adaptability and endurance have

once more come to the fore as if to confirm the notion that the Diaspora spirit is still one of the fundamental elements of Greekness. A closer look, however, indicates that we are dealing with a somewhat different phenomenon. The old Diaspora was not a simple migration of Greeks but a complex movement that enabled the emerging mercantile bourgeoisie of a small and infertile land to participate with distinction in a wide network of international trade. It led to the establishment of Greek communities that often occupied key positions in the economic, social and sometimes political life of the countries where they were implanted. This clearly has not been the case with the new type of emigration, which can be seen both as a solution to a problem created by the socio-economic structural changes in Greece and a result of the opening up of certain fast-developing countries in the core of the international economy.

The immediate cause of the new exodus was the so called 'currant crisis' that hit the Peloponnese at the end of the 19th century. It was a severe agricultural crisis that was to last, in less acute forms, until the present day as more and more land-holders abandoned their small and unproductive plots, which had ceased to be economically viable. The mass migration to the USA which accounted for 96 per cent of all emigrants until 1921 alleviated some of its most unpleasant effects. Instead of flocking to the rather small Greek cities which could not have absorbed them, many peasants headed for the New World, the land of endless opportunities. The Diaspora communities in America were augmented by a constant stream of arrivals up to the outbreak of the First World War. More came after the Asia Minor disaster in 1922 and the civil war in 1949. Eventually there were more Greeks in America than in the older Diaspora concentrations of south-east Europe and the Levant. But the Greeks who went to America were not expected to provide entrepreneurial talent in the US economy. Instead they were forced to turn to small businesses in the service sector, gradually working their way up and achieving a certain degree of prosperity, but never the prominence that the Greeks enjoyed in Egypt, Asia Minor or Romania. This is hardly surprising in view of the fact that America was a fast developing industrial nation richly endowed with almost everything except labour power. Despite the wild rumours circulating in Greece about the golden opportunities available in the New World, the Greek American communities did not produce millionaires but restaurant owners, hoteliers and grocers.

It is extremely difficult to calculate the number of Greek Americans although it has been said that they are as many as one million and a half. The line that divides the member of the Greek Diaspora communities in the USA from the American of Greek origin is extremely hard to draw. Society in America is less homogeneous and more inclusive than in other countries and has the ability to assimilate new blood from overseas at a remarkable speed. On the other hand the absence of a clearly defined national identity tends to preserve a more or less pronounced sense of ethnicity which may rise to the surface.

The same may be said of the Greek communities in Australia. Emigration to this country began after the end of the civil war in the 1950s and coincided with the new policy of the Australian government to encourage Europeans to settle in its vast and underpopulated continent. Large numbers of Greeks took up the opportunity and today there are about 200,000 Greeks in Australia. They are concentrated in Sydney, where their number has reached 90,000. The Australians started with a policy of assimilation which later gave way to a more broad-minded approach that encourages diversity among the various ethnic groups.

Emigration to north-west Europe is a relatively recent phenomenon occasioned by the post-war economic boom. First Belgium and then West Germany solved the problems created by labour shortages by importing workers from southern Europe. This new type of immigrant has very little in common with his ancestors who settled in western and central Europe in the 17th and 18th centuries. In fact the 200,000 Greek 'guest-workers' (*Gastarbeiter*) in Germany can hardly be included in an account of the Greek Diaspora. Their function was to satisfy the needs of the West German economy for unskilled labour; the onset of the economic crisis in the 1970s and the subsequent rise of unemployment meant that the 'guests' had outstayed their welcome and the time had come for them to return home. The old Diaspora began with the exportation of commodities; the new one seems to have ended with the exportation of people.

Diaspora and homeland: the creative paradox

The geographical spread of overseas emigration in the 20th century has been much greater than in previous centuries but it has taken place in a fast-shrinking world. Today distances have grown shorter and communications have improved, making contact between the Diaspora communities and Greece much easier than in the past. This development has helped enormously the cultural activities of the Diaspora, which have always been essential for the continuation of the original ethnic identity abroad. On the other hand this very identity has come under increased pressure because its patterns of traditional behaviour that have been proved effective in the past are becoming increasingly unsuitable in the modern consumer societies of the developed countries where the 20th-century Greek Diaspora is concentrated.

It is extremely difficult to summarize in brief the significance of the Diaspora phenomenon in post-Byzantine Greece. Many historians have rightly underlined the contradictory effects created by a strong mercantile middle class operating outside Greece and having relatively little contact with the national economy. In almost every respect except numbers it was overwhelmingly stronger than the national heartland. The communities that flourished abroad absorbed most of the human potential that might have achieved a more rapid and integrated development in Greece itself, although it must be pointed out that it was the comparative lack of opportunities at home which drove them abroad in the first place. The Diaspora's economic vitality contrasted sharply with the precarious finances of the Greek state, and it was this vitality, rather than the anaemic performance of Greece, that sustained the myth of the commercial genius of the race.

Perhaps the most important and certainly the most elusive contribution of the Diaspora was in the field of ideology and culture. It provided the main impetus for the Greek enlightenment in the 18th century and prepared the ideological ground for the Greek War of Independence. For the Greek merchants who lived abroad, the national identity was something that had to be elaborated, maintained and sometimes constructed. The great emphasis that the Diaspora community placed on its cultural, educational and religious activities can be seen as a response to the stimuli or threats to which it was exposed, an attempt to secure a degree of ideological coherence that was vital for its survival as a community. This resulted in highly original ideological combinations that have fertilized Greek culture until this day. In this and every other important sense the Greek Diaspora has been one of the major factors that shaped the face of modern Greece, a face whose features are still far from settled.

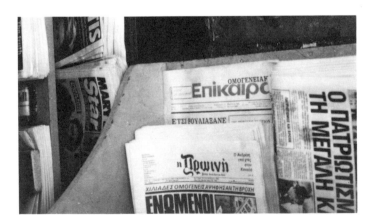

Greek newspapers published in New York. Although most Americans of Greek origin are now thoroughly assimilated, their ties with the home country remain strong and they exert influence socially and culturally if not politically.

12
Eclipse and Rebirth

from the Ottoman period to
modern Greece

RICHARD CLOGG

CONSTANTINOPLE, or 'The City' as it is known in the Greek world, fell to the Ottoman Turks on 29 May 1453, a Tuesday, a day of the week that continues to be regarded as ill-fated by the Greeks. Although the fall of this bastion of Christian civilization to the infidel had a great symbolic significance in the west, the reaction of the inhabitants of the pitiful rump of the Byzantine empire that fell to the Turks was mixed. The bulk of the Greek populations of the eastern Mediterranean had already had a long experience of Ottoman rule, while, of the remainder, many regarded the imposition of Ottoman rule as less objectionable than submission to the papacy, which had been the price that western Christendom had demanded for military assistance during the declining years of the empire. This attitude had been succinctly expressed by the Grand Duke Loukas Notaras in his famous assertion that it would be preferable for the turban of the Turk to prevail in 'The City' rather than the mitre of the Latin cardinal. For the Ottomans, at least, would allow the Greeks to maintain their faith untrammelled by the taint of Latin heresy. The mood of resignation with which many Greeks greeted the fall of Constantinople was enhanced by the widespread view that the disaster formed part of the pattern of divine retribution for the manifold sins of the empire and that, in any case, the end of the world would occur at the end of the seventh millennium since Creation, which was calculated as the year 1492.

Such isolated pockets of Greek settlement as remained outside the *Pax Ottomanica* were gradually overrun, although it was some time before the Ottomans were able to consolidate their rule over the Aegean islands. Rhodes did not fall until 1522, Chios and Naxos until 1566, Cyprus until 1571, while Crete, the 'Great Island', did not succumb until 1669, after an epic twenty-year siege. The Ottomans were able to establish only a brief foothold in the Ionian Islands, which were to remain Venetian dependencies until 1797. Frankish and Ottoman Greece were not sealed off from one another; people and ideas moved freely between them. In many areas of the Greek lands under Ottoman rule, particularly in the remote mountain fastnesses, the control exercised by the Ottoman central government was relatively light. The *Agrapha* villages of the Pindos range, for instance, were so named because they were 'unwritten' in the imperial tax registers. Other areas of the Greek world, such as the rich mastic-growing island of Chios, enjoyed a high degree of autonomy and special privileges.

The camp of the Klepht chieftain Karaiskakis, who became one of the leaders in the War of Independence. He was killed in 1827 and was revered as a national hero. This painting of the mid-19th century is by Theodoros Vryzakis.

Ottoman rule in the Greek lands

Once they had consolidated their hold over the Byzantine empire, the Ottomans, whose state had essentially been geared towards military expansion, were faced with the problem of ruling over very substantial non-Moslem populations, Christian and Jewish. This they overcame by organizing them into *millets*, on the basis not of ethnic origin but of religious confession. In addition to the ruling Moslem *millet*, there was an Orthodox *millet*, a Gregorian Armenian *millet*, a Jewish *millet* and a Catholic *millet*. The Orthodox *millet* was known as the *Millet-i-Rum*, or 'Greek' *millet*. This was a misleading title, for it embraced, besides the Greeks, all the Orthodox Christian inhabitants of the empire, whether Serb, Bulgarian, Romanian, Vlach, Albanian or Arab. But the ecumenical patriarch, who was the head of the *Millet-i-Rum*, and the higher reaches of the hierarchy of the Orthodox church, through which it was administered, were always Greek, a fact that came increasingly to be resented by the Orthodox Christian but non-Greek subjects of the sultan.

Some uncertainty exists as to the exact nature of the privileges granted by the Sultan Mehmed the Conqueror to the first ecumenical patriarch of the post-conquest period, Georgios Gennadios Scholarios. But the powers and privileges of the Orthodox church under Ottoman rule were certainly more extensive than they had been during the days of the Christian empire. The patriarch, moreover, came to exercise considerable powers over the Orthodox Christian flock and by no means only in strictly religious matters. In many areas of the empire Orthodox Christians would have had more dealings in their daily lives with their own religious authorities than with the Ottomans. In return for the granting of this extensive jurisdiction over the Orthodox faithful, the patriarch and the hierarchy were expected to act as guarantors of their loyalty. The execution in reprisal of the patriarch Grigorios V on the outbreak of the Greek War of Independence in 1821 occasioned outrage in the Christian west. But to the Ottomans Grigorios had manifestly failed to perform his primary duty, that of ensuring the loyalty of his followers to the Ottoman state.

If the Greeks under Ottoman rule were accorded, following Islamic tradition, a wide degree of religious toleration, they were none the less subject to a number of disabilities which had the effect of turning them into second-class citizens. A Christian could not, for instance, marry a Moslem woman. His word was not accepted in a court of law against that of a Moslem. He was required to pay a special tax, the *harac*, in lieu of military service and was barred from bearing arms. The most onerous imposition was undoubtedly the *paidomazoma* or janissary levy. This was the obligation, imposed on Christian families in the Balkans at irregular intervals, to deliver a certain proportion of their most intelligent and best-looking male children to be raised, after being forcibly converted to Islam, as bureaucrats or élite troops. Some Greeks, subjected to intolerable local oppression, converted, sometimes *en masse*, to Islam. But some of these secretly adhered to the precepts and practices of Orthodox Christianity.

The concentration of power, civil as well as strictly religious, in the hands of the patriarch and the hierarchy of the church, led to the development of furious rivalries for high office. The Ottomans themselves had a vested interest in such competition, for it soon became customary for an enormous *peşkeş*, or bribe, to be paid to the grand vizir, the sultan's chief minister, whenever the office of patriarch changed hands. Despite the fact that a patriarch in theory enjoyed life tenure it was not uncommon for the same individual to hold office more than once. Dionysios IV Mouselimis, during the later 17th century, was five times elected to the office of patriarch, while the 'Ethnomartyr' Grigorios V, was three times patriarch before his execution in 1821. The office of patriarch was by no means the only high office in the church which could be secured through bribery alone, and the church as an institution was no exception to the rapacity and corruption that was endemic to the Ottoman system of government as it went into decline. Corruption in the higher reaches of the church meant increased impositions on the mass of the faithful. This, in turn, led to the development of popular anti-clericalism, which was reinforced, as the centuries passed, among the small minority of educated Greeks by a growing resentment at the way in which the hierarchy of the church had so closely identified its interests with those of the Ottoman powers that be. Some Orthodox clerics, indeed, were to argue, as did the patriarch of Jerusalem in 1798, that the Ottoman empire was itself part of the divine dispensation, that it had been raised up to protect the Orthodox faith from contamination by the Catholic (and revolutionary) west.

The 16th and 17th centuries are a particularly shadowy period in the history of the Greek people. Occasionally, however, Greeks emerged into prominence. One such, a descendant of the great Byzantine family of the Kantakouzenoi, was known by the Turks as Şeytanoğlu, or 'the Son of the Devil'. Through his control of the fur trade and of the salt monopoly in the empire he acquired a fortune large enough to enable him to purchase sixty galleys for the Sultan's navy. Even this gesture, however, was unable to save him from execution in 1578. Şeytanoğlu, however, was very much the exception. The mass of the Greeks at this time were overwhelmingly concerned with the daily struggle for existence. Where they thought of eventual emancipation from the Hagarene yoke of the Ottomans it was in terms of prophecies and oracles foretelling the eventual liberation of the Greek people through divine intervention. Widespread credence was attached to the notion of the *xanthon genos*, a fair-haired race of liberators from the north, widely identified with the Russians. Even during the darkest days of the *Tourkokratia* or period of Turkish rule, however, there were sporadic revolts, sometimes stimulated by hopes of foreign deliverance, sometimes not. Examples of these were the uprisings on the mainland and in the islands of the archipelago stimulated by the crushing defeat inflicted on the Ottoman navy at the Battle of Lepanto in 1571 and the revolt launched by Dionysios Skylosophos in Epirus in 1611. Moreover, throughout the period of the *Tourkokratia*, the *klephts* afforded a suggestive example of pre-nationalist armed resistance to the Turks. The *klephts* were essentially outlaws who attacked Greek and Turk alike. But, in that their attacks were launched against such visible symbols of Ottoman authority as tax collectors, they came to be identified in the popular mind as defenders of the oppressed Greeks against their Moslem overlords. Moreover, the existence of the *klephts*, together with the *armatoloi*, the Christian militia created by the Ottomans in an effort to control the depredations of the *klephts* (the dividing line between the two was never very rigid), was to ensure that when the Greeks did begin to fight for their independence they could call on armed formations with a long and invaluable experience of irregular warfare.

It was not, however, until the 18th century that there appeared to be a realistic chance that the Greeks might hope to regain their freedom through their own efforts. Following the failure of the Siege of Vienna in 1683, the Ottoman empire was increasingly forced on the defensive, coming under pressure from the Austrians in the west, the Russians to the north and the Persians to the east. Russia, in particular, during the 18th century posed a particular threat to the territorial integrity of the empire and claimed, as a consequence of the Treaty of Küçük Kaynarca, which concluded the Russo-Turkish war of 1768–74, a spurious protectorate over all the Orthodox Christians of the empire. The shrinkage of the territorial base of the empire was paralleled by a break-down in the control exercised by the Ottoman Porte, or government, over its far-flung provinces. Whole swathes of imperial territory came under the control of *ayans* and *derebeys*, provincial notables who, while Moslem and professing to recognize the suzerainty of the sultan, in effect usurped the authority of the central government. These Turkish usurpers often made concessions to their Christian subjects, whose support they sought to help maintain their authority. The successful defiance of the Porte, for years on end, by *ayans* such as Ali Paşa of Jannina afforded a suggestive example to the Greeks, and together with the empire's apparent inability to resist the external threat, demonstrated that the Ottomans were no longer, as they once had appeared, invincible.

Although by the 18th century the Ottoman empire was manifestly in decline, the notion of the Greeks being able to throw off the Ottoman yoke would have appeared fanciful indeed had not a number of highly

The Greek spirit of independence under the Ottomans was manifested in many ways. At one end of the scale was the Orthodox church, the visible embodiment of Greek culture, represented by its hierarchy of bishops. At the other were the Klephts (right), outlaws whose attacks on Turkish officials and tax-collectors made them symbols of resistance.

significant developments taken place during the course of that century. The growing external pressure on the empire meant that the Ottomans could no longer, as they had during the zenith of their power, merely dictate peace terms to defeated adversaries. They now needed the services of skilled diplomats who could mitigate the consequences of military defeat. These they found in the Phanariots, a kind of *noblesse de robe*, drawn from a small group of families of Greek or Hellenized Albanian and Romanian origin, and living in the Phanar quarter of Constantinople, where the patriarchate was situated. From the time of the Peace of Carlowitz in 1699 until the outbreak of the Greek War of Independence in 1821, these Phanariots came to monopolize the office of *tercüman başı*. Strictly the title implied that they were the principal interpreters to the Porte, but their influence on the conduct of the empire's external relations was in practice far wider. Likewise the Phanariot Greeks who acted as interpreters to the *kapudan paşa* (the admiral of the Ottoman fleet) came to act as *de facto* governors of the Aegean islands. Throughout the 18th century, Phanariots acted as *hospodars*, or princes, of the Danubian principalities of Wallachia and Moldavia, ruling on behalf of the Ottomans in the vice-regal splendour of their courts in Jassy and Bucharest. These Phanariot *hospodars* acquired a reputation for rapacity and oppression but some introduced important reforms into the princip-

alities and acted as patrons of Greek education and culture. Competition for the various positions monopolized by the Phanariots was as fierce as that for high office in the church and the corruption and intrigue that surrounded them was as intense. The average tenure in office of a *hospodar* was less than three years. This Phanariot service aristocracy was firmly locked into the power structure of the Ottoman state and the Phanariots as a caste had a vested interest in the continuation of Ottoman power. None the less the political experience acquired by these grandees in some of the very highest offices of the Ottoman state was subsequently to stand the Greeks in good stead. The courts of the Phanariot rulers of Wallachia and Moldavia became centres of Greek education and culture, which flourished more freely there than under direct Ottoman rule. Teachers and pupils came to Bucharest and Iaşi from other parts of the Greek world, and often brought back with them some acquaintance with western thought and the first stirrings of a critical and inquiring spirit.

Of greater importance, however, to the development of the Greek national movement than the rise to power and influence of the Phanariots was the emergence of a prosperous and widely dispersed Greek mercantile class, as active outside as within the Ottoman empire. Greek entrepreneurs had been quick to exploit the absence of an indigenous merchant class in the principalities of Moldavia and Wallachia and in the territories newly lost to the empire such as Hungary or southern Russia, where they had been actively encouraged to settle by Catherine the Great. The general arbitrariness of Ottoman rule during the period of the empire's decline inhibited the development of manufacturing industry. The example of the Thessalian hill-town of Ambelakia, which at the turn of the 18th century engaged in the highly profitable manufacture, on cooperative lines, of spun red cotton for export to central Europe, was very much the exception. Greek entrepreneurs during the 18th century were very largely engaged in the export of raw materials from the Ottoman empire to western Europe and with the importation of western manufactured foods and colonial produce. By the end of the century Greek merchants had come virtually to monopolize the commerce of the empire, in the process presenting a formidable challenge to the established interests of British, French, Dutch and Italian merchants who enjoyed a privileged status under the capitulatory regime. By this time Greek had effectively become the *lingua franca* of Balkan commerce, and Greek mercantile *paroikies*, or communities, had been established throughout the Mediterranean, southern Russia and central Europe and as far afield as Calcutta in India and New Smyrna in Florida. At the same time a flourishing mercantile marine developed in the three 'nautical' islands of Hydra, Spetsai and Psara, with Greek sea-captains and their crews making huge profits breaching the continental blockade imposed during the French revolutionary and Napoleonic wars. The venerable tradition of Greek piracy in Aegean waters, coupled with the fact that Greeks made up a large proportion of the crews of the Ottoman fleet, was to prove an invaluable asset during the War of Independence.

The existence of this prosperous and widely dispersed Greek mercantile bourgeoisie during the decades before independence is an established fact. But the political consequences of such a development were ambiguous. Some merchants, contrasting the order and positive encouragement to trade they encountered in the states of western Europe with the lawlessness and obstacles to the development of an orderly commerce within the Ottoman dominions, were moved to give their support to the nascent national movement. The majority of these merchants, however, particularly the more prosperous among them, were reluctant to jeopardize their newly found wealth. But where these merchants did unquestionably contribute to the development of a Greek national consciousness, to an awareness of a specifically Greek rather than merely Orthodox Christian identity, was in providing the material base for the intellectual revival that was such a pronounced feature of the late 18th and early 19th centuries. Besides endowing schools and libraries and subsidizing a growing literature in modern Greek, published almost exclusively outside the Ottoman dominions, these merchants enabled young Greeks to study in the universities of western Europe. Here they came into contact not only with societies where the rule of law prevailed but also with the intoxicating ideas of the European Enlightenment, the French Revolution and Romantic Nationalism.

They became aware, moreover, of the hold which the language and civilization of ancient Greece had over the minds of their educated European contemporaries and this, in turn, helped to stimulate within them an awareness that they were the heirs to a heritage that was universally admired throughout the civilized world. A key role in this effort to re-awaken a 'Sense of the Past' in his compatriots was played by Adamantios Korais. Korais was born in Smyrna in 1748. After an unsuccessful stint as a merchant in Amsterdam, he studied medicine at Montpellier and in 1788 settled in Paris where he remained until his death in 1833. Here he established a formidable reputation as a classical scholar and prepared editions of classical texts for his compatriots in the Greek lands. These he prefaced with improving exhortations in which he sought to instil a sense that the Greeks were the inheritors of the incomparable cultural heritage of ancient Greece and urged them to cast off the mantle of Byzantine ignorance in which they had been enveloped. He believed passionately that only through education could the Greeks prepare themselves for emancipation from the double tyranny of the Ottoman Turks and the monkish ignorance of the hierarchs of the Orthodox church.

By the early decades of the 19th century, then, Greek society was undergoing a process of rapid social change and (as Professor Svoronos has described in an earlier chapter) a small but growing number of Greeks, besides becoming increasingly resentful at the continuance of Ottoman rule, were developing a distinct sense of ethnic identity. But many of the élites of Greek society, the Phanariots, the hierarchy of the Orthodox church, the wealthier merchants, the *kocabaşis*, or provincial notables, were comfortably wedded to the Ottoman *status quo*. Moreover, the nationalist enthusiasms of the small intelligentsia, which was to be found more in the Greek communities of the Diaspora than within the Greek lands, largely passed over the heads of the great mass of the Greek people. It was only towards the very end of the 18th century that the first efforts were made towards concerting an armed revolt against the Ottomans.

The struggle for independence

The first to develop plans for a co-ordinated revolt against the Ottomans was Rigas Velestinlis, a Hellenized Vlach from Thessaly who had acquired his earliest political experience in the service of the Phanariot *hospodars* of the Danubian Principalities. During his stay in Vienna in the 1790s he had been strongly influenced by the French Revolution. The French example is clearly apparent in a number of political tracts which he had printed and with which he intended to revolutionize the Balkans, inciting not only the Greeks but the other Balkan peoples to throw off the insufferable tyranny of the Turks. The most important of these were the *Declaration of the Rights of Man* and the *New Political Constitution of the Inhabitants of Rumeli, Asia Minor, the Islands of the Aegean and the Principalities of Moldavia and Wallachia*. This latter was essentially a blueprint for a revived Byzantine empire but with republican institutions on the French model in the place of monarchical, and with the Greek element in the empire in firm control. This was not yet a plan for a Greek national state. Nothing came of his grandiose schemes, however, for he was betrayed before he had even left Habsburg territory and, after being handed over with a handful of fellow conspirators, was strangled by the Ottoman authorities in the fortress of Belgrade in May of 1798. If Rigas' achievement in practical terms was nil, none the less his activities alarmed both the Ottoman Porte and the hierarchy of the Orthodox church. The apprehensions of both were further heightened by the French occupation in 1797, with all the panoply of revolutionary 'liberation', of the Ionian Islands, which had hitherto formed part of the Venetian Republic. The occupation of the Ionian Islands and Bonaparte's subsequent invasion of Egypt in 1798 brought the pernicious doctrines of the French Revolution to the very borders of the empire. Moreover, the fact that the Ionian Islands after 1815 constituted, notionally at least, an independent state under British protection afforded a suggestive example of an area of free Greek soil not under Ottoman control.

Although Rigas Velestinlis' achievement was much more symbolic than real, he was to inspire those Greek nationalists who believed that intellectual revival and an increasingly conscious Greek nationalism must be followed up by concrete plans for an armed revolt. The lead in such an undertaking was assumed by three somewhat marginal members of the Greek mercantile Diaspora, Emmanouil Xanthos, Nicholas Skouphas and Athanasios Tsakaloff. These founded in 1814, significantly not within the Greek lands themselves but in Odessa, one of the important centres of the Diaspora, the *Philiki Etairia* or Friendly Society. The Philiki Etairia had but one aim, namely the 'liberation of the Motherland' through an armed and co-ordinated uprising. Strongly influenced by Freemasonry, the Philiki Etairia embraced four categories of membership, who were initiated into the society with elaborate rituals. In its early years the Society made relatively little headway in its efforts to recruit members. From 1818 onwards, however, membership grew apace, particularly among the Greek communities of the Diaspora. From the beginning, the *Arche*, or leadership of the society, sought to cultivate the impression that it enjoyed the blessing of Russia, which the Greeks at large had been nurtured to consider as the most likely external power to emancipate their Orthodox co-religionists. Two attempts were made to prevail upon Count Ioannis Capodistrias, a Corfiote Greek who since 1816 had been the Tsar Alexander I's joint foreign minister and a man thoroughly versed in the ways of international diplomacy, to assume the overall leadership of the conspiracy. Capodistrias, however, considered the whole enterprise to be foolhardy and doomed to failure and counselled instead that the Greeks should await the outcome of the next in the seemingly interminable series of Russo-Turkish wars, when they might aspire to the kind of semi-autonomous status within the

A shadow puppet representing the Klepht leader Theodoros Kolokotronis. In the complicated manoeuvres after the war, Kolokotronis supported the Russian interests, rebelling against King Otto in 1833.

Ottoman empire enjoyed by Serbia. He did not, however, betray the conspiracy and, in 1820, the Society persuaded Prince Alexander Ypsilantis, a Phanariote serving as an aide-de-camp to Tsar Alexander, to assume the supreme leadership of the society. Nothing came of the elaborate schemes engineered by the leadership to stimulate an uprising that would also be supported by the Bulgars and the Serbs, for in many parts of the Balkan peninsula there was a growing resentment at Greek ecclesiastical and cultural hegemony. The Philiki Etairia's chance was to come, however, when in 1820 the Sultan Mahmud II, as part of his policy of seeking to restore the authority of the central government, launched a campaign to destroy the power of Ali Paşa, the *ayan* who controlled much of mainland Greece. Such a campaign would inevitably tie up a substantial part of the Sultan's armies and presented an opportunity that was not to be missed. Ypsilantis, therefore, launched an invasion of the Danubian Principalities across the river Pruth in March 1821, issuing a call to arms with an appropriate invocation of the glories of ancient Greece. He had hoped to exploit a concurrent uprising of the native Rumanian inhabitants of the Principalities against the local *boyars*, or notables. But those who had rallied to the standard of Tudor Vladimirescu showed little enthusiasm for fighting on behalf of Greeks, whom they regarded as quite oppressive as the Ottoman Turks. It was not long, therefore, before Ypsilantis' ragged army of emigré Greeks and students was routed by Ottoman forces at the Battle of Drăgăşani in June and Ypsilantis himself was forced to flee across the borders into the Habsburg empire.

Soon afterwards (the precise degree of co-ordination between the two uprisings is not clear) scattered outbursts of violence culminated in a fully fledged revolt in the Peloponnese, an uprising which was to meet with considerable initial success. The fighting was marked by atrocities committed by both sides and it was not long before the Turks, very much in a minority in this area of the Sultan's domains, retired to their coastal fortresses. To the initial element of surprise, the Greeks' long tradition of klephtic warfare and the rapidity with which their sea-captains were able to gain command of the sea, enabled the insurgents to seize the initiative during the early years of what was to prove a protracted struggle. The news of the uprising, moreover, aroused the enthusiasm of liberal opinion throughout the civilized world and it was not long before foreign philhellene volunteers, the most prominent of whom was Byron, began to arrive to offer their services to the embattled insurgents. These philhellenic volunteers came from a number of countries (a solitary Cuban is recorded) and numbered in their ranks, besides the genuine idealists, a number of do-gooders who saw in Greece a kind of laboratory for their various enthusiasms, together with a sprinkling of downright rogues. Some, indeed, became disillusioned when they discovered that the modern Greeks bore precious little resemblance to the worthies of Periclean Athens. Throughout Europe philhellenic committees were set up to raise money for the Greek cause and to relieve distress and these activities had some limited effect in eventually moving the governments of the Europe of the Holy Alliance, which initially looked upon the revolt with ill-disguised horror, to intervene in the conflict.

The initial successes of the insurgents were soon to raise the question of the governance of the newly acquired. territories. It was not long before three provisional governments came into existence. Early in 1822 a highly democratic constitution was adopted, which reflected the aspirations of the westernizing intelligentsia and which was clearly intended to present an attractive image to enlightened opinion in Europe. It was not, however, until 1823, when a revised constitution was promulgated, that the three local governments were suppressed in favour of a unified central authority. But long before a successful outcome to the war was in sight factionalism began to threaten the whole enterprise. Power in the new central government was contested between rival groups and by 1824 outright civil war between the feuding factions had broken out. The underlying causes of this factionalism, which was to manifest itself during later periods of national crisis, are complex, and during the course of the war political alignments and alliances were in a state of continuous flux. The Peloponnesian *kocabaşis*, or local notables, sought to retain the power and privileges that they had traditionally enjoyed under the Turks, while the klephtic leaders such as Theodoros Kolokotronis were no less determined that their vital military contribution should be rewarded with an appropriate share of political power. The small group of westernizing intellectuals, while they lacked political and military muscle, fought to ensure that Greece was endowed with the trappings of a liberal constitutional state on the European model. The island shipowners, whose contribution to the war at sea was substantial, also demanded their share of the political spoils. Broadly speaking the cleavage can be interpreted in terms of a struggle for power between the 'military' or 'democratic' party, in which the former klephtic leaders represented, if only by default, the interests of the broad mass of the Greek population, and the 'civilian' or 'aristocratic' party. The 'civilian' party was centred on the Peloponnesian primates, the island shipowners and the small group of Phanariot politicians who had gained their political experience under the Ottomans but who had chosen to side with the insurgents.

Another dimension to the cleavage was the confrontation that emerged between the modernizers, largely western-educated and dressing in the western fashion, *alafranga*, and the élites that had hitherto dominated Greek society and whose traditional outlook was reflected in their dress. These westernizers sought to develop a regular army on European lines and were anxious to equip Greece with the full panoply of the institutions of a liberal constitutional state and to place a firm limit on the powers traditionally enjoyed by the Orthodox church. The traditional élites, unlike the westernizers, had no fully articulated national consciousness. Instead they tended to see the war in terms of a religious crusade against the Moslem Turks. They had no concept that they were fighting for political democracy. Rather they were anxious to cling on to their traditional prerogatives and to protect the privileged position that they already enjoyed within Greek society. Essentially they thought in terms of substituting their own oligarchical rule for that of the Turks.

While these political divisions were dividing the insurgents, the military situation took a drastic turn for the worse. For the Sultan Mahmud II, in his determination to crush the Greek rebellion, had enlisted the support of his nominal vassal, Mehmet Ali, the ruler of Egypt, and of his son Ibrahim Paşa. The price demanded for their cooperation was high, but Ibrahim Paşa rapidly established himself in early 1825 in the Peloponnese and began mercilessly to harry the insurgents. With the military position fast deteriorating, the desperate Greeks looked increasingly to the Great Powers for help in resolving the crisis. By this stage of the war, the Powers, each increasingly fearful lest the other should profit from the continuing conflict, and with their commercial interests in the region severely affected, began to move towards a policy of cautious involvement. The Protocol of St Petersburg of 1826 provided for joint British and Russian mediation in the conflict, mediation to which France became a party by the Treaty of London of 1827. This policy, described by Canning, the British prime minister, as one of 'peaceful interference', was to culminate in the destruction by a joint British, Russian and French fleet of the Ottoman and Turco-Egyptian fleets at the Battle of Navarino in October 1827. This decisive, if not entirely planned,

'Mrs Greece and her rough lovers', an English caricature of 1828. Turkey: 'Down on your knees and beg my sublime pardon.' Russia: 'Leave that ugly old ruffian and I'll manage your affairs, my pretty dear.' Greece: 'Oh Lord, gentlemen, I'd rather have nothing to say to either of you.' In the background Britain and France quarrel over the lady. The medal, above right, sees the same situation from the opposite point of view. After the Battle of Neocastro, England, France and Russia raise an exhausted Greece from the ground.

intervention by the Great Powers was to ensure that some form of independent Greece was to come into existence, although it was to be several years before the borders of the new state were fixed and the precise terms of its governance and sovereignty settled. In 1827, a third constitution, again of markedly liberal hue, was enacted at the Assembly of Troezen and Count Capodistrias, who had resigned from the Russian service in 1822, was elected *kyvernitis*, or governor, of the liberated territories. He effectively deployed his very considerable diplomatic skills in negotiating the boundaries of the new state. These ran from Arta in the west to Volos in the east and included a number of the Aegean islands nearest to the mainland. Capodistrias was faced, however, with formidable problems in creating the basic institutions of the state and his refusal to be bound by the 1827 constitution, combined with his paternalist and authoritarian ways, alienated influential groups, including many of those who had been most active in prosecuting the war. Unrest culminated in his assassination in October 1831. Britain, France and Russia, who had taken upon themselves the role of protecting powers, had already decreed that Greece should be ruled by a European prince and their choice lighted on Otto of Wittelsbach, the seventeen-year-old son of King Ludwig of Bavaria.

The new state: aspirations and problems

The inheritance into which Otto entered in 1833 was not a promising one. The territories of the new state had been ravaged by the best part of a decade of intermittent hostilities and Capodistrias' efforts to create the basic institutions of a state where none had hitherto existed had met with only partial success. Most problematic of all, the new nation, with its population of some three-quarters of a million, contained scarcely a third of the Greeks under Ottoman rule. Virtually all the great commercial centres of the empire, Smyrna, Constantinople and Thessalonica, in which Greek merchants had flourished and continued to do so, remained outside its bounds. This had as a consequence that, from the beginning, the *Megali Idea*, or Great Idea, of uniting all the areas of compact Greek population within the Near East, was to dominate the external and, to a substantial degree, the internal politics of the new state. The *Megali Idea* in its extreme form, which envisaged that Constantinople, in the words of the popular ballad, would with the passing of time 'once again be ours', was never in fact to be achieved, although for a time in the early 20th century it did not appear the fantastic dream it does with hindsight. It was to be nearly a century before the borders of Greece more or less reached their present extent. Moreover, during the course of the 19th century Greece's irredentist objectives, which consistently outstripped the physical means at her disposal, were to bring her into frequent conflict with the three 'protecting' Powers who had guaranteed the territorial integrity of the new state in a treaty, to which Greece was not a party, with the Ottoman empire in 1832. A pattern was thus established of Great Power interference in the internal affairs of Greece which has existed until the present day.

As Otto had ascended the throne when he was a minor, until 1835 the country was governed on his behalf by a three-man Bavarian regency. These regents showed little understanding of the aspirations of those Greeks who had actually fought for independence. Moreover, they ignored Greek sensitivities by fashioning the institutions of the new state on the west European model, by importing legal codes and administrative practices wholesale from the west, and by

307

subordinating the state to the civil power, bringing about a breach with the ecumenical patriarchate in Constantinople that was not to be healed until 1850. Even after the *Bavarokratia* or period of Bavarian rule, strictly speaking, had come to an end in 1835, there remained a considerable Bavarian presence in Greece, particularly in the army, a fact that was to cause understandable resentment on the part of the stalwarts of the armed struggle for independence, who felt that their efforts had received insufficient recognition. Many of the irregular troops who had fought in the war refused to be incorporated into a national army commanded by foreigners, and not a few reverted to their traditional occupation of brigandage. Throughout the 19th century brigandage was to constitute a major problem confronting successive governments, although politicians were by no means above contracting alliances with brigands when it proved opportune, particularly when electoral pressure was required in their constituencies.

The settlement by which Greece had emerged as an independent state had provided for Otto to grant a constitution. This he resolutely refused to do. None the less, rudimentary political parties, which found their origins during the period of the struggle for independence, came into existence. Significantly these came to be known as 'English', 'French' and 'Russian' parties and their leaders retained close ties with the respective ministers of the 'protecting' Powers in Athens. The 'English' party attracted the support of those who resented most bitterly Otto's refusal to institute constitutional government. The 'French' party likewise strongly supported constitutionalism but at the same time advocated a forward policy in pursuing Greece's irredentist aims. The 'Russian' party, on the other hand, became the natural focus for the more conservative-minded Greeks, and, in particular, for those who resented the breaking of administrative (but not spiritual) links with the ecumenical patriarchate and who found Otto's failure to convert to Orthodoxy most galling. By the early 1840s there had developed a considerable undercurrent of unrest with Otto's authoritarian style of government. Even if since 1837 the prime minister had always been a Greek, Bavarians continued to hold sensitive positions, and the minister of war, for instance, was a Bavarian. There was growing resentment over Otto's refusal to concede a constitution, which alienated the westernizing intellectuals who had believed that they were fighting for liberal constitutionalism as well as for freedom from the hegemony of the Ottomans. Financial incompetence, onerous tax burdens, and the substantial portion of the state's modest income that was devoted to military expenditure and to the servicing of Greece's foreign debt, added to the groundswell of discontent. Many continued to feel cheated of the recognition and the spoils of office that they considered to be their due. Even those who had no interest in constitutional government were disappointed that Otto had not

converted to Orthodoxy and that he remained without any heir, let alone an Orthodox one.

These various strands of discontent prompted the army to intervene in the bloodless *coup d'état* of 3 September 1843. This was the first of many occasions during Greece's independent history in which the armed forces intervened directly in the political process, although in this case there is considerable evidence that the move enjoyed widespread popular support. As a result Otto was constrained to concede a constitution in 1844 that was, in the context of its times, a remarkably liberal document. Greece, then, from a remarkably early period was equipped with all the trappings of liberal parliamentary democracy, including virtually universal manhood suffrage. From the beginning, however, problems arose from this attempt to graft the forms of western constitutionalism, which had slowly emerged in societies whose historical experience had been radically different from that of Greece, onto a traditional society with very different values from those prevailing in the industrialized or industrializing societies of the west. This tension between democratic forms and traditional practices has manifested itself right up until modern times. From the beginning Otto, ably assisted by the wily Vlach politician Ioannis Kolettis, was able to subvert the new constitution by instituting what amounted to a 'parliamentary dictatorship'. Kolettis' political sleights of hand and the universal resort to *rousfeti* (the dispensing of offices and favours to secure votes, in parliament or in the country at large), combined to alienate a new generation that was entering politics and which had had no direct involvement in the struggle for independence. By the mid-1850s the old political groupings, focused on the 'English', 'French' and 'Russian' parties, had faded away. This new political élite once again began to hold Otto responsible for their frustrations. There had been a brief upsurge in the king's popularity during the Crimean War, when Otto had enthusiastically espoused the irredentist cause and sought, unsuccessfully, to exploit the fact that the Ottoman empire was embroiled with Russia during the Crimean War. But Otto's forward policy prompted an Anglo-French occupation of the Piraeus between 1854 and 1857, one of the most flagrant examples of intervention in Greek affairs by the 'protecting' Powers until the protectorate was formally abolished in 1923. In the aftermath of the Crimean War, however, all the old resentments against Otto that had prompted the 1843 *coup d'état* came to the fore. Following an unsuccessful attempt against Queen Amalia's life, Otto was ousted in a *coup* launched in Athens in October 1862 while he and Queen Amalia were on a tour of the Peloponnese. Otto made no attempt to resist and, following the advice of the representatives of the Powers, he retired to his native Bavaria, where until his death a few years later he manifested a genuine but unrequited affection for his erstwhile subjects, frequently insisting on wearing Greek traditional dress.

A change of dynasty

With the departure of Otto, the Powers were faced with the problem of finding a new monarch for Greece. This was not an easy task for there was no great rush of candidates, given the fate of Otto at the hands of his former subjects. The overwhelming choice of the Greek people themselves was Prince Alfred, the second son of Queen Victoria. But he was ruled out as he belonged to the ruling dynasty of one of the protecting powers. Instead their choice lighted on Prince Christian William Ferdinand Adolphus George of the Danish Glücksburg dynasty, which has intermittently reigned until recent times. He assumed the title of King George I of the Hellenes and throughout his fifty-year reign he was often able to exploit his family connections with many of the ruling dynasties of Europe. His reign began auspiciously with the cession to Greece by Britain of the Ionian Islands, a gesture intended to dampen irredentist fervour. This first accession of territory to the small rump of a Greek state that had come into existence in the early 1830s increased its population by some quarter of a million inhabitants, and led to the incorporation of an area of the Greek lands that had never effectively formed part of the Ottoman empire. In the same year, 1864, a new constitution was promulgated which was even more democratic than that of 1844. It conceded universal adult male suffrage, but women were not to be entitled to vote in national elections until as recently as 1955.

The politics of the early part of George's reign were confused, with political parties, such as existed, revolving around prominent personalities rather than ideologies and engaging in the relentless pursuit of office. For only by acquiring office could politicians hope to satisfy the insatiable demands of their voters-cum-clients. As the 19th-century satirist Emmanuel Roidis aptly put it:

Elsewhere, parties are born because people exist disagreeing, each wanting different things. In Greece, the exact opposite occurs; the cause of party formation and struggle is the admirable accord with which all want the same thing: to be fed at the public expense.

Given the rudimentary state of development of the Greek economy in the 19th century, the state assumed a disproportionate importance as a source of employment, and competition for political power, and hence patronage, was particularly intense, with politicians ever willing to form kaleidoscopic and shifting coalitions in the unceasing pursuit of office. The network of patron–client relationships that permeated 19th-century society and which have continued to be a marked feature of Greek society originally developed as a kind of defence mechanism against the harshness and, above all perhaps, the arbitrariness of Ottoman rule. Greeks felt the need for patrons and protectors to mediate on their behalf with the Ottoman authorities and these kinds of attitudes not only carried over into

The canal across the Isthmus of Corinth, a project mooted since antiquity, was begun in 1881 and finished twelve years later. Together with a railway system, it was a clear sign that Greece had entered the modern world.

the independence period but proved perfectly compatible with the formal institutions of parliamentary democracy. Right up until modern times a parliamentary deputy has seen it not only as an obligation, but as an indispensable pre-condition of political survival, to mediate with a state generally regarded as hostile and an unresponsive bureaucracy on behalf of his voters. Although there was a considerable divergence between the realities and the forms of political life in 19th-century Greece, Greek society was essentially open, and doors were not closed on grounds of social origin alone, while the press enjoyed a freedom that bordered on licence. Few politicians enriched themselves at the public expense. In addition, from the prime minister downwards, they were expected to, and did, make themselves available to the humblest supplicant.

Moreover, during the last quarter of the 19th century the political system took some hesitant steps in the direction of modernization. The turning point came in 1875 when, following a major political crisis, King George was forced to concede the fundamental principle that the formation of a government should be entrusted to whichever politician was able to command the support of the majority in parliament. It was not until 1882, however, that Charilaos Trikoupis, the chief proponent of this principle, known as the *dedilomeni*, was able to form a government. For most of the remaining two decades of the century the essence of a two-party system operated, with Trikoupis alternating in power with his great rival, Theodoros Deliyannis. Trikoupis essentially represented the westernizing element in Greek political life, Deliyannis the traditional. Trikoupis sought to consolidate the Greek state politically and economically before embarking on irredentist adventures. His efforts to establish Greece's international creditworthiness, to improve communications through railway construction and the building of the Corinth canal, and to modernize the army and navy, necessarily involved higher taxation. This in turn afforded an easy target for the demagoguery of Deliyannis, who openly declared that he was against everything that Trikoupis stood for. Deliyannis' populist rhetoric and enthusiastic espousal of the cause of a 'Greater Greece' undoubtedly reflected more faithfully the views of the mass of the Greek electorate at the time but his adventurist policies when in power were to place a severe strain on the economy, as in the case of the abortive mobilization during the Bulgarian crisis of 1885, and were to result in a disastrous defeat during the thirty-day Greek–Turkish war of 1897.

As throughout so much of Greece's independent history, questions of foreign policy tended to dominate the domestic political scene in the last decades of the 19th century. Periodic uprisings in Crete in pursuit of *enosis*, or union with the kingdom, and to a greater or lesser degree supported from Athens, were to place a permanent strain on relations with the Ottoman empire and also occasioned intervention on the part of the Powers. Towards the end of the century, moreover, rivalry between the Greeks, Bulgarians and Serbs over their respective claims to Macedonia was to prove the main focus of Greek foreign policy. Greece had only been marginally involved in the great eastern crisis that had convulsed the Balkans between 1875 and 1878 and had resulted in a crushing defeat for the Ottoman empire at the hands of Russia. As an indirect outcome of the ensuing settlement at the Congress of Berlin, Greece acquired the rich agricultural region of Thessaly, together with the Arta region of Epirus. Greece's frontiers now shifted northwards, bringing the border that much closer to Macedonia, with its inextricably mixed populations of Greeks, Bulgars, Serbs, Vlachs, Turks and Albanians. The Greek effort in Macedonia was for the next thirty years directed as much against the competing nationalisms of the Bulgarians and Serbs as against the Ottoman Turks, who were indeed to exploit these intra-Balkan rivalries. Initially these rivalries manifested themselves in ecclesiastical, educational and cultural propaganda, but from the 1890s onwards all of the parties to the struggle resorted increasingly to violence, which was in turn

supported and subsidized by the governments of the respective motherlands. A further consequence of the Balkan crisis of the 1870s was the acquisition by Great Britain, through the Cyprus Convention of 1878, of the right to administer the predominantly Greek-populated island of Cyprus. Until the Ottoman empire entered the war on the side of the Central Powers in 1914, the island remained under Ottoman sovereignty. In that year, however, Britain formally annexed the island, which acquired the status of a Crown Colony in 1925.

When Deliyannis, seeking to exploit the Bulgarian crisis in 1885, ordered a general mobilization, this in turn led to the imposition of a naval blockade by the Powers. When the Cretans demand for *enosis* had once again in the mid-1890s become insistent, Deliyannis once more responded to popular agitation by mobilizing the country's armed forces. On this occasion, however, Great Power pressure was ineffectual and hostilities broke out between Greece and the Ottoman empire. These resulted in a rapid and humiliating defeat for Greece. The terms of the peace settlement were not, however, onerous. Crete was granted autonomous status, although an International Financial Control Commission was established. This had the task of overseeing the payment of interest on Greece's large external debts, for the Greek government had been forced to declare itself bankrupt in 1893, in the wake of a severe economic crisis which had been precipitated by a collapse in the world price of currants, one of the country's main exports.

The decade following the defeat of 1897 was one of introspection and self-doubt, while, following the death of Trikoupis in 1896, Greek politics reverted to their traditional pattern. The political malaise of the early years of the 20th century was, however, abruptly terminated by the military *coup* of Goudi of 1909, which brought the Military League to the forefront of the political stage. The formation of the Military League reflected various strands of discontent within the armed forces, not least that arising from the blighted promotion prospects of those who did not enjoy the patronage of the royal princes. The Young Turk revolution of 1908 in the Ottoman empire, which was to lead to the deposition of the Sultan Abdul Hamid, had afforded a suggestive precedent, while an economic crisis, coupled with renewed *enosist* agitation in Crete had created a domestic climate in which the Military League's appearance in the political arena appears to have attracted wide popular support. The League's action signified the emergence of the military as a major force in the political life of 20th-century Greece and was but the first of a number of overt military interventions in the political arena.

Although the Military League did not openly assume power, it effectively controlled developments and was instrumental in projecting Eleftherios Venizelos to the forefront of Greek politics. Venizelos had already made his mark on the politics of his native Crete, where he had emerged as a strong champion of the union of the

The break-up of the Turkish empire in the Balkans made the area a constant source of anxiety to the great powers, expressed in this 'Punch' cartoon of October 1912. By the end of 1913, Greece had extended her territory virtually to her present borders. 'Venizelos Triumphant' (far right) is a naive painting expressing the national rejoicing.

THE BOILING POINT.

island with the Kingdom. The fact that he was untainted by association with the politicians of the Kingdom enabled the Military League to step down in his favour without appearing to capitulate to the old political cliques of which it had been so critical. In elections held in 1910 Venizelos secured a massive majority in a parliament empowered to revise the 1864 constitution, a process duly completed in 1911. Once his power had been legitimized through elections Venizelos soon demonstrated that he was no mere puppet of the Military League. The early years of his premiership were distinguished by an ambitious programme of constitutional and social reform, together with a determined effort, as the final struggle over the remaining European territories of the Ottoman empire appeared increasingly imminent, to improve the fighting efficiency of the army and navy. The Italian–Turkish war of 1911 (which resulted in an Italian occupation of the Dodecanese Islands that was to last until 1947) encouraged the Balkan states to combine to drive the Turks out of Europe. Venizelos had certainly absorbed the lesson of the 1897 war, namely that Greece had little chance of success in a single-handed attack on the Ottoman empire and he certainly wished to participate in any scramble for Macedonia. On the other hand he was conscious that the very large Greek populations in Asia Minor were vulnerable to reprisals by an Ottoman government that was becoming increasingly nationalistic.

None the less Greece, under Venizelos' leadership, became an enthusiastic member of the Balkan alliance and joined with Serbia, Bulgaria and Montenegro in launching an attack in European Turkey in October 1912. The Balkan allies, whose alliance was always somewhat fragile, given their mutually irreconcilable territorial claims in Macedonia, made sweeping gains at the expense of the Ottoman armies, over whom they enjoyed a large numerical superiority. Thessalonica, in which Spanish-speaking Sephardic Jews, the descendants of those expelled from Spain in 1492, formed the largest element in the population, was occupied by

Greek troops in November, only a few hours before the arrival of their Bulgarian allies. Greek naval superiority in the Aegean enabled her to liberate the Greek-inhabited islands that remained under Ottoman rule, while the *enosis* of Crete with the Kingdom was formally recognized. Following a temporary cessation of hostilities, the Greek armies were able to push on to capture Jannina and much of Epirus, although northern Epirus, a region long coveted by Greece, was incorporated within the frontiers of the newly independent Albania. The Ottomans were forced to accept the division of the spoils by the Balkan states at the Treaty of Bucharest of August 1913. Bulgaria, however, felt that although she had borne the brunt of the fighting against the Ottoman armies she had been unfairly rewarded in terms of territory. When she turned against her erstwhile allies, the Greeks were able to push on to capture Drama, Serres and Kavala.

Greece's territorial gains as a result of the First and Second Balkan Wars were dramatic. The annexation of the territories that comprised 'New Greece' increased her land area by some seventy per cent, while her population increased by some seventy per cent, from 2,800,000 to 4,000,000. A shadow was cast over this achievement by the assassination by a madman of King George I during a visit to the newly acquired port of Thessalonica in 1913. But when his son, Constantine, succeeded to the throne the old prophecy that the Greeks might once again occupy Constantinople when a Constantine once more ruled over Greece no longer appeared to be beyond the bounds of the possible.

Schism, catastrophe, republic

The reforming impetus of Venizelos' first administration, coupled with Greece's truly spectacular successes during the Balkan wars, had forged an unprecedented degree of unity and national identity on the part of the Greek people, a unity that was demonstrated by Venizelos' winning of 146 out of 181 seats in parliamentary elections held in 1912. Yet the high expectations that had been aroused that Greece was poised to displace the Ottoman empire as the major power in the eastern Mediterranean were to be dashed by the National Schism that was to divide the country into two antagonistic and, at times, warring camps during the First World War, and by the disastrous outcome of her post-war venture into Asia Minor. Greece was to emerge from the First World War and the ensuing catastrophe in Asia Minor a country divided against herself, a fact that was to colour the entire history of the inter-war period.

The first manifestations of this cleavage were the differences that developed in 1914 between Eleftherios Venizelos and King Constantine over Greece's wartime alignment. Venizelos identified himself wholeheartedly with the Entente and believed that French, and particularly British, support was essential to the fulfilment of Greece's remaining irredentist aspirations. King Constantine, on the other hand, believed that Greece's interests would best be served by neutrality, while his opponents charged that his neutralism was influenced by his marriage to a sister of the Kaiser Wilhelm II. But underlying these differences over foreign policy were more profound cleavages. The supporters of Venizelos represented an uneasy alliance between an entrepreneurial middle class, intent on capitalist modernization, and a mass base attracted by Venizelos' identification with social reform and territorial expansion. The supporters of Constantine, on the other hand, reflected an essentially defensive reaction to the interests represented by Venizelos. From the very outbreak of the war, Venizelos sought to commit Greece on the side of the Entente. But the British foreign secretary, Sir Edward Grey, in his anxiety to keep the Ottoman empire and Bulgaria out of the war, was unwilling to embrace the support of a country which had only recently ceased to be engaged in a bitter war with both states.

Even after the Ottoman empire had entered the war Grey was anxious to maintain Greek neutrality. It was for this reason that he proposed to Venizelos that Greece yield up to Bulgaria some of her recently acquired Macedonian territory, offering in return the promise of important, but vague, territorial concessions in Asia Minor. Venizelos was anxious to accept the offer, as indeed he was to commit troops to the ill-fated Dardanelles campaign. When the king began to have doubts about such a commitment Venizelos felt that he had no option but to resign in March 1915. Despite the fact that he was returned to power by a convincing margin in further elections held in June it was not long before Venizelos felt obliged to resign for the second time within six months. On this occasion the differences between Venizelos and the king arose out of their differing interpretations of Greece's obligations to Serbia arising out of her 1913 treaty, now that Bulgaria had aligned herself openly with the Central Powers. Before his departure, however, Venizelos invited Britain and France to land troops in the region of Thessalonica in support of the Serbs, although Greece

was technically to remain neutral. This second resignation, in October 1915, marked the beginning of an irreparable rift between the king and his prime minister. The supporters of King Constantine argued that the crown had traditionally enjoyed a wide discretion in matters of foreign policy. The supporters of Venizelos, on the other hand, maintained that the dismissal of a prime minister enjoying the support of a clear majority in a newly elected parliament was a flagrant breach of constitutional practice. Venizelists were by now convinced that the king was bent on preserving neutrality at all costs, whatever the damage to the country's honour and to constitutional propriety. Constantinists were no less convinced that Venizelos was bent on committing Greece to the Entente cause on one pretext or another. Venizelos now withdrew from political life while relations between the Entente Powers and the royalist government in Athens continued to worsen. A *coup* by Venizelist officers in August 1916 prepared the way for Venizelos to establish his own provisional government of national defence in the city in October. Initially the Entente powers withheld recognition from the Venizelos govenment. But the situation changed after French and British landings in the Athens region to enforce neutrality, perhaps the most blatant of numerous interventions by the Protecting Powers in the internal affairs of Greece, had been rebuffed. France and Britain now instituted a naval blockade of the royalist-controlled areas of Greece, mainly those areas of 'Old' Greece that had formed the heartland of the independent state, and in June of 1917 King Constantine was forced to leave Greece, although he did not formally abdicate. Venizelos now became prime minister of a country that, while it was once again united geographically, remained divided politically, particularly as royalists were the subject of widespread purges.

Once in power Venizelos hastened to commit Greek forces to the Entente cause and these participated in the successful offensive launched on the Macedonian front in September, that contributed decisively to the collapse on the western front. As a further token of his pro-Entente zeal he despatched Greek troops to join in the anti-Bolshevik campaign in Russia. At the Versailles Peace Conference Venizelos, whose charm and diplomatic skill were universally recognized, sought to capitalize on his consistently pro-Entente stand. Even before the peace settlement with the Ottoman government had been agreed, Venizelos received the authorization of Lloyd George, Clemenceau and President Wilson to land Greek troops in Smyrna (Izmir), ostensibly to protect the very substantial local Greek population from Ottoman reprisals but in fact to forestall a possible occupation of the region by Italian troops. For Italy, as well as Greece, had been promised territorial concessions in Asia Minor as an inducement to enter the war. When the peace treaty was finally signed at Sèvres in August 1920, Greece was confirmed in her occupation of the Smyrna region for a period of five years, after which the inhabitants of the region would be able to opt for incorporation either into Greece or Turkey. Greece was also awarded almost all of western and eastern Thrace, while her sovereignty over the Aegean islands captured during the Balkan wars was formally recognized. With Turkey seemingly prostrate, the treaty was greeted with great enthusiasm by Venizelos' supporters who triumphantly proclaimed the creation of a Greater Greece of 'the two continents and of the five seas'. Irredentist triumphs, however, did not prevent Venizelos from suffering a humiliating defeat in elections held in November 1920, at the hands of an electorate that was not only war-weary but also resentful of the arbitrariness of Venizelos' supporters and which identified him with the flagrant breaches of Greece's sovereignty perpetrated by the Entente allies during the war. Venizelos' electoral defeat was the signal for the restoration of King Constantine and a further twist was given to the National Schism by the persecution of Venizelists.

The royalists continued Venizelos' forward policy in Asia Minor despite the fact that the Greek landings had proved the catalyst for a revived Turkish nationalism inspired by Mustafa Kemal (Atatürk). Neither the western allies nor their Greek proxies appear to have had a clear idea as to the likely political and military consequences of Greece's Anatolian entanglement. As Kemal reached an accommodation with the French, Italians and Bolsheviks, Greece found herself increasingly exposed and isolated both diplomatically and militarily. After inconclusive negotiations for a compromise settlement, the Turks in August 1922 launched an offensive which rapidly turned into a total rout of the Greek armies. Smyrna, 'Infidel Smyrna' as it was known by the Turks, was captured and devasted by fire and massacre in which thousands of Christians, Greek and Armenian, perished. The defeated and demoralized Greek armies, accompanied by tens of thousands of panic-stricken and destitute refugees, withdrew to the islands. Thus, with the 'Catastrophe', as it is referred to in Greece, ended a two-and-a-half thousand year presence in Asia Minor. The dream of the *Megali Idea*, or Great Idea, had been irretrievably shattered.

Inevitably, a defeat of this magnitude could not but have major repercussions on Greece's domestic politics. Following the seizure of power by a military junta, King Constantine abdicated, and it was not long before his successor, George II, took the path of exile. In the search for scapegoats, five prominent royalist politicians, including the former prime minister, and the military commander in Asia Minor were sentenced to death by court martial on a charge of high treason, although there was no evidence of wilful treachery. The 'Trial of the Six' was to cast a long shadow over the politics of the inter-war period and was in effect to give the Venizelist/Royalist schism something of the nature of a blood feud. Venizelos was not a member of the revolutionary government but laboured valiantly to salvage what he could from the disaster in the negotiations that culminated in the Treaty of Lausanne in 1923,

by which Greece forfeited almost all the gains that had been enshrined in the Treaty of Sèvres. Agreement was also reached on an exchange of populations between Greece and the new Republic of Turkey. Not only the Greek communities of western Asia Minor, which had been occupied by the Greek army, were expelled, but also those of Pontus, Cappadocia, Lycia and elsewhere, who had been remote from the area of Greek operations. The exchange was based on religion, which produced some odd anomalies. For many of the Orthodox Christians of Asia Minor, for instance, knew no other language than Turkish, while many of the Moslems of Crete spoke only Greek. The massive uprooting of populations, passionately devoted to their ancestral lands, caused untold human misery. On the other hand, the intensity of nationalist passions, which had led to the commission of atrocities by both sides, rendered the centuries-old symbiosis of Christian and Moslem essentially unviable. Only the Greeks of Constantinople, which continued to house the ecumenical patriarchate, and Imbros and Tenedos, straddling the entrance to the Dardanelles, and the Turks of Western Thrace were exempted from the exchange.

The arrival of some 1,300,000 refugees (including significant numbers from Russia and Bulgaria) into a Greece prostrated and virtually bankrupted by war inevitably placed enormous strains on the social and political fabric of the country. Despite the antagonism encountered by many of the refugees on the part of the native inhabitants, the physical problems of their resettlement were resolved with a remarkable degree of success. The last of the remaining large landholdings were distributed among the in-comers, consolidating rural Greece as a society of peasant smallholders. Although indubitably these widely scattered smallholdings militated against agricultural efficiency, Greece was spared the politically de-stabilizing problem of a landless peasantry. Moreover, the refugee influx helped to give the newly acquired territories of Macedonia and Thrace a clear Greek majority, whereas previously Greeks in these territories had been in a minority. Henceforth Greece, by the standards of the Balkans, was without significant minority problems. Those refugees from flourishing urban centres such as Smyrna were to inject welcome entrepreneurial skills into a still much underdeveloped economy, although many of the urban refugees were faced for decades by a hard struggle for existence. While the recently established Communist Party of Greece (KKE) made some headway in recruiting among the uprooted and impoverished refugees, by and large these remained loyal to Venizelos, whom they continued to regard as their liberator, and the refugees, together with the army, acted as the arbiters of Greek political life during the inter-war period. The refugees vote was clearly instrumental in the formal establishment of a republic in 1923 and in the return to power of Venizelos in 1928, following a period of political confusion interrupted by the outright and somewhat absurd military dictatorship

General Ioannis Metaxas held dictatorial power from 1936 to 1941, openly modelling his regime on those of Hitler and Mussolini. He won widespread popularity during the struggle against Italy in 1940.

established by General Pangalos in 1925–6.

The Venizelos government of 1928–32 introduced a needed element of stability. Significant steps were made in improving relations with Italy, with Greece's Balkan neighbours and above all with Turkey, which, despite all the bitterness engendered by the recent past, Venizelos visited in 1930, ushering in two decades of good relations. Significant steps were also made in the direction of greater Balkan cooperation in the face of an increasingly menacing international situation. But Venizelos had no answer to the dire consequences for Greece of the great slump of the 1930s, which hit particularly badly a country dependent to an unusual degree on the export of agricultural products such as olive oil, tobacco and currants and on the remittances of emigrants in the United States. Following elections in 1933, which were won by the anti-Venizelist People's Party, some of Venizelos' supporters, headed by Colonel Nicholas Plastiras, the chief protagonist of the 1922 *coup*, launched a *coup* aimed at restoring him to power. This failed and was followed soon afterwards by a dramatic attempt on Venizelos' life. The increasingly polarized political atmosphere gave rise to talk of a royalist restoration. This in turn promoted a further unsuccessful *coup* by Venizelist officers in March 1935. On this occasion Venizelos was directly implicated and was forced to flee to France where he died soon afterwards.

In the wake of the failed *putsch* the king returned to Greece, following a manifestly rigged plebiscite. Undoubtedly, however, many Greeks hoped that the restoration of the monarchy would lead to a greater political stability, while the king himself appears to have returned to the country from his twelve-year exile in Britain genuinely determined to act as a conciliator.

But the elections, held in early 1936 under a system of straightforward proportional representation, which the king had hoped would resolve the crisis, had the opposite effect. For they resulted in a disastrous deadlock, with the Communist-controlled Popular Front, with fifteen seats (in a three-hundred-seat parliament) holding the balance between the evenly matched Venizelist and royalist blocs. Each of the main *parataxeis*, or political camps, negotiated with the Communists, who had hitherto been very much on the margin of Greek political life. Public disillusionment grew apace when it was revealed that both sides had been negotiating with the far left and this facilitated the rise to power of General Ioannis Metaxas, who succeeded the non-political caretaker prime minister, Constantine Demertzis, who died at a critical juncture in the crisis. Metaxas managed to persuade the king that a threatened general strike in early August 1936 was the prelude to a Communist bid to seize power. The king was prevailed upon to agree to a suspension of key articles of the constitution on 4 August 1936. These measures, in theory at least, were temporary. But Metaxas soon made clear his intention to rule the country as a dictatorship and parliament was not to convene for a further ten years.

Dictatorship, occupation, civil war

Once installed in power, and enjoying the benevolent toleration of the king and of the army, and, initially at least, the acquiescence of the population at large, Metaxas was able to vent his spite against the parliamentary system in general and Greek politicians in particular, and to attempt to refashion the Greek character in conformity with what he termed 'the serious German spirit'. Although he shared to the full the contempt felt by Hitler and Mussolini for liberalism, Communism and democracy, Metaxas' nationalism was neither aggressive nor racially inspired. Moreover the ideological basis of his regime was transparently thin. In conscious imitation of Hitler's Third Reich, he developed the concept of the Third Hellenic Civilization, the first being the pagan civilization of ancient Greece, the second the Christian civilization of Byzantium. The third, to be fashioned by Metaxas, was in some way to reconcile and synthesize the contradictory values of both and to perpetuate his essentially paternalist and authoritarian style of government. In keeping with his populist, anti-plutocratic rhetoric, which was frequently belied by the practice, he styled himself 'National Father', 'First Peasant' and 'First Worker'. For all his admiration for Fascist regimes, Metaxas, influenced by the king, showed no inclination to steer his country away from the traditional British connection. Indeed, in 1938, he offered to conclude a formal treaty with Britain. This was turned down, although Britain in April 1939 did offer Greece a guarantee of her territorial integrity in the wake of the Italian invasion of Albania.

On the outbreak of the Second World War Metaxas

struggled to preserve his country's neutrality, while making clear his sympathies towards Britain. Greece, however, came under increasing pressure from an Italy anxious to demonstrate that she could match Hitler's victories in Poland and the west. Even when an Italian submarine torpedoed the cruiser *Elli* while it was anchored off the island of Tinos in honour of the Feast of the Dormition (Assumption) of the Virgin on 15 August 1940, Metaxas chose not to respond. But he could not, and did not, ignore a humiliating ultimatum delivered by the Italian ambassador in the early hours of 28 October 1940. In rejecting this ultimatum out of hand Metaxas reflected the refusal of the overwhelming majority of the Greeks to capitulate to Italian bullying. In a great wave of national exaltation the Greek people, despite their political divisions, united in the common struggle against the invaders. The Italian advance was soon checked and within weeks the Greek army had pushed deep in Albanian territory, occupying most of the region of 'northern Epirus' to which Greece had long-standing territorial claim. Even if the disparity in men and equipment between the two sides was not as great as it seemed at the time, the 'Albanian epic' afforded a stirring example of a small state successfully resisting the Axis juggernaut at a particularly dark period of the Second World War. Until his death in January 1941 Metaxas struggled to avoid provoking German intervention but it became increasingly obvious that the Germans were in any case determined to extend their control of much of the Balkan peninsula to Greece. Metaxas' successor therefore agreed to the despatch of a British expeditionary force (primarily composed of Australians and New Zealanders). This was sent more out of a sense of *noblesse oblige* than with any realistic hope of stemming the German tide. And indeed the combined Greek and British forces were unable to put up more than a brief resistance to the German invasion when it came in April 1941. Within a matter of weeks the country, including Crete, captured after a daring German airborne landing, was overrun and a harsh tripartite German, Italian and Bulgarian occupation established. The requisitioning of food stocks rapidly resulted in a terrible famine and huge inflation, while Greece's Jewish population was virtually wiped out during the course of the occupation.

From the very earliest days of the occupation, however, resistance to the occupiers was to manifest itself. Although the Communists had taken an ambiguous attitude towards the German and Italian invasions, they were to take the lead in organizing this resistance, while seeking to maintain the appearance of a broadly based anti-Axis coalition. A National Liberation Front (EAM) was created, together with its military arm known by the initials ELAS, both under the control of the Communist party. A number of much smaller non-Communist groups, the most significant of which was known by the initials EDES, came into being. Much the largest of these groups was EAM, which by the end of the occupation numbered some

two million supporters. Whether of Communist or non-Communist inspiration, virtually all these groups, however, shared a common antipathy towards the exiled King George II, who was held responsible both for the Metaxas dictatorship and the horrors of the ensuing occupation. With the assistance of a military mission parachuted into Greece by the British authorities in the Middle East, some spectacular acts of resistance were accomplished but almost from the beginning the disunity that had characterized the Greeks at criticial junctures in their post-independence history began to manifest itself. For it soon became clear that the Communist leadership of EAM/ELAS, besides organizing resistance against the Axis, was also bent on assuming power on liberation. This brought it into opposition not only with anti-Communist Greeks but with the British authorities, who, for much of the war, were determined to ensure the eventual return of King George II. In pursuit of its ultimate objective, EAM/ELAS sought to monopolize the resistance and, during the winter of 1943–4, outright civil war broke out in the mountains of 'Free Greece' between ELAS and the much smaller EDES. British support, however, prevented EDES from being overrun and British mediation restored a fragile peace to the mountains. By the summer of 1944 it was clear that the liberation of the country was imminent. It was equally clear that this was likely to be accompanied by a furious struggle for power between EAM/ELAS and their opponents, republican and royalist.

As so often in the past, however, the course of events in Greece was to be determined not so much by the balance of forces within the country as by the complexities of Great Power relations. For Churchill, with his strong commitment to the cause of the king and his fear lest a Communist-controlled Greece might interrupt Britain's vital communications with the Middle East and India, became increasingly haunted by the fear of a Communist take-over. For this reason he was prepared to come to an agreement with Stalin over the division of the Balkans into Russian and British spheres of influence. The essence of the agreement was reached in May 1944 and was finalized by Churchill and Stalin at their Moscow meeting of October 1944. In return for Stalin's consent to a 90 per cent British preponderance in Greece, Churchill was prepared to allow a 90 per cent Soviet preponderance in Romania and a 75 per cent preponderance in Bulgaria, two countries the control of which, unlike Greece, Stalin regarded as vital to Soviet security interests. The precise interpretation of this agreement is the subject of continuing debate, but Churchill always considered that Stalin had kept his word in giving Churchill what he termed 'freedom of action' in Greece. Although the evidence is not conclusive it would seem that Stalin, true to the spirit of this unusual deal, ordered the KKE not to make an outright bid for power in the autumn of 1944 as the Germans began their final withdrawal from the country. As it was, the left overcame its original reluctance

12.OKTωBPIOV 1944

A woodcut by the painter Spiros Vassiliou celebrating the return to Greece of the government of national unity in October 1944.

and entered the government of national unity that returned to Greek soil in October 1944.

But in effect the seemingly inevitable conflict between Communists and anti-Communists, whose rivalry now overlaid the older division between Venizelists and anti-Venizelists, had merely been postponed. For within a matter of weeks of the triumphal return of a government of national unity under the leadership of the Venizelist George Papandreou fierce fighting had broken out in Athens between the forces of ELAS on the one hand and the small forces at the command of the government of national unity, backed up by the British troops that had accompanied it to Greece on liberation, on the other. Churchill had always been anxious that there should be a British military presence in Greece in view of his fears of a Communist take-over. The occasion of the clash was a failure to reach agreement as to the terms under which ELAS, which represented a formidable fighting force and was in physical control of much of the country, would agree to disarm. What the Communist leadership had in mind in launching the insurgency is not clear. For, despite the preponderance of ELAS in much of the remainder of Greece, its onslaught was restricted to the Papandreou government in Athens. What the leadership of the left seems to have had in mind is not so much an outright seizure of power as an attempt to destabilize the Papandreou government and, in particular, to remove the wily and fiercely anti-Communist Papandreou from office, so as to pave the way for a constitutional or quasi-constitutional accession to power. But Churchill, whose obsession with Greek affairs is strikingly illustrated by his impulsive and dangerous trip to Athens on Christmas Eve 1944 in a basically unsuccessful attempt to mediate in the crisis, was determined to thwart any such bid. Gradually, as reinforcements that could be ill-

spared from the Italian front poured into Athens, the British secured the upper hand, although the Varkiza agreement of February 1945, which ended the insurgency, was relatively generous to the left.

The Varkiza agreement was to provide only a temporary respite from the impending clash between left and right. For it was followed by a right-wing backlash against the left. This, in turn, had been fuelled by the barbarous treatment of hostages taken by the ELAS forces during the December fighting. A series of governments, effectively controlled by the British authorities, proved incapable of controlling the climate of terror and the left, in protest, boycotted the elections held in March 1946, the first elections to be held since 1936. Given the highly polarized state of Greek politics at this time, the sweeping victory gained by elements grouped around the right-wing and pro-royalist People's Party is not surprising. Nor was the very substantial vote for the return of King George to Greece in a plebiscite held in September 1946. The elections and the plebiscite, neither of which could be regarded as a true test of public opinion, did nothing to check the disastrous slide towards civil strife during the summer of 1946. A critical stage was reached with the establishment in October of the Communist-controlled Democratic Army. The left was now clearly engaged in an outright bid for power by armed force.

Support from Greece's Communist neighbours, Yugoslavia, Bulgaria and Albania, enabled the Democratic Army to engage in an effective guerilla war leading to the control of large areas of northern Greece. But, despite repeated efforts, the Democratic Army was unable to hold any substantial town near the country's northern borders which might act as the seat of a provisional government. This did not inhibit, however, the establishment in December 1947 of a Provisional Democratic Government of Greece, headed by Markos Vaphiadis, who during the occupation had been a prominent ELAS leader. None of the eastern bloc countries, however, recognized the provisional government. Moreover, the aid which the Democratic Army received from its Communist neighbours to the north was much more than matched by the aid which the national government, for most of the war a coalition between centre and right-wing politicans, received from the United States. For, in March 1947, with the enunciation of the Truman Doctrine, the United States assumed the protectorate over Greece that had hitherto been traditionally exercised by Britain. American involvement resulted in a massive build-up of military and economic aid to a Greece ravaged by occupation and civil war. The flow of military equipment, the advice of American military advisers and the total control which it enjoyed of the air, gradually enabled the national government to turn the tide against the Democratic Army. Moreover, internal dissension undermined the military potential of the insurgent army. Its commander, Markos Vaphiadis, who advocated the tried methods of guerilla warfare, was

Andreas Embiricos, born 1901, lived in Paris between the wars and joined the Surrealist movement, writing poems and short prose pieces, often erotic in content, exploring the unconscious in rich, dream-like imagery. His collection called 'Personal Mythology' was published in 1960, with drawings by Minos Argyrakis.

purged by Nikos Zakhariadis, the secretary-general of the KKE, who favoured organization on traditional military lines. As the situation worsened, the KKE advocated, as it had done to its cost during the inter-war period, the establishment of an autonomous Macedonia, which could be established only by detaching Greek territory. A further blow to the insurgents was the closing of the frontier with Yugoslavia in the summer of 1949, after the KKE had sided with Moscow in the split with Belgrade. This cut the insurgents off from their primary source of logistic support. By the summer of 1949 an increasingly better trained and better equipped National Army had penned the Democratic Army against the Grammos–Vitsi range, on the Albanian border. By the autumn the defeated remnants of the army had fled into exile in eastern Europe and the Soviet Union.

A changing society

Despite the difficulties experienced in achieving stable and acceptable government, the processes of economic, social and cultural change that had begun in the period between the wars continued after the Second World War and were, in the end, to transform Greece. The refugees of 1922 from Asia Minor were not only successfully absorbed, but emerged as a lively professional middle class – something that had previously been largely lacking in Greek society. The skill and experience which many brought with them helped to develop and diversify the economy and to enlarge the country's cultural horizons. New opportunities drew men and women from the villages to the rapidly expanding cities. The role of agricultural exports in the foreign trade of Greece diminished, while that of shipping, tourism and mining increased. The old

locally based patron–client relations began to break down, and, in the seventies, new, ideologically orientated political parties with a mass basis began to arise.

Greek culture became more self-assertive, freeing itself from dependence on foreign models. National sources and their relation to Byzantine and popular traditions were re-examined and revalued. Literature, perhaps the most important and most distinctive cultural activity of Greece, had first to come to terms with the complex problem of the language: disputes continued between those who clung to the conservative 'purist' Greek (*katharevousa*) and those who championed demotic Greek, the ordinary language of the man in the street. It was the latter which prevailed, and for the first time new and highly accomplished writers emerged who won recognition and acclaim outside Greece itself.

In poetry, the seminal influences were folksongs and ballads, the great 19th-century poets Dionysios Solomos and Kalvos, and the early 20th-century Alexandrian Constantine Cavafy. The 1930s saw the emergence of a great number of remarkable and diverse poets whose work came to be widely appreciated both in Greece and abroad after the war. These included Costis Palamas (the most important poet before the war, he died during the German occupation of Greece), Angelos Sikelianos, Costas Varnalis, George Seferis (who received the Nobel Prize in 1961), Andreas Embiricos, Nikos Engonopoulos, Takis Papatsonis, Yanis Ritsos and Odysseus Elytis, who in 1981 became the second Greek poet to receive the Nobel Prize within twenty years.

The same period saw the maturity of the Greek novel. Nikos Kazantzakis is the best-known novelist

317

Constantine Cavafy, 1863–1933, became the best known of modern Greek poets internationally, in spite of his relatively sparse output and in spite of having spent all his life outside Greece, in Alexandria. His poems are both intensely personal and intensely conscious of the presence of history. This etching from his love poems is by Yannis Tsaruchis.

outside Greece, but others too – George Theotokas, Stratis Myrivilis, Elias Venezis, Angelos Terzakis, Stratis Tsirkas, Pantelis Prevelakis and their younger successors – all offered in their various ways a sensitive and critical reflection of Greek society in the process of change.

Yannis Ritsos is perhaps the most important, as well as being among the most prolific and popular, poets of the present generation. A Communist, he suffered years of 'internal exile' under the Colonels. It was during this time that he wrote 'The Poet's Profession' (below) with its dark allusions to atrocities, in his fine Byzantine script. He is also an artist, using natural objects such as stones (right) to evoke the classical past.

Τό ἐπάγγελμα τῦ ποιητῦ

Στό διάδρομο οἱ ὀμπρέλες, οἱ γαλόσες, ὁ καθρέφτης.
μές στόν καθρέφτη τό παράθυρο πιό ἥσυχο κάπως.
στό παράθυρο ἡ πύλη τῦ ἀντικρυνῦ νοσοκομείν. Ἐκεῖ
ὁλόκληρη σειρά οἱ ἀνυπόμονοι, γνωστοί αἱμοδότες-
οἱ πρῶτοι ἔχουν συνωθίσει κιόλας τά μανίκια τους
ἐνῶ ὁλη μέσα νύχτα νόμαρες οἱ πέντε τραυματίες εἶναι νεκροί.

Ἀθήνα. 30. ΙΙΙ. 72.

The composers Nikos Skalkottas (although barely known in his lifetime), Yannis Xenakis, Manos Hadzidakis and Mikis Theodorakis, and the film director Theodore Angelopoulos have also brought Greek themes before international audiences.

Crisis and resolution: a near balance

Greece emerged from the 1940s a country ravaged by war, occupation and civil war, with its economy and transport system in ruins. Serious work in the direction of reconstruction got under way only after the establishment in 1952 of a stable right-wing government under Marshal Papagos. The style of the Papagos government (1952–5) and of its equally conservative successor (1955–63), headed by Constantine Karamanlis, was distinctly authoritarian in character although it was during this period that the foundations were laid for the astonishingly high rate of economic growth that has characterized the Greek economy during the period since the end of the Civil War. This development may have been unbalanced, with serious inequalities in the distribution of the country's growing prosperity, but none the less the living standards, together with the expectations, of the great mass of the Greek people increased spectacularly. The bulk of investments in Greece during this period were channelled into the service industries and into property development, with frequently deleterious consequences for the country's physical environment. Tourism began to assume an ever increasing importance to the economy so that by the 1980s some two tourists visited Greece for every three of the native inhabitants of the country. Many Greeks, in their search for material stability, either took the traditional road of emigration beyond the Greek borders or moved from the villages to the towns, which grew at a remarkable pace. By the 1980s a third of Greece's total population of nine million was concentrated in the area of Greater Athens.

It was during the 1950s that the demand of the Cypriots for the *enosis*, or union, of the island with mainland Greece reached a critical stage. British refusal initially even to contemplate the possibility of self-determination, and a growing interest on the part of the

Turkish government in the fate of the Turkish minority on the island, which constituted some eighteen per cent of the total population, together with a violent terrorist campaign on the island waged by General Grivas, all contributed to a crisis of growing intensity. The outcome of this in 1960 was not *enosis*, but the establishment of an independent state of Cyprus, the powers of whose president, Archbishop Makarios, were circumscribed by a complicated and essentially unworkable constitution. Independence was to bring only a temporary peace to the island, for within three years the 1960 constitutional settlement had broken down and relations between the Greek and Turkish communities had become increasingly antagonistic.

By the early 1960s there were clear signs that many Greeks hankered after a more liberal style of government as the bitterness that was the inevitable consequence of a hard-fought civil war began to fade. This changing political climate was reflected in the victory of George Papandreou's Centre Union in the elections of November 1963, following which Constantine Karamanlis, whose eight-years premiership had been the longest since Greece became an independent state, went into a self-imposed exile. In further elections, held a few months later in February 1964, Papandreou substantially increased his majority and embarked on a cautious programme of reform. Within fifteen months, however, the septuagenarian Papandreou had become embroiled in a major constitutional conflict with the young King Constantine II, who had succeeded his father Paul in 1964, and who now refused to allow Papandreou to take over the Ministry of Defence. The crisis of July 1965, the forced resignation of George Papandreou and the ensuing split in the Centre Union party gave rise to a period of intense political instability, which in turn afforded the pretext for the mounting of a *coup d'état*, on 21 April 1967, by a small group of ultra right-wing officers. The pretext for the *coup* was the non-existent threat of a Communist take-over. The immediate purpose of the conspirators was to forestall the holding of elections which had at last been agreed as affording the only way out of a political impasse that had more than a passing similarity with that which immediately preceded the establishment of the Metaxas dictatorship in 1936. It appeared likely that George Papandreou would be returned to power and that the group of radical Centre Union deputies centred on his son, Andreas Papandreou, would enjoy an increasing influence. The Colonels, as the regime came to be known, were at all costs anxious to avoid such an eventuality. Unlike most previous military interventions in the political arena in Greece, the Colonels were not acting on behalf of a particular group of politicians or of the king. It soon became clear that they were anxious to maintain a tight grip on power for themselves.

In the context of Greece's post-war political development, the military regime of 1967–74 has a peculiarly anachronistic flavour, representing as it did an attempt to stem the tides of social and political change. Although the 'Regime of the 21 April 1967' sought to develop an ideology of its own, this was but a reflection of the sterile mix of authoritarianism and paternalism that had been offered by Metaxas. The predominant elements in what passed for its ideology were a virulent anti-Communism, an undisguised contempt for politicians across the political spectrum and a populist rhetoric that was persistently belied by economic policies that clearly favoured business interests and foreign capital. In gratitude for the concessions extended to them, the Association of Greek Shipowners, for instance, made the leader of the 'revolution', Colonel George Papadopoulos, president for life of their association. If, as in 1936, the regime initially enjoyed a measure of acquiescence on the part of those wearied by the seeming inability of the politicians to resolve their differences, the unpopularity of the regime soon became apparent. Any manifestations of open opposition were efficiently and brutally repressed. The essential bankruptcy of the regime was demonstrated by the savage suppression by the army of a sit-in at the Athens Polytechnic in November 1973, which resulted in 34 deaths. Although by this time it was clear that the regime manifestly had no basis in popular support, it was not brought down by pressure from below. Rather, the Colonel's regime collapsed under the weight of its own incompetence in July 1974. This collapse was precipitated by an ill-judged attempt to overthrow Archbishop Makarios as president of Cyprus and thus bring about the *de facto*, if not *de jure, enosis* of the island with Greece. This crude move gave the Turkish government precisely the pretext it needed, as one of the guarantor powers of the 1960 constitutional settlement, to invade the island, ostensibly to protect the Turkish minority. Although this minority numbered only some eighteen per cent of the population, the Turkish army occupied almost forty per cent of the most productive regions on the island. After an attempted mobilization on the part of the military regime had collapsed in chaos, and with Greece totally isolated internationally, a section of the army, including General Gizikis, whom the Junta had appointed president, together with a group of civilian politicians called on Constantine Karamanlis to return from his eleven-year exile in Paris to salvage what he could from the crisis and to oversee the process of return to democratic government.

The problems facing Karamanlis were manifold. His immediate task was to defuse the real risk of an outright war between Greece and Turkey and to ensure that an army that had, for seven-and-a-half years, enjoyed the fruits of power, not only returned to the barracks but that it stayed there. In this immensely difficult task he was armed only by his great prestige and moral authority. Responding to a wave of anti-American feeling, arising from the perception of most Greeks that it had been the US administration that had been the main external support of a brutal, inefficient and unpopular regime and that the US had manifestly failed to stem the invasion of Greek-inhabited territory by one of Greece's NATO allies, he withdrew Greece from the military command-structure of the alliance. In a striking departure from his authoritarian style of the 1950s and early 1960s he now legalized the Communist Party, which in 1968 had split in two, the KKE and the much smaller Communist Party of the Interior.

When he sought to legitimize his power by holding elections in November 1974 it is not surprising that he should have won a substantial majority of the popular vote. For many Greeks, of all political persuasions, saw in him the best and, indeed, the only guarantor against a return of the tanks. Immediately after the elections he held a plebiscite on the constitutional issue which resulted in a substantial vote (sixty-nine per cent) against a return of King Constantine, who had been in exile since 1967. Greece's poor relations with Turkey, arising partly out of the continuing Turkish occupation of northern Cyprus and partly out of a complex of bilateral problems caused by conflicting claims in the Aegean, and her poor relations with the United States, for the previous thirty years Greece's principle external patron, made Karamanlis seek compensation in accelerating Greece's accession to the European Community. Greece already had a treaty of association with the EEC dating back to 1961. The reasons underlying the Greek wish for entry were at once economic, political and psychological. For it was argued that membership would bring with it not only economic benefits but would also serve to consolidate Greece's newly found economic freedoms and to provide protection against the Turkish threat. It would, moreover, legitimize Greece beyond doubt as a 'European' country. Karamanlis' drive for membership met with a successful outcome, with the signing in May 1979 of Greece's Treaty of Accession to the European Community, which provided for full membership in January 1981.

During the years following the downfall of the Colonels' regime, Karamanlis' attention was focused primarily on the various external problems facing Greece, with the country's manifest social and economic difficulties taking second place. The political opportunity this afforded was cleverly exploited by Andreas Papandreou who, on his return to Greece, had founded a new political party, the Panhellenic Socialist Movement (PASOK), whose centrist antecedents were apparent but which held out the prospect of radical socialist transformation. Following the collapse of the traditional centre in the elections of 1977, PASOK emerged as the principal opposition party. Papandreou's idiosyncratic form of populist socialism, enshrined in the slogan *Allagi* or 'Change', was allied to a vociferously proclaimed determination to break the cycle of dependence and foreign interference that had bedevilled so much of Greece's independent history. This combination proved increasingly attractive to those Greeks, particularly perhaps the recent migrants to the towns, who felt excluded from the country's burgeoning prosperity and who were most immediately affected by inadequate education, welfare and health provision. Papandreou's manifest ability to articulate not only the aspirations, but also the frustrations, of what he termed the 'non-privileged' Greeks was reflected in his sweeping victory in the elections of 1981. The rival New Democracy party, headed by George Rallis after Karamanlis had himself elected president in May 1980, proved unable to match Papandreou's charismatic appeal. 1981, then, saw two developments of major importance for Greece: her entry into the European Community as the tenth member and the election of the first socialist government in the country's history. Whether the high expectations of many Greeks aroused by either or both of these events would be fulfilled remained to be seen. But at least it could be said that Greece's democratic institutions had seemingly been established on a firmer footing than at any time in its post-independence history.

Fotis Kontoglou, writer and painter, saw the unchanging Greek landscape in terms of a continuing Byzantine tradition. 'Taygetos' is from his 'Travels in Greece', published in 1928.

Prologue: Land and People

General Studies: A. Philippson, *Die griechischen Landschaften*, 4 vols. (Frankfurt, 1950–59) is the most detailed descriptive and interpretative geography of Greece; it is by a distinguished historical geographer. A modern study of the whole Mediterranean region can be found in P. Birot and J. Dresch, *La Méditerranée et le Moyen-Orient*, 2 vols. (Paris, 1964). For a general introduction dealing with the classical and Hellenistic periods, see M. Cary, *The Geographical Background of Greek and Roman History* (London, 1949). J. L. Myres, *Geographical History in Greek Lands* (Oxford, 1953) is a discussion of particular historical problems of antiquity. See also B. G. Spyridonakis, *Essays on the Historical Geography of the Greek World in the Balkans during the Turkokratia* (Thessalonica, 1977). B. Kayser, *Social and Economic Atlas of Greece* (Athens, 1964) contains useful material on modern Greece. A still valuable study of the formation of nations in south-eastern Europe is J. Ancel, *Peuples et nations des Balkans* (Paris, 1925). A. Philippson, *Das griechische Klima* (Bonn, 1948) is a major study of climatic conditions and variations and their effects.

Studies of particular areas or problems: R. Carpenter, *Discontinuity in Greek Civilisation* (Cambridge, 1966) is a study of the possible influence of climatic changes. For a detailed study of population movements, see Hélène Antionadis-Bibicou, 'Villages désertes en Grèce – un bilan provisoire', in *Villages désertes et histoire économique, XIe–XVIIIe siècles* (Paris, 1965), pp. 343–417. N. P. Diamandouros and others (eds.), *Hellenism and the First Greek War of Liberation (1821–1830): Continuity and Change* (Thessalonica, 1976), pp. 19–58, discusses land and people at the birth of the Greek state. The most detailed study of a particular region is E. Y. Kolodny, *La Population des îles de Grèce: essais de géographie insulaire en Méditerranée orientale*, 2 vols. (Aix-en-Provence, 1974). R. V. Schoder, *Ancient Greece from the Air* (London, 1974) contains striking photographs of different types of Greek landscape. W. B. Turrill, *The Plant-Life of the Balkan Peninsula* (Oxford, 1929) is a thorough geographical study of the Balkan area, including Greece. A. Jardé, *Les Céréales dans l'antiquité grecque* (Paris, 1925) discusses the cultivation and processing of cereals in Greece in antiquity. For a useful guide to the identification of Greek plants, with excellent colour photographs, see A. Huxley and W. Taylor, *Flowers of Greece and the Aegean* (London, 1977).

1   The Age of the Heroes

P. M. Warren, *The Aegean Civilisations* (Oxford, 1975) and A. W. Johnston, *The Emergence of Greece* (Oxford, 1976), two volumes of the series 'The Making of the Past', give a stimulating introduction to the periods. See also M. I. Finley, *Early Greece: the Bronze and Archaic Ages* (2nd ed., London, 1981), which is selective and critical. A conspectus of two generations of earlier scholarship can be found in *The Cambridge Ancient History* (3rd ed., Cambridge, 1973–5), vol. I.2, especially Chapter xxvi(a) 'Greece, Crete and the Aegean islands in the Early Bronze Age' by J. L. Caskey and vol. II.1–2. C. Renfrew, *The Emergence of Civilisation* (London, 1972) is a pioneer effort to bring a wider range of approaches into Aegean archaeology; J. T. Hooker, *Mycenaean Greece* (London, 1977) is exceptional for its readiness to question the comfortable assumptions of Aegean prehistorians. The new possibilities of Aegean island archaeology are exemplified by J. L. Davis and J. F. Cherry (eds.), *Papers in Cycladic Prehistory* (Los Angeles, 1979), and an important test case is discussed in C. Renfrew and M. Wagstaff (eds.), *An Island Polity: the Archaeology of Exploitation in Melos* (Cambridge, 1982). P. P. Betancourt, 'The end of the Greek Bronze Age' in *Antiquity* 50 (1976), pp. 40–47, is one of the more credible accounts of Mycenaean decline. A. M. Snodgrass, *The Dark Ages of Greece* (Edinburgh, 1971) covers the period of the next two titles, with some attention to the historical implications. V. R. Desborough, *The Greek Dark Ages* (London, 1972) and J. N. Coldstream, *Geometric Greece* (London, 1977) set out the archaeological evidence in greater detail than Snodgrass. They cover the 11th/10th and the 9th/8th centuries BC respectively. See also A. J. Toynbee, *The Greeks and their Heritages* (Oxford, 1981).

2   Between the Persian Wars and Alexander

For a general view of the period and an outline of events, see: *The Cambridge Ancient History*, vol. V: *Athens, 479–401 BC* and vol. VI: *Macedon 401–301 BC* (Cambridge, 1927); E. Will, *Le Monde grec et l'Orient*, vol. I: *Le Vème siècle* (Paris, 1972) and (with C. Mossé and P. Goukowsky), *Le IVème siècle et L'époque hellénistique*, 2 vols. (Paris, 1975).

On the institutions of the state and political history: V. Ehrenberg, *The Greek State* (2nd ed., London, 1969) is essential reading on the Greek states as a whole. **On Athenian institutions**, see C. Hignett, *A History of the Athenian Constitution* (Oxford, 1958), which traces the evolution of the Athenian constitution from its beginnings to the 4th century BC. W. R. Connor, *The New Politicians of 5th century Athens* (Princeton, 1971) throws light on the crucial period of the Peloponnesian War in the political history of Athens. M. H. Hansen, *The Sovereignty of the People's Court in Athens in the 4th century BC* (Odense, 1974) analyses the role of the People's Court in the political life of 4th-century Athens. P. J. Rhodes, *The Athenian Boule* (Oxford, 1972) discusses one of the central institutions of Athenian democracy. **On Sparta**, three works stand out from a mass of publications. For the principal stages of Sparta's history, see W. G. Forrest, *A History of Sparta 950–192 BC* (London, 1968). P. Cartledge, *Sparta and Lakonia. A Regional History* (London, 1979) excellently addresses the central issues. On the difficulties posed by the special character of Spartan society, see P. Oliva, *Sparta and her Social Problems* (Prague, 1971).

On social and economic life, see M. Austin and P. Vidal-Naquet, *Economic and Social History of Ancient Greece* (London, 1977), which looks at the range of problems posed by Greek societies, with a selection of texts. G. E. M. de Ste. Croix, *The Class Struggle in the Ancient Greek World* (London, 1981) is a survey which uses Marxist analysis to explain the evolution of the Greek world. M. I. Finley, *The Ancient Economy* (London, 1973) is a remarkable examination of the problems faced by modern historians attempting to understand the economic systems of antiquity; the same author's *Ancient Slavery and Modern Ideology* (London, 1979) is an account of the controversies surrounding the study of slavery in the ancient world; and his *Economy and Society in Ancient Greece* (London, 1981) is a collection of articles by one of the greatest contemporary historians.

On the 'crisis' of the 4th century, see C. Mossé, *Athens in Decline* (London, 1976).

3   Thinking about the cosmos

This highly selective list of books covers many aspects of the subject which have had to be omitted from the chapter.

General: the whole period is comprehensively studied by W. K. C. Guthrie, *A History of Greek Philosophy* (Cambridge, 1962–82). Vols. i–iii deal with pre-Platonic philosophy and Socrates; iv and v with Plato, and vi with Aristotle. Guthrie offers a judicious and elegant account with copious references to scholarly controversies. For a view of the subject in relation to the history of science, see S. Sambursky (a physicist by early training), *The Physical World of the Greeks* (2nd ed., London, 1960) and G. E. R. Lloyd, *Early Greek Science, Thales to Aristotle* (London, 1970). The latter's *Magic, Reason and Experience* (Cambridge, 1979) is a detailed study of the origins and development of Greek science, which considers the methodological issues touched on in the last pages of this chapter.

Presocratic Philosophy: my references are to the 'B' sections of Diels-Kranz, *Die Fragmente der Vorsokratiker*, 6th ed. onwards. G. S. Kirk and J. E. Raven, *The Presocratic Philosophers* (2nd ed., Cambridge, 1983) is an historical review based on the original texts, which are translated. E. Hussey, *The Presocratics* (London, 1972) is an interesting introduction, more penetrating in argument than Guthrie. For an ambitious and philosophically demanding interpretation see J. Barnes, *The Presocratic Philosophers* (paperback ed., London, 1982). Much of the best work on Greek philosophy is published in article form. Useful collections on the Presocratics are D. J. Furley and R. E. Allen (eds.), *Studies in Presocratic Philosophy*, 2 vols. (London, 1970, 1975) and A. P. D. Mourelatos (ed.), *The Pre-socratics* (New York, 1974).

Socrates and Plato: most general accounts of Plato's philosophy include discussion of Socrates. A good starting-point for more precise discussion is a collection of essays edited by G. Vlastos, *The Philosophy of Socrates* (New York, 1971). Plato's dialogues are usefully, if outdatedly, summarized by A. E. Taylor, *Plato, the Man and his Work* (paperback ed., London, 1960). The arguments are helpfully studied by I. M. Crombie, *An Examination of Plato's Doctrines*, 2 vols. (London, 1962, 1963), and by J. Annas, *An Introduction to Plato's Republic* (Oxford, 1981). For more specialized study see the collections of articles edited by R. E. Allen, *Studies in Plato's Metaphysics* (London, 1965) and by G. Vlastos, *Plato*, 2 vols. (New York, 1971). Commentaries on some Platonic dialogues, with translations, are available in the Clarendon Plato Series (Oxford), ed. M. J. Woods.

Aristotle: good introductions include D. J. Allan, *The Philosophy of Aristotle* (London, 1957) and J. L. Ackrill, *Aristotle the Philosopher* (Oxford, 1981). For a more detailed new approach see A. Edel, *Aristotle and His Philosophy* (Chapel Hill, 1982). Specialized work is represented in *Articles on Aristotle*, ed. J. Barnes, M. Schofield, and R. Sorabji, 4 vols. (London, 1975–9). Commentaries on many of Aristotle's works, with translation, are available in the Clarendon Aristotle Series (Oxford), ed. J. L. Ackrill.

Miscellaneous: For a stimulating general discussion of Greek philosophy see B. Williams, in *The Legacy of Greece*, ed. M. I. Finley (Oxford, 1981); *Language and Logos. Studies in Ancient Greek Philosophy Presented to G. E. L. Owen*, ed. M. Schofield and M. Nussbaum (Cambridge, 1982) exemplifies the latest scholarly work. (Both of these books are referred to in the chapter.) Books which consider Greek thought from a wider perspective include E. R. Dodds, *The Greeks and the Irrational* (Berkeley and Los Angeles, 1951), and M. Détienne and J.-P. Vernant, *Cunning Intelligence in Greek Culture and Society* (Hassocks, Sussex, 1978).

4   Classical Art

General: the fullest survey of the whole subject (excluding architecture) is now [C.] M. Robertson, *A History of Greek Art* (Cambridge, 1975); a one volume version in the author's own abridgement has appeared as *A Shorter History of Greek Art* (Cambridge, 1981). Among numerous single-volume books recently published, the most measured, fact-orientated handbook is R. M. Cook, *Greek Art* (London, 1972). Substantial, copiously illustrated surveys of Greek art include G. Becatti, *The Art of Ancient Greece and Rome* (London, 1968); for the archaic period, E. Homann-Wedeking, *Archaic Greece* (London, 1968); for the classical (appealing to a high-brow readership), K. Schefold, *Classical Greece* (London, 1967); for the relatively ill-charted Hellenistic period, T. B. L. Webster, *Hellenistic Art* (London, 1967), with a broad cultural sweep, and C. M. Havelock, *Hellenistic Art* (London, 1971); on sculpture, architecture and painting, by J. Charbonneaux, R. Martin and F. Villard respectively, the three successive main periods each occupying a volume: *Archaic Greek Art 620–480 BC* (London, 1971), *Classical Greek Art 480–330 BC* (London, 1972), and *Hellenistic Art 330–50 BC* (London, 1973).

Vase-painting and painting: E. Pfuhl, *Malerei und Zeichnung der Griechen* (Munich, 1923) has a big volume of plates, mainly of vases. A. Rumpf, *Malerei und Zeichnung* (Munich, 1953) remains an important survey with numerous small illustrations. F. Villard (in the three volumes of the work cited above) gives a balanced survey. **For vase-painting**, R. M. Cook, *Greek Painted Pottery* (London, 1960 and 1972) is fundamental. P. Arias, M. Hirmer and B. B. Shefton, *A History of Greek Vase Painting* (London, 1961) is informative and copiously illustrated. As regards the different classes of Greek painted vases, appropriate references will be found in the bibliographies of recent works cited above; two specialized studies with exceptionally full illustration are J. Boardman's *Athenian Black Figure Vases* (London, 1974) and *Athenian Red Figure Vases* (London, 1975).

Sculpture: still indispensable are G. M. A. Richter, *The Sculpture and Sculptors of the Greeks* (New Haven, 1930) and A. W. Lawrence, *Classical Sculpture* of 1929 which has been remodelled in his *Greek and Roman Sculpture* (London, 1972). For serious study G. Lippold, *Griechische Plastik* (Munich, 1950, with numerous small illustrations) is unlikely to be superseded. R. Carpenter's *Greek Sculpture* (Chicago, 1960) continues to be provocative of thought. R. Lullies and M. Hirmer, *Greek Sculpture* (London, 1957 and 1965) is a copiously illustrated introduction. **On archaic sculpture** H. Schröder *Archaische griechische Plastik* (Breslau, 1933) is a sensitive brief survey; for archaic East Greek E. Akurgal in his *Die Kunst Anatoliens* (Berlin, 1961) is helpful. For Hellenistic sculpture, M. Bieber, *The Sculpture of the Hellenistic Age* (New York, 1961) is most comprehensive. Well illustrated books concerned with the Olympia temple sculptures centre on the sets of photographs by W. Hege and by A. Frantz: W. Hege and G. Rodenwaldt, *Olympia* (London, 1936); B. Ashmole, N. Yalouris and A. Frantz, *Olympia, the Sculpture of the Temple of Zeus* (London, 1967). On the Parthenon sculptures F. Brommer's work is magisterial; it is published in English as *The Sculptures of the Parthenon* (London, 1979); for the sculptures and buildings on the Acropolis, W. Hege and G. Rodenwaldt, *The Acropolis* (London, 1957). B. Ashmole, *Architect and Sculptor in Classical Greece* (London, 1972) is worth reading on the Olympia, Parthenon, and Mausoleum sculptures. For sculptural technique see S. Adam, *The Technique of Greek Sculpture in the Archaic and Classical Periods* (London, 1966). For works covering portrait sculpture, grave reliefs and other genres, references to books of substance will be found in the bibliographies of the general works cited above.

Miscellaneous: for other arts not touched on in this chapter a short list of full surveys may include Å. Åkerström, *Die Architektonischen Terrakotten Kleinasiens* (Lund, 1966); J. Boardman, *Archaic Greek Gems* (London, 1968); J. Boardman, *Greek Gems and Finger Rings* (London, 1970); R. A. Higgins, *Greek and Roman Jewellery* (London, 1961); R. A. Higgins, *Greek Terracottas* (London, 1967); C. M. Kraay and M. Hirmer, *Greek Coins* (London, 1966); R. M. Cook, *Clazomenian Sarcophagi* (Mainz, 1981). Also, on craftsmen generally, A. Burford, *Craftsmen in Greek and Roman Society* (London, 1972).

Architecture: two substantial handbooks of Greek architecture are W. B. Dinsmoor, *The Architecture of Ancient Greece* (London and New York, 1950), and A. W. Lawrence, *Greek Architecture* (Harmondsworth, 1957 and 1967); for more photographs H. Berve, G. Gruven and M. Hirmer, *Greek Temples, Theatres and Shrines* (London, 1963). Among books dealing with city design and building complexes may be mentioned R. E. Wycherley, *How the Greeks built Cities* (London, 1949 and 1962), and R. Martin, *L'Urbanisme dans la Grèce antique* (Paris, 1956); J. Travlos, *A Pictorial Dictionary of Ancient Athens* (London, 1970); H. A. Thompson and R. E. Wycherley, *The Agora of Athens: the History, Shape and Uses of an ancient City Centre* (Princeton, N.J., 1972); R. A. Tomlinson, *Greek Sanctuaries* (London, 1976); and not least R. V. Schoder, *Ancient Greece from the Air* (London, 1974).

5   The Foundations of Literature

Translations from Greek and books about Greek literature are innumerable. A systematic bibliography would be as long as this book. **Homer** can still be read with enjoyment in the versions by Chapman (1616, repr. Oxford, 1930) or Pope (1715, 1726, repr. New York, 1965), or in the Victorian prose translations of the *Iliad* by A. Lang, W. Leaf and E. Myers (London, 1883) and of the *Odyssey* by S. H. Butcher and A. Lang (London, 1879). The best

modern version of the *Odyssey* is by Walter Shewring (Oxford, 1980); few other modern translations of Homer are successful and the Penguin version by E. V. Rieu is perhaps the least successful. **Tragedy** has sometimes been splendidly translated, e.g. Sophocles' *Oedipus Tyrannus* and *Oedipus Colonus* by W. B. Yeats (in his *Collected Plays*, London 1952 and New York, 1953 and often reprinted), Sophocles' *Women of Trachis* by Ezra Pound (London, 1956) and Aeschylus' *Oresteia* by Hugh Lloyd Jones (Englewood Cliffs, N.J., 1970) and by Robert Lowell (New York, 1978; London, 1979). There are two recent translations of the whole of Greek tragedy – D. Grene and R. Lattimore, *The Complete Greek Tragedies*, 4 vols. (Chicago, 1953–9), and W. Arrowsmith (ed.), *The Greek Tragedy in New Translation* (1974–   ). Translations of **Pindar** by C. M. Bowra (Harmondsworth, 1969) and R. Lattimore (Chicago, 1947) are excellent, as is Peter Jay's *Poems from the Greek Anthology* (London, 1973). **Prose** gives the translator fewer problems than poetry. Some older translations are admirable, e.g. Thomas Hobbes' *Thucydides* (1629; adapted by D. Grene, 2 vols., Ann Arbor, 1960), Thomas North's *Plutarch* (1579; revised version by A. H. Clough, London, 1864, and reprinted in the Everyman Library), and the 17th-century versions of the Greek romances, of which R. Stoneman offers a selection in his *Daphne into Laurel* (London, 1982). Benjamin Jowett's Plato is a masterly Victorian translation (3rd ed., Oxford, 1892). The Penguin Classics provide useful translations, with introductions, of many Greek authors; their quality varies. The Loeb Classical Library – Greek text with facing English translation – is sometimes dull, occasionally inaccurate, but never sinks below a solid, plodding level.

History: the best and fullest history of Greek literature is that of Albin Lesky (London, 1966). C. M. Bowra's *Landmarks in Greek Literature* (London, 1966 and paperback reprints) is good on the key figures. *The Oxford Classical Dictionary* (2nd ed., Oxford, 1970) is a useful work of reference. C. A. Trypanis' *Greek Poetry from Homer to Seferis* (London, 1981) is full of insights and unexpected pleasures. Sir Kenneth Dover's books – *Lysias and the Corpus Lysiacum* (Berkeley, 1968), *Aristophanic Comedy* (London, 1972), *Ancient Greek Literature* (Oxford, 1980), and *Greek Popular Morality in the Time of Plato and Aristotle* (Oxford, 1975) – are dry but informative.

Criticism: on Homer, G. S. Kirk's *The Songs of Homer* (Cambridge, 1962) and Jasper Griffin's *Homer on Life and Death* (Oxford, 1980) are reliable and exciting, and Gilbert Murray's *The Rise of the Greek Epic* (4th ed., London, 1934) has not lost its thrilling sense of discovery. On tragedy, Albin Lesky's *Greek Tragic Poetry* (New Haven and London, 1983) is balanced and informative. Brian Vickers' *Towards Greek Tragedy: Drama, Myth, Society* (London, 1973) offers the point of view of an expert on modern drama. R. Lattimore's *The Poetry of Greek Tragedy* (Baltimore, 1958) is a lively critical study. P. Walcot's *Greek Drama in its Theatrical and Social Context* is a useful guide to staging and audience (Cardiff, 1976). See also *The Cambridge History of Classical Literature*, volume 1: *Greek Literature*, edited by P. E. Easterling and B. M. W. Knox (Cambridge, 1984).

6   The Age of Kings

The best introduction to the Hellenistic age in English is F. W. Walbank, *The Hellenistic World* (London, 1981), which has an up-to-date bibliography; see also W. W. Tarn and G. T. Griffith, *Hellenistic Civilization* (London, 3rd ed., 1952). The *Cambridge Ancient History* volumes VI–VIII (Cambridge, 1927–30), covers the Hellenistic period; a new edition is in preparation. M. Rostovtzeff, *The Social and Economic History of the Hellenistic World*, 3 vols. (Oxford, 1941), is a classic work on its theme, richly documented and illustrated, though some of Rostovtzeff's views now need modification; see also the important survey by C. Préaux, *Le Monde hellénistique*, 2 vols. (Paris, 1978). **On political history** E. Will, *Histoire politique du monde hellénistique*, 2 vols. (Nancy, 1966 and 1967, 2nd ed. 1979–   ), gives the best account, with detailed references to ancient sources and modern bibliography. **For the political institutions** of the Hellenistic world see V. Ehrenberg, *The Greek State* (2nd ed., London, 1969) and A. H. M. Jones, *The Greek City from Alexander to Justinian* (Oxford, 1940). **For the ancient sources** see M. M. Austin, *The Hellenistic World from Alexander to the Roman Conquest* (Cambridge, 1981).

On Alexander see J. R. Hamilton, *Alexander the Great* (Oxford, 1973) and U. Wilcken, *Alexander the Great*, ed. E. N. Borza (New York, 1967). **On the hellenistic kingdoms:** Antigonids: F. W. Walbank, *Philip V of Macedon* (Cambridge, 1940). Seleucids: E. Bikerman, *Institutions des Séleucides* (Paris, 1938). Attalids: E. V. Hansen, *The Attalids of Pergamum* (2nd ed., Ithaca, N.Y., 1971). Ptolemies: C. Préaux, *L'économie royale des Lagides* (Brussels, 1939), supplemented by her survey cited above, and P. M. Fraser, *Ptolemaic Alexandria*, 3 vols. (Oxford, 1972), essential also for cultural and literary history.

Economic aspects: M. I. Finley, *The Ancient Economy* (Berkeley and Los Angeles, 1973); G. E. M. de Ste. Croix, *The Class Struggle in the Ancient Greek World* (London, 1981). **Military aspects:** G. T. Griffith, *The Mercenaries of the Hellenistic World* (Cambridge, 1935); M. Launey, *Recherches sur les armées hellénistiques*, 2 vols. (Paris, 1949–50); D. W. Engels, *Alexander the Great and the Logistics of the Macedonian Army* (Berkeley and Los Angeles, 1978). **Philosophy and thought:** A. A. Long, *Hellenistic Philosophy* (London, 1974). **Science:** G. E. R. Lloyd, *Greek Science after Aristotle* (London, 1973). **The Hellenistic world and the east:** S. K. Eddy, *The King is Dead. Studies in* *the Near Eastern Resistance to Hellenism* (Lincoln, Nebraska, 1961); A. Momigliano, *Alien Wisdom. The Limits of Hellenization* (Cambridge, 1975).

7 Rome and the Greek East

A reliable general introduction to the period from Augustus to the 3rd century AD will be found in F. Millar, *The Roman Empire and its Neighbours* (2nd ed., London, 1981). M. I. Rostovtzeff, *Social and Economic History of the Roman Empire* (2nd ed. English translation, Oxford, 1957) is still good reading, but presents an over-hostile view of the later empire. On Rome and the Greek world, see G. W. Bowersock, *Augustus and the Greek World* (Oxford, 1965) and his *Greek Sophists in the Roman Empire* (Oxford, 1969). R. K. Sherk, *Rome and the Greek East to the Death of Augustus* (Cambridge, 1984) collects and translates some of the epigraphic evidence. For Aphrodisias, see Joyce Reynolds, *Aphrodisias and Rome* (London, 1982). For the imperial cult in Asia Minor in the early empire, see S. F. Price, *Rituals and Power* (Cambridge, 1984). The classic work on 'euergetism' (ostentatious giving) is in French: P. Veyne, *Le pain et le cirque* (Paris, 1976). For the cities of the Greek east under Roman rule see A. H. M. Jones, *The Greek City from Alexander to Justinian* (Oxford, 1940). Clive Foss, *Ephesus after Antiquity* (Cambridge, 1979) is a study of an individual city and its changing fortunes and physical appearance. From the countless books on early Christianity see W. H. C. Frend, *Martyrdom and Persecution in the Early Church* (Oxford, 1965) and Henry Chadwick, *The Early Church* (Harmondsworth, 1967). E. Patlagean, *Pauvreté sociale et pauvreté économique à Byzance, 4e au 7e siècles* (Paris, 1977) is a mine of information on the impact of Christianization on the cities of the Greek east. For the development of Constantinople, see G. Dagron, *Naissance d'une capitale* (Paris, 1974) and for the age of Justinian, R. Browning, *Justinian and Theodora* (London, 1971). Finally, G. E. M. de Ste. Croix's *The Class Struggle in the Ancient Greek World* (London, 1981) offers a major interpretation of the reasons for the ending of classical antiquity (coinciding with the Islamic conquests of the 7th century) from a strictly Marxist point of view.

8 A Christian Millennium

The basic history of this period is best recorded in George Ostrogorsky's *History of the Byzantine State* (revised English edition, Oxford, 1980); *The Cambridge Medieval History*, vol. IV.1 (Cambridge, 1966), edited by J. M. Hussey, also has useful chapters on the empire's relations with foreign powers; part 2 (1967) is devoted entirely to institutions and culture. A more idiosyncratic introduction to Byzantium is given in A. P. Kazhdan and G. Constable, *People and Power in Byzantium, an Introduction to Modern Byzantine Studies* (Washington, D.C., 1982). *Byzantium, The Empire of New Rome* by Cyril Mango (London, 1980), and *The Byzantine Empire* by Robert Browning (London, 1980) present highly readable general accounts. The relevant volumes of the *Tabula Imperii Byzantini* establish the geographical framework of medieval Greece: see vol. I, *Hellas und Thessalia*, edited by J. Koder and F. Hild (Vienna, 1976); vols. on the Peloponnese and Thrace are in preparation.

For the Byzantine peasantry, P. Lemerle's *Agrarian History of Byzantium* (English translation, Galway, 1979) and A. Laiou-Thomadakis, *Peasant Society in the Late Byzantine Empire* (Princeton, 1977) are helpful. **The development of the Greek language** during the medieval period is best studied through Robert Browning's *Medieval and Modern Greek* (Cambridge, 1983); and **the art and architecture of medieval Greece** through O. Demus's *Byzantine Mosaic Decoration* (London, 1948, reprinted 1976), Cyril Mango, *Byzantine Architecture* (New York, 1976), G. Millet, *L'école grecque dans l'architecture byzantine* (Paris, 1916, reprinted London, 1974), A. Grabar, *Byzantine Painting* (Geneva, 1979) and D. Talbot Rice, *Art of the Byzantine Era* (London, 1963). H. Hunger documents the pervasive Christian influence in Byzantine civilization in his *Reich der Neuen Mitte* (Graz/Vienna/Cologne, 1965).

Several important Byzantine sources can be read in translation: in the Penguin Classics series, *The Alexiad of Anna Comnena* (Harmondsworth, 1969), and Michael Psellus's *Fourteen Byzantine Rulers* (Harmondsworth, 1966, repr. 1979). The epic poem of Digenis is translated by J. Mavrogordato (Oxford, 1956, repr. 1970); the Chronicle of Morea by H. Lurier in *Crusaders as Conquerors* (New York, 1964), and Benjamin of Tudela's diary by M. N. Adler, *The Itinerary of Benjamin of Tudela* (London, 1907).

The complex history of **Slavonic and Bulgar incursions into Greece** is treated in a detailed review article by S. Vryonis in *Balkan Studies* 22 (1981); see also Robert Browning, *Byzantium and Bulgaria* (London, 1975); Judith Herrin, 'Aspects of the process of hellenization in the early Middle Ages', in *Annual of the British School at Athens*, 68 (1973). The middle Byzantine period and Macedonian Renaissance is surveyed in A. J. Toynbee's *Constantine Porphyrogenitus and his World* (Oxford, 1973), and the role of the capital or 'Queen city' in D. A. Miller's *Imperial Constantinople* (New York, 1969). Life in the Greek provinces is analysed by Judith Herrin, 'Realities of Byzantine Provincial Government: Hellas and Peloponnesos, 1180–1205', in *Dumbarton Oaks Papers*, 29 (1975).

On the history of **western activities in Greece**, William Miller's *The Latins in the Levant, 1204–1566* (London, 1908, repr. 1964) remains fundamental. The Assizes of Romania are carefully published by David Jacoby, *La Féodalité en Grèce* (Paris, 1971), whose article 'The encounter of two societies: Western conquerors and Byzantines in the Peloponnese after the

Fourth Crusade', in *American Historical Review*, 78 (1973) provides a stimulating picture. The Greek states can be studied in Donald M. Nicol's *The Despotate of Epiros 1267–1479*, (Cambridge, 1984) and Sir Steven Runciman's *Mistra, Byzantine capital of the Peloponnese* (London, 1980). Relations between the eastern and western churches are treated by Sir Steven Runciman, *The Eastern Schism* (Oxford, 1955) and Joseph Gill, *Byzantium and the Papacy, 1198–1400* (New Brunswick, 1979), and the latter author's study of the Council of Florence (Cambridge, 1959) deals authoritatively with the projects for union. The empire's decline is narrated by D. M. Nicol in *The End of the Byzantine Empire* (London, 1979), and vividly portrayed by Sir Steven Runciman in *The Fall of Constantinople 1453* (Cambridge, 1965).

9 The Impact of Hellenism

Greek influence on the Moslem world: critical discussion of what texts were available to Arab translators is available in P. Lemerle, *Le premier humanisme byzantin. Notes et remarques sur enseignement et culture à Byzance des origines au Xe siècle* (Paris, 1971), pp. 22–42; English translations of Arab texts showing Greek influence are given in F. Rosenthal, *The Classical Heritage in Islam* (Berkeley, 1965). S. Vryonis, 'Byzantium and Islam. Seventh–Seventeenth Century.' in *East European Quarterly* 2 (1968), pp. 205–40, is a survey of relations through one thousand years. There is a critical examination of the aims and achievements of the translators of Greek philosophical texts in A. Badawi, *La transmission de la philosophie grecque au monde arabe* (Paris, 1968). For a study of the influence of Aristotelian and Platonic thought in the Moslem world, see I. Opelt, *Griechische Philosophie bei den Arabern* (Munich, 1970). De L. O'Leary, *How Greek Science passed to the Arabs* (2nd ed., London, 1951) is a useful outline of the subject. A critical survey of research in the mid-20th century is provided by R. Paret, 'Notes bibliographiques sur quelques travaux récents consacrés aux premières traductions arabes d'oeuvres grecques' in *Byzantion* 29–30 (1959–60), pp. 387–446.

Greek influence on the Slav world: for a broad survey of Byzantine political and cultural influence, see D. Obolensky, *The Byzantine Commonwealth: Eastern Europe 500–1453* (London, 1971). There is a clear and authoritative introduction to the work of the Apostles of the Slavs in F. Dvornik, *Byzantine Missions among the Slavs: SS. Constantine-Cyril and Methodius* (New Brunswick, 1970). A. P. Vlasto, *The Entry of the Slavs into Christendom. An Introduction to the Medieval History of the Slavs* (Cambridge, 1970) is a detailed examination of the contacts of the Slav peoples with Greek and Latin Christian culture. The transmission of Greek secular culture to the Slavs is examined in I. Ševčenko, 'Remarks on the diffusion of Byzantine scientific and pseudo-scientific literature among the Orthodox Slavs' in *Slavonic and East European Review* 59 (1981), pp. 321–45.

Additional references: C. Becker, *Islamstudien. Vom Werden und Wesen der islamischen Welt* (Leipzig, 1924), I, 1–39; al-Nadīm, *The Fihrist of al-Nadīm, A Tenth-Century Survey of Muslim Culture*, trans. B. Dodge (New York and London, 1970); M. Meyerhof, 'New Light on Hunain ibn Ishaq and his Period' in *Isis*, VIII (1926), 685–724.

10 Towards Nationhood

Two books by A. E. Vakalopoulos, *Origins of the Greek Nation 1204–1461* (New Brunswick, 1970) and *The Greek Nation 1453–1669* (New Brunswick, 1976), provide a rich and fascinating study of the changing situation of the Greek people from the Fourth Crusade to the capture of Crete by the Turks. Nikos Svoronos, *Histoire de la Grèce moderne* (2nd ed., Paris, 1964), pp. 5–41, is a survey of the main factors in the development of the Greek nation up to 1821. There is a brief but excellent study of the emergence of the Greek nation from the Byzantine empire in D. A. Zakythinos, *The Making of Modern Greece: From Byzantium to Independence* (Oxford, 1976). D. J. Geanakoplos, *Interaction of the 'Sibling' Byzantine and Eastern cultures in the Middle Ages and Italian Renaissance (330–1600)* (New Haven and London, 1976) is an analysis of the cultural relations of Greece and the west. There are studies of Greeks and Romans, Greeks and Turks and of the continuity of Hellenism in T. Winnifrith and Penelope Murray (eds.), *Greece Old and New* (London, 1983), pp. 65–128. For an examination of the continuity of Byzantine institutions under the Ottoman empire, see S. Vryonis, 'The Byzantine Legacy and Ottoman Forms' in *Dumbarton Oaks Papers* 23–24 (1969–70), pp. 251–308. A. J. Toynbee, *The Greeks and their Heritages* (Oxford, 1981), pp. 73–270, is a critical study of what the modern Greek nation inherited from its ancient and Byzantine past.

11 Beyond the Frontiers

The only comprehensive account of the Greek Diaspora can be found in the *Great Hellenic Encyclopaedia*, vol. 10 (n.d.). There are separate chapters for each country which contained a Greek community, with detailed information about its history and activity. What is missing is a theoretical framework that would enable us to analyse the Diaspora as a social, economic and cultural phenomenon. This gap was filled for the first time by two studies which mark the turning point in the historiography of the Diaspora. N. Psyroukis, *The Diaspora Phenomenon* (Athens, 1974; in Greek) is an attempt at a Marxist analysis, and a similar but far more sophisticated approach can be found in K. Tsoukalas, *Dépendance et Reproduction. Le Rôle social des appareils scolaires en Grèce* (Paris, 1975). Tsoukalas is mainly concerned with the Greek educational system from 1830 to 1922 but in the third chapter (pp. 267–362) he provides an in-depth analysis of the Greek communities abroad, based on a number of extremely valuable insights.

General surveys of the Balkans during the period in question can be found in C. and B. Jelavich (eds.), *The Balkans in Transition* (Los Angeles, 1963), P. F. Sugar and I. J. Lederer (eds.), *Nationalism in Eastern Europe* (Seattle and London, 1969) and L. S. Stavrianos, *The Balkans since 1453* (New York, Chicago and London, 1958). For the role of the Greek Orthodox church see S. Runciman, *The Great Church in Captivity: a Study of the Patriarchate of Constantinople from the Eve of the Turkish Conquest to the Greek War of Independence* (Cambridge, 1968) and for a non-Greek approach to Balkan history N. Iorga, *Byzance après Byzance* (Bucharest, 1935) is very useful. Trajan Stojanovitch, 'The Conquering Balkan Orthodox Merchants', in *Journal of Economic History*, vol. 20, March 1960, provides a valuable corrective to the rather hasty generalizations about the Greekness of the Balkan merchants.

There are numerous accounts of **individual Diaspora communities**, mostly in Greek. The most detailed account of the Greeks in Egypt can be found in A. Politis, *Greeks and Modern Egypt*, 2 vols. (Alexandria, 1931; in Greek). On Turkey, see Leon Makas, *L'Hellénismede l'Asie Mineure* (Paris and Nancy, 1919) and for the Greeks in America, T. Salutos, *The Greeks in the United States* (Cambridge, Mass., 1964). S. Prokopiou, *Modern Greek in Asia and Africa* (Athens, 1930; in Greek) gives a colourful account of Greek communities in the two continents and at the same time illuminates rather well the image that the Greek immigrants had of themselves.

12 Eclipse and Rebirth

R. Clogg, *A Short History of Modern Greece* (2nd ed., Cambridge, 1985), is an up-to-date introduction to modern Greek history, while J. Campbell and P. Sherrard, *Modern Greece* (London, 1968) is particularly valuable for its attention to society and culture. The gradual enlargement of the Greek state is described in D. Dakin, *The Unification of Greece 1770–1923* (London, 1972). Steven Runciman covers the history of the Orthodox church at a time when it had a central role in the history of the Greek people in *The Great Church in Captivity: a Study of the Patriarchate of Constantinople from the Eve of the Turkish Conquest to the Greek War of Independence* (Cambridge, 1968), while C. M. Woodhouse, *Capodistria: the Founder of Greek Independence* (Oxford, 1973) is a thorough study of the first president of Greece. On the early years of the independent state, J. A. Petropulos, *Politics and Statecraft in the Kingdom of Greece 1833–1843* (Princeton, 1968) is essential. The 19th century is not well covered in English but M. Llewellyn Smith, *Ionian vision: Greece in Asia Minor 1919–1922* (London, 1975) and G. Mavrogordatos, *Stillborn Republic: Social Coalitions and Party Strategies in Greece, 1922–1936* (Berkeley and London, 1983) throw much light on Greece during the first four decades of the 20th century. C. M. Woodhouse, *The Struggle for Greece 1941–1949* (London, 1976) is an account of one of the most troubled decades in Greece's independent history by a historian who was closely involved in Greek affairs during the Second World War. W. H. McNeill, *The Metamorphosis of Greece since World War II* (Oxford, 1978) gives a good indication of the pace of economic and social change in Greece during recent decades. N. P. Mouzelis, *Modern Greece: Facets of Underdevelopment* (London, 1978) is a thoughtful study by a Marxist economist, with rich bibliographical references. A comprehensive annotated listing of works in English on all aspects of Modern Greece is contained in Mary Jo and Richard Clogg, *Greece* (Oxford, 1981).

Sources of Illustrations

Where no photographer's name is mentioned, the copyright belongs to the museum or institution holding the object depicted. Abbreviations: BL = British Library, London; BM = British Museum, London; BN = Bibliothèque Nationale, Paris; ML = Musée du Louvre, Paris; NAM = National Archaeological Museum, Athens; SMB = Staatliche Museen, Berlin.

Page 7 Drawing by Fotis Kontoglou, *Travels in Greece*, 1928. **9** Photo Roloff Beny. **10–11** 2, Photo Alison Franz. 3, BM. 4, Photo S. V. Skopelitis. 5, Signed by Nikosthenes, *c.* 520 BC. ML. Photo Hirmer Verlag. **12–13** 6, Photo Roloff Beny. 7, Photo Ian Mackenzie-Kerr. 8, Photo David South/Cameron Press. **14–15** 9, Archaeological Museum, Reggio, Calabria. Photo Leonard von Matt. 10, SMB. 11, Sermons of St Gregory of Nazianzus, BN. 12, BM. 13, Photo Popperfoto. 14, Archaeological Museum, Reggio, Calabria. **16–17** 15, Photo André Held. 16, Photo Scala. 17, Photo Charles Walker/Barbara Heller Archive. 18, Photo S. V. Skopelitis. **18–19** 19, Photo R. V. Schoder. 20, 21, Photo Archives Gad-Boissonnas. 22, Photo Popperfoto. **20–21** 23, BM; and Theophilos Museum, Varia, Mytilene. Photo Harissiades. 24, Photo Daniel Schwartz. **22–3** 25, SMB. Photo Hirmer Verlag. 26, Detail of icon by Emmanuel Lombardos. Byzantine Museum, Athens. 27, Photo Doros Partissides. 28, Acropolis Museum, Athens. Photo Hirmer Verlag. 29, Kestner Museum, Hanover. 30, Photo Daniel Schwartz. **24** 31, Photo Pierre Couteau. **26** BM. **27** BM. **29** Archaeological Museum, Volos. **32** Antikensammlung, Munich; **34** BM. **35** BN. **37** Victoria and Albert Museum, London. **41** 1, Heraklion Archaeological Museum. Photo Leonard von Matt. **42–3** 2, Goulandris Collection. 3, Photo Leonard von Matt. 4, Heraklion Archaeological Museum. Photo Hirmer Verlag. 5, Heraklion Archaeological Museum. Photo Josephine Powell. 6, Heraklion Archaeological Museum. Photo Leonard von Matt. **44–5** 7, NAM. Photo Nikos Kontos. 8, NAM. Photo Nikos Kontos. **46–7** 9, NAM. Photo Roloff Beny. 10, NAM. Photo Nikos Kontos. 11, Greek National Tourist Office. 12, Photo Hirmer Verlag. **48** 13, NAM. Photo Nikos Kontos. **49** Coin showing the labyrinth, from Knossos. BM. **50** NAM. **52** NAM; and J. Chadwick, *The Decipherment of Linear B.* **53** Marinatos, *Crete and Mycenae.* **54** Thames and Hudson Archive; Carl W. Blegen. **55** Greek National Tourist Office. Piet de Jong, *BSA* 25. **57** After Wace. Drawing by Martin Weaver. **58** NAM. **59** NAM. **61** NAM. **65** 1, Musei e Gallerie Pontificie, Vatican. **66–7** 2, SMB. 3, National Museum, Copenhagen. 4, Antikenmuseum, West Berlin. 5, Metropolitan Museum of Art, New York. 6, Thorvaldsen Museum, Copenhagen. 7, BM. 8, SMB. 9, Museum of Fine Arts, Boston. **68–9** 10, BM. 11, Museo Nazionale di Villa Giulia, Rome. Photo Scala. 12, BM. Photo John Webb. **70–71** 13, Antique copy of an original of 440–430 BC. BM. 14, Copy of statue by Polykletos made about forty years after his death. Musei e Gallerie Pontificie, Vatican. Photo Alinari. 15, National Museum, Copenhagen. 16, Agora Museum, Athens. Photo Roloff Beny. **72–3** 17, BM. 18, BM. 19, BM. Photo John Webb. 20, Musées Royaux, Brussels. Photo Hirmer Verlag. **74–5** 21, Photo Roloff Beny. 22, Detail from volute crater by Karmeia Painter, *c.* 410 BC. Photo Hirmer Verlag. 23, Detail of crater from Spina, 420–410 BC. Archaeological Museum, Ferrara. Photo Hirmer Verlag. 24, Archaeological Museum, Reggio, Calabria. Photo Scala. **77** Foot soldier with spear and shield, from the inside of Black Figure plate, 5th cent. BC. **78** Photo Leonard von Matt. **80, 81** Photo Leonard von Matt. **82** ML. BM. **85**

Photo Hirmer Verlag. **86, 87,** Agora Museum, Athens. **89** BM. Photo Hirmer Verlag. **91** BM. **93** Photo Hirmer Verlag. NAM. **94** Archaeological Museum, Ferrara. **95** Museo Nazionale, Naples. **96** Metropolitan Museum of Art, New York. **97** NAM. **99** Diagram of the Universe according to Ptolemy. From Oronce Finé, 1528. **100** Museo Nazionale, Naples. **103** SMB. **105** Archaeological Museum, Trier. **107** Österreichische Nationalbibliothek, Vienna. **109** Museo Nazionale, Naples. **111** BM. **113** St John's College, Oxford. **117** 1, NAM. Photo André Held. **110–119** 2, NAM. 3, NAM. 4, NAM. 5, BM. 6, SMB. 7, Archaeological Museum, Eleusis. Photo German Archaeological Institute, Athens. 9, NAM. **120–21** 10, Archaeological Museum, Florence. 11, 12, ML. Photo André Held. 13, Musei e Gallerie Pontificie, Vatican. Photo Hirmer Verlag. **122–3** 14, NAM. 15, SM. 16, SM. 17, ML. Photo Hirmer Verlag. 18, NAM. 19, Acropolis Museum, Athens. Photo Hirmer Verlag. 20, 21, Olympia Museum. Photo Hirmer Verlag. 22, Olympia Museum. Photo German Archaeological Institute, Athens. 23, Ostia Museum. Photo German Archaeological Institute, Rome. **124–5** 24, Museo Nazionale, Naples. Photo André Held. 25, Photo David Schwartz. **126–7** 26, Photo Roloff Beny. 27–31, BM; and Acropolis Museum, Athens. Photo German Archaeological Institute, Athens. 32, Photo Edwin Smith. **128** 33, Museo Nazionale, Naples. Photo Scala. **129** Vase painting showing a sculptor at work. See p. 66 (3). **130** Museo delle Terme, Rome. Photo Georgina Masson. **132** Agora Museum, Athens. Watercolour by Piet de Jong. From R. Hampe, *Ein frühattischer Grabfund*, pl. 21. **133** Fragments from Aegina. **135** Heraklion Museum. ML. SMB. Photo Hirmer Verlag. **136** Archaeological Museum, Florence. **137** Boulogne Museum; BN. **138** Metropolitan Museum of Art, New York. **139** Acropolis Museum, Athens. **140** From *Olympia, Die Ergebnisse . . .* **141** Olympia Museum. Photo Hirmer Verlag. **142** Acropolis Museum, Athens. Photo Hirmer Verlag. **143** Drawn by Donald Bell Scott. Drawn by Jon D. Wilsher, after Stevens. **145** American School of Classical Studies, Athens. **146** After a drawing by John Travlos. BM. **147** Olympia Museum. Photo Hirmer Verlag. **148** BM. **149** Pergamon Museum, Berlin. **151** Lyre: obverse of a coin of the Chalcidian League, *c.* 410 BC. Photo Hirmer Verlag. **152** ML. **154** Museum of Fine Arts, Boston. **155** BM. **157** SMB. **158** SMB. **159** BN. **160** BM. **163** Flaxman, illustration to Hesiod's works. Maillol, *Daphnis and Chloe*, 1937. Hans Erni, *Plato's Banquet*. **165** BL. **166** BL. **169** 1, Photo Roloff Beny. **170–71** 2, Museo delle Terme, Rome. Photo Alinari. 3, Musei e Gallerie Pontificie, Vatican. 4, Museo Nazionale, Naples. Photo Mansell/Alinari. 5, Museo delle Terme, Rome. Photo Georgina Masson. 6, BM. 7, Metropolitan Museum of Art, New York. Collection Walter C. Baker. 8, Glyptothek, Munich. Photo Hirmer Verlag. **172–3** 9, Photo Greek National Tourist Office. 10, Archaeological Museum, Thessalonica. Photo Nikos Kontos. **174–5** 11, BN. 12, Museo Nazionale, Naples. Photo Mansell/Alinari. 13, Archaeological Museum, Kabul. Photo BM. 14, BM. 15, ML. Photo Giraudon. **176–7** 16, Photo Ian Mackenzie-Kerr. 17, Photo Sonia Halliday/F.H.C. Birch. 18, Photo Peter Fraenkel. 19, Photo Charles Walker/Barbara Heller. 20, Photo Charles Walker/Barbara Heller. **178–9** 21, Private collection. 22, Archaeological Museum, Istanbul. Photo Hirmer Verlag. 23, Schweizerisches Landesmuseum, Zürich. 24, Academia de la Historia, Madrid. Photo Giraudon. 25, Photo Josephine Powell. **180–181** 26, Monastery of St Catherine, Sinai. Photo Roger Wood. 27, Biblioteca

Apostolica, Vatican. **28**, Photo Erich Lessing/John Hillelson. **182–3** 29, Pushkin Museum, Moscow. 30, Greek National Tourist Office. 31, Photo Hirmer Verlag. 32, Photo Georgina Bruckner. 33, Photo Hirmer Verlag. 34, Photo Sonia Halliday. 35, Acropolis Museum, Athens. Photo Alison Franz. 36, Museo Laterano, Rome. Photo Hirmer Verlag. 37, Bardo Museum, Tunisia. 38, Metropolitan Museum of Art, New York. 39, Benaki Museum, Athens. 40, Photo Popperfoto. 41, Photo German Archaeological Institute, Rome. **184** 42, Photo André Held. **185** Base of the Portland Vase. BM. **186** Archaeological Museum, Istanbul. **188** Archaeological Museum, Pella. **189** Photo Leonard von Matt. Archaeological Museum, Kabul. Photo Josephine Powell. BM. **190** BM. Photo John Webb. **191** BM. **192** A. von Gerkan. **193** SMB. **194** BM. **195** BM. **197** Metropolitan Museum of Art, New York. **198** Bibliothèque Bodmer, Geneva. **199** NAM. Photo Daniel Schwartz. **201** Triumphal entry into Antioch, 313 AD. BN. **202** Kunsthistorisches Museum, Vienna. **205** SMB. **207** SMB. **209** ML. **210** Photo Hirmer Verlag. **213** Landesmuseum, Trier. **217** 1, Diözesenmuseum, Bamberg. **218–19** 2, Museum of Fine Arts, Moscow. 3, BN. 4, BN. 5, Biblioteca Marciana, Venice. Photo Hirmer Verlag. 6, Biblioteca Nacional, Madrid. Photo Werner Forman/Barbara Heller. **220–21** 7, Monastery of St John, Patmos. Photo André Held. 8, Church of St Cassian, Nicosia. Photo André Held. 9, Photo André Held. **222–3** 10, BM. 11, From the Sermons of St Gregory Nazianzus. BL. 12, From the Book of Job. BN. 13, From the Book of Job. BN. 14, Pierpont Morgan Library, New York. 15, 16, From the Book of Job. BN. **224–5** 17, Photo Werner Forman. 18, Photo Lala Aufsberg. 19, Photo Daniel Schwartz. 20, Photo Werner Forman/Barbara Heller. **226–7** 21, Photo from UNESCO. 22, Photo Josephine Powell. 23, Photo G. Berengo Gardin. 24, Photo Laskarina Bournas. 25, 26, Photo G. Berengo Gardin. **228–9** 27, Photo Wim Swaan/Camera Press. 28, Photo Daniel Schwartz. 29, Photo Yanni Petsopoulos/Barbara Heller. **230–31** 30, Biblioteca Nacional, Madrid. 31, Biblioteca Apostolica, Rome. 32, Hungarian National Museum, Budapest. 33, Biblioteca Nacional, Madrid. 34, BL. 35, Oesterreichische Nationalbibliothek, Vienna. 36, BL. **232** 37, Photo Sonia Halliday. **233** Marble roundel of a Byzantine emperor. Dumbarton Oaks Collection, Washington. **234** Library of the Great Meteora Monastery. **237** Treasury of St Mark's, Venice. Photo O. Bohm. **238** Staatsbibliothek, Munich. **241** Biblioteca Apostolica, Vatican. **243** Photo Josephine Powell. **244** BN. **247** Photo Hirmer Verlag. **249** Bodleian Library, Oxford. **251** Detail of mosaic decoration showing strong Greek influence, in the Great Mosque of Damascus. Photo J. E. Dayton. **253** BN. **254** Metropolitan Museum of Art, New York. Photo Werner Forman. **257** Oesterreichische Nationalbibliothek, Vienna. **259** Biblioteca Nacional, Madrid. **261** Bulgarian National Library, Sofia. **265** 1, From the Zographos Album. **266–7** 2, Museum of Fine Arts, Boston. 3, BL. 4, From the Schwartz Mansion, Ambelakia. Photo Greek National Tourist Office. 5, Print after Edward Dodwell. BM. 6, Drawing by Peityer. BM. 7, Print in BM. 8, Print after Dupré. **268–9** 9, Folk Art Museum, Nauplion. 10, From the Zographos Album. 11, Painting by Peter von Hess. Neue Pinakothek, Munich. **270–71** 12, National Historical Museum, Athens. Photo S. V. Skopelitis. 13, Painting by T. Vryzakis. Benaki Museum, Athens. 14, Painting by L. Lipparini. Benaki Museum, Athens. 15, Popular print. **272–3** 16, Photo Popperfoto. 17, Photo Daniel Schwartz. 18, Photo S. V. Skopelitis. 19, Painting by Giorgio Peritelli. Private collection, Athens. 20, Photo Daniel Schwartz. **274–5** 21, Kunsthistorisches Museum, Vienna. 22, Victoria and Albert Museum, London. 23, Painting by L. J. Weller. Stadthistorisches Museum, Vienna. 24, Photo Michel Desjardins/Réalités/Camera Press. 25, Photo Lucinda Guinness. 26, Photo Anne Bodi. **276–7** 27, Photo S. V. Skopelitis. Tsaruchis Museum. 28, Artist's collection. 29, Artist's collection. **278–9** 30, Painting by Orlov. National Historical Museum, Athens. Photo S. V. Skopelitis. 31, Photo Benaki Museum, Athens. 32, German propaganda photograph. 33, Radio Times Hulton Picture Library. 34, Radio Times Hulton Picture Library. 35–38, Photo Bunte/Camera Press. **280** 39, Photo Daniel Schwartz. **281** Detail from the Veroli Casket. Victoria and Albert Museum, London. **282** BN. **287** Woodcut by Spiros Vassiliou. **288** Oesterreichische Nationalbibliothek, Vienna. **291** BM. Museo Correr, Venice. **293** Germanisches Nationalmuseum, Nuremberg. BM. **295** *Illustrated London News*. **296** Photo Richard Haughton. **298** Photo Lucinda Guinness. **299** Medal by K. Lange, showing the National Assembly at Epidauros. **300** Painting by T. Vryzakis. National Gallery of Painting, Athens. **303** From De Tournefort, *Relation d'un Voyage du Levant*, 1717; from F. C. H. L. Pouqueville, *Voyage de la Grèce*, 1826. **305** Folk Art Museum, Nauplion. **307** BM. Medal by K. Lange celebrating the Battle of Neocastro. **309** Photo Greek National Tourist Office. **310** *Punch*; Benaki Museum, Athens. **314** Poster issued at the time of Metaxas's death, 1941. **316** Woodcut by Spiros Vassiliou. **318–19** Drawing by Minos Argyrakis. Drawing by Yannis Tsaruchis. Manuscript by Yannis Ritsos. Drawing on stone by Yannis Ritsos. **320** Drawing by Fotis Kontoglou, *Travels in Greece*, 1928.

Index

Page numbers in *italic* refer to illustrations and captions.